FLORIDA ON FILM

Florida A&M University, Tallahassee
Florida Atlantic University, Boca Raton
Florida Gulf Coast University, Ft. Myers
Florida International University, Miami
Florida State University, Tallahassee
University of Central Florida, Orlando
University of Florida, Gainesville
University of North Florida, Jacksonville
University of South Florida, Tampa
University of West Florida, Pensacola

UNIVERSITY PRESS OF FLORIDA

Gainesville · Tallahassee · Tampa · Boca Raton
Pensacola · Orlando · Miami · Jacksonville · Ft. Myers

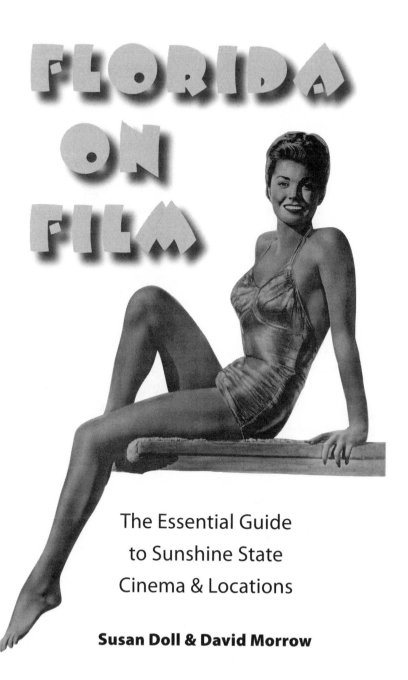

FLORIDA ON FILM

The Essential Guide
to Sunshine State
Cinema & Locations

Susan Doll & David Morrow

11 10 09 08 07 06   6 5 4 3 2 1

Library of Congress Cataloging-in-Publication Data
Doll, Susan, 1954–
Florida on film: the essential guide to Sunshine State cinema
and locations / Susan Doll and David Morrow. p. cm.
Includes bibliographical references and index.
ISBN-13: 978–0–8130–3045–6 (alk. paper)
1. Motion picture industry—Florida—History. 2. Florida—
In motion pictures. 3. Motion picture locations—Florida.
I. Morrow, David, 1962– II. Title.
PN1993.5.U73D65 2007
384.'8097599–dc22   2006030880

The University Press of Florida is the scholarly publishing
agency for the State University System of Florida, compris-
ing Florida A&M University, Florida Atlantic University,
Florida Gulf Coast University, Florida International
University, Florida State University, University of Central
Florida, University of Florida, University of North Florida,
University of South Florida, and University of West Florida.

University Press of Florida
15 Northwest 15th Street
Gainesville, FL 32611-2079
http://www.upf.com

This book is dedicated to our mothers,
Anita B. Doll and Eileen Morrow.
Thank you for a lifetime of unwavering
love and support.

CONTENTS

ACKNOWLEDGMENTS

We want to thank all of those who helped make possible *Florida on Film*. We are most grateful to our agent, Julie Hill, for her faith in our project. We would like to thank Rhonda Fleming and Ricou Browning for granting us exclusive interviews about their Florida-related film experiences. A special thank-you goes to Jody McDaniel, the planning and grants coordinator of Jacksonville's Department of Parks, Recreation, and Entertainment, for her information on the Norman Studios. Thanks to those who provided us with copies of hard-to-find films, including Facets Multi-Media of Chicago for access to forgotten silents, Maryann Dahlen for sending us a copy of *Where the Boys Are* on a moment's notice, and Steve at Picture Palace (www.picpal.com) for coming up with a copy of the rare *Hell Harbor*.

We would also like to thank those who helped us with the film stills that illustrate *Florida on Film*, including Sharon Fox, who offered valuable suggestions for tracking down photos and memorabilia. And thanks to Brian Warling of Warling Studios for photographing the posters and lobby cards.

INTRODUCTION

> Florida! The name conjures images of exotic beauty and
> adventure. Such fantasies have been as strong for the peo-
> ple of the motion picture and television industries as for
> the millions of tourists and new residents who regularly
> flock southward. The mesmerizing call of swaying palms,
> and sun-drenched beaches, has lured moviemakers to
> the Sunshine State since the earliest days of the century,
> creating a fascinating screen history.
>
> —Richard Alan Nelson, *Lights! Camera! Florida!*

In 1898 a motion picture camera captured images of soldiers receiving a train-
load of medical supplies for the Ninth U.S. Calvary who were fighting the
Spanish-American War in Cuba. This early newsreel marks the beginning of
Florida's rich and complex association with the movies.

The warm climate and exotic locales of the Sunshine State lured filmmakers
and their studios long before Hollywood became synonymous with American
film. In the winter of 1908–9, the Kalem Company set up an operation in
Jacksonville, opening the door for other companies to follow. The film colony
in Jacksonville thrived throughout the 1910s, while other Florida cities, including Miami and Tampa, attracted their share of film production. After World
War I, however, circumstances would turn the tide in favor of the West Coast
as the center of American filmmaking.

Even after Hollywood became America's filmmaking mecca, writers and
directors and producers continued to recognize that Florida locations are layered with meaning: they can evoke mystery, suggest romance, or provide a
backdrop for fun in the sun. During the Golden Age, studios recreated Florida
on their soundstages and back lots, hoping to add the unique flavor of this
state to their movies.

After the 1950s, the industry was no longer bound to studio shooting, often
preferring to film on location. During this time, Florida gradually regained its

Figure I.1. Silent film crew in Florida. (State Archives of Florida)

standing as a center of filmmaking. By 1979 it had become the third largest film production center in the United States.

Florida on Film examines in detail more than eighty films that were shot within the borders of the Sunshine State or that use Florida as a primary setting. In exploring these films, information and insight into the American cinema are combined with the history and culture of Florida. Examinations of popular genres such as film noir, horror, action, and science fiction appear alongside entertaining background information on the locations used for specific films. Whether reading about the symbolic use of swampland imagery in *Just Cause* or the practical need to shoot in the clear waters of Wakulla Springs for *The Creature from the Black Lagoon*, readers come away with a deeper understanding of how Florida's geography and popular image affected the films that were shot there.

In addition to the movie lore and literature, *Florida on Film* is a fount of information on the state itself, including its history, culture, image, geography, flora and fauna, climate, and industries. The book also fits neatly into a recent trend within the tourism industry in which movie buffs plan vacations based on the shooting locations of popular films. Called movie tourism, the trend was jump-started by the many fans who visited the baseball diamond carved out of an Iowa cornfield for *Field of Dreams*. *Florida on Film* embodies the essence of movie tourism by providing not only insight into cinema but also tourist information for those who desire a unique vacation.

Examining films from the standpoint of locations differs from both academic discussions and popular reviews. While the former can entail arcane analysis that lacks broad appeal, the latter's emphasis on evaluative judgment based on personal taste is superficial and unsatisfying. With its unique emphasis, *Florida on Film* offers accessible interpretations of films that both challenge and entertain the reader. The book revisits familiar classics, recalls forgotten gems, and revitalizes recent films initially dismissed by reviewers.

The book is divided into nine chapters, each covering a film genre, a historical era, or some aspect of Florida and film. For example, "Fun in the Sun" is devoted to comedy, "Florida as Paradise" is about the use of the Sunshine State as a symbol for paradise, and "The Golden Age" contains films from Hollywood's most legendary era, the 1930s through the 1950s.

One of the richest chapters in *Florida on Film* actually focuses on films trashed by critics and ignored by scholars. The critical and financial failures examined in "Florida Bust" range from the obtuse to the ridiculous, yet each flop offers perspective into the film industry, an entertaining behind-the-scenes story, or a tidbit about Florida history. While films such as *The Fat Spy*, *The Cape Canaveral Monster*, and *Blood Feast* may be dreadful viewing experiences, readers will be fascinated by the revelations they have to offer.

Another chapter is devoted to silent films shot in Florida, because the state hosted such a vital film industry in the 1910s. Film scholars have examined the silent era from every possible angle, yet surprisingly little has been written about Florida's role in that era. Also forgotten are the many women who contributed to the growth of American cinema in the chaotic days before the industry regimented itself along gender lines. "Silent Florida" addresses both of these topics, with such entries as Kathlyn Williams's *Lost in the Jungle* and Gene Gauntier's *Girl Spy* series.

Before the mega–theme parks became synonymous with Florida, the state was famous for its kitschy tourist attractions with such unforgettable names as Weeki Wachee, Wakulla Springs, and the Waltzing Waters. Many have been bypassed by more modern attractions or forced to close down because of financial difficulties. Several films in *Florida on Film* were shot in these one-of-a-kind locations, and as long as they are preserved on film, they will never be forgotten.

This last point is a reminder that popular films are a unique form of history. They preserve aspects of the past that few think are important at the time; they record the contributions of talented individuals who may later be forgotten; they are meaningful snapshots of another place and another time.

Within each chapter, the films are arranged alphabetically. Each film is individually profiled in an analytical essay that includes a plot synopsis and a cast and credit list. Some entries also include sidebars that focus on a fascinating detail related to the film.

A useful feature of *Florida on Film* is the Movie Tourist's Guide that concludes each chapter. These guides contain brief entries on Florida sites and locales that were spotlighted in that chapter's films. We hope these entries will encourage adventurous movie tourists to travel to the places and settings of their favorite films. Visiting the locations where famous—or, in some cases, not-so-famous—films were shot can add depth to the viewing experience and make everyone's favorite movies even more meaningful.

More than eighty films are discussed in detail in *Florida on Film*, with dozens of others mentioned in introductions and sidebars. Selection was based on how well the films fit into the central topic of each chapter and on what unique characteristics they could add to the coverage of Florida. Care was taken to ensure that all regions of the state would be represented. Special attention was paid to people with a direct connection to Florida filmmaking, such as Burt Reynolds, Ricou Browning, and Victor Nunez.

Still, it was impossible to include every movie that was ever shot in Florida, and the book was not intended to be a complete account of Florida films. To keep the list down to a manageable number, only narrative features were included; there are no shorts, animated films, or documentaries. We also eliminated films that we felt would repeat a historical perspective or illustrate a point already made by a previous entry. Another entire book could have been written on the films that were excluded from *Florida on Film*, and if we have left out one of your favorites, we apologize.

Like Hollywood, perhaps we should consider a sequel. . . .

FLORIDA ON FILM

1

SILENT FLORIDA

> We were Florida bound, the first company
> to be sent out of New York. . . . Our depar-
> ture created a sensation in the industry.
> —Gene Gauntier, *Blazing the Trail*

To the American public, "Hollywood" is much more than a geographic locale, or even a reference to the film industry. The name conjures up everything
magic and mythic about the movies. Yet the production of motion pictures did
not originate in Hollywood; it began in the entertainment centers of New York
and Chicago. And when established film companies began to expand outside
the North, they didn't necessarily flock to the West Coast right away. Instead,
many headed for Florida, congregating in Jacksonville, which served for several years as the winter capital of the industry. While it is hard to imagine any

other city but Hollywood evoking the glamour, excitement, and magic of the movies, it could very well have been Jacksonville.

Kalem, the first production company to set up in Florida, arrived in Jacksonville—or Jax, as it was nicknamed—in the winter of 1908–9. In those pioneering days of cinema, most major film companies had multiple troupes, or stock companies, that were sent to various locations in search of diverse backdrops for films. Kalem sent a troupe to Florida in order to continue film production during the winter months, which was difficult to do in the North. Some companies set up shop in Texas around the same time, but Florida would prove to be more popular because of the diversity of its landscape, as well as its low labor costs and inexpensive land.

While some producers shot in Miami and Tampa, Jacksonville quickly became the city of choice for film companies. At the time, Jax was the largest city in Florida as well as a financial, manufacturing, distribution, and transportation center for the Southeast.[1] It was also picturesque. Gene Gauntier, one of Kalem's top scriptwriters and premiere actresses, described the appeal in her memoir titled *Blazing the Trail*:

> There were wonderful stretches of sand at Pablo and Manhattan Beach, facing the open sea, uninhabited and desolate, with their scrubby palmettos, which served as settings for many desert island scenes. There were fishing villages . . . quaint old-time Florida houses with their "galleries" of white Colonial columns, orange and grapefruit groves, pear and peach orchards . . . formal gardens and Spanish patios; the gorgeous Ponce de Leon hotel and gardens, and the picturesque old fort at St. Augustine.[2]

In that first winter in Jacksonville, Kalem produced the first narrative film to be made in Florida, *A Florida Feud; or, Love in the Everglades*. Though the film depicted the poor whites of Florida in unflattering stereotypes, it was a box-office and critical success because of the location work, which was noted in the trade publications of the day. The success of this film prompted Kalem to return to Florida regularly and encouraged other companies to follow suit.

Arthur Hotaling brought his company Lubin to Florida and the West Indies in 1909, settling permanently in Jacksonville in 1912. Lubin gave Oliver "Babe" Hardy his start in films that year—well over a decade before the rotund comedian teamed with Stan Laurel. In 1910 the Selig Polyscope Company arrived in Jacksonville, followed by Majestic, Vim Studios, the Thanhouser Film Company, Gaumont Productions, and Metro, among others. Selig found Florida perfect for its series of jungle films starring the adventurous Kathlyn Williams.

Several production companies purchased land in Jacksonville in order to build permanent stages or studios. Kalem built an outdoor staging area in 1913, followed by a glass-roofed studio with a $20,000 lighting system in 1914. By that time, Lubin's Jacksonville studio was operating eight months out of the year, keeping a staff of fifty full-time employees.

Legend has it that most film companies came to Florida to escape the repressive tactics of the Motion Picture Patents Companies, a business organization that consisted of the top ten film companies of the day. Little better than a monopoly, the MPPC attempted to run small and middle-sized independent companies out of business through intimidation and violence. However, Kalem, Selig, and Lubin were all part of the MPPC, so the oft-told tale is a misassumption. Jax attracted both the established companies and the independents.

Jacksonville was also home to the Norman Film Manufacturing Company, which specialized in race movies—films made with all-black casts for black audiences in segregated theaters. Race movies featured black actors and actresses in a variety of heroic starring roles, providing a much-needed alternative to the standard stereotyped depictions of African-Americans. The Norman studios remain intact today, making them the only surviving evidence of Jacksonville's once-thriving film industry.

The mayor of Jacksonville, J. E. T. Bowden, supported the film industry because it created jobs. He lobbied hard to attract more companies and more investment to his little town. At first, residents and businesses readily cooperated, with the city's leading department store going so far as to open a movie department to assist new filmmakers in learning about the city.

It wasn't long, however, before the antics of the movie people set the townsfolk against them. Staged car chases through the city's streets seemed reckless to residents, while the filming of crime scenes on Sundays upset their sensibilities. Filmmakers seemed insensitive to the chaos they caused when they deliberately set off fire alarms in order to get shots of authentic fire trucks for free, or when they planted false stories of tragic events in order to draw hordes of people for crowd scenes. The film industry also attracted a criminal element, including gamblers and con men selling fraudulent stock in nonexistent film ventures.

In 1917 Mayor Bowden lost his reelection bid to the reform candidate John Martin, who ran largely on opposition to the film industry. Jacksonville merchants began to hike their prices when selling to the movie colony, while local banks refused to underwrite the growth of the film industry. Without political support or an established economic infrastructure, the industry quickly pulled out of Jacksonville. By that time, a sleepy little suburb of Los Angeles called Hollywood had attracted the attention of some major film companies, who had already established big studios there. Most of the Jacksonville colony relocated to the West Coast. Los Angeles supported the burgeoning film industry by offering financial backing, fostering a massive talent pool of technicians and artists, and promoting the industry to attract more independents. Unlike Jacksonville, Hollywood was more than willing to become a company town.

Filmmaking in Florida did not immediately disappear with the collapse of the Jacksonville colony. Norman continued to produce its race films in Jax during the 1920s, and the tiny Klutho company stayed on as well. Small production companies and studios had been established in Tampa and in Miami during the early 1910s, and they provided support and space for the production of a variety of films, including D. W. Griffith's *The White Rose* in 1923.

Periodically, businessmen in Florida attempted to build new studios to lure filmmakers. But without public or political support, little came of their efforts. With the hurricane of 1926, then the collapse of the land boom, and finally the Depression, hopes of reestablishing a film industry in Florida vanished.

THE BATTLE ROYAL

Even though I am in California, my heart is in Florida as
the best times of my life were spent in Jacksonville.
—Oliver Hardy, letter to Halle Cohen, in *Stan and Ollie*,
by Simon Louvish

THE STORY

The Plumps and the Runts live happily in the hills of Old Kentucky. Robert Runt woos Polly Plump, while Peter Plump has fallen for Robert's sister. When a quarrel over a fish escalates into a full-blown feud between the two families, the couples' courting comes to an abrupt halt. But then the Runts and Plumps decide to bury the hatchet in order to rid the area of pesky revenue agents.

THE FILM

Oliver Hardy reached a pinnacle of show-business success after he teamed with Stan Laurel for a string of comedy shorts and features. Their union began in 1927, when the movies were still silent, and lasted until 1951, when they made their last feature, *Atoll K*. Their comedy has continued to delight subsequent generations through exposure on television, video, and DVD.

A decade before there was a Laurel and Hardy, however, there was a Stan

Figure 1.1. Comedian Oliver Hardy. (Doll/Morrow Collection)

Jefferson and a Babe Hardy. Each had enjoyed a separate career, either as a solo comedian or as part of another team or ensemble. Oliver Hardy's career as a silent film comedian actually began in Florida, when Jacksonville rivaled Hollywood as America's film capital.

Oliver Norvell Hardy was working as a projectionist at the Electric Theatre in Milledgeville, Georgia, when a friend who had recently vacationed in Florida returned with exciting tales of moviemaking in the streets of Jacksonville. Young Hardy, a singer whose ambitions had been kindled by the vaudeville troupes that toured his native Georgia, was inspired to move to Florida and try his luck in the flickers. Initially unsuccessful, Hardy left briefly but returned to Jacksonville in 1914 with a new wife and better luck. In April 1914 he appeared in his first film, *Outwitting Dad*, produced by Lubin, one of the movie companies that had established a permanent branch in the Florida city the movie colony called Jax.

Unlike most of the great silent comedians, who had polished their acts and established their personas in vaudeville or music halls, Oliver Hardy learned his craft in front of the camera, primarily in Jacksonville. The Lubin Company was producing four one-reelers per week when Hardy joined up, and he was quickly thrown into the frenetic pace of production. By the fall of 1914, Babe Hardy—as he was often billed at the time—appeared in advertising for Lubin, suggesting he was a permanent fixture in their comic ensemble. Arthur Hotaling, who headed the Florida unit of Lubin, directed Hardy in a variety of small and secondary parts. Hardy weighed about three hundred pounds at the time, which was heavier than he would be in the Laurel and Hardy films, and often Hotaling made comic use of his girth.

Lubin closed its Florida studio in February 1915, but Hardy was hired by another Jacksonville-based production company, Vim Comedies, in early 1916. In the sixty-five one-reelers he made for Vim, Hardy developed his talent for physical comedy through larger parts and more consistent characterizations. Immediately, he was tossed into the Pokes and Jabbs film series, starring Bobby Burns and Walter Stull, in which the rotund comedian played a secondary character named Plump. When Billy Ruge joined the series as Runt, Hardy and Ruge became a comedy team with its own potential. Vim spun off the pair into their own Plump and Runt series, consisting of thrity-five one-reelers. As Peter Plump and Robert Runt, Hardy and Ruge played the same characters from film to film, with their comic identities based primarily on their contrasting size. The plot and setup of each film differed, however: *Frenzied Finance* took place in the world of banking, *Busted Hearts* was a comic romance, and *The Battle Royal* was a stereotypical view of backwoods folks in Appalachia.

Like most of the production companies based in Jacksonville, Vim took advantage of the sunny weather and diverse landscape to shoot their films outdoors. The Plump and Runt shorts were shot in streets, along the beaches, and in the wooded areas close by. To simulate the mountains of Old Kentucky, *The Battle Royal* was shot in a wooded area, though no attempt was made to get rid of the Spanish moss hanging from the trees. The one-reeler featured an ensemble cast, with several comedians filling out the Plump and Runt families, including some male actors in drag. Hardy handled the physical gags as deftly as any of the cast, stumbling over logs, wrestling with a fish on a line, and bolting through the woods. Despite his weight, he was agile, good with props, and spry, which were talents that separated the good silent film comedians from the mediocre. Hardy furthered his craft by directing a few shorts for Vim, including *The Guilty Ones*, *He Winked and Won*, *Fat and Fickle*, and *The Boycotted Baby*, which helped him understand screen comedy from the other side of the camera.

Offscreen, Babe Hardy enjoyed a warm relationship with his adopted home city of Jacksonville. He and his wife Madelyn, who was a musician, often worked together in hotels and nightclubs in the evening after he was done filming. At one time the couple lived in the Klutho Building, a modern three-story apartment building intended to entice movie people to reside permanently in Jax. He also joined the Masons in Jacksonville and retained that affiliation until he died.

By the end of 1916 Vim Comedies had collapsed, probably because of accounting irregularities by upper management. Vim was taken over by a company called Caws, which quickly changed its named to the King Bee Film Corporation. Like most of the Vim family, Hardy signed with the new company and relocated with it to Bayonne, New Jersey, and then to California in 1917. In California, Babe Hardy, who eventually changed his billing to Oliver, enjoyed a steady rise to the top. He worked his way through various production companies until he landed at Hal Roach's studio, where director Leo McCarey teamed him with Stan Laurel in 1927.

Unlike Laurel, who liked to talk about his background and past experiences with the press, Hardy did not freely discuss his early days. Consequently, few know of his close connection to Florida's short-lived film colony during the 1910s. But it was in Jacksonville that Oliver Hardy honed his talents as a silent film comedian and gained experience and confidence through the dozens of comedy shorts he shot there between 1914 and 1916. Likewise, Hardy's name and lasting fame helped Jacksonville elbow its way into film history books, even if that place rests in the shadow of Hollywood.

THE CREDITS	THE CAST	
Released in 1916 by Vim Comedies	Babe Hardy	Plump
Produced by Louis Burstein	Billy Ruge	Runt
Directed by Will Louis	Elsie MacLeod	Runt's sister
	Billy Bletcher	Grandpa Runt
	Will Louis	Revenue officer

A FLORIDA ENCHANTMENT

[The Ponce de Leon is] the most amusing of hotels.
—Henry James, *The American Scene*

THE STORY

While visiting her aunt in Florida, Lillian Travers discovers an antique chest containing magic seeds with the power to turn women into men, and men into women. In a fit of jealousy over a suitor, she swallows one of the seeds and awakens the next morning to find that she needs a shave! Now a man, Lillian goes out on the town, courts sweet Bessie Horton, and turns her female maid into a male valet by forcing her to swallow one of the seeds. The story comes full circle when Lillian's suitor downs one of the seeds and turns into a woman.

THE FILM

The gender-bending aspects of *A Florida Enchantment* tend to grab most of the attention whenever this oddity from the silent era is examined. Rediscovered by gay and lesbian film festivals, the film generated a great deal of academic discourse during the 1990s over its use of sexual reversals. Because the character of Lillian Travers was played by actress Edith Storey, even after the character turns male, and because the regendered Lillian continues to dress like a woman, at least for a while, the gay community interpreted the change Lillian undergoes as one of sexual orientation, rather than one of biology. Thus, when the regendered Lillian dances with women or actively courts Bessie Horton, it is interpreted as lesbian desire.[3]

Other scholars have offered a social interpretation of the sex reversals. Lillian swallows the seed because she suffers at the whim of a man, who is free to flirt and be attentive to all women. As the note in the chest states, herein lies "a secret for all women who suffer." By becoming a man, Lillian will obtain all the social and economic privileges and benefits of males in society. The author of the novel on which the film is based, Archibald Clavering Gunter, claimed he wrote the story to point out that "men have a better time than women amid the social environment of our present civilization."[4] However well-intended his social critique might have been, his implied solution to this inequality—that women should become men—was very male-centric in its assumption that masculinity is an ideal we all aspire to, and that women would not miss being women.

Barely mentioned in the many articles and commentaries on *A Florida*

Figure 1.2. Postcard of the Hotel Ponce de Leon. (Doll/Morrow Collection)

Figure 1.3. Postcard of the Hotel Alcazar. (Doll/Morrow Collection)

Enchantment is the film's unique setting, the magnificent Hotel Ponce de Leon in St. Augustine. Yet the setting provides a key to understanding the film in another capacity—as a chronicle of a specific moment in Florida's history. During the Gilded Age, the Ponce de Leon was one of several luxurious resort hotels where the leisure class of the East Coast spent the winter months. The construction of these resorts and other hotels not only jump-started the state's tourism and agricultural businesses but also attracted the type of guest who figured prominently in Florida's future.

Henry Flagler had made his millions as a partner to John D. Rockefeller in Standard Oil, but when Standard Oil reorganized its business structure, Flagler was free to pursue a second career in Florida. In 1885 he bought a small train line and turned it into the Florida East Coast Railroad (FEC), expanding it southward along the Atlantic coast. He also built three winter resorts and several luxury hotels along his railroad line, including the Hotel Ponce de Leon, which opened in 1888. In doing so, Flagler, along with rival Florida railroad baron Henry Plant, transferred the culture and sophistication of the East Coast to Florida by attracting the elite urban class to their hotels. The Ponce de Leon was a jewel in Flagler's crown of resorts and hotels, which also included the Hotels Alcazar and Cordova in St. Augustine and the Royal Poinciana in Palm Beach.

The Gilded Age, which was the era of the robber barons and the nouveaux riches, extended from America's centennial year to World War I. The wealthy socialites of this era dominated business and culture, but they were best known for their practice of conspicuous consumption. No party was too lavish, no home too full of plush European furnishings, no leisure resort too indulgent of its guests. *A Florida Enchantment*, with its upper-crust characters enjoying the winter season in St. Augustine, captured the era just as it was ending.

The Hotel Ponce de Leon was not just a luxurious resort; it was a magnificent stage where the guests displayed themselves for the benefit of other guests. The sumptuous 450-room Ponce de Leon and its grounds were constructed on six acres at a cost of $2.5 million. The Spanish Renaissance exterior design evoked St. Augustine's historical past by recalling the splendor of Old World Spain, giving the hotel an aura of fantasy and exoticism. Guests entered the hotel grounds from King Street between two brick gateposts decorated with lions' heads. From here they stepped into a pavilion, and then into the large courtyard with its central fountain and lush gardens. Finally they entered the main hotel through one of three arched entrances framed with such Floridian motifs as sea scallops and mermaids. Inside, the hotel was resplendent with plush furnishings, allegorical paintings, figured columns, and stained glass. It also had all the modern conveniences, including electricity, a telegraph and ticker tape office, and telephones. Flagler sought to create a different world—an indulgent world of convenience and extravagance—and he succeeded.

It is fitting that director Sidney Drew used the Ponce de Leon as the setting for *A Florida Enchantment* not only to signify the luxurious lifestyle of his characters but also to offer a suitable backdrop for a whimsical fantasy, an "enchantment." The film takes advantage of some of the hotel's most exotic features: characters in white lace dresses and summer suits lounge and converse in the lush gardens; Lillian and Bessie pause in front of one of the beautiful arched entrances; Dr. Cassadene stops to ponder a plot twist near the dolphin fountain by the ladies' entrance. The dance where Lillian so boldly courts Bessie takes place in the hotel's rotunda, with its carved caryatids visible in the background. Even the character of Dr. Cassadene reflects the indulgences of this era, because he is not a guest at the hotel but a doctor employed by the Ponce to tend to the whims and illnesses of the wealthy guests—an amenity Flagler actually supplied at his hotels.

By World War I, the fantasy lifestyle and conspicuous consumption of the Gilded Age had ended, curtailed by congressional investigations into questionable business practices, by costly upkeep on mansions and summer homes, and by the dwindling of fortunes squandered on excessive lifestyles. Understanding the significance the Hotel Ponce de Leon in the lives of the leisure class of the Gilded Age adds another layer of meaning to the title of *A Florida Enchantment*. It was not just the magic seed that was enchanted, it was also the lives of the characters—and, by extension, those of the real-life leisure class who were once so fortunate.

THE CREDITS	THE CAST	
Released in 1914 by the Vitagraph Company	Sidney Drew	Dr. Fred Cassadene
Produced by Sidney Drew	Edith Storey	Miss Lillian Travers
Directed by Sidney Drew	Charles Kent	Major Horton
Written by Marguerite Bertsch and Eugene Mullin,	Jane Morrow	Miss Bessie Horton
from a novel and play by Archibald Clavering	Ada Gifford	Miss Stella Lovejoy
Gunter	Ethel Lloyd	Jane
Cinematography by Robert A. Stuart	Grace Stevens	Miss Constancia Oglethorpe

THE FLYING ACE

Thrills. Action. Punch! The Greatest Airplane Mystery Thriller Ever Produced.
—poster for *The Flying Ace*

THE STORY

Asked by his former boss to track down a missing paymaster and the company payroll, Captain William Stokes quickly gets on the case. Stokes, a former railroad detective and World War I hero, eventually discovers the misjudged paymaster, uncovers the true villain, and recovers the payroll.

THE FILM

The Flying Ace became the fifth film with an all-African-American cast produced by Richard E. Norman at the Eagle Studios in Jacksonville, Florida. The Norman Film Manufacturing Company had begun making films with all-black casts in 1919 with the release of the romantic melodrama *Green-Eyed Monster*, originally produced in 1916 with a white cast. While there is no written evidence to reveal why Norman, who was white, decided to make films with African-American casts, the release of his films coincided with the initial wave of "race movies."

Race movies were films with all-black casts made for black audiences. Many were produced by independent black filmmakers or production companies, including the Lincoln Motion Picture Company in Los Angeles and the Micheaux Film Corporation of Chicago. Race movies first flourished after the release of D. W. Griffith's *Birth of a Nation* in 1915, partly in response to the offensive portrayal of African-Americans in that film. Soon dozens of small companies cropped up in urban markets to make low-budget films for African-American audiences in segregated or black theaters. The Norman Film Manufacturing Company made films for segregated theaters across the Deep South, from Florida and Alabama to Texas.

Norman, a Florida native, had been trying to find his niche in the film industry since 1912, when he traveled through the Midwest producing films for very localized markets. During this time he visited small towns and villages and offered to shoot a fictional film incorporating local events, residents, and businesses. After the film was completed, he sold tickets to screenings held at schools, churches, and theaters for a 60–40 split. In the mid-teens, he returned to Jacksonville to make feature films for national distribution. When the African-American version of *Green-Eyed Monster* did well at the box office, Norman saw the financial advantage of making race movies.

Most of Norman's race movies were genre films with exciting, adventurous story lines. *The Crimson Skull* and *The Bull-Dogger* were Westerns that included

Figure 1.4. Advertisement for *The Flying Ace*. (State Archives of Florida)

scenes of legendary black cowboy Bill Pickett roping and riding. *Regeneration* was a South Seas tale involving sunken treasure, while *Black Gold* was about oil riggers in Oklahoma. *The Flying Ace*, also known as *The Fighting Ace* or *The Black Ace*, took advantage of the post-WWI craze for tales of flying.

Like most races movies, Norman's films were shot on very low budgets. While the protagonist of *The Flying Ace*, Captain William Stokes, is a champion flier who returns from the war a bona fide hero, actor Lawrence Criner, who played Stokes, never left the ground. Much of the action occurred on the airfield around the plane, and the few "flying stunts" in the film were simulated. *The Flying Ace* was shot primarily at the Eagle Studios, located in the suburb of Arlington, with the opening scenes shot at the Mayport train station in Jacksonville.

The lack of actual flying stunts did not seem to interfere with the box office success of the film. *The Flying Ace* was in circulation for almost a decade, grossing approximately $20,000 for Norman.[5] Part of the appeal of the film was Criner, a featured actor with the famous Lafayette Players, who had also starred in Norman's *Black Gold* and Oscar Micheaux's *The Millionaire*. Costarring with Criner was character actor Steve "Peg" Reynolds, a one-legged performer who was a Norman favorite. Criner's real-life wife Kathryn Boyd, a prominent black actress of the period, played his love interest in the film.

Those who look for historical accuracy in films will be disappointed in *The Flying Ace*. The protagonist could not have flown missions in France for the U.S. Air Force because African-Americans were not allowed to train as pilots in the armed services until 1940. However, there were a few real-life black flying aces who might have inspired the fictional character, including Eugene Bullard, a volunteer in the French Foreign Legion and the French army, and Hubert Fauntleroy Julian, who learned to fly as a member of the Royal Canadian Air Corps. Julian and black aviatrix Bessie Coleman, who learned to fly in France, barnstormed around America during the 1920s performing daredevil stunts. In 1924 Norman contacted Coleman and another black stunt flier, Captain Edison C. McVey, about making a film. McVey owned his own production company, Afro-American Film Producers of Galveston, Texas, and had footage of himself performing a variety of dangerous stunts. While the deals with Coleman and McVey did not work out, these barnstormers influenced Norman to make a film about a black flying ace, even if he failed to include actual flying footage.

Norman released his last race movie, *Black Gold*, in 1927. He continued to operate Eagle Studios and distribute the films of others for years after Jacksonville ceased to be a filmmaking capital, eventually turning to the production of industrial training films to make a living. The race movie market was always highly competitive, partly because theater owners tended to pit the production companies against each other to try to get the best deal. But the expense of synch sound at the end of the 1920s led to the demise of almost all black production companies. Only the tenacious Oscar Micheaux survived the coming of sound.

Race movies were an important part of film history because they provided both an alternative view of African-Americans on the big screen and creative opportunities for African-Americans behind the camera. Mainstream commercial films offered limited roles for black actors and provided no opportunities for black writers, directors, or craftsmen. At best, black actors in Hollywood were relegated to supporting parts or cameo performances as singers and dancers; at worst, they were offered derogatory stereotyped roles as maids, porters, or the comic relief. In race movies, black actors starred as a variety of heroic characters—from cowboys to detectives to flying aces. Like any audience, African-Americans benefited by seeing positive images of themselves in popular culture. While *The Flying Ace* was not historically accurate, it offered a view of blacks as daring and heroic as that of white protagonists in Hollywood films.

THE CREDITS	THE CAST	
Released in 1926 by the Norman Film Manufacturing Company	Lawrence Criner	Captain William Stokes
Directed by Richard E. Norman	Kathryn Boyd	Ruth Sawtelle
	George Colvin	Thomas Sawtelle
	Harold Platts	Finley Tucker
	Steve "Peg" Reynolds	Peg
	Boise DeLegge	Blair Kimball
	Lyons Daniels	Jed Spivens

THE GIRL SPY SERIES

I wrote a picture called *The Adventures of the Girl Spy*, which embodied all the difficult and sometimes dangerous stunts I could conjure up.... It made a tremendous hit and exhibitors wrote in for more. Thus began the first series made in films.

—Gene Gauntier, *Blazing the Trail*

THE STORY

Disguised as a boy, a spunky Southern girl named Nan becomes a spy for the Confederate Army. The intrepid Girl Spy survives many a hair-raising adventure as she carries out her missions on behalf of her beloved South.

THE FILMS

A plucky heroine on a perilous adventure seems like the setup for a contemporary film starring one of today's actresses who might train for weeks with a variety of experts to get in shape for the reel-to-reel stunts. Few remember that in the pioneering days of the cinema, plucky heroines populated the big screen in a variety of serials and series. Actresses whose names have long since been forgotten gingerly stepped into these energetic roles, doing their own stunt work before stunt men, trainers, or action coordinators even existed. Gene Gauntier not only starred in such a series, she also wrote each episode.

In the earliest days of the silent cinema, many women were actively involved behind the camera. Generally starting out as actresses in small production companies, women often found themselves helping out in whatever capacity was needed. Most of the troupes were small, with a family-like atmosphere in which all company members did a variety of tasks. The informality of the early days resulted in an egalitarianism in which actresses learned to write, direct, and even manage the details of production. Like Gauntier, many actresses turned to writing scenarios—to the point where women scenarists outnumbered men ten to one during the silent era.[6]

Gauntier joined the Kalem Company in 1906 as an actress, but the following year Kalem cofounder Frank Marion asked her to write an original story for a romantic melodrama. Though her first effort turned out to be "not filmable," she decided to try again by adapting Mark Twain's *Tom Sawyer* into a one-reel adventure. From that point on, Gauntier became Kalem's premiere writer, eventually penning more than three hundred scenarios for one-reelers, sometimes at the rate of three a day.[7] In addition, she continued to appear in films, often writing and starring in action-packed adventures based on stories she found in books, magazines, or poems.

Gauntier's entry into the movies came at a very early moment in film history, and her career made an impact on the emerging industry in more ways than one. She preceded D. W. Griffith—the Father of American Film—into the business, and the story goes that it was Gauntier who recommended to American Biograph that they use Griffith as a director. According to her autobiography, *Blazing the Trail*, she assigned Griffith his first film to direct, *The Adventures of Dollie*, during her brief stint as a scenarist for Biograph. She supposedly assigned legendary cameraman Billy Bitzer to help him. If this is true, she brought together the most famous director-cinematographer team in history.[8] Whether apocryphal or not, the story points to Gauntier as a seasoned veteran in the "picture business" when Griffith was still a struggling actor-playwright.

Gauntier also wrote the scenario that would spark the test case responsible for amending American copyright laws to include movies. In the early days, scenario writers freely borrowed from novels, plays, poems, short stories, and even other movies without acknowledging the original author or source. After Gauntier's adaptation of *Ben-Hur* was released by Kalem in 1907, the estate of author Lew Wallace sued the film company for copyright infringement. The case was eventually settled in 1912 with Kalem paying the Wallace estate $25,000. From that point forward, all films had to be registered for copyright, and movie companies had to submit material related to their movies at the Copyright Office of the Library of Congress. Adapting scenarios from outside sources became a more structured and accountable enterprise.

Most important, Gauntier was a true pioneer in the evolution of filmmaking practices and conventions. In 1912 she wrote and appeared in a five-reel adaptation of the Christ story shot on location in Palestine and titled *From the Manger to the Cross*. An early example of the multireel film, *Manger* preceded any of Griffith's forays into longer films, a distinction that landed it on the National Film Registry in 1998. Far less known but also significant are her Girl Spy adventures (1909–12), which Gauntier claimed were the cinema's first true series.[9] Series are not to be confused with serials; in the former, each entry is complete in itself but the characters are the same from film to film, while the latter consists of a continuing story told in several episodes. During the silent era, both series and serials stressed action, adventure, and stunts, and many featured female characters in the role of the heroic protagonist.

The Girl Spy films were produced in Florida by Kalem, which had sent a stock company to Jacksonville in 1908 to make films during the winter months. The company included Gauntier as a leading lady and key writer and Sidney Olcott as the main director. The group headquartered in the Jacksonville suburb of Fairfield at the Roseland Hotel, a large ramshackle establishment on the banks of the St. Johns River. The founders of Kalem had always insisted on location shooting, because it was conducive to action and looked picturesque on the big screen. Kalem's directors and writers specialized in capturing the atmosphere of a location and utilizing geography to the best advantage. The area across the St. Johns River from the Roseland was relatively undeveloped and became a major location for Kalem's one-reelers. Strawberry Creek was particularly useful, because it captured the look and feel of the Deep South, with its swamps, Spanish moss, palmettos, and water hyacinths. The only problem was the snakes—rattlers, moccasins, and copperheads—which required the cast and crew to carry medicine kits on a steady basis.

From the beginning of her days with Kalem, Gauntier had appeared in action-oriented films, with lots of thrills and spills. When she wrote scenarios for herself, she concocted stories of great adventure with numerous stunts. One such film was 1909's *The Adventures of the Girl Spy*, which used Florida's geog-

Figure 1.5. Gene Gauntier *(second row, center)* in a publicity poster for the Kalem Company. (State Archives of Florida)

raphy as an integral part of its action. The main character, Nan, was inspired by the famous Confederate spy Belle Boyd, who had disguised herself as a boy to spy for the South during the Civil War. *Girl Spy* became a hit, and Gauntier continued Nan's exploits in such films as *The Further Adventures of the Girl Spy* and *The Girl Spy Before Vicksburg*, with Olcott as the director. Gauntier, as Nan, found herself being hurled through the air by exploding ammunition dumps, trapped in burning buildings, and stuck in either snake-infested or shark-infested waters. Eventually the difficult stunt work took its toll, and she decided to end the series by marrying Nan off and ending the war. However, the Girl Spy proved so popular that Gauntier was persuaded to resurrect her one more time, despite the fact that the war had ended in the last entry to the series. The clever writer solved this dilemma by titling the new film *A Hitherto Unrelated Incident of the Girl Spy*, implying the story took place prior to the previous film—a very early example of a prequel. (Later, Reliance produced *The Girl Spy's Atonement*, starring Norma Phillips, which was not part of Gauntier's series.)

Aside from the series format, the stunt work by Gauntier, and the effective use of location, the Girl Spy films are also notable as Civil War narratives. The year 1911 marked the fiftieth anniversary of the start of the Civil War, and the years surrounding this anniversary saw a proliferation of Civil War movies. At first, most of these films were shot in the North and their stories unfolded from the Northern perspective, but the Girl Spy series countered the trend by using a Southern heroine, a Confederate point of view, and Southern locations. By the end of 1911, the trend had reversed and more Civil War films were presented from the Southern perspective.[10]

Soon after the Girl Spy series ended, Gauntier formed her own production company in Florida with director Sidney Olcott, but the venture was short-lived. In 1918 she retired from making films to work as a war correspondent. By the time she penned her memoirs for *Woman's Home Companion* in 1928, so much had changed in the film industry that her name was no longer recognized. Afterward, she became a relatively successful novelist, preferring to live outside the United States—never once looking back on the industry that had so completely forgotten her.

THE CREDITS	THE CAST	
Released from 1909 to 1912 by the Kalem Company	Gene Gauntier	Nan, the Girl Spy
Directed by Sidney Olcott	various others	
Written by Gene Gauntier		
Cinematography by George Hollister		
Art direction by Henry Allen Farnham		

THE IDOL DANCER

A story burning with primeval love, teem-
ing with the hot passions of the jungle.
—advertisement, *New York Times*

THE STORY

On Romance Beach, an island under the Southern Cross, native girl White
Almond Flower lives a carefree life with her adopted father. Untamed and uninhibited, she dances in front of her pagan idol, stirring the passions of two
men, Dan, a drunken beachcomber, and Walter, the nephew of the island's
missionary.

THE FILM

In 1919 the name D. W. Griffith was synonymous with the highest level of
American filmmaking. Within the industry, particularly among filmmakers
and exhibitors, he was credited with raising "the flickers" above the level of an
arcade amusement. Griffith must have felt pressured to make a masterwork
each time he stepped behind the camera, because reviewers were quick to judge
whether his work was up to the Griffith standard, and exhibitors expected his
films to bring in the crowds.

The years just after World War I were very busy for Griffith. He had production deals with three different studios or companies—Artcraft, First National,
and United Artists. Between the three companies, he owed at least ten films.
Griffith had recently purchased and renovated the old Henry Flagler estate
in Mamaroneck, New York, which he planned to turn into a production facility where he and his troupe of regulars could work smoothly and quickly.
However, the first film to be shot at Mamaroneck was actually directed by actress Lillian Gish. Griffith left her in charge in the winter of 1919–20 after he
decided to shoot two films in Florida back to back as part of his commitment
to First National.

The veteran filmmaker opted for this course of action primarily because
First National had already given him the start money for two of the three films
he owed them, but also because he wanted a break from winter shooting. He
selected material that was well suited to a warm climate and tropical locale and
turned it into two films about love in the South Seas islands, *The Love Flower*
and *The Idol Dancer*. *Dancer* was based specifically on two stories by Gordon
Ray Young titled *Heathens* and *Blood of the Covenanters*, which were owned by
Griffith's company but probably unpublished. Griffith took most of his regu-

lar troupe with him to Florida, including actors Richard Barthelmess, Clarine Seymour, Carol Dempster, and Porter Strong, in addition to cinematographer G. W. "Billy" Bitzer and assistant director Elmer Clifton. The two films would star virtually the same cast, except that Seymour was selected to play the leading lady in *The Idol Dancer* while Dempster would star in *The Love Flower*.

The Griffith cast and crew disembarked at Ft. Lauderdale, which was a small town of swamps and coconut groves in 1919. Evidently deciding that Lauderdale did not provide the backdrop he needed, Griffith sent location scouts to the Bahamas and Cuba to find picturesque settings. A spot on New Providence Island was chosen, and plans were made for the cast and crew to sail there. Despite his disappointment, Griffith did shoot a variety of establishing shots and exteriors in the Lauderdale area, and some of them showed up in *The Idol Dancer*, including a long shot of an industrious harbor with a variety of boats and ships, and a few shots of tangled scrub brush peppered with palmetto bushes.

The most memorable part of Griffith's Florida excursion turned out to be the sea voyage from Miami to the Bahamas to shoot the principal action of both films. Griffith hired a young sailor to take his group to the location aboard a yacht called the *Grey Duck*. According to Billy Bitzer, the sailor hoped to use Griffith's money as a down payment to buy the *Grey Duck* for rum-running—a lucrative livelihood in Florida during Prohibition.[11]

The trip should have taken about two days, but the young captain and his inexperienced crew soon veered off course. The decision was made to anchor in the Berry Islands. The next day a storm blew up, and the group, which numbered thirty-seven, decided to weather it where they were. Despite a shortage of food, the spirits of the group were kept up by spirits of another nature.

With near-hurricane force, the storm blew along the original course of the *Grey Duck*. The coast guard in Miami grew alarmed when the yacht did not reach its destination on time, and boats and planes were dispatched to search for the wayward film people. Actor Richard Barthelmess had stayed behind in Florida for a few extra days with his mother, and when he found out about his friends, he chartered a former minesweeper to join the coast guard in the search. Meanwhile, the lack of food and sanitation pushed Griffith to ask the captain to set off once again. The *Grey Duck* finally anchored in the Bahamas on the fifth day of their adventure.

The flurry of activity surrounding the *Grey Duck* was noted by the newspapers, who tried to turn the search into a big story. When the film people showed up unharmed, the newspapers felt cheated out of major headlines. Hints were dropped that perhaps the whole escapade had been a publicity stunt, because Griffith's most recent film, *The Greatest Question*, was about life

Figure 1.6. Director D. W. Griffith *(seated)* and cameraman
Billy Bitzer in Florida. (State Archives of Florida)

after death. Perhaps he was trying to drum up business for the film, which
was failing at the box office, by staging a near-death experience. However, in
a letter to Navy Secretary Josephus Daniels thanking him for the search party,
Griffith declared, "We were in some peril."[12]

The adventures of the *Grey Duck* proved a more interesting tale than the
one that unfolded in *The Idol Dancer*, a torrid melodrama with flat direction
and florid performances. Melodramas had always been Griffith's specialty, but
this film lacked the controlled pacing and solid characters of his best work.
Young leading lady Clarine Seymour, who died shortly after the film was released, was being groomed for stardom by Griffith, but she lacked the skill of
his other leading ladies, Lillian Gish and Mae Marsh. The film's editing was

clunky and repetitious, and the cinematography failed to take advantage of the exotic locations. The many weaknesses of *The Idol Dancer* have caused some to speculate that assistant director Elmer Clifton may have done more than assist on this film; rushed because of the contracts hanging over his head, Griffith may have handed most of the directorial chores over to Clifton, while shooting *The Love Flower* himself. After the photography was completed, Griffith returned to Mamaroneck, where he hurried through the editing of both films.

Despite the promises of posters and ads, *The Idol Dancer* and *The Love Flower* failed to ignite audiences with the "hot passions of the jungle." After his contract with First National was fulfilled, Griffith seemed to be through with filming humdrum material by hack writers. He returned to stories with strong characters in familiar settings, releasing one of his masterpieces, *Way Down East*, later that year.

THE CREDITS

Released in 1920 by First National
Directed by D. W. Griffith
Written by E. V. Taylor, from two stories by
    Gordon Ray Young
Edited by James Smith
Cinematography by G. W. Bitzer and Paul H. Allen

THE CAST

Clarine Seymour	Mary, aka White Almond Flower
Richard Barthelmess	Dan McGuire
George MacQuarrie	Rev. Franklyn Blythe
Creighton Hale	Walter Blythe
Kate Bruce	Mrs. Blythe
Porter Strong	The Reverend Peter
Walter James	Chief Wando
Anders Randolph	The Blackbirder

The Love Flower

Another film shot by D. W. Griffith on location in Florida and the Bahamas in 1919–20 was *The Love Flower*, a romantic melodrama based on a story by Ralph Stock originally published in *Collier's Weekly*. Carol Dempster, who was romantically involved with Griffith at the time, starred as a young woman who escapes to a South Seas island with her father, who has just shot her mother's lover. Once on the island, Dempster is torn between an idle-rich playboy and the dogged detective pursuing her. Reviews made note of the film's remarkable use of locations and atmospheric photography, suggesting that Griffith himself directed this production, undoubtedly because Dempster was in the starring role.

IT'S THE OLD ARMY GAME

> The picnic scene tells us part of what is wrong with
> the country, though it does not go so far as to tell
> us what to do about it.
> —Carl Sandburg, review of *It's the Old Army Game*

THE STORY

Elmer Prettywillie must contend with the whims and antics of the customers who frequent his small-town drugstore, from the haughty matron who wakes him up in the middle of the night for a two-cent stamp to the freeloading firemen who want sodas on the house. When a fast-talking real estate speculator talks him into a Florida land scheme, Elmer jumps at the chance to get rich quick.

THE FILM

A vaudeville headliner with the George White Scandals and the Ziegfeld Follies, W. C. Fields hoped to duplicate his stage success on the silver screen when he starred in *It's the Old Army Game* in 1926. Fields's first venture into the movies had been in a one-reeler titled *Pool Sharks* back in 1915. More recently he had appeared in a few feature films, including *Sallie of the Sawdust*, which was a re-creation of his acclaimed stage hit *Poppy*. But he was not yet a movie star.

Famous Players–Lasky, later known as Paramount, signed the comedian to a long-term contract intending to make him the next Charlie Chaplin or Harold Lloyd. With *It's the Old Army Game*, the plan was to adapt some of the comedian's recent vaudeville skits to the big screen. The most famous bit in the film was the "back porch sketch," in which Fields's character, a druggist with the slightly off-color name Elmer Prettywillie, tries to nap on the back porch but has his beauty sleep interrupted by a noisy baby, a fruit peddler, and the ice man. The sketch had been the best part of a short-lived play called *The Comic Supplement*, and when the play folded, Fields adapted the bit to the Ziegfeld Follies. Eight years later, the sketch would be reworked for *It's a Gift*, one of the comedian's classic sound films.

The final sequence in the film was the "picnic sketch," in which Elmer and his obnoxious family picnic on the lawn of a grand estate, trashing the place in the process. The picnic sketch had also been featured in the Follies. Adapting Fields's recent routines was a smart strategy, because it was less stressful for the comedian to tailor familiar work to the cinema than it was for him to invent entirely new sketches for a medium he was not used to. Also, any viewers who had seen Fields on the stage would be primed to enjoy his well-known routines on film.

It's the Old Army Game threaded together Fields's comic bits with the barest of plots, exposing a disadvantage of adapting his sketches to film. Compared with vaudeville or musical comedy reviews, movies required more attention paid to narrative. Consequently, *Army Game* suffers from its weak plotting.

It is the plot, however, that gives the film its Florida connection. The second half of the film finds Elmer Prettywillie involved in a real estate scheme with a conniving New York speculator. Florida during the Roaring Twenties was in the midst of a major land boom. The feverish activity in land sales that brought new development to the state also brought out so many unscrupulous speculators that "buying swampland in Florida" became a joke in numerous plays, comedy sketches, and films of the period (see *The Cocoanuts*, chapter 7).

Scriptwriter Tom Geraghty, who also acted as the film's supervisor, not only set the story in Florida but decided to shoot part of the film there as well. The cast and crew spent a month in Ocala and Palm Beach shooting the picnic sketch, a romantic scene between secondary players Louise Brooks and William Gaxton, and a few exteriors of Ocala streets. Though the palm trees and lush vegetation gave the film a distinct sense of location and some much needed vibrancy, the crew lacked discipline and focus while they were shooting these scenes.

The picnic sketch was shot at El Mirasol, the Palm Beach estate of Edward T. Stotesbury, a senior partner in J. P. Morgan and Company. Stotesbury and his wife, Eva, also owned two other luxury homes—a small mansion in Bar Harbor, Maine, and their main estate in Philadelphia. According to some sources, the Stotesburys were a bit starstruck, and they gladly lent the grounds of their Florida estate to Paramount for the film's production.[13] The sketch called for Prettywillie, his spinster sister, and his bratty nephew to drive onto the lawn and picnic in front of the main house, ignorant of the damage they were inflicting on private property. "A motorist has no rights anymore," complains Elmer. "Imagine a man building a house in the middle of a beautiful lawn like this!" The crew shot for five days at El Mirasol, and during that time a great deal of actual damage was done to the grounds. Three separate takes were done of Fields driving through the gates of the estate, across the manicured lawn, and then through the tall hedges, destroying part of the hedges in the process and cutting deep ruts into the lawn. The cast and crew littered the grounds with newspapers, food wrappers, and cigar butts, while the servants looked on aghast. Fields supposedly took great delight in the disrespect shown the Stotesbury estate.[14] A native of Philadelphia, he had experienced an abysmal

Figure 1.7. Poster for *It's the Old Army Game*. (Doll/Morrow Collection)

childhood of poverty and abuse, leaving home at age eleven to struggle on his own. Scarred and embittered by his early life, Fields undoubtedly remembered the privileged Stotesburys of Philadelphia's highest rung of society and exacted a minor revenge.

According to costar Louise Brooks, the residents of Ocala treated the movie people to some down-home Southern hospitality, which included an unending supply of alcohol. Brooks recalled, "Nobody in Ocala seemed to have heard of Prohibition, and if there was a company that needed no help in the consumption of liquor, it was ours."[15] One wild night, Fields and two friends drove all the way to Miami to buy six cases of gin from a gangster, with Fields packing a .38 in case of trouble. The carousing took its toll on the film, with the production falling a week behind schedule. When producer William LeBaron, who had remained behind in New York, noticed that some of the rushes were out of focus and tilted because one of the cameramen was repeatedly hung over, he yanked the cast and crew home.

Not surprisingly, Fields was dissatisfied with the final film. The narrative was undeveloped and disjointed, while his character teetered between being a lovable curmudgeon and a cruel bully. The experience taught the savvy performer the value of a tightly constructed script and a consistent screen character. By the time of the sound era, W. C. Fields would emerge as one of Hollywood's premiere screen comedians, with a firmly established comic style and persona.

THE CREDITS	THE CAST	
Released in 1926 by Famous Players–Lasky Corporation, distributed by Paramount Pictures	W. C. Fields	Elmer Prettywillie
	Louise Brooks	Mildred Marshall
Produced by William LeBaron	Blanche Ring	Tessie Overholt
Directed by Edward Sutherland	William Gaxton	George Parker
Written by Thomas J. Geraghty and J. Clarkson Miller, from a story by Joseph P. McEvoy and William LeBaron	Mary Foy	Sarah Pancoast
	Mickey Bennett	Mickey
Edited by Thomas J. Geraghty		
Cinematography by Alvin Wyckoff		

LOST IN THE JUNGLE

Death was her leading man, not once, but many times.
—*Movie Weekly*, on Kathlyn Williams's work
in animal films

THE STORY

Meta Kruga and her father live an idyllic existence fifty miles into the interior of Africa. Mr. Kruga wants his daughter to marry a neighbor, Hans, but Meta refuses because she has fallen for a young Englishman. After Kruga throws her out of the house, Meta becomes lost in a jungle infested with vicious animals and hidden dangers.

THE FILM

Selig Polyscope, one of the industry's pioneering companies, developed a reputation for producing jungle adventures and animal films, especially after a Selig troupe established a studio in Jacksonville in 1910. Selig rented its menagerie of exotic animals from a showman and trainer named Big Otto, eventually purchasing the animals sometime before the entire studio operation relocated to Los Angeles around 1912. The jungle and animal adventures proved quite successful for the studio, while the star, Kathlyn Williams, became Selig's biggest sensation between 1910 and 1916.

A native of Montana, the athletic Williams was an animal lover who thrived on adventure for much of her life. She gamely agreed to do her own animal stunts during her Selig years, despite a lack of training or experience with exotic animals. In this early era of filmmaking, the industry had no standard safety policies to protect actors, nor was there any organization to monitor the use of animals on the set. While the Selig producers would never have deliberately put Williams in harm's way, the lack of standard procedures and stunt coordinators on these films was an invitation to trouble.

Lost in the Jungle was shot in Jacksonville in 1911, using the tropical landscape of the area to suggest deepest, darkest Africa. Populating Selig's Jacksonville jungle was a collection of animal stars, who provided the adventure in the story. Sharing the big screen with Williams were Toddles the elephant, Charlie the lion, Elmer the camel, and four unnamed leopards. Despite the presence of a dashing young newcomer named Tom Mix, Toddles was the big hero of *Lost in the Jungle*. After Williams's character is attacked by a leopard, the elephant picks up the injured girl with his trunk and carries her home on his head. To judge from the remembrances of several cast members, Toddles was quite the

Figure 1.8. Silent film actress Kathlyn Williams.
(Courtesy of the Academy of Motion Picture Arts and Sciences)

character on the set, though undoubtedly his antics have been exaggerated by the haze of memory and nostalgia. The big male elephant's best trick was to inhale a substance and then spray it through his trunk. When no one was paying attention, Toddles liked to dip his trunk into the coffee pots and shower the unsuspecting cast and crew with cold coffee and grounds.

Two months prior to shooting *Lost in the Jungle*, Williams began winning the trust and affection of Toddles by tossing him oranges every morning. She knew that her safety in her big scenes with Toddles was dependent on forging a connection with the elephant. Though Toddles often heaved the oranges back at her during these bonding sessions, the ploy worked well enough that the climactic sequence occurred without a hitch. One reviewer remarked about the final film, "Everyone who views the picture will feel like hugging the ponderous brute when he kneels and assists the helpless girl. . . . It is a thrilling rescue and fairly startles one by its novelty and realism."[16]

Though Toddles proved to be an amiable costar, the same could not be said for the leopards. One incident with the big cats resulted in severe scalp lacerations as well as a mountain of publicity for Kathlyn Williams and could have cost her life. Conflicting accounts of the story have evolved over the years, but the most consistent versions include a leopard, Williams, and some chickens. While shooting the scene of the leopard attack, Williams lay down behind a log. A chicken was to be tossed over her as a way to entice one of the trained leopards to leap over her and the log. The camera would then capture the leopard leaping over her in midair, making it look like it was on the attack. This strategy worked well enough in rehearsal, but during the actual shooting, the leopard became distracted when Williams's hair (which was light blond and about the same color value as the chicken) blew in the wind. The big cat struck the actress in the head with his massive paw, severely cutting her scalp. Williams was covered in blood to her waist.[17]

The incident with the big cat did not deter Williams from starring in other animal pictures—or from handling other adventurous stunts, for that matter. After leaving Florida, she starred in a handful of aviation films for Selig in Chicago that required her to fly with stunt pilots. She was so intoxicated by flight that she took flying lessons and eventually received a pilot's licence. In 1912 Williams moved with the Selig organization to the Los Angeles area, where she continued as the studio's premiere adventure actress. There the studio expanded its operations, even constructing the Selig Jungle Zoo opposite Eastlake Park in Los Angeles to house animals for its films, including *The Adventures of Kathlyn*, an early serial starring Williams.

As the industry evolved and audience tastes expanded beyond one- and two-reel escapades, Williams established herself as a serious actress. Not unlike Gene Gauntier (see "The Girl Spy Series" above), she also wrote several screenplays for herself and produced a few of her films. She eventually left Selig for other production companies and studios, settling into character parts in the 1920s. Offscreen, she became known for entertaining the elite of Hollywood with sophisticated dinner and cocktail parties. A series of personal tragedies in the mid-1920s curtailed her socializing and caused her to retire from the screen. In 1949 Williams was involved in a car accident that left her in a wheelchair for the rest of her life—a cruel fate for someone who thrived on adventure—and she withdrew into isolation and depression. Like so many other pioneering women from the early days of the film industry, Kathlyn Williams was forgotten and then lost to the history books.

THE CREDITS	THE CAST	
Released in 1911 by the Selig Polyscope Company	Kathlyn Williams	Meta Kruga
Directed by Otis Turner	William V. Mong	Jan Kruga
Written by Otto Breitkreutz and William V. Mong	Frank Weed	Sir John Morgan
	Charles Clary	Hirshal
	Ernest Anderson	Hans
	Tom Mix	Bit part

MIDNIGHT FACES

Midnight—the innocent little hour that is blamed for everything.
—title card in *Midnight Faces*

THE STORY

Lynn Claymore arrives in the Florida Everglades to claim a deserted mansion that he inherited from a long-lost uncle. His arrival attracts the attention of several offbeat characters, who all find reasons to visit the newly opened mansion. Then the guests begin to disappear one by one in a mysterious chain of events.

THE FILM

Midnight Faces, also known as *Midnight Fires*, was not produced by a major studio or directed by a prominent filmmaker. It starred no well-known actors, nor did it feature particularly high production values. How it came to be shot in Florida and why it survived when so many acclaimed silents have been lost or destroyed are bigger mysteries than those found in the movie's feeble plot. Yet it is obscure films like *Midnight Faces* that sometimes throw wrenches into the works of cinema scholarship, proving that history is never static, never a closed book.

The film's narrative is an early cinematic example of the "old dark house" tale, in which a group of characters spend one or more nights in a supposedly haunted house. In this subgenre of the horror film, the old dark house is seldom truly haunted. Instead, nefarious members of the group are often involved in a scheme to bilk others out of the property, or out of a treasure located there.

In *Midnight Faces*, the characters who come together for a night or two in "the old dark house" make such a motley crew that it becomes unintentionally humorous. Arriving at his newly acquired mansion, Lynn Claymore is accompanied by his African-American personal man, Trohelius, and the estate attorney, Richard Mason. They are joined by the mansion's former butler, Useless McGurk, and its housekeeper, Mrs. Hart, followed quickly by old Samuel Lund, who is paralyzed and confined to a wheelchair. A cute and vivacious flapper, Mary Bronson, pops up, catching the eye of Lynn, who seems not to notice that she has no explanation for being there. Mary seems to be in cahoots with Suie Chang, a Mandarin Chinese man who is accompanied by two brutes named Otis and Red. The group are preyed upon by a mysterious figure in a long, dark cape and wide-brimmed hat who appears and disappears from secret passageways and dark corners of the house. Eventually the plot unfolds—or rather unravels—to reveal that Lynn's dead uncle, Peter Marlin, is still alive and not really his uncle after all. The mysterious man in black is Samuel Lund, who is not really paralyzed, and Chang turns out to be Peter Marlin's good friend and not really the villain. The whole affair was a ruse on the part of Lund and attorney Mason to get the Marlin mansion.

Though an unexceptional film at best, *Midnight Faces* is of interest because it was released the year before Paul Leni's well-known film version of *The Cat and the Canary*. Leni's film is generally considered the prototype for the old dark house subgenre,[18] not only because of the plot but also because of its expressionist style. Leni had achieved great success in Germany with the expressionist films *Waxworks* and *The Student of Prague*. *The Cat and the Canary* was his first Hollywood film after immigrating to America, and he brought to the film the low-key lighting, symbolism, and heavy use of atmosphere associated with German expressionism. The direct influence of expressionism on the emergence of the American horror genre has been well documented, and Leni's film makes a nice clean starting point for that documentation.

Figure 1.9. *Midnight Faces* star Kathryn McGuire, as she appeared with Buster Keaton in *The Navigator*. (Doll/Morrow Collection)

However, *Midnight Faces* also uses the old dark house plot, while exhibiting some of the visual motifs and characteristics of German expressionism. Many interior scenes are rendered in low-key lighting, though it is sloppily handled and falls short of creating the requisite heavy atmosphere. Expressionist lighting cues abound, including the use of bar shadows to suggest entrapment and the depiction of the killer in silhouetted shadow to suggest he is the evil doppelganger of one of the characters. The shadowy hand of the killer, shown as he goes about his deadly business, is a reminder of the expressionists' preference for using the outstretched, clawlike hand in scenes of great tension or strife. While the release of *Midnight Faces* a year before *The Cat and the Canary* does not detract from the latter's influence on American horror films, it does weaken *Cat*'s position as the prototype of this subgenre in Hollywood.

Bennett Cohen (sometimes Cohn), the writer-director of *Midnight Faces*, could have lifted the old dark house plot from the play version of *The Cat and the Canary*, which had been a popular stage production since 1922. But where he picked up the expressionist influence is not known. Was he familiar with German films, some of which were released in the States? Or did *Midnight Faces* emulate other American horror films, now lost, that had already begun using the expressionist style?

Cohen deviated from the German style in deciding to shoot on location in the swamps of Florida. Most German expressionist films are products of studio production—the better to control the lighting, set design, and camera work, which are central to the German style. But Cohen set and shot *Midnight Faces* in the "bayous" of Florida (as one of the film's intertitles puts it). The characters arrive at the mansion in canoes and rowboats via a swamp, with Spanish moss overhanging the murky water. An actual frame house set in a brushy, wooded area is used for the exterior shots of the mansion, though interiors were more than likely shot in a studio or controlled environment. The Florida location adds an aura of seclusion and an atmosphere of exotic eeriness.

Midnight Faces is by no means a lost classic, but its existence serves as a reminder that the tenets of film history are not written in stone, and they can evolve or change at the discovery of any little-known or lost film. It also demonstrates that any film—no matter how odd or mediocre—is worthy of serious consideration.

THE CREDITS

Produced in 1926 by Otto K. Schreier Productions,
  distributed by Goodwill Pictures
Directed by Bennett Cohen
Written by Bennett Cohen
Photographed by King Grey
Edited by Fred Bain
Electrical effects by Edward Bush,
  technical effects by Clyde Whittaker

THE CAST

Ralph Bushman, aka	
Francis X. Bushman Jr.	Lynn Claymore
Jack Perrin	Richard Mason
Kathryn McGuire	Mary Bronson
Edward Peil Sr.	Suie Chang
Charles Belcher	Samuel Lund
Nora Cecil	Mrs. Hart
Martin Turner	Trohelius Snapp
Eddie Dennis	Useless McGurk
Andy Waldron	Peter Marlin
Al Hallett	Otis
Larry Fisher	Red O'Connor

THE WHITE ROSE

[A] tale of the Old South.
—opening title card of *The White Rose*

THE STORY

Joseph Beaugarde, the son of a distinguished Louisiana planter, is studying to be a minister when he meets and courts young Bessie Williams, a flighty but good-hearted girl who works in a resort hotel. Joseph eventually returns home to his new ministry and his waiting fiancée, but he is unaware that Bessie is carrying his child.

THE FILM

In early 1923 the legendary D. W. Griffith returned to Florida to shoot *The White Rose*, the story of a fallen minister who finds redemption after accepting his responsibilities as a man. Everything about the project, from the setting in the antebellum South to the theme of moral hypocrisy, was material close to Griffith's heart. He personally connected to this film in a way he had not with many of his post–World War I projects.

The director penned the script himself, under the pseudonym Irene Sinclair, after researching news stories about clergymen who committed sexual transgressions. While less complicated than the narratives of his masterpieces, the story line neatly intertwines the lives of four characters, who mature from naive youth to responsible adults in the course of the film. The story begins with Joseph, who is betrothed to wealthy Marie Carrington. While away from home to study for the ministry, he finds that he is smitten with the vivacious Bessie, who wins his heart and then breaks it in a misunderstanding. Meanwhile, Marie is attracted to childhood friend John White, but they can never be together because he is from a family far beneath her station. The story's moral indiscretions, unrequited love, near-death experiences, and final redemption are pure melodrama—Griffith's specialty since the era of one-reelers.

Three of the major roles were filled by actors who had been guided or groomed by Griffith to some degree. Mae Marsh starred as Bessie, the naive young girl whose head is turned by the free-wheeling jazz babies who frequent the hotel where she works. Marsh had been a Griffith regular ten years earlier, culminating her years with the old master when she costarred in *Birth of a Nation* and *Intolerance*. Marsh had taken up the theater after leaving Griffith, but she gladly returned to the fold for this role, which was tailor-made for her. Carol Dempster, with whom Griffith was romantically involved, played Marie,

Figure 1.10. *The White Rose* star Neil Hamilton.
(Doll/Morrow Collection)

the gentle plantation heiress who is betrothed to Joseph. While the actresses were Griffith stalwarts, the actors were relative newcomers. Neil Hamilton costarred in the part of John White, which was the smallest of the significant roles. Griffith was grooming Hamilton to be his new leading man, and this minor part was one step along the way to potential stardom. The unknown actor in the *White Rose* ensemble was Ivor Novello, a newcomer from Wales whom Griffith hired to play the earnest minister Joseph Beaugarde. Novello later moved to London to play in a variety of British films, including Alfred Hitchcock's first important effort, *The Lodger*.

Given his personal connection to the material, it is not surprising that Griffith decided to shoot in the Deep South, specifically Louisiana and Florida. Griffith had been born and raised in Kentucky, and the history and culture of the South were a major part of his childhood. His father, Roaring Jake Griffith, had been a Confederate officer during the Civil War, and though a distant and remote parent, Roaring Jake liked to regale his children with stories of his adventures and of his beloved South. D. W. had a way of making the locations in his films integral to the atmosphere and narrative, but never more so than when he was spinning a yarn of the Old South.

The scenes showing exteriors of the Beaugarde mansion were shot in New Iberia, in the Bayou Teche region of Louisiana, on the grounds of an actual plantation called the Shadow. Built in 1830, the Shadow was owned by Weeks Hall, who invited Griffith to stay while shooting. The company then moved to South Florida to shoot around Ft. Lauderdale for exteriors for the fictional Blue River Inn, the resort hotel where Bessie and Joseph meet and finally succumb to their passion.

The locations were so integral to the narrative of *The White Rose* that Griffith adjusted his style slightly to showcase them. In lieu of his customary dependence on close-ups, well-planned pacing, and tightly structured sequences of parallel editing, Griffith opted to compose in a tableau style, focusing on atmosphere and lighting. He used three cameramen to shoot the film: the reliable Billy Bitzer, newcomer Hal Sintzenich, and Henrik Sartov, who specialized in soft-focus photography. The result was an exquisitely beautiful film, with carefully lit images of exotic gardens, sun-kissed rivers, and open fields. Backlighting was used to add a misty atmosphere to some scenes, highlighting Griffith's interpretation of the romantic South—a perfect backdrop to Bessie and Joseph's ardor. A few years earlier Griffith had come to the Ft. Lauderdale area to shoot two films set in the South Seas (see *The Idol Dancer*), but he was dissatisfied with the locale and moved on to the Bahamas. This time, the New River offered the exact locations Griffith needed to paint a portrait of lazy summer days and hot romantic nights at a Southern resort hotel.

Interior sets for the film were constructed at a new studio facility, Miami Studios in Hialeah. The studio had been opened the previous year by Chamber of Commerce president E. G. Sewell, who hoped to bring film production to the Miami area by providing a fully supplied, professional facility. Occasionally the studio even offered financing. Sewell's plan worked for a brief time. There was an upsurge in production in Florida between 1922 and 1926, with Griffith's decision to shoot there a definite boost to their efforts.

Griffith seemed particularly happy while shooting *The White Rose*, thoroughly enjoying his time in the South.[19] While the company filmed along the New River, many local residents turned out to watch the proceedings, and the director recruited them as extras, including a few Seminole Indians. The crew stayed at the newly built Broward Hotel, which pushed up its opening date to accommodate the film company. D. W. Griffith became the very first guest to sign the hotel's register.

Unfortunately, Griffith's good spirits while shooting *The White Rose* did not last. When he returned to his production facility at Mamaroneck, New York, to begin the editing, he was dissatisfied with the footage.[20] Despite the powerful cinematography, the film was flawed. The performances were uneven, as though Griffith had not directed the actors with his usual sure hand: Dempster seemed too low-key, while Marsh was too fidgety. In addition, the African-American characters were rendered in broad strokes, either as comic stereotypes or as self-sacrificing servants. The lack of subtlety stands out in comparison with the other actors, particularly because the black characters were most often played by white actors in blackface. This was a convention Griffith had always used in his films, but by 1923 the rest of the film industry was using more and more black actors. Critics were generally kind to *The White Rose*, but some reviews, such as those in the *New York Times* and *Motion Picture Magazine*, commented on the oddity of white actors playing black characters. They also noted that the humor in those scenes was forced, coarse, and incongruous with the movie's overall tone.

The White Rose did become a modest success at the box office, but reviewers and audiences seemed disappointed or unsatisfied. Ultimately, they could not articulate the real problem with the film, because they couldn't foresee what was just over the horizon. The story, the themes, and the imagery may have been well suited to Griffith, but they were not suited to the changing mores of the Jazz Age. *The White Rose* signaled the beginning of a permanent decline for Griffith, in which his films and production methods were increasingly out of step with the times.

THE CREDITS	THE CAST	
Released in 1923 by United Artists	Mae Marsh	Bessie "Teazie" Williams
Produced by D. W. Griffith	Carol Dempster	Marie Carrington
Directed by D. W. Griffith	Ivor Novello	Joseph Beaugarde
Written by Irene Sinclair	Neil Hamilton	John White
Photographed by G. W. "Billy" Bitzer,	Lucille LaVerne	Auntie Easter
Hendrik Sartov, and Hal Sintzenich	Porter Strong	Apollo
Edited by D. W. Griffith		
Production design by Charles M. Kirk		
Special effects by Edward Scholl		

THE MOVIE TOURIST'S GUIDE TO SILENT FLORIDA

The silent era has long since passed, and little remains of Florida's history as a once-thriving filmmaking center. However, movie tourists with a passion for the past can find a few sites where legends such as Oliver Hardy and Tom Mix once honed their craft. With just a little imagination, visitors might sense the fun and excitement of cinema's earliest pioneers as they helped develop this new medium of entertainment.

THE BATTLE ROYAL

Jacksonville

Comedian Oliver Hardy enjoyed the time he spent in Jacksonville while making one-reel comedies for the Lubin Company and for Vim Studios. At one point Hardy and his first wife lived in the Klutho Building, an apartment building built in 1913. Tom Mix, who appeared in a small role in *Lost in the Jungle*, also stayed at the Klutho for a while.

Henry J. Klutho had been a student of Frank Lloyd Wright's, and his three-story building was designed in the prairie style made famous by Wright. Klutho constructed other buildings in Jacksonville, including the Klutho Studios (a movie studio on Main Street), the St. James Building (now City Hall), and the Morocco Temple (now occupied by Cecil W. Powell and Company). In the modern era the Klutho Building fell into disrepair, but it was purchased by Fresh Ministries in 1999 to house the Center for Urban Initiatives. A significant architectural site, the Klutho Building is located on North Main Street in Jacksonville.

A FLORIDA ENCHANTMENT

St. Augustine

The primary setting of this unusual comedy was Henry Flagler's magnificent Ponce de Leon Hotel, the first of the grand hotels that Flagler built in St. Augustine. Designed in the Spanish Renaissance style by young architects John Carrere and Thomas Hastings, the Ponce influenced architectural style in Florida during the Gilded Age. In 1968 the hotel became Flagler College, a small liberal arts college, which offers tours of the grounds from May to August. Now called Ponce de Leon Hall, the main hotel covers the entire block bounded by King, Valencia, Sevilla, and Cordova Streets. It is reached by traveling east on King Street from U.S. 1.

Old St. Augustine

One of the main characters in *A Florida Enchantment* is pursued by an angry mob through the Castillo de San Marcos, the seventeenth-century Spanish fort that has long been St. Augustine's most honored attraction. The fort, the oldest masonry fort in the continental United States, is constructed of coquina. Coquina is a limestone rock formed by billions of compacted seashells and corals. There are plenty of bastions and dungeons to explore at the fort; in addition, the National Park Service stages several events each year, including torchlight tours and reenactments.

THE FLYING ACE

Jacksonville

Much of this film was shot at the Eagle Studios, owned by Florida native Richard E. Norman, who made movies with African-American casts for African-American audiences. One of the few silent film studios still intact, the main building became a dance studio operated by Mrs. Norman after her husband no longer used it. Later it housed a plumbing company and then a telephone answering service, among other businesses.

In 2000 the National Trust for Historic Preservation deemed it nationally significant; in 2003 a local group called Old Arlington persuaded the City of Jacksonville to purchase it. The complex includes an old darkroom, a screening room, an indoor studio, and a prop storage room. The Department of Parks, Recreation, and Entertainment has cleaned and repaired the buildings and eventually plans to open the site, now called the Norman Film Studios, to the public. The Norman Film Studios are located at 6337 Arlington Road.

THE GOLDEN AGE

> Those who now look back on the Hollywood of the 1930s, '40s,
> and early '50s with nostalgia and regret for its passing are cer-
> tainly looking back on what, for all its faults, was indeed a
> golden age for filmmakers; an age which perhaps could only
> have existed when it did and which can never come again.
> —Barry Norman, *The Story of Hollywood*

In a scratchy clip from an old newsreel, a tram full of tourists is ushered
through the famous gates of Paramount Pictures. As the bulky vehicle lumbers
across the lot, the studio bustles with daily activities. The doors of soundstages
open and close as crew members enter and exit; grips carry equipment from
one door to another; extras dressed in exotic costumes stroll about; and stars
Gary Cooper and Fredric March wave congenially to the visitors. Even with

the flat lighting and grainy film stock, the clip captures the glamour, energy, and excitement of moviemaking during the Golden Age when the studios ruled the industry.

From the early sound era through the 1940s, the Hollywood industry operated using the most efficient and complex system of filmmaking ever devised. Each major studio consisted of a large compound of soundstages and back lots where vast resources were coordinated to make a large number of films each year. The studio had authority over every aspect of film, from the beginning of a story idea to the actual showing of the film in theaters. This highly controlled process was known as the studio system.

Eight studios dominated the film market—Paramount, MGM, Twentieth Century–Fox, Warner Brothers, RKO, Universal, Columbia, and United Artists. In Hollywood, these film factories produced movies with an army of highly skilled craftspeople who were locked into exclusive, long-term contracts. From New York, the corporate offices of the studios controlled marketing and distribution. And around the country, studio-owned theater chains determined what films would be shown in which theaters and for how long. The studio system allowed the big eight to control 95 percent of the industry's revenue, without ever losing their facade of glamour and showmanship. The domination of the American film market was so absolute that few films received a national release outside the eight major distributors.

The studios were managed by such ruthless moguls as Louis B. Mayer, Harry Cohn, Jack Warner, and Darryl F. Zanuck, who affectionately referred to their productions as "pictures," a quaint and modest term that was a shortened form of "motion pictures." While the studio heads could not literally oversee every facet of production for every film, they knew that their associate producers would do it for them. In some of the larger studios, like Paramount and MGM, another level of producers beneath the associates, called unit producers, directly supervised the production of several films per year. In the studio system, the producer reigned.

However, the producer was greatly dependent on the talents of the craftspeople within each department to complete his slate of films. This pool of specialists—from cinematographers to costume designers to gaffers to prop masters—could construct the physical environment and create the appropriate mood for any story from any era in any genre. And they generally did it within the confines of the studio soundstages or back lots. By working at the same task on dozens of films every year, they became expert in their crafts.

While the studio's researchers supplied each department with accurate and valuable background information, the settings created for Hollywood films were generally more dependent on aesthetics and imagination than on historical accuracy. In other words, the researchers at Paramount undoubtedly supplied the art directors on *Reap the Wild Wind* with photographs and illustrations of Key West and Charleston, South Carolina, in the 1840s. However, the art directors' exaggerated use of saturated reds and oranges to illustrate a Key West sunset behind the criss-crossed masts of wooden sailing ships provided the perfect romantic backdrop that director Cecil B. DeMille wanted for a passionate love scene between John Wayne and Paulette Goddard. Though the craftspeople at the big studios labored under strict orders from above, their combined efforts constituted a unique kind of collaboration that truly serviced the films.

The bulk of film production during the Golden Age was done on the studio lots of the big eight not only because the craftspeople could re-create any part of the world during any era of history with style and imagination but also so the producers could micromanage all facets of making a film. This was an important element, considering that each studio averaged fifty feature films per year during the Golden Age. Thus the fictional Caribbean island that provides the setting for *Mr. Peabody and the Mermaid* reflects the imaginative efforts of a studio staff more than it resembles the real Caribbean. However, the soft lighting, rounded archways, and exotic touches fit the magical story about a mythical creature. Likewise the interior of the Largo Hotel in *Key Largo* was constructed inside a studio because director John Huston and master cinematographer Karl Freund could control the lighting, which was essential in creating the mood of the film.

Of all the talent under contract, the actors probably resented the studios the most. Stars were locked into exclusive long-term contracts, and they did not have control over what films they were to appear in, or how many. Their careers and even their personal lives were managed by the studios, often causing anger and rancor. Studios constructed images for their stars and used them to lure audiences to their films, a strategy now called the star system. While the stars may have resented this manipulation, producers understood how to use their stars' images to help construct characters and advance the narratives in their films. Casts were carefully selected so that a film's narrative benefited from its stars' images and talents; often vehicles were tailored to showcase these. The star system resulted in a legacy of delightful performances that continue to move audiences to this day. One need only watch William Powell in *Mr. Peabody and the Mermaid*, Claudette Colbert in *Palm Beach Story*, or Humphrey Bogart in *Key Largo* to get an idea of the star system at its best. Casting actors on the basis of their images is still a Hollywood practice, but few of today's producers can match the old studios at exploiting stars to their best advantage.

The studio system survived economic depression, the growth of organized labor, and World War II, but it did not survive the Supreme Court. At the end of the 1940s, the highest court in the land declared the studios' domination of the industry an oligopoly, which occurs when a few companies cooperate to influence the market. The court's decision required that the studios sell their theater holdings and cease other trade practices that were legally questionable. At the same time, outside distractions such as television and lifestyle changes began to lure urban audiences away from the movies. The absolute power of the studios eroded throughout the 1950s as the studio bosses retired, died, or were fired, and the boards of directors who replaced them struggled to produce films that would bring audiences into the theaters. To compensate for the loss of revenue, the studios loosened their grip over the industry by reducing the length of contracts for stars or by letting many actors, directors, producers, and crew members out of their contracts completely. Many producers, directors, and stars eagerly formed their own small production companies to make films with the creative control denied them under the studio system. During the transition period of the 1950s, the studios turned more toward the distribution and financing of motion pictures and pulled away from production. The practice of a studio controlling a film from the script stage through exhibition gradually disappeared.

Many small production companies chose to shoot the principal photography of their films on location, a practice influenced by European filmmakers and made easier by advances in equipment. During the 1930s and 1940s, studios had sometimes sent second units to actual locations to get background shots or to shoot a few key scenes, as was the case with *Key Largo*, but principal photography was done in Hollywood. As the 1950s progressed, location shooting became the norm, even for studio productions. Several films in this chapter were improved by the producers' decisions to shoot primarily in Florida, which added authenticity to their stories. *Distant Drums* provides an excellent example from the transition period: the film is an ordinary Western that dutifully follows the conventions of the genre, including the racist depiction of Native Americans as two-dimensional savages, but the location shooting in the Everglades and a star turn by Gary Cooper make it creditable viewing. Likewise, *Beneath the 12-Mile Reef* and *The Rose Tattoo* thrived on their authentic Florida settings.

By the 1960s the studio system had completely died, and with it the last vestiges of the Golden Age. Today the studios are still mighty forces in the Hollywood industry, but the Mayers, the Cohns, and the Warners are all gone, replaced by marketing graduates and businessmen who call their films "product."

BENEATH THE 12-MILE REEF

This is a sponge fisherman, a special breed of man
dedicated to the most dangerous of all occupations.
—narration from *Beneath the 12-Mile Reef*

THE STORY

Two seafaring families, one from Tarpon Springs and the other from Key West, battle over the lucrative sponge beds that lie off the coast of Florida. When romance blooms between the younger generations of the families, tensions escalate within and between the clans.

THE FILM

In the early 1950s Hollywood executives were reeling from the threat posed by the new medium of television. Every year, more and more sets were appearing in American homes and fewer and fewer movie tickets were being sold at the box office. The variety, quality, and quantity of television programming steadily increased, and the American film industry found itself facing a competitor that gave away for free what they were trying to sell.

The industry responded in two ways. Recognizing the potential of the medium, studios carved out a piece of the new market through deals with the television networks, selling rights to old films or renting out their production facilities. They also modified their own product, bringing to the fore technologies that had been tinkered with or used only sparingly in the past in the hope of giving viewers something they could not get in their living rooms. The first of these was color. Rudimentary systems for producing color film had been available since the mid-1910s, and more effective technologies were developed and occasionally used in the 1920s, most often only for key sequences in a film. *Toll of the Sea*, a drama based loosely on the story of *Madame Butterfly*, became the first widely distributed Technicolor film in January 1922. Disney began to make extensive use of an improved Technicolor process for its animated releases in the early 1930s, and 1935's *Becky Sharp* was the first full-length motion picture to use the technology. Though audiences responded well to these strikingly saturated images, color films remained the exception rather than the rule for the next fifteen years, until Hollywood began using them heavily to draw viewers away from their television sets.

The novelty of 3-D projection, which again had been available for years, surfaced in the 1952 film *Bwana Devil*, an otherwise forgettable African adventure that drew audiences in droves. Studios jumped on the bandwagon, releasing numerous 3-D films and heavily marketing the technology over the next two years, until viewers lost interest.

Finally, in 1953, Darryl F. Zanuck and Twentieth Century–Fox took a bold and wildly successful step forward by embracing another film technology that had been around in one form or another for thirty years—the anamorphic lens. When added to the front of a standard movie camera, the anamorphic lens compressed the image horizontally onto the film, allowing the essentially square frame of the negative to capture an image much wider than it was tall. With a comparable lens mounted on the front of a projector, the image could then be replayed without distortion on a rectangular screen, creating a broader canvas for the filmmaker that more closely duplicated the natural human field of vision. With the addition of stereophonic sound, the new process, dubbed CinemaScope, promised a whole new level of realism for the moviegoer. Best of all, filmmakers and exhibitors could offer this wide-screen spectacle without having to invest in entirely new equipment and techniques for recording and projecting.

Fox signed an exclusive agreement with Frenchman Henri Chrétien, who had invented the anamorphic film lens in 1927, and announced to the world in February 1953 that all of its future films would be released in CinemaScope. To their chagrin, the studio learned that Chrétien had only three working anamorphic lenses left from the originals he produced in the twenties. They commissioned Bausch and Lomb to manufacture more, and in the meantime assigned one Chrétien lens to each of three carefully selected upcoming films— the biblical epic *The Robe*, the romantic comedy *How to Marry a Millionaire*, and the family adventure *Beneath the 12-Mile Reef*. Fox's announcement set the other major studios scrambling to develop wide-screen processes of their own, and for the next six months entertainment reporters wrote endlessly about the efforts of each studio and the promised benefits of the new wide-screen technologies, whipping up a frenzy of anticipation in the public. Fox's competitors took turns announcing their own wide-screen systems, but most eventually recognized the benefits of an industrywide standard and made arrangements with Fox to shoot in CinemaScope.

The Robe premiered at New York's Roxy Theater on September 16, 1953, and the CinemaScope process created a sensation among viewers, critics, and movie technicians alike. The process was—and remains—heralded as the most significant technological development in filmmaking since the advent of sound. For all of Hollywood, there was no turning back.

Each of the first three CinemaScope films made use of the new system's advantages in a different way. A sweeping saga based on classical material, *The Robe* offered a story that held up to the grandeur of the new screen experience.

Figure 2.1. Lobby card from *Beneath the 12-Mile Reef*. (Doll/Morrow Collection)

How to Marry a Millionaire was a sophisticated romance constructed around Lauren Bacall, Marilyn Monroe, and Betty Grable, three of Hollywood's hottest female properties, whose charisma and natural attributes were more than a match for the scale of CinemaScope. *Beneath the 12-Mile Reef* had a simple story and a cast of unknowns or performers who had long since passed their peak, but it offered instead the breathtaking grandeur of Florida's natural beauty both above and below the water.

Reef opens with a stunning underwater sequence that follows one of the many Greek sponge divers of Tarpon Springs as he plies his dangerous trade on the Gulf seafloor. The segment runs three minutes and features a variety of exciting marine creatures, among them sharks, eels, and giant sea turtles. Altogether the film offers seven extended underwater scenes, including a friendly competition among the young men of the village, the young lovers at the heart of the story frolicking beneath the waves, and two fights involving the film's protagonist, one against an octopus and the other against a rival sponger from Key West.

In addition to these segments, the film takes full advantage of Florida's terrestrial beauty, depicting the inviting beaches, sparkling waters, and stunning sunsets across the Gulf in sumptuous Technicolor and expansive CinemaScope. Fox ensured it would fully capture the scale and beauty of the region by assigning one of its top cinematographers, Edward Cronjager, to apply its new technology to what would otherwise have been a second-tier production.

The Greek culture and sponging industry depicted in the film had been a part of Florida's history since the early 1900s, just after the extensive sponge beds near Tarpon Springs were discovered. American fisherman began harvesting the sponges in shallow waters by snagging them from their boats with long hooked poles. In 1905 a Greek immigrant named John Corcoris introduced the diving techniques used in the Mediterranean for gathering the valuable animals and encouraged experienced Greek divers to come to the area. In a few short years the small town had a well-established Greek culture and had become the country's leading producer of sponges. The area's sponge beds were blighted by disease in the 1940s, dooming the industry, but the town has remained true to its Hellenic heritage and boasts the largest percentage of Greek residents of any city in the United States.[1]

If not for the advent of CinemaScope and Technicolor, *Beneath the 12-Mile Reef* might have been just another minor, long-forgotten film from Hollywood's Golden Age. Instead, by demonstrating the potential of a revolutionary entertainment technology, it became a significant installment in American film history.

THE CREDITS	THE CAST	
Released in 1953 by Twentieth Century–Fox	Robert Wagner	Tony Petrakis
Produced by Robert Bassler	Terry Moore	Gwyneth Rhys
Directed by Robert D. Webb	Gilbert Roland	Mike Petrakis
Written by A. I. Bezzerides	J. Carrol Naish	Socrates
Cinematography by Edward Cronjager	Richard Boone	Thomas Rhys
Original music by Bernard Herrmann	Angela Clarke	Mama Petrakis
Edited by William Reynolds	Peter Graves	Arnold
Art direction by George Patrick and Lyle R. Wheeler	Harry Carey Jr.	Griff
Set decoration by Fred J. Rode		
Costume design by Dorothy Jeakins		

DISTANT DRUMS

The rescue—the throbbing jungle drums—the man-devouring
marsh-wilderness aflame with unseen menace!
—poster for *Distant Drums*

THE STORY

A small band of U.S. soldiers set off to destroy the stronghold of gunrunners
who are supplying arms to Native Americans during Florida's Second Seminole
War. They succeed in their mission and rescue a group of civilian prisoners,
but when their escape route is compromised, they are forced to retreat into the
dangerous Everglades with a band of Seminole warriors on their heels.

THE FILM

The image of the American cowboy—capable, independent, honorable, asser-
tive—has come to define the American persona of the rugged individualist for
the entire world. This iconic cowboy figure was propagated in popular culture
through dime novels and Wild West shows even as the Western era was un-
folding in the latter half of the nineteenth century. With the advent of film,
however, the Western hero became one of the most well-defined and recognizable archetypes in American culture.

The American West has provided fodder for filmmakers since the earliest
days of commercial moviemaking, but the Western genre reached its apex during the Golden Age of Hollywood in the 1930s and 1940s. Following a clear set
of filmic conventions, the horse opera proved to be one of the most durable,
successful, and flexible genres created by the American film industry.

A typical Western is set in the American West between 1865 and 1890 in a
frontier region where white American settlers attempt to establish their presence in keeping with the doctrine of Manifest Destiny. This effort inevitably
leads to conflict between the forces of civilization and the wilderness, the major dramatic theme of the standard Western. The typical Western hero is a
product of both these worlds but belongs completely to neither. While he has
clear cultural ties to the community, he also possesses skill with weapons and
a knowledge of nature that associates him with the violent wilderness. Most
often, the hero's expertise allows the forces of civilization to carry the day, but
in the end he remains outside the bounds of the community and must either
give up his way of life, move on to a new frontier, or die.

Distant Drums is a classic Western in almost all respects. The plot focuses
on an armed conflict between the U.S. Army and Native Americans who are

Figure 2.2. Publicity photo from *Distant Drums*. (Doll/Morrow Collection)

harrassing white settlers in a dispute over land. The hero, played by Gary Cooper, lives apart from the civilized whites on an inland island he shares with friendly natives. He wears buckskins, subsists off the land by hunting, and was even married to a Native American princess who bore him a son before she was mistakenly killed by soldiers. Cooper's character leads a small force into the wilderness to attack a fort being used by gunrunners who are supplying the native uprising. After successfully taking the fort and finding a number of settlers being held prisoner, he must lead the group through hostile territory and back to civilization. The only deviation from the established Western conventions is the setting—Florida in the 1840s.

The backdrop for *Distant Drums* is drawn from a formative chapter in the history of Florida. In the early 1800s the southeastern peninsula was a possession of Spain, a once great imperial power that now struggled to control its dwindling colonies. The northern Panhandle area was inhabited by various Native American groups that had been driven out of the Southeast by white encroachment. Referred to by whites as Seminoles, these groups developed a loose collective culture and managed to maintain significant autonomy under the weak Spanish rule. The United States had long coveted Spain's last possession in eastern North America and, using the Seminole practice of harboring runaway slaves as an excuse, sent 1,700 troops led by Andrew Jackson into Florida in 1818. In what became known as the First Seminole War, Jackson attacked several Seminole strongholds only to find that the elusive natives had slipped away before his arrival. He then attacked a Spanish outpost and illegally claimed western Florida for the United States. The following year, Spain signed a treaty for the sale of the region, and the United States officially took possession of the territory in 1821.

Under American rule, the Seminoles moved to the central and southern parts of the peninsula and lived in relative peace until Andrew Jackson ascended to the White House. With the passage of the Indian Removal Act in the 1830s, Jackson ordered all Native American groups in the Southeast to be relocated west of the Mississippi River, and Seminoles led by Osceola resisted, beginning in 1835. The American military had no more success during the Second Seminole War than Jackson himself had achieved fifteen years earlier. Shrewdly using the treacherous, swampy terrain to their advantage, the Seminoles carried out a highly successful guerrilla campaign that dragged on for seven years. After $20 million and nine different military commanders failed to oust the determined natives, the U.S. Army simply gave up. During the course of the war, several thousand Seminoles were captured and moved west, and by the time hostilities ended only a few hundred remained in the state. But two soldiers died for every one Seminole that was relocated, and in the end they remained one of the few native groups not to have been exterminated or conquered by whites.

While Florida is a far cry from the American West, the Everglades offered an appropriately forbidding wilderness setting for *Distant Drums* that maintained the traditions of the Western. In the film, the dense, treacherous swamp holds danger at every turn from deadly inhabitants such as alligators and snakes. To successfully survive this unforgiving wilderness and elude the relentless Seminole pursuit, Cooper's character draws on all his knowledge and skill as an outdoorsman.

The film also made use of a significant historical landmark from the days of Spanish rule. The gunrunners' stronghold that serves as the target of Cooper's commandos was actually the Castillo de San Marcos, a fort built in the late seventeenth century for the defense of the Spanish colony at nearby St. Augustine. Over its two-hundred-year history as an active fortification, the fort stood under four different flags—those of Spain, Britain, the United States, and the Confederacy—but was never once taken by force. It played a role in the Second Seminole War, serving as the prison in which Osceola was first kept when he was captured in 1837. Two years after *Distant Drums*, Universal Pictures would release their own "eastern Western." *Seminole*, starring Rock Hudson, Barbara

Hale, and Anthony Quinn, made similar use of the Everglades as an unconquerable wilderness. While *Distant Drums* suffers from a typically unenlightened depiction of Native Americans, *Seminole* offers a more sympathetic and sophisticated interpretation of their role in American history.

THE CREDITS	THE CAST	
Released in 1951 by Warner Brothers	Gary Cooper	Capt. Quincy Wyatt
Produced by Milton Sperling	Mari Aldon	Judy Beckett
Directed by Raoul Walsh	Richard Webb	Lt. Richard Tufts
Written by Niven Busch and Martin Rackin	Ray Teal	Pvt. Mohair
Cinematography by Sidney Hickox	Arthur Hunnicutt	Monk
Edited by Folmar Blangsted	Robert Barrat	Gen. Zachary Taylor
Original music by Max Steiner	Larry Carper	Chief Oscala
Art direction by Douglas Bacon		
Set decoration by William Wallace		

The Wilhelm Scream

About halfway through *Distant Drums*, one of the soldiers is savaged by an alligator and lets out a piercing death scream. Added to the film during post-production, the sound effect had been recorded in the studio in six takes. Several of the other takes were used earlier in the film during the shoot-out between Cooper's men and the gunrunners. According to the Web site <hollywoodlostandfound.net> Warner Brothers archived the tape in its sound effects library, and it was frequently reused over the next fifteen years in films including *The Charge at Feather River*, *Them!*, *Sergeant Rutledge*, and *PT 109*.

Sound effects engineer Ben Burtt noticed the ubiquitous scream as a film student in the early 1970s, and when he was hired to work on *Star Wars* in 1977, he found the original recording in the Warner archives and incorporated it into the film. Burtt dubbed the effect the Wilhelm Scream after the character it was used for in *The Charge at Feather River*, and many of his colleagues have since made a point of using the sound bite as an homage to the Golden Age. Over the last thirty years, characters have let loose the Wilhelm Scream as a death knell or cry of terror in all the *Star Wars* and *Indiana Jones* movies and in such diverse features as *Poltergeist*, *Beauty and the Beast*, *Batman Returns*, *Toy Story*, *A Goofy Movie*, *The Majestic*, *The Fifth Element*, and *Pirates of the Caribbean*.

EASY TO LOVE

Never had plumbing been put to a more glamorous use.
—Esther Williams, *Million Dollar Mermaid*, on the
MGM pool used for her aqua-musicals

THE STORY

Julie Hallerton is a top advertising model and the star of the water show at Florida's famed Cypress Gardens. She's pursued by both a handsome fellow swimmer and a national crooning idol, but her true feelings lie with Cypress Gardens owner Ray Lloyd, who thinks of her only as one of the employees.

THE FILM

Easy to Love is a typical Golden Age musical filled with light comedy, strained romance, expert choreography, and beautiful, beautiful Hollywood stars. Set amid the glamour and elegance of the entertainment and advertising industries, the familiar story follows the romantic travails of a beautiful young girl and the many men in her life. The film also brings together two of the greatest institutions in the history of aquatic entertainment—Esther Williams and Florida's Cypress Gardens.

As a teenager, Williams was a national swimming champion who earned a berth on the Olympic training team only to have her hopes shattered when World War II resulted in the cancellation of the games. While working as a sales clerk for I. Magnin on Wilshire Boulevard in Beverly Hills, she decided to audition for the Billy Rose Aquacade, a swimming and diving show that had been the hit of the 1939 World's Fair and was preparing to open in San Francisco. Williams earned the lead female spot in the show and found herself sharing billing with famed actor and athlete Johnny Weissmuller.

She spent several years debating whether to pursue a career in show business and ultimately decided to take the chance with a contract at MGM. The studio had been keen to sign the statuesque young swimmer, as they were looking to answer the success of Sonja Henie and her ice-skating musicals at Twentieth Century–Fox. After months of acting classes and voice lessons, Williams made her debut in *Andy Hardy's Double Life*, showing off her elegant athleticism in pool scenes with Mickey Rooney. Fans responded positively to the young starlet, and MGM quickly began work on the first swimming musical, *Bathing Beauty*. The film proved a huge success, and the studio invested a quarter of a million dollars to build an elaborate pool for Williams on Sound Stage 30 that featured underwater fountains and geysers and was rigged for fireworks, smoke, and other special effects.

ESTHER WILLIAMS
METRO·GOLDWYN·MAYER

Figure 2.3. Poster of Esther Williams. (Doll/Morrow Collection)

Over the next fifteen years, Williams appeared in one of the most success-ful strings of musicals to come out of Hollywood's leading studio for musicals. Often working with the same pool of actors—Van Johnson, Ricardo Montalban, Red Skelton, Cyd Charisse, Howard Keel, Xavier Cugat—she became one of the top box-office stars of her time. In films such as *On an Island with You*, *Neptune's Daughter*, *Million Dollar Mermaid*, and *Dangerous When Wet*, she wore glamorous costumes, cavorted in the water, wooed Hollywood's smooth-est leading men, and captured the hearts of audiences around the world.

During the course of this career, Williams filmed three movies in Florida—*On an Island with You* in 1948, *Neptune's Daughter* in 1949, and *Easy to Love* in 1953. The 1948 film used Florida as a stand in for Hawaii in a self-reflexive story about the making of an aquatic musical. *Neptune's Daughter* offers a light tale of a former champion swimmer who goes into the swimsuit business and falls in love with a dashing South American; oddly, the story previews Williams's own life, as she would later design her own line of swimwear and enter into a tempestuous marriage with Latin heartthrob Fernando Lamas. *Easy to Love*, however, is the Williams film that makes the most prominent use of its Florida location, with most of the story taking place at Cypress Gardens, the state's first theme park.

Cypress Gardens opened on January 2, 1936, and earned owner Dick Pope the title Father of Florida Tourism for the remarkable achievement of turning a tract of worthless swampland into a lush and inviting paradise that would become one of the state's top tourist attractions. The gardens offered more than eight thousand exotic plants on meticulously landscaped grounds that could be viewed from small boats that glided across a network of canals. In 1940 one of the park's signature attractions was added when comely young girls were hired to stroll the grounds wearing colorful antebellum hoop skirts. Three years later, Pope's wife Julie added the spectacle that the park would become most famous for—the water ski show. According to the Popes, the idea was born of a misunderstanding when soldiers on leave saw a newspaper photo of a water skier at the park and assumed that there was a show. They arrived at Cypress Gardens and inquired about the skiers, and Julie Pope persuaded her children and their friends to put on a demonstration. The following week several hundred soldiers showed up, and the park has been offering elaborate water carnivals ever since.

In *Easy to Love*, Williams portrays Julie Hallerton, the fictional star of the Cypress Gardens water show. Her heart's desire is Ray Lloyd, the dashing owner of the park, played by Van Johnson. Despite Julie's obvious affections, Lloyd remains focused only on the park and his ancillary business of promoting his attractive employees as advertising models. The scenario offers ample opportunity for Williams to display her athletic talents—swimming languidly in a Florida-shaped pool that was built on the grounds for the film, performing an aquatic clown routine, and of course water skiing. Despite Williams's expertise in the water, she was not an experienced water skier and needed to work hard to perform the elaborate routines, which included a daring jump over an entire orchestra on a platform and an eighty-foot dive from a helicopter. Williams was accustomed to performing dangerous stunts for her films—she broke three vertebrae in her neck doing a fifty-foot dive for *Million Dollar Mermaid*. She gamely accepted the challenge and performed most of her own stunts in *Easy to Love*, including the orchestra jump, but she drew the line at the dangerous leap from the helicopter. To the chagrin of master choreographer Busby Berkeley, she insisted on using a double for that because she was three months pregnant.

THE CREDITS

Released in 1953 by Metro-Goldwyn-Mayer
Produced by Joe Pasternak
Directed by Charles Walters
Written by William Roberts and Laszlo Vadnay
Cinematography by Ray June
Edited by Gene Ruggiero
Art direction by Cedric Gibbons and Jack Martin Smith
Set decoration by Richard Pefferle and Edwin B. Willis
Choreographed by Busby Berkeley

THE CAST

Esther Williams	Julie Hallerton
Van Johnson	Ray Lloyd
Tony Martin	Barry Gordon
John Bromfield	Hank
Edna Skinner	Nancy Parmel
King Donovan	Ben
Carroll Baker	Clarice

THE GREATEST SHOW ON EARTH

You are here to please me. Nothing else on earth matters.
—DeMille to his crew, in *The Autobiography of Cecil B. DeMille*

THE STORY

Hit by financial problems, circus manager Marc "Brad" Braden hires egotistical aerialist the Great Sebastian to bring in the crowds. The rivalry between Sebastian and Braden's girl, Holly, livens up the center ring but threatens Holly and Brad's relationship. The ups and downs of circus life are depicted on an epic scale in this colorful drama set under the Big Top.

THE FILM

When John Ringling decided that his world-famous circus should spend its winters in Sarasota, the state of Florida and the Greatest Show on Earth began a relationship that exists to this day. The Ringling Brothers and Barnum & Bailey Circus wintered in Sarasota from 1927 through 1959, when it relocated to Venice, Florida. In 1992 the circus moved its winter headquarters to the state fairgrounds just outside Tampa. Today Sarasota is the site of John Ringling's mansion, Cà d'Zan, the Ringling Museum of Art, and the Circus Museum.

Given Sarasota's love and support of its circus heritage, it was only logical that legendary Hollywood producer-director Cecil B. DeMille decided to shoot a large portion of his circus drama, *The Greatest Show on Earth*, in Florida. But it was more than history that DeMille was after; he wanted to capture the atmosphere and camaraderie inside the circus as well as the spectacle and sen-

Figure 2.4. Publicity photo from *The Greatest Show on Earth*. (Doll/Morrow Collection)

sation of its surface. Many of the circus's most famous performers lived and rehearsed in Sarasota during the winter months, including clowns Emmett Kelly and Lou Jacobs and aerialists Antoinette Concello and Fay Alexander. These performers provided DeMille with endless anecdotes about circus life, trained the film's stars to do their circus acts during the winter of 1949–50, and offered the producer a glimpse into the everyday world of the circus performer.

Star Betty Hutton had lobbied DeMille endlessly for the role of Holly, the aerialist in love with the big boss, Charlton Heston. And to prove her worth, Hutton was determined to master the trapeze. Antoinette Concello taught her how to do a crossover, in which the performer flies from the swinging bar to a catcher, and then from the catcher to the pedestal. However, costar Cornel Wilde, who played rival aerialist the Great Sebastian, discovered that he had a fear of heights and could not bring himself to do even the simplest of stunts. DeMille was thrilled with Hutton's enthusiasm for her role, but he was disappointed in Wilde, whom he teased relentlessly during production. Male aerialist Fay Alexander did Wilde's stunts, but he also donned a blond wig to double for Hutton during the more dangerous parts of Holly's act.

For his role as Buttons the clown, Jimmy Stewart worked with Lou Jacobs, who was famous for his bits with a miniature car and a motorized bathtub. Other troupers in the cast included Gloria Grahame and Dorothy Lamour.

Figure 2.5. Publicity photo from *The Greatest Show on Earth*. (Doll/Morrow Collection)

Grahame played the Elephant Girl, who rode around the ring on the back of an elephant or hung from a hoop in its mouth. She also placed her head beneath its massive foot. The latter proved too much for the film's insurance company, and DeMille was forced to use a phony elephant leg in the close-up. Lamour, a show-biz veteran, gamely gripped a ring with her teeth and was hoisted high into the air to dangle above the crowds.

DeMille, who had traveled with the Ringling circus in 1949 as part of his research, was just as game. On his sixty-eighth birthday, while the circus was in Madison, Wisconsin, he was hauled up in a bosun's chair to the peak of the Big Top, where he remained for more than an hour, checking the lighting conditions to prepare the shooting script. Small wonder that he had no sympathy for Wilde's phobia.

The stars of the film performed their newly acquired circus skills for the residents of Sarasota in early 1950. DeMille also staged an old-fashioned circus parade down the main street of Sarasota, capturing on the big screen the delight of more than fifty thousand Florida residents who turned out to see the spectacle. To complete the film, DeMille shot the Ringling circus in performance in Philadelphia and Washington, D.C., before heading to the Paramount studios in Hollywood to stage the climax—a spectacular train wreck created largely with special effects.

The Greatest Show on Earth won the Oscar for Best Picture of 1952, an honor that recent critics suggest is undeserved. As might be expected, the film's show-biz sentiment and old-fashioned glamour do not mesh with contemporary tastes, but viewers should scratch beneath the surface. Though brimming with the pageantry and color of the circus, the film does not lose sight of its "plumbing," the word DeMille used for story. Like the three rings of a circus, the story consists of three threads skillfully interwoven into a whole—the romance of Holly and the big boss, the rivalry between Sebastian and Holly, and the mystery behind Buttons the clown. The climax, while thrilling and action-packed, simultaneously resolves each thread of the story coherently and organically. DeMille, who had been directing films for forty years, had long since mastered the craft of spinning a tightly woven tale.

The name Cecil B. DeMille is synonymous with "spectacle," and in this film the director's sense of spectacle and drama included some behind-the-scenes moments that have turned out to be the film's enduring strength. From unloading the circus train to parading through Main Street to raising the Big Top, DeMille captured moments of circus life that were already disappearing. By 1952 circus parades were no longer common, as circuses began to bypass small towns in favor of larger venues. Then in 1956 Ringling abandoned the Big Top in favor of staging the show inside big-city civic centers. In retrospect, *The Greatest Show on Earth* has become a chronicle of the circus from an era long gone—not just the Ringling show but the circus as an institution.

THE CREDITS

Released in 1952 by Metro-Goldwyn-Mayer
Produced by Cecil B. DeMille and Henry Wilcoxon
Directed by Cecil B. DeMille
Screenplay by Fredric M. Frank, Barre Lyndon, and
   Theodore St. John
Cinematography by George Barnes and J. Peverell
   Marley
Costumes by Edith Head
Art direction by Hal Pereira and Walter Tyler
Visual effects by Devereaux Jennings, Gordon
   Jennings, and Paul Lerpae

THE CAST

Charlton Heston	Marc "Brad" Braden
James Stewart	Buttons
Betty Hutton	Holly
Cornel Wilde	The Great Sebastian
Dorothy Lamour	Phyllis
Gloria Grahame	Angel
Lyle Bettger	Klaus
Henry Wilcoxon	Gregory, FBI agent
Lawrence Tierney	Mr. Henderson

Circus performers as themselves:
Emmett Kelly, Cucciola, Antoinette Concello,
John Ringling North, Tuffy Genders, Felix Adler,
Merle Evans, Lou Jacobs, and Buzzy Potts

KEY LARGO

RALPHIE: Hey Curly, what all happens in a hurricane?
CURLY: The wind blows so hard the ocean gets up on its
hind legs and walks right across the land.

—*Key Largo*

THE STORY

Frank McCloud arrives one summer day shortly after World War II at the Key Largo hotel of James Temple. McCloud, who was the commanding officer of Temple's son George, killed in the war, has dropped by to check on Mr. Temple and George's widow, Nora. When a hurricane suddenly blows up, Frank, Nora, and Mr. Temple find themselves trapped in the Largo Hotel with a ruthless gangster and his men.

THE FILM

Master director John Huston and screen legend Humphrey Bogart teamed up for six films during their careers. While *The Maltese Falcon* generally receives the most attention in film history books, *Key Largo* is one of those beautifully crafted classics that are ageless in theme and style. The strength of this postwar drama is its soothing message of healing, which would surely have resonated with audiences when *Key Largo* was released in 1948.

Bogart starred as former army officer Frank McCloud, an example of the cynical, world-weary character type he made so famous. McCloud had been a newspaper reporter before the war, but since his discharge he has drifted around the country vaguely dissatisfied and dislocated from mainstream life. He comes to Key Largo because he served with George Temple during the war and wants to pay his respects to George's widow, Nora, and his father, James Temple. A crisis occurs when a hurricane blows up unexpectedly. Not only is the "big blow" a powerful one, but the Largo Hotel's guests are revealed to be Johnny Rocco and his gang of ruthless thugs. Rocco is in the midst of a counterfeiting deal, but the hurricane changes his plans, making the ferocious gangster edgy and dangerous. Nora expects Frank to do something to stand up to Rocco, but Frank has become a cynical loner, probably from his wartime experiences, and he refuses to stick his neck out.

As the film progresses, the increasingly violent storm becomes a metaphor for the intensifying crisis as the gangsters become more and more nervous. Throughout the ordeal, Frank observes Nora and her wheelchair-bound father-in-law standing up to the bully Johnny Rocco, and he begins to understand the value of home and family through his respect for Mr. Temple's courage and his increasing affection for Nora. He is reminded that these are values worth fighting for—just as they were when he went off to war years earlier. Frank then changes his mind about the necessity of standing up to what Mr. Temple calls "the Roccos of the world," a veiled reference to Hitler, among others. He agrees to sail the gangsters to Cuba to get them away from the hotel. Aboard ship, he defeats the tough guys through a combination of courage and wits. As he sails back to the Temples at the Largo Hotel—his new family and home—the sunlight breaks through the clouds to light his return. The storm, which served as a metaphor not only for the crisis with the gangsters but also for Frank's own postwar turmoil, is over.

Though based on a 1939 play by Maxwell Anderson, *Key Largo* was updated for a contemporary audience to a post–World War II story. The idea that Frank McCloud needed to be reminded that he had fought the war to preserve the ideals and basic institutions of our society, and that these are values worth fighting for, was relevant to audiences still weary from a major world conflict. More important, the idea that Frank had become alienated from mainstream society by the experiences of war was a reality ex-soldiers and their families could relate to. Finally, at the end of the film, when Frank agrees to stay on at the hotel to help Mr. Temple and to be with Nora, the Temple family is restored. The theme of restoration would resonate with families that had been torn apart when fathers, sons, brothers, and husbands died in the war. Like many households of the era, the Temple family is not the same as it was before the war, but in regrouping, the survivors find hope and a new resolve to go on.

Despite its support of American ideology and the plight of soldiers, *Key Largo* is no simplistic tale of jingoistic flag-waving. Director John Huston had just been in Washington the previous year, along with *Key Largo* stars Humphrey Bogart and Lauren Bacall, to denounce the HUAC investigations—the infamous congressional witch-hunts into supposed communist activity in America. The film's line of dialogue regarding the need to stand up to the "Johnny Roccos of the world" could easily be applied to the members of HUAC, which stepped on the rights of its witnesses by bullying them into accusing or incriminating others as communists.

Huston's shaping of the Frank McCloud character as an ex-soldier suffering from the psychological effects of war was influenced by his own wartime experiences. Huston had been a lieutenant in the Signal Corps, and he directed three documentaries to support the war effort. However, two of those films were eventually banned by the U.S. Army because their realistic depiction of war and its effects made the documentaries almost antiwar films.[2] *Let There Be Light*, which showed the emotionally disturbed war veterans at Mason General Hospital on Long Island, was confiscated and restricted until 1980, and *The Battle of San Pietro*, which chronicled the bloody attack on San Pietro Infine in December 1943, was edited by the army and then banned.

Figure 2.6. Lobby card from *Key Largo*. (Doll/Morrow Collection)

Knowing Huston's liberal political background helps to understand the emphasis he gives to a bit of real-life Florida hurricane lore during the scene in which the storm is at its peak. Mr. Temple needles the nervous gangsters by telling them about the great Labor Day Hurricane, an actual category-5 hurricane that hit the Upper Keys in 1935. In low-key lighting, with storm sounds howling in the background, Temple—expertly played by veteran actor Lionel Barrymore—lays it on thick about the fury of the wind, the loss of life, and the way dead bodies were found in the mangroves for weeks afterward. Sadly, most of the gruesome details written into Barrymore's speech were true.

Spotted on August 31, that hurricane was considered mild at first, and experts predicted it would move between the Lower Keys and Cuba, probably to the south of Key West. Instead it blew up through Lower and Upper Matecumbe Key, Plantation Key, and Tavernier Key with such ferocity that it wiped out much of the region's agricultural industry. Upper Matecumbe had once been a leading lime and pineapple center, but the plantations and groves were permanently destroyed by the hurricane's 200–250 mph winds and a 25–foot storm surge.[3] Much of the Florida East Coast Railroad, completed by Henry Flagler in 1912, was destroyed as well, particularly its concrete spans and the stone embankments. The most devastating result, however, was the loss of life; almost five hundred people were killed.

Most of the victims were World War I veterans who were living on Matecumbe while building a highway through the Keys. Many had been part of the 1932 Bonus March, in which disgruntled WWI vets marched on Washington, D.C., to demand early payment of a bonus Congress had promised them for their service. Instead, President Herbert Hoover had them forcibly dispersed by the U.S. Army. Newspaper photographs of current soldiers routing WWI veterans, and reports of the injuries and trauma inflicted, shocked the nation. To make it up to the vets, President Franklin Roosevelt gave them jobs in the Civilian Conservation Corps (CCC), with many of them assigned to build the highway through the Keys. There was a hurricane evacuation plan in effect for these men, who lived in the flimsiest of temporary barracks on Matecumbe, but the plan failed on Labor Day of 1935. The train that was supposed to pick them up and take them back to the mainland did not arrive on time, showing up only in the midst of the hurricane. On arrival, the train was derailed by the storm surge, and most of the veterans on the island were drowned, whipped to death by the wind, or crushed by debris. Ernest Hemingway, who was among the first to visit Matecumbe after the storm, wrote a scathing article titled "Who Murdered the Veterans?" His outrage helped push Congress to hold hearings into why the government-contracted rescue train failed to follow the plan.[4] However, the hearings were little more than a smokescreen, for nothing was learned and no one was held accountable.

Mr. Temple does not tell the whole story in *Key Largo*, but Huston, who experienced firsthand the sacrifices veterans make for their country, must have known that the reference to the train blown off the track would be enough to remind many of this terrible tragedy. It was tragedy compounded by the deaths of so many WWI vets who had been let down by their country—twice.

THE CREDITS	THE CAST	
Released in 1948 by Warner Brothers	Humphrey Bogart	Frank McCloud
Produced by Jerry Wald	Edward G. Robinson	Johnny Rocco
Directed by John Huston	Lauren Bacall	Nora Temple
Written by Richard Brooks and John Huston, from	Lionel Barrymore	James Temple
a play by Maxwell Anderson	Claire Trevor	Gaye Dawn
Cinematography by Karl Freund	Thomas Gomez	Curly Hoff
Edited by Rudi Fehr	Harry Lewis	Toots Bass
Special effects by Robert Burks and William	William Haade	Ralphie Feeney
McGann	John Rodney	Deputy Clyde Sawyer
	Monte Blue	Sheriff Ben Wade
	Jay Silverheels	Tom Osceola
	Rodd Redwing	John Osceola

MR. PEABODY AND THE MERMAID

> We're not like other women
> We don't have to clean an oven
> And we never will grow ollllllllld. . . .
> We've got the world by the tail!
> —official Weeki Wachee mermaid anthem

THE STORY

Polly Peabody takes her husband, Arthur, on a Caribbean holiday to recover from a bout with the flu and to reflect on turning fifty. While fishing, Mr. Peabody snags a bona fide mermaid and becomes mesmerized by her youth and beauty.

THE FILM

Light and simple on the surface, *Mr. Peabody and the Mermaid* is a charming commentary on aging, particularly its psychological reverberations. In the film, Arthur Peabody is whisked away to an exotic paradise for rest and relaxation just before his fiftieth birthday. Already dejected by the approaching milestone, Peabody is dealt a low blow when his wife, Polly, admits that she doesn't mind that he is getting older. She startles him with the revelation "A wife doesn't really feel safe, you know, until her husband turns fifty," implying that older husbands don't pester their wives for conjugal rights. The admission emasculates him, and he feels estranged from Polly. Not long after, Arthur snags a mermaid, whom he calls Lenore, while fishing in the ocean near Key Aura. He brings her back to the resort where he's staying and hides her in the decorative pool.

The mermaid represents the passion and desire of youth, which becomes apparent as Peabody tries to rekindle his feelings of romance and desire through Lenore. He teaches her how to kiss and cuddle, and she becomes more than a willing pupil. "My age means nothing to you, does it?" he murmurs to her. It is significant that Lenore cannot speak, so that Arthur's dialogue in their scenes together is not so much conversation as it is his thoughts and reflections on the meaning of attraction and desire—and the loss of it. No one else actually sees that Lenore is a mermaid, which suggests that she is a figment of Peabody's imagination as he works through his midlife crisis. Polly and the butler do see Arthur carry something that resembles marine life, but they see only her tail. That Lenore is an idealized version of womanhood for Peabody is underscored by the use of soft focus and romantic lighting effects. Her features are softened by a gauzy haze, while her hair sparkles with points of light.

Figure 2.7. Lobby card from *Mr. Peabody and the Mermaid*. (Doll/Morrow Collection)

Polly finds clues to Arthur's involvement with another woman, though she mistakenly believes his paramour to be pushy party girl Cathy Livingston. She leaves him behind in the Caribbean, where he becomes more and more enchanted by Lenore. When a nosy neighbor almost discovers her, Peabody realizes he must release her back into the ocean. Complications occur when local authorities believe that Arthur may have killed his wife, but he insists that Polly left him because he was harboring a mermaid. Eventually Lenore returns to the depths of the ocean, and Arthur returns to Boston. He spills his tale to Dr. Harvey, a psychiatrist, who assures Peabody that he is normal, whether Lenore was real or not. Peabody realizes the significance of his enchantment with his mermaid and gives Polly one of Lenore's beautiful hair combs, transferring his romantic desires from Lenore to his wife.

Star William Powell was the perfect choice to play Arthur Peabody; indeed, the film seems a vehicle constructed around Powell's image. On the written page, Peabody is not a particularly sympathetic character. He is a self-absorbed fifty-year-old married man who becomes involved with a female who—mermaid or not—looks less than half his age. Powell, however, brings to the role his history of playing genteel, mature men of great charm and sophistication—

a star image built from such films as *My Man Godfrey*, *Libeled Lady*, *Life with Father*, and the *Thin Man* series. He imbues Arthur Peabody with the attributes of vulnerability, morality, and civility, and these characteristics help to excuse the character's weaknesses and signal that Peabody will carry his obsession only so far. *Mr. Peabody and the Mermaid* provides a perfect example of the strengths of the star system, in which films were cast and marketed according to the images of their stars.

The Caribbean resort where the Peabodys vacationed, as well as most of the ocean sets, were created on a soundstage and on the back lot of Universal Studios in Hollywood. The resort features exotic flora and fauna and a classy design of arches and porticos to give the hotel a vaguely foreign ambiance. Most of the ocean scenes were done on the large pond on the back lot of Universal, which film crews still use to shoot ocean scenes. The underwater sequences, however, were shot in Weeki Wachee Springs, Florida.

When Lenore is submerged in the decorative pond at the vacation resort, the audience can see her cavort around a castlelike structure that looks like an illustration for a fairy tale. Just after Lenore hears Peabody declare his strong feelings for her, she dives below the surface and executes several impressive turns and maneuvers. Though she cannot speak, her playful behavior is enough to express her joy at Peabody's revelation. Her water dance was actually part of the choreographed routine of the Weeki Wachee mermaids, who doubled for actress Ann Blyth in the underwater scenes. Lenore's watery home was part of the Weeki Wachee set.

Weeki Wachee, nicknamed the City of Mermaids, is home to a Florida tourist attraction that features women in mermaid costumes swimming underwater in carefully choreographed routines. The attraction was opened in 1947 by ex–navy frogman Newton Perry, who had a theater constructed fifteen feet underwater in a natural spring. The mermaid show had been open only a year when *Mr. Peabody* was released, and Weeki Wachee benefited from the publicity surrounding the film. For the premiere of *Mr. Peabody* at Southern theaters, a small tank containing mermaid Nancy Tribble was used to cross-promote the film and Weeki Wachee Springs.

At Weeki Wachee the mermaids—and a few mermen—take part in an elaborate underwater ballet that consists of graceful turns, effortless spins, and breathtaking stunts. From 1947 to 1960, the main show consisted of demonstrations of choreographed movements, but beginning in 1961, the shows took on themes and narratives. Not surprisingly, their staple was an interpretation of *The Little Mermaid*, but other shows have included *The Mermaids and the Pirates* (1962–63), *Mermaids on the Moon* (1969–70), *The Spirit of '76/Perils of Pearls* (1976–77), and *Pocahontas Meets the Little Mermaid* (1995–97).

While performing the ballets, the mermaids discreetly breathe from submerged air hoses along the sides of the theater. They swim over to the hoses, breath in air, hold their breath while executing their spins, turns, and tricks, and then rush back for more air. The mermaids and mermen are underwater for the entire thirty-minute show without a break in the open air. To prepare for this unique show, the performers train for about a year, first taking instruction on land and then learning the routine in the water without the mermaid costume. The final exam requires trainees to hold their breath for two and a half minutes while changing out of a costume underwater. To be a mermaid requires not only gracefulness but also incredible stamina.

The Weeki Wachee park consists of several hundred acres, including a natural spring with clear water at a constant 72 degrees. The spring is the headwater of the Weeki Wachee River, and the mermaids and mermen perform alongside fish and turtles—as well as the occasional snake and alligator! However, their greatest danger comes not from the wildlife but from the ravages of time and the insensitivities of big business. Weeki Wachee fell upon hard times in recent years as a result of declining attendance, high maintenance costs of the aging facilities, and other problems. Just after the millennium, the owners of the 440 acres around the spring attempted to close the attraction and replace it with a state park. But a vigorous effort from the mayor of Weeki Wachee, a former mermaid, staved off closing, at least temporarily.

In comparison to the mega–theme parks that have invaded the state in recent years, Weeki Wachee, the City of Mermaids, is a uniquely Floridian attraction that was once considered a wonder and a marvel. *Mr. Peabody and the Mermaid* reminds us that it still is.

THE CREDITS

Released in 1948 by Universal Pictures
Produced by Nunnally Johnson and Gene Fowler Jr.
Directed by Irving Pichel
Written by Nunnally Johnson, from a novel by Guy and Constance Jones
Cinematography by Russell Metty
Underwater cinematography by David S. Horsley
Edited by Marjorie Fowler
Art direction by Bernard Herzbrun and Boris Leven
Costumes by Grace Houston

THE CAST

William Powell	Arthur Peabody
Ann Blyth	Lenore
Irene Hervey	Polly Peabody
Andrea King	Cathy Livingston
Clinton Sundberg	Mike Fitzgerald
Art Smith	Dr. Harvey
Hugh French	Major Ronald Hadley

THE PALM BEACH STORY

And they lived happily ever after . . . or did they?
—last line of *The Palm Beach Story*

THE STORY

Gerry Jeffers decides to leave her charming but unsuccessful husband, Tom, in order to help his career as an inventor and satisfy her own material desires. She runs off to Palm Beach, planning to divorce Tom and marry a millionaire who can then back Tom's business ventures. Tom follows, and the two pose as brother and sister in order to court two eccentric members of the wealthy Hackensacker family.

THE FILM

For more than a century, Palm Beach has been America's premiere bastion of wealth and luxury. Boasting some of the most extravagant mansions ever built, the sixteen-mile-long barrier island off the southeast coast of Florida has long served as the winter residence of families including the duPonts, Posts, Vanderbilts, and Kennedys. Local lore holds that the island sprang from far humbler beginnings, however. The famous trees lining the beaches and avenues that give the island its name were planted by industrious local scavengers in 1878, when a Spanish ship bearing a load of coconuts from Havana wrecked on the island. The settlers hoped to use the flotsam to launch a commercial coconut industry. Though those dreams never materialized, many of them earned tidy sums a few years later when Henry Flagler's Florida East Coast Railway began buying up land on the island to create a resort. Flagler opened his Royal Poinciana Hotel in 1894 and heavily promoted it as a winter playground for America's idle rich of the East and Midwest.

Architect Addison Mizner was the next to shape Palm Beach's future. After creating some of New York's most talked about mansions, Mizner moved south for health reasons and crafted a grand plan for the small island. Early in the twentieth century, he brought his distinctive architectural vision to a number of palatial homes and buildings, such as the Everglades Club, the Bath and Tennis Club, and hotels including the Brazilian Court, the Colony, and the Biltmore. With such luxurious amenities, the island quickly became a center of the winter social season for America's upper classes. From December to February, Palm Beach was *the* place to be.

Over time, that social season has extended to run from November through April but remains focused on charitable fund-raising thanks in large part to the efforts of cereal heiress Marjorie Merriweather Post. In the 1920s, Post built Mar-a-Lago, one of the most decadent of the many decadent homes on the island, and used it to host what became the peak event of the season, the Red Cross Ball. Today, more than a hundred charity galas are hosted on the island each year.

Despite this long tradition of giving, Palm Beach has also earned a reputation as a cliquish, exclusionist community where dilettantes and sycophants rest on family fortunes and focus their energies on snobbish social machinations. As such, the island provided a perfect setting for *The Palm Beach Story*, a classic Preston Sturges comedy that skewered sex, marriage, and the rich.

Sturges began his Hollywood career in the 1930s as a highly desired scriptwriter who sold his services to several major studios. After much effort, he persuaded Paramount to let him try his hand at directing his own scripts, clinching the deal by accepting a nominal fee of ten dollars for the screenplay he was to helm, *The Great McGinty*. Released in 1940, this comedy of concealed identity offered a biting satire of the American political system and became a huge hit with audiences. The success paved the way for Sturges and other top talents such as Billy Wilder and John Huston to both write and direct, a practice not typical in the studio system.

Much admired for the razor-sharp wit and snappy dialogue of his scripts, Sturges used the director's chair to bring his writing to the fore. As Sturges said himself, "[I] did all my directing when I wrote the screenplay."[5] From this position, he crafted a body of work over the next several years that would enshrine him as the undisputed master of the screwball comedy. Though this genre is generally credited as beginning with Frank Capra's *It Happened One Night* and was ably executed by many other directors, Sturges is the one who perfected the art of combining the lunacy of farce, the physical humor of slapstick, and the literate wit of romantic comedy in such films as *The Lady Eve* and *The Palm Beach Story*. In addition to humor, his films offered sly satire on various social institutions and mores.

The Palm Beach Story is one of the shining examples of his skill. Joel McCrea and Claudette Colbert star as Tom and Gerry Jeffers, a struggling young couple living beyond their means in a New York penthouse who break up at the wife's insistence so they can each have more secure financial futures. Gerry reasons that as a single young woman, she can easily find a wealthy provider, whom she will charm into offering business opportunities to Tom. She runs off with no belongings or money, convinced that her charms will allow her to travel to Palm Beach, arrange a divorce, and court a millionaire. Since this is a screwball comedy, she is able to achieve her hare-brained scheme with ease.

Tom pursues her, intent on winning her back, and during the chase they encounter a variety of wild characters that lampoon the wealthy class. For ex-

Figure 2.8. Publicity photo from *The Palm Beach Story*. (Doll/Morrow Collection)

ample, Gerry finagles a train ticket by flaunting her distress to the members of the Ale and Quail Club, a group of well-to-do sportsman heading south on an annual hunting pilgrimage. Though chivalrous, the men prove to be little more than drunken reprobates who raise such havoc on the train that the conductor uncouples their private car and leaves it on a sidetrack. Gerry then enlists the assistance of one of the wealthiest men in the world, the naively eccentric John D. Hackensacker III, who buys her an entire wardrobe in Jacksonville and then takes her to Palm Beach on his yacht.

Tom finally catches up with her on the pier, but Gerry, still determined to carry out her plan, introduces him to Hackensacker and his oft-married sister Princess Centimillia as her brother, Captain McGlew. Smitten with Tom, flighty Centimillia casually begins to ignore her current paramour, a zany fop named Toto who speaks an undetermined European language that none of them understand. She blithely accounts for her shifting affection by announcing to Gerry that she thinks she'll marry an American this time because that would be more patriotic. In the end, of course, all problems appear to be resolved, and the final image shows three appropriately paired couples standing before the altar. In keeping with the wry Sturges wit, however, a coda appears on the screen over the couples: "And they lived happily ever after . . . or did they?"

The film's Palm Beach setting provides a perfect backdrop for parody, presenting an illogical universe that serves to highlight the inherent logical flaws of real life. Amid the madcap humor, *The Palm Beach Story* offers piercing commentary on the restrictions of marriage and the idleness of privilege, undermining a pair of social institutions often accepted at face value.

THE CREDITS	THE CAST	
Released in 1942 by Paramount Pictures	Claudette Colbert	Geraldine "Gerry" Jeffers
Produced by Paul Jones	Joel McCrea	Tom Jeffers ("Capt. McGlew")
Directed by Preston Sturges	Mary Astor	The Princess Centimillia
Written by Preston Sturges	Rudy Vallee	John D. Hackensacker III
Cinematography by Victor Milner	Sig Arno	Toto
Edited by Stuart Gilmore	Robert Warwick	Mr. Hinch, Ale and Quail Club
Music by Victor Young	William Demarest	First member, Ale and Quail Club
Art direction by Hans Dreier and Ernst Fegte	Robert Dudley	Wienie King
Costume design by Irene	Fred Toones	George, club car bartender

REAP THE WILD WIND

To gain her first each eager strives,
To save the cargo and the peoples' lives;
Amongst the rocks where the breakers roar,
The wreckers on the Florida shore.
—"The Wreckers' Song," a folk tune

THE STORY

Jack Stuart, a sea captain for Commodore Devereaux's shipping line, works out of Key West, sailing the route between Cuba and the Keys. Jack's job is dangerous: on the treacherous reefs along the Straits of Florida, many a ship has wrecked and gone down. When one of Stuart's ships is purposely scuttled by his first mate, Devereaux representative Stephen Tolliver is sent to Key West to keep a watchful eye on Jack—and on Jack's beautiful fiancée, Loxi Claiborne.

THE FILM

In 1942 Cecil B. DeMille turned a minor short story from the *Saturday Evening Post* into the rousing box-office sensation *Reap the Wild Wind*. In bringing to the screen the tale of Key West's sea trade and salvage operators, the veteran director offered his audiences romance, high-seas adventure, thrills, history, and spectacle, which was DeMille's stock in trade. Helping him achieve his vision on such a grand scale were all of Paramount Pictures' resources, from the expert camera crew to the clever prop masters. *Reap the Wild Wind* provides an excellent example of one of the strengths of the studio system: the hundreds of skilled craftsmen on staff in the various departments of each studio. For the big-budget spectacles that DeMille was famous for, each department—costumes, makeup, props, special effects, set design, cinematography—was called upon to contribute its expertise to the whole. And one of DeMille's strengths as a director was the way he used these resources to best advantage.

The climactic scene in *Reap the Wild Wind* finds Captain Jack Stuart and Stephen Tolliver investigating a wreck at the bottom of the sea. The two make their way to the floor of the ocean by using deep-sea diving gear, which was a new and dangerous technology in the 1840s, when the story takes place. There they discover evidence that the cousin of love interest Loxi Claiborne was drowned when the ship sank, and if that is not dramatic enough, a huge squid emerges from the wreckage and reaches for the two men with its creeping tentacles. Tolliver cannot escape the grasp of the squid, but Stuart attacks one of the beast's huge tentacles with a knife. The squid turns its attention to Stuart, who is killed while saving the life of Tolliver.

According to DeMille in his autobiography, the squid sequence was one of the reasons for the film's popularity with the public, partly because it was exciting and partly because most people were unfamiliar with the monsters of the deep.[6] Paramount's prop department was responsible for coming up with a realistic-looking squid that could move and attack underwater. The burnt-red monster, made of sponge rubber and powered by an electric motor, was brought to life by a twenty-four-button control panel atop the huge tank of water where the sequence was filmed. The squid's tentacles were fourteen feet long and capable of wrapping themselves around a human.

While underwater in diving gear, John Wayne and Ray Milland, who played Stuart and Tolliver, took direction from DeMille through telephone wires rigged into their diving helmets by the capable Paramount crew. The wreckage of the nineteenth-century cargo ship had been built underwater in the studio's water tank, where the scenes for many a sea adventure had been shot. The tank was about the size of a football field and was twenty-five feet deep. Designed by Hans Dreier and Roland Anderson, the underwater set also featured a mass of ship's cables and cargo baskets that floated in and out of frame, creating a sense of danger. Part of the sunken ship's cargo was brightly silk cloth that drifted eerily about the wreckage. Unfortunately, the silk lost its pigment in the salt water of the tank, but the costume department handled the problem, redyeing the silk at the end of each day.

The special underwater photography was accomplished by cinematographer Dewey Wrigley, while Gordon Jennings was in charge of the special effects, which included everything from creating the illusion of a giant wave

Figure 2.9. *Reap the Wild Wind* star John Wayne.
(Doll/Morrow Collection)

pummeling a ship to constructing a beautiful Key West sunset in the studio. The only "staff" that did not cooperate with DeMille was the school of fish in the water tank, who would never stay in camera range. As DeMille quipped, "Rehearsal did not do them much good."[7]

Though not a very glamorous department compared to set design or special effects or cinematography, Paramount's research department did a stellar job on *Reap the Wild Wind*. They not only provided the prop masters with information on giant squids, they researched sea slang of the 1840s, the dangers of ocean storms, and when stick matches were first available to the public. They also provided details about Key West as the capital of salvage operators and wreckers in the early nineteenth century.

Wreckers, or salvage operators, were men who sailed to the sites of shipwrecks in small vessels to rescue the crew, then claimed a percentage of the cargo as salvage to be sold at auction. The coral reefs in the Florida Straits along the south side of the Keys were dangerous to navigate, and cargo ships going to and from New Orleans, Cuba, or Jamaica faced great peril as they passed through the Straits. A lighthouse constructed on Key West was not enough to keep the ships off the reefs or out of the shallow inlets during storms. The wreckers of the Keys were famous for their daring sailing of small craft through treacherous storm waters to reach imperiled ships. Their first efforts involved attempts to save the ship, because if the ship could be maneuvered off the reef intact, then the wreckers' fee was substantially higher. Fees were determined by one of three methods: direct agreement with the distressed ship's owner, friendly arbitration, or a hearing in a court with admiralty jurisdiction. While many wreckers saved the lives of passengers and crew members, the occupation also attracted brigands and pirates who lit false lights to lure ships to their destruction for plunder and profit. Fights broke out frequently among competing salvage crews, and murder was not an uncommon occurrence.

In the late 1820s the wreckers in the Florida Keys began to prosper. Key West rapidly grew into the capital city of salvage, with wrecks bringing in as much as $100,000 every year, and by the 1830s it was the wealthiest city per capita in the United States.[8] The town grew around the salvage operations: five lawyers set up practices that argued nothing but salvage cases; finery from around the world recovered from wrecks was available to the residents of the Keys; customs officials collected taxes on all the goods; shipyards were bustling with activity; shopkeepers prospered by selling salvaged goods; and saloons and grog shops opened to entertain the sailors. The most successful salvage captains constructed beautiful two-story white homes in Key West, complete with balconies and shutters to stave off the heat. Tropical plants surrounded the houses, offering shade and an exotic atmosphere.

The heroism and romance of this nineteenth-century salvage industry inspired Cecil B. DeMille to spin a thrilling yarn with a host of colorful characters against a sweeping ocean backdrop. *Reap the Wild Wind* provides a fitting, if romanticized, tribute to the wreckers of the Keys, who represent an exciting footnote generally left out of the textbooks of American history.

THE CREW	THE CAST	
Released in 1942 by Paramount Pictures	Ray Milland	Stephen Tolliver
Produced by Cecil B. DeMille	John Wayne	Captain Jack Stuart
Directed by Cecil B. DeMille	Paulette Goddard	Loxi Claiborne
Written by Alan LeMay, Charles Bennett, and	Raymond Massey	King Cutler
Jesse Lasky Jr., from a story by Thelma Strabel	Robert Preston	Dan Cutler
Cinematography by Victor Milner and	Susan Hayward	Drusilla Alston
William V. Skall	Lynne Overman	Captain Phillip Philpott
Underwater cinematography by Dewey Wrigley	Walter Hampden	Commodore Devereaux
Art direction by Hans Dreier and Roland Anderson	Louise Beavers	Maum Maria
Edited by Anne Bauchens	Hedda Hopper	Aunt Henrietta Beresford
Music by Victor Young		
Special photographic effects by Gordon Jennings,		
with W. L. Pereira and Farciot Edouart		
Costumes by Natalie Visart		
Marine consulting by Captain Fred F. Ellis		

THE ROSE TATTOO

I like living here. I like living in a house. I like to travel and stay
in hotels and order room service but after I get the traveling
out of my system, I like to come home and cook spaghetti.

—Tennessee Williams, in *Key West Writers
and Their Houses*, by Lynn Kaufelt

THE STORY

Serafina Delle Rose, a Sicilian immigrant living in the Deep South, is so passionately in love with her husband Rosario that she fails to see his faults. When he dies in a truck accident, Serafina closes herself off from the world and devotes herself to his memory. Disheveled and unkempt, she stays in her house, sewing dresses to support herself and her teenage daughter, Rosa. A turning point occurs when Serafina discovers that Rosario had been having an affair, and she finds herself drawn to another robust, carefree truck driver.

THE FILM

Tennessee Williams finished *The Rose Tattoo* in 1949, and the play opened on Broadway in February 1950 after several out-of-town previews. Though Williams had written the play with Italian actress Anna Magnani in mind, Maureen Stapleton starred as Serafina Delle Rose on the stage, with Eli Wallach costarring as the hearty truck driver Alvaro Mangiacavallo. *The Rose Tattoo* is a valentine to sexual passion as a life-affirming force, because Serafina is brought back to life by the sexual stirrings she feels for the funny but virile Alvaro. The play also made use of bold comedy through the larger-than-life antics of Alvaro, which was a feature not common in Williams's previous work. The play's success was measured by its accolades: *The Rose Tattoo* won the highly coveted Tony Award for best play, while Stapleton and Wallach won for their performances in the starring roles.

In the mid-1950s *The Rose Tattoo* was picked up for adaptation to film by respected producer Hal Wallis. Both Wallis and Williams wanted Anna Magnani to play Serafina, and she agreed. She had been reluctant to accept the stage role because of her lack of fluency in English, but the nature of film work made that less of a problem. Burt Lancaster was signed to costar as Alvaro, which added energy and star charisma to the production.

Unfortunately, the film severely scales down most of the play's passion. The references to sex in the dialogue are eliminated or heavily veiled, while marriage replaces sexual desire as the guiding force in the story. Daughter Rosa's

Figure 2.10. Publicity photo from *The Rose Tattoo*. (State Archives of Florida)

sexual awakening by a sailor in the play becomes the need to sanctify young love through a socially acceptable union in the film. Alvaro's lusty bawdiness is turned into overblown comic antics for the big screen. A neighbor's goat, used as a potent symbol of unbridled lust in the play, is little more than comic relief in the film. The changes were undoubtedly made because the Production Code, the censorship code that had governed Hollywood films since the Golden Age, was still very much in place during the mid-1950s, though some directors had begun to push its limits. The code not only forbade open references to sexuality, it mandated that the only legitimate relationship between a man and a woman was marriage. All the Hollywood films based on Williams's plays were reworked to fit the code's guidelines and restrictions, but the *The Rose Tattoo* seemed to suffer from the changes more than most.

One change that was well suited to a Tennessee Williams story was the decision to shoot the film in Key West, Florida, where the colorful writer owned a home. In the public consciousness, the name Tennessee Williams is largely associated with a wild and exotic New Orleans, where all residents "take a streetcar named Desire, and then transfer to one called Cemeteries and ride six blocks and get off at Elysian Fields."[9] While the South's most famous playwright did live in New Orleans, he also made a home for himself in Key West.

Williams visited the city for the first time in 1941, checking into a boarding house called the Trade Winds, owned by Mrs. Cora Black. The writer, who became good friends with Mrs. Black's daughter, Marion, liked the unconventional atmosphere of Key West, which was tolerant of bohemian lifestyles and gay relationships. He rented one of Mrs. Black's guest cottages behind the main house for $8 per week. Key West had always been a refuge for all manner of writers and artists, including Williams's favorite, Hart Crane. During the 1940s, when the playwright began to visit the Keys, such artists and writers as Grant Wood, Doris Lee, John Dewey, James Farrell, and Max Eastman could be found in this tropical paradise, though Ernest Hemingway had already moved on by that time. Other writers and artists, including Gore Vidal, Carson McCullers, Christopher Isherwood, and Françoise Sagan, drifted in and out of town as visitors and tourists. Williams eventually rented an old Bahamian house on Duncan Street, finally buying it around 1950. Over the years, he added a patio, a swimming pool, a guest cottage, and a small writing studio that he called the Mad House. In the late 1970s he purchased a second house on Van Phister Street for his sister Rose, who had been mentally handicapped by a lobotomy decades earlier. Unfortunately, the situation did not work out, and Rose returned to the care facility where she had spent most of her adult life. Though Williams traveled the country a great deal, frequently staying in one city for many weeks, even months, Key West was the only place he owned property until 1972 when he bought a second home in New Orleans.

The Rose Tattoo took place "somewhere along the Gulf Coast between New Orleans and Mobile," but Wallis and Williams thought hot, sunny Key West provided an appropriate backdrop. The crisp photography by James Wong Howe did not romanticize the tropical atmosphere; instead, the veteran cinematographer opted for a hard-edged, realistic style that would emphasize the dirt and dust of a small Southern community of working class immigrants.

When Wallis arrived in Key West to help scout locations, Williams was in New York on other business. Wallis and his crew drove around the area looking for a wood frame house to be Serafina's home and found one that had a small backyard where the animal wrangler could keep the goats. Wallis wondered if the neighboring homeowner would mind if the film crew pushed his fence back a few feet, so that Serafina's backyard could be bigger. The Key West representative that had accompanied Wallis smiled and said he was sure he wouldn't mind, because the neighbor was Tennessee Williams. Wallis had actually selected Williams's neighborhood for the principal location without realizing it.

Williams was involved in the production of the film in several ways. During shooting, he allowed the actors to use his home as a dressing room where they could prepare for their scenes or relax between takes. He, Wallis, and Williams's companion, Frank Merlo, appeared in the bar scene in which Serafina searches for her husband's lover. The sequence was shot in an actual bar in downtown Key West called the Mardi Gras, and Wallis and Williams appear as two patrons who watch a furious Serafina march into the seedy establishment. The handsome man who tries to stop the fight between the angry wife and the defiant lover is Merlo.

Several locals were used as extras in *The Rose Tattoo*, and the scene in which Serafina meets Alvaro was shot at St. Paul's Episcopal Church on Duval Street. Though other actual Key West locations are visible in the *The Rose Tattoo*, including a Japanese tattoo parlor where Alvaro gets a rose tattooed on his chest, a diner called Jack's Chili Bowl, the Casa Marina Hotel, and a school, director Daniel Mann did not make memorable use of them.

Though less remembered in retrospect than other films adapted from the plays of Tennessee Williams, *The Rose Tattoo* did provide a showcase for Anna Magnani's considerable talent. Earthy, intense, and volatile, the actress tore through the role of Serafina Delle Rose, instantly making it her own. Her efforts garnered her an Academy Award as best actress.

THE CREDITS		THE CAST	
Released in 1955 by Paramount Pictures		Anna Magnani	Serafina Delle Rose
Produced by Hal B. Wallis		Burt Lancaster	Alvaro Mangiacavallo
Directed by Daniel Mann		Marisa Pavan	Rosa Delle Rose
Screenplay by Tennessee Williams and Hal Kanter		Ben Cooper	Jack Hunter
Cinematography by James Wong Howe		Virginia Grey	Estelle Hohengarten
Edited by Warren Low		Jo Van Fleet	Bessie
Art direction by Tambi Larsen and Hal Pereira		Sandro Giglio	Father De Leo
Costumes by Edith Head			
Music by Alex North and Harry Warren			

THE MOVIE TOURIST'S GUIDE TO GOLDEN AGE FLORIDA

The Golden Age of Hollywood may be long gone, but visitors to Florida can still find many spots where the era left its mark. Many of these movies were filmed on location in the Sunshine State. Others were shot on sets re-created on a Hollywood soundstage, but they were at least inspired by actual Florida locales.

Tarpon Springs

Though demand for natural sponges has dwindled, Tarpon Springs retains a waterfront district that preserves the look and feel of the Greek community when it was the sponge capital of the United States. Visitors can dine, shop, and purchase sponges and other souvenirs at the Sponge Docks and observe the same kind of sponge auctions that served as the town's economic engine one hundred years ago. Boat tours that include diving demonstrations are available, as are ecological tours of the nearby Anclote River. During the Feast of the Epiphany in January, the community holds an annual competition in which young men dive to retrieve a simple wooden cross from the waters of Spring Bayou. The winner is carried to St. Nicholas Greek Orthodox Church to receive a special blessing. The competition was recreated in *Beneath the 12-Mile Reef* and, of course, Robert Wagner won.

DISTANT DRUMS

Everglades National Park

As the only remaining subtrobical habitat in North America, the Everglades offers an array of unique flora and fauna for the intrepid explorer. The park's main entrance on Palm Drive just outside Florida City provides a doorway to a primeval place that remains as dangerous today as it was for U.S. soldiers and their Seminole foes in the early 1800s.

Seminole Sites

Seminole Indians remain in Florida to this day and welcome tourists to learn about their culture, history, and land. Visitors can learn the true story of the Seminole people and their success against the U.S. Army by visiting such Seminole-run sites as the Bilie Swamp Safari and the Ah-Tah-Thi-Ki Museum near Clewiston, and the Okalee Indian Village near Hollywood.

EASY TO LOVE

Cypress Gardens Adventure Park

In 2003, after sixty-seven years, Florida's Cypress Gardens abrubtly closed its doors as a result of financial troubles, much to the dismay of Florida residents who fondly remembered the park from their childhoods. A Georgia amusement park owner stepped in to save the landmark attraction, and the refurbished park opened in 2005. Located midway between Orlando and Tampa off U.S. Highway 27, the park still offers its signature attractions of Southern belles, water ski spectacles, and fabulously landscaped gardens as featured in

Easy to Love. It now also offers concerts on a regular basis in addition to an adjoining water park.

THE GREATEST SHOW ON EARTH

Sarasota

In 1927, Ringling Brothers and Barnum & Bailey Circus selected Sarasota as its winter home. Though the circus has since moved on, the town has retained its big-top heritage through the John and Mable Ringling Museum of Art. Located in the former estate of John Ringling at 5401 Bay Shore Road, Sarasota, the museum displays Ringling's personal art collection, featuring twenty-one galleries of works by Rubens, Van Dyck, and other Baroque masters. In addition to the fine art, the facility houses a Circus Museum focusing on the memorabilia and history of America's most famous traveling entertainment.

KEY LARGO

Key Largo

The greater part of this film was shot inside the studio in Hollywood, but a bit of second unit work depicted Highway 1 as it snaked along Key Largo. Most of this footage appears at the beginning of the film and captures the Key Largo of the 1940s. Though nothing exists on the Key to remind movie tourists of this particular film, there is a John Huston–Humphrey Bogart connection to visit. The boat used in *The African Queen* is moored at Mile Marker 100 on Highway 1 and offers short pleasure trips.

Lower Matecumbe Key

At Mile Marker 81.6, visit the pale coral limestone monument to the victims of the Labor Day Hurricane of 1935. The bodies of 423 of the hurricane's victims rest here. A relief carved on the front depicts high seas and wind-battered palms.

MR. PEABODY AND THE MERMAID

Weeki Wachee Springs

Weeki Wachee Springs is one of the state's largest freshwater springs. In 1946 Newton Perry, an ex–navy frogman, built an underwater theater at the springs, which would house one of Florida's most famous tourist attractions—the mermaid show. Women swimmers in mermaid costumes perform underwater with the benefit of strategically placed air pipes for them to take in air. Weeki Wachee is located at U.S. 19 and Highway 50, forty-five miles north of Clearwater.

Palm Beach

As a playground for the richest of the rich, Palm Beach can be a pricey vacation destination. Rooms at The Breakers can top $2,000 per night, and private clubs like Marjorie Merriweather Post's former residence Mar-a-Lago require a six-figure initial membership fee. Travelers on more limited budgets can find reasonably priced accommodations in nearby communities and still enjoy the shops and fine dining of the jet set. One noteworthy Palm Beach attraction is the Flagler Museum, converted from the palatial residence of one of the state's great visionaries.

REAP THE WILD WIND

Key West

The Shipwreck Historeum Museum on Whitehead Street honors the memory of Key West's brave and industrious wreckers and the role they played in shaping the island's history. The museum presents films and live performances that tell the story of the island's wreckers and displays artifacts recovered from a ship that foundered on the reef in 1856.

THE ROSE TATTOO

Key West

The Rose Tattoo was filmed on location in Key West in the same neighborhood where Tennessee Williams made his home. The Williams home at 1431 Duncan Street is not open to the public, but the Tennessee Williams Theater on the Florida Keys Community College campus offers plays, musical performances, and other cultural events year round. The theater has also sponsored an annual Tennessee Williams Festival since 2003 that draws luminaries including Eli Wallach and Glenda Jackson.

St. Paul's on Duval Street, the oldest Episcopal church in Florida, appeared in the film as the Catholic church attended by Serafina Delle Rose. The small cemetery behind the building, a regular stop on local ghost tours, is known for the mysterious orbs of light that appear in photos taken on the grounds.

FLORIDA NOIR

The streets were dark with something more than night.
—Raymond Chandler, *The Simple Art of Murder*

Chandler's poetic description for the milieu of his private detective, Philip Marlowe, perfectly captures the essence of film noir. It at once evokes the melancholy of the characters, the corrupt atmosphere of the environs, and the idea that there is more to this type of movie than meets the eye. Dark, moody, and forbidding, film noir is beloved by movie buffs, mystery lovers, and those who prefer their heroes with an edge.

Film noir is a type of mystery thriller characterized by a dark visual style and a pessimistic outlook. The dark look derives from the chiaroscuro lighting, called low key if the shadows are evenly depicted, or high contrast in scenes with a sharp distinction between lights and darks. Besides being beautiful to look at, the lighting has a symbolic purpose, cluing the viewer to the unscrupulous and immoral actions of the characters—even the good ones. A tour de force of film techniques, film noir also uses a variety of angles, distorting lenses, and offbeat compositions. In addition, the set designs feature bar motifs and weblike patterns to suggest entrapment or imprisonment. Distortion—be it from lighting, angles, or set design—dominates the visual style and conveys that the noir world is corrupt, debased, and just a little mad.

Mysteries ache to be solved, and the primary character in film noir is the detective figure. Though most often a private eye, the character can also be a cop, a lawyer, a reporter, or anyone who assumes an investigative role. But the noir detective is no Sherlock Holmes; instead he is weak, flawed, or ineffectual and thus incapable of putting the clues together. Unlike other types of crime stories, film noir does not focus on answers. The quest, or the journey the detective takes to solve the mystery, defines the genre. The quest reveals that the crime that began his investigation is misleading in its simplicity; crime and corruption become an ever-widening web too big for any one person to resolve.

If the crime represents a web of corruption, then the femme fatale weaves that web. She stands at the center of this world holding a cigarette and a cocktail glass, looking for the quickest route to money and power. The detective knows she's bad, but he is not strong enough or smart enough to resist her. Fumbling his way through the mystery, the detective discovers he is on his own. Even those who claim to be on his side generally fail or betray him, and they leave him with physical and emotional wounds.

Though the first noir films appeared during World War II, the genre fed on the malaise, disillusionment, and fears of postwar America. Unemployment, the emerging cold war, urban strife, and tension over women in the workforce generated an undercurrent of discontent and alienation beneath a surface of complacency. By the end of the 1950s, when times began to change, noir had disappeared. In the early 1970s the genre resurfaced, fueled by the political discord and social upheaval of the era. Young directors who had learned about noir in film school expressed their anger and discontent through neurotic, ineffectual protagonists drawn from the dark corners of film noir. In the early 1990s neo-noir emerged, less tied to the specific politics and social traumas of the period, but proving that the genre could speak to new generations.

Classic film noir of the 1940s and 1950s borrowed its primary settings— Los Angeles and San Francisco—from the stories and novels of the writers who originated hard-boiled detective fiction in the 1920s, including Dashiell Hammett and Raymond Chandler. The history, politics, and image of Los Angeles in particular made that town an inspired choice for stories of lost dreams, impenetrable mysteries, and moral decay.

Los Angeles experienced rapid growth and development during the 1910s and 1920s, which set the stage for corrupt politics and backroom deals. Because L.A. is situated in a desert, much of its history involves fierce battling over control of water sources and water rights; additionally, land booms, transportation development, and the discovery of oil contributed to the rampant corruption and sordid deals—all hidden beneath the glamour and glitz of Hollywood.

L.A. never completely lost its appeal as a setting for film noir, even for those produced in later eras. But times change, and a new noir setting emerged, once again borrowed from hard-boiled crime fiction.

During the 1960s John D. MacDonald introduced a series of crime novels with *The Deep Blue Good-By*. Set in South Florida, the series features a detective figure named Travis McGee, a self-proclaimed "salvage expert" who tracks down large sums of money stolen from Florida's residents. Through McGee's misadventures, MacDonald exposed the ill effects of Florida's rapid growth after World War II. Shady land development deals, increased air and water pollution, ecological disasters, the proliferation of high-rises, and greedy politicians had turned Florida into the new L.A., at least by noir standards.

Later writers including Elmore Leonard, Charles Willeford, and Carl Hiaasen followed in MacDonald's wake, depicting a Florida that is at once a beckoning paradise and a lurid hotbed of crime. The Florida School of crime novelists embroidered the Sunshine State's most noted characteristics, focusing on its fluid population and ethnic diversity and exaggerating its greedy developers and low-life criminals to create an exotic, subtropical world where a flexible morality is not only expected but natural.

In 1981 Lawrence Kasdan effectively visualized that world with his modern-day film noir *Body Heat*. The small beach town, Spanish-style mansion, tropical vegetation, thick fog, and interminable heat seemed to paint an authentic portrait of Florida, but these elements also typecast it as the perfect setting for film noir. With *Body Heat*, Florida locales became as much a part of noir conventions as L.A. or California had been during the 1940s. Soon after, *A Flash of Green*, *Cape Fear*, *China Moon*, and others followed suit. By 1998, when *Palmetto* was released, critic Roger Ebert declared that, with its tacky theme bars, humid nights, ceiling fans, and greedy losers, "Florida is the ideal state for film noir."[1]

The films in this chapter represent a wide range of what recent noir has to offer—from the classic *Body Heat* to the tongue-in-cheek *Palmetto*, from the independently produced *A Flash of Green* to the slick Hollywood thriller *Out of Time*. All make effective or clever use of Florida's locales, imagery, cliches, and idiosyncracies. While some tourists may prefer Florida's theme parks and souvenir shops, movie tourists embrace the region's more colorful history and edgier culture, fully aware that, even in the Sunshine State, the streets can be "dark with something more than night."

BODY HEAT

THE STORY

During a scorching heat wave, small-time lawyer Ned Racine finds trouble when he falls under the spell of Matty Walker, the wife of a wealthy Florida developer. When the affair leads to the murder of Matty's husband, Ned realizes his troubles have only started.

THE FILM

Body Heat reworked the genre of film noir, updating it for a new generation. With its brazen sex scenes, cynical tone, and rich atmosphere, the film became a hit with modern audiences who had little knowledge of the original noir films of the 1940s and 1950s. Writer-director Lawrence Kasdan, who had mined the serials and adventure films of the 1930s and 1940s to cowrite *Raiders of the Lost Ark*, similarly borrowed from the original cycle of film noir to construct *Body Heat*.

Often misrepresented and misunderstood, film noir is a type of crime drama that is famous for its dark visual style. In the low-key lighting that dominates most scenes, the rich, black shadows are used to suggest mystery, corruption, or hidden desires. The story involves a crime and the solving of the crime by a detective figure who is flawed. Though the initial crime may be solved, the detective uncovers in the course of his investigation an ever-widening web of deceit and mendacity that he is powerless to stop. At the end of most noir films, things are much worse than they were at the beginning, suggesting the world is a quagmire of corruption and the lone individual can do little about it.

The agent of the deceit and destruction in film noir is the femme fatale—the irresistible spider woman who lays a trap for the detective hero, tempting him with her sensuality and sexuality. And he succumbs to her temptations, because he is weak or flawed. The femme fatale is not interested in love; instead, she seeks money and power, and the detective is either the quickest path to getting what she wants or a minor obstacle that she easily removes.

So when *Body Heat*'s Matty Walter purrs to Ned Racine, "You're not too bright. I like that in a man," she not only reveals her predatory nature but also picks up where past film fatales left off—Barbara Stanwyck in *Double Indemnity*, Jane Greer in *Out of the Past*, Lana Turner in *The Postman Always Rings Twice*. But the viewers do not catch on at first because, like Ned, we are

Figure 3.1. Kathleen Turner in *Body Heat*. (Doll/Morrow Collection)

too intoxicated by Matty, the Florida setting, the jazzy score, and the steamy atmosphere to grasp her warning.

The film was shot in Delray Beach, Lake Worth, and Hollywood, Florida, located in the southern part of the state along the Atlantic coast. The three locales stand in for the fictional communities of Miranda Beach and Pine Haven, where a summer heat wave is igniting the passions of some of the residents. As Oscar, the local police chief, observes, the heat wave creates a "crisis time," in which people gradually abandon the rules of proper behavior that normally keep compulsions and obsessions in check.

The depiction of "tropical" in *Body Heat* is so rich that it has a sultry, erotic connotation. Each of the three locations offers something "Floridian" that adds to the exotic flavor, so that the environment, the characters, and their

Figure 3.2. Lobby card from *Body Heat*. (Doll/Morrow Collection)

motivations are all intertwined. Hollywood, Florida, provides the locale for Ned's introduction to Matty. The two meet along the Hollywood Beach boardwalk after listening to big-band music at the Beach Theater bandshell. The 1940s-style music recalls the time frame of the original noir films, while the hot, breezy evening along the boardwalk fuels the sexually charged conversation between Matty and Ned. "Don't you want to lick it?" Matty coos, after Ned offers to wipe up the spilled snow cone on her dress.

The piers in the Lake Worth area provided the locales for several key scenes. Ned likes to jog along beaches and piers, giving the illusion that he is healthy and fit. However, he usually stops at some point to smoke a cigarette, suggesting the weaker, self-destructive side to his character. One night while jogging, Ned meets a friend along an empty pier that extends far out into the water. As the friend warns Ned about Matty's treachery, the idea that Ned is out on a limb is suggested by the long pier that disappears into an empty, black night.

A liftbridge in Delray Beach was used to prolong the suspenseful climax to the film. While Oscar rushes to arrest Ned for murder, he is delayed by the bridge lifting to allow boats to pass beneath it. Oscar makes it just in time to witness Ned's fate being sealed.

Aside from these very specific locales, the Florida setting serves the story in more general ways. Land development is a major moneymaking venture in the state. The fact that it has always had a shady connotation is suggested by the old line "If you believe that, then I have some swampland in Florida to sell you." In the film, Matty's husband, Edmund, has become wealthy through nefarious business associates who engage in real estate development and speculation. That this "business" can be violent is suggested when Edmund explains that he is wealthy and powerful because he is willing "to do what's necessary."

Surprisingly, the story was originally set in New Jersey. But given the impressive use of locales—from the empty piers to the tropical mansions—it is inconceivable that *Body Heat* could take place anywhere but Florida.

THE CREDITS	THE CAST	
Released in 1981 by Warner Brothers	William Hurt	Ned Racine
Produced by Fred Gallo and Robert Grand	Kathleen Turner	Matty Walker
Directed by Lawrence Kasdan	Richard Crenna	Edmund Walker
Written by Lawrence Kasdan	Ted Danson	Peter Lowenstein
Cinematography by Richard H. Kline	J. A. Preston	Oscar Grace
Edited by Carol Littleton	Mickey Rourke	Teddy Lewis
Production design by Bill Kenney	Kim Zimmer	Mary Ann Russell
Original music by John Barry	Lanna Saunders	Roz Kraft
	Carola McGuinness	Heather Kraft

CAPE FEAR

The South has a fine tradition of savoring fear.
—detective Claude Kersek in *Cape Fear*

THE STORY

Released after fourteen years in a Georgia prison, Max Cady tracks down his former lawyer, Sam Bowden, to seek revenge. Sam lives in a small Southern town with his wife and daughter, who are also stalked by the maniacal Cady. At first Sam turns to the legal system for protection, but he finds that the system is no match for the shrewd and dangerous ex-convict. The two finally face off on the Bowdens' houseboat as it drifts along the Cape Fear Coast during a raging thunderstorm.

THE FILM

Located in southeastern North Carolina, the Cape Fear Coast was named for the area's rugged shoals and forbidding waters. The state is also home to the Cape Fear River and a small town of the same name. However, Martin Scorsese's film noir thriller *Cape Fear* is set in the fictional town of New Essex, and was shot mostly in and around Hollywood, Florida. Scorsese could have shot the film in the beautiful North Carolina coastal region, but he was not interested in duplicating a specific area in North Carolina, or Florida for that

Figure 3.3. Publicity photos from *Cape Fear*. Top *(left to right)*: Robert De Niro, Jessica Lange, Nick Nolte. Bottom: Gregory Peck *(left)* and Robert Mitchum *(right)*. (Doll/Morrow Collection)

matter. Instead, it was the "Fear" in *Cape Fear* that appealed to Scorsese, and he created a setting that depicted the darkest regions of a mythical South—a place of primitive behaviors, exotic characters, and nightmare landscapes.

Cape Fear is a remake of a 1962 near-classic directed by J. Lee Thompson. To pay homage to Thompson's film, Scorsese cast the actors from the original in small roles: Robert Mitchum, who starred as the psychopath in the 1962 film, plays a police lieutenant; Gregory Peck, who played the innocent victim of Mitchum's wrath, appears as a slimy lawyer; and Martin Balsam, a detective in the original, plays a judge. The 1962 version does not comfortably fit into the film noir genre, but Scorsese's remake is closer to noir. The master director makes vivid use of the genre's dark, exaggerated visual style, and he emphasizes the theme of corruption. However, rather than focusing on the corruption of social institutions, Scorsese exposes the personal corruption that infects the members of the Bowden family. In depicting the family as imperfect, even damaged, Scorsese changes the meaning of the material. In effect, he is reworking the original *Cape Fear*, not remaking it.

In Scorsese's film, lawyer Sam Bowden is tainted personally and professionally. Years earlier, Sam had unsuccessfully defended Max Cady against charges of rape and aggravated assault. Recognizing Cady as a brutal sexual predator, Sam suppressed evidence of the victim's promiscuity, which might have resulted in a lighter sentence. Yet Sam's job was not to be judge and jury; his job was to defend his client. Cady's eventual discovery of Sam's breach is the catalyst for his revenge, but it also points up the lawyer's lapse in professional integrity. Sam is further sullied by his improper relationship with court clerk Lori Davis, who is in love with him. Before the Bowdens moved to New Essex, Sam's dalliances with women almost broke up his marriage. His failure to learn from his indiscretions reveals a moral weakness.

Sam's family is also troubled and dysfunctional. Wife Leigh is neurotic, hostile, and distant to both her husband and daughter. After making love with Sam, she fidgets at her night stand, poking at her face and smearing lipstick across her mouth, obviously disappointed and unfulfilled. Teenage daughter Danielle is defiant and closed off, clearly wounded by her parents' troubled relationship. Instead of discussing their problems, however, the family buries them, just as Sam buried evidence to get rid of Cady. All things repressed must surface eventually, at least in storytelling, and Max Cady emerges to push his way into the Bowdens' lives—a powerful symbol, or even projection, of their troubles and problems.

The embodiment of the discord plaguing the Bowdens, Max Cady is depicted as a potent, malevolent force of nature. As he strolls out of prison, a storm brews in the background—at once an effective symbol and a portent of the film's violent climax in a raging thunderstorm. Dialogue reinforces his primal brutality, as when Lieutenant Elgart compares Cady to a tiger who needs to be lured out of the woods and then destroyed. Cady himself tells Lori Davis, "I'm one hell of an animal," before biting off a piece of her cheek while raping her. In the film's most controversial scene, Cady pretends to be Danielle's acting teacher, seducing her with kind words of understanding before thrusting his thumb into her mouth. The scene takes place in the school auditorium, where the set on the stage recalls the backdrop for a fairy tale, suggesting that Cady is the proverbial Big Bad Wolf who has huffed and puffed his way into the Bowden household.

If Cady is a predator of mythic proportions, then Florida's junglelike foliage and exotic Spanish moss provide a suitably threatening terrain for him to prowl. Early in the film, Cady sits on a stone fence that surrounds the Bowden property. Like an animal stalking his prey, he is silhouetted against a burst of fireworks lighting up the night sky, with palm trees, Spanish moss, and thick foliage visible in the background. Originally there was no Spanish moss on the grounds of the house used for the Bowden residence, so production designer Henry Bumstead had it trucked in, creating a wild, primordial atmosphere straight out of a nightmare.

Aside from the flora and fauna, the South contributes to the frightening nature of Max Cady in other ways. He is depicted as a barbarous redneck, whose accent is an exaggerated version of a rural Southern drawl. His body is covered in tattoos that echo the phrases of a fire-and-brimstone sermon. Cady tells the Bowmans that his grandfather and grandmother were part of a backwoods religious sect that handled deadly snakes and drank poisons as a way to prove their sanctity and devotion to Jesus. As scriptwriter Wesley Strick explains in a documentary on the film, he wanted to make Cady "a monster out of the South," using "aspects of the South that are most primitive and most frightening."[2]

Strick and Scorsese paint the South as a repository of fear and torment—an apt place for a not-so-innocent family to face its literal and figurative demons. In a haunting monologue, a detective hired to protect the Bowdens tells Sam to "savor his fear." Played by Joe Don Baker, who speaks in a true Southern accent that contrasts with Cady's exaggerated drawl, the detective confesses that the South evolved in fear, first of the Indians, then of the slaves, and then of the Union. "The South has a fine tradition of savoring fear," he claims, alluding to the region's history of violence, discord, and hostility. By the time Sam finally faces Cady, fear has pushed him over the edge, and he reverts to Cady's primitive level. The two battle hand to hand with rocks and fists in the raging water and oozing muck of Cape Fear.

Strick, who was born and raised in New York City, found the South a darkly exotic place with an alien, forbidding history and culture. He and Scorsese exaggerated these elements of the South through the character of Cady, just as they exploited the exotic flora and fauna of Florida to create a setting that was at once frightening and mythic. While that strategy worked to create a provocative story about a family facing a primal force that threatens to destroy it, it also paints a dark portrait of the South, one dependent on disturbing stereotypes and exaggerations.

THE CREDITS	THE CAST	
Released in 1991 by Universal Pictures	Robert De Niro	Max Cady
Produced by Kathleen Kennedy and Frank Marshall,	Nick Nolte	Sam Bowden
and Barbara De Fina	Jessica Lange	Leigh Bowden
Directed by Martin Scorsese	Juliette Lewis	Danielle Bowden
Written by Wesley Strick, based on the screenplay	Joe Don Baker	Claude Kersek
by James R. Webb, adapted from the novel	Robert Mitchum	Lieutenant Elgart
The Executioners by John D. MacDonald	Gregory Peck	Lee Heller
Cinematography by Freddie Francis	Martin Balsam	Judge
Edited by Thelma Schoonmaker	Illeana Douglas	Lori Davis
Production design by Henry Bumstead	Fred Dalton Thompson	Tom Broadbent
Original music by Bernard Herrmann, arranged		
and conducted by Elmer Bernstein		

CHINA MOON

[Murderers] always screw up, sooner or later.
—Detective Kyle Bodine in *China Moon*

THE STORY

Kyle Bodine, veteran detective in the small Florida town of Braden, falls hard for Rachel Munro, wife of a philandering and abusive banking millionaire. When Rachel shoots her husband during a violent domestic encounter, Bodine uses his expertise to clean up the crime scene and protect Rachel. As Bodine and his colleagues investigate, a trail of planted evidence leads back to him, and he begins to realize he's been set up.

The opening scene of *China Moon* is thick with the trappings of film noir. Against a backdrop of harsh neon and rain-slicked streets, a couple meet in a seedy motel. An unseen observer approaches to photograph the illicit tryst, capturing the lovers amid the barred shadows of their rented room. Though all of the characters are unknown at this point, it's clear that we are entering a world of passion, betrayal, and deceit, and it's clear that not everyone is coming out alive.

Detective Kyle Bodine lives at the center of this world, a bastion of jaded integrity. Professional, even-tempered, and intelligent, he uses disciplined observation to solve crime after crime and has earned a reputation for first-rate police work. A loner grown hard from the violence he sees and bored with the witless criminals he catches, Bodine is clearly ready for something more. He adopts a promising young detective as his protégé, but it isn't until he meets wealthy Rachel Munro slumming in a bluesy beer joint that his life begins to regain meaning.

Married to a despicable cad, Rachel seems to be a vulnerable, tortured beauty in need of saving, and Bodine finds the combination irresistible. She deflects his attentions at first, playing the role of good girl, but one night the two sneak through a barbed wire fence to a secluded, pristine lake, and beneath a "moon like a big old plate of china," passion ignites. Layered in symbolism, this scene shows Bodine transgressing a barrier to enter a primal land characterized by two symbols of female power—the moon above and the still waters below.

Before long, Rachel's husband is dead, and Bodine finds himself destroying evidence and disposing of the body—in the very lake he and Rachel visited earlier. This is only the beginning of Bodine's troubles, as events quickly spiral beyond his control. His young partner proves a more apt pupil than he anticipated, uncovering information about Rachel that even Bodine didn't know. When planted evidence incriminating him turns up, Bodine finally sees he's been trapped in a web of lies, and he scrambles through one plot twist after another in search of the truth.

Though much of *China Moon* is classic noir, the two main characters deviate slightly from the formula. Bodine is not a corrupt antihero; he's very much a straight arrow, living on the right side of the law. As the story unfolds, it becomes clear that his only weakness is, in fact, his greatest strength; his skill as a detective makes him believe he can beat the system, and it's also what made him a target in the first place. For most femmes fatales, weakness is merely an act and vulnerability a weapon, but the manipulative Rachel proves to be a sympathetic figure who develops genuine feelings for her patsy.

Though a first-time director, John Bailey certainly had adequate experience

Figure 3.4. *China Moon* star Ed Harris.
(Doll/Morrow Collection)

for handling the film. He had been a top-tier cinematographer for two decades, working on a variety of successful independent productions, studio films, and documentaries. He was a favored cameraman for a wide range of directors, from auteurs such as Paul Schrader (*American Gigolo, Cat People, Mishima*) and Robert Redford (*Ordinary People*) to Hollywood heavyweights Walter Hill (*Crossroads*), Michael Apted (*Continental Divide*), and Lawrence Kasden (*The Big Chill, The Accidental Tourist, Silverado*). His work on the western *Silverado* may have established the connections that led to this opportunity to direct. Kasden also directed *Body Heat*, the first of the high-profile Florida noirs and clearly an influence on *China Moon*. More important, though, *Silverado* featured Kevin Costner as a quirky, likeable young gunslinger, and *China Moon* was the second film produced by Costner's Tig Productions, after *Dances with Wolves*.

Bailey has only rarely taken the director's role since *China Moon*, preferring the autonomy he enjoys as a respected cinematographer. The few films he has directed have proven difficult experiences for him, such as *Mariette in Ecstasy*, a 1996 labor of love that the studio decided not to release. *China Moon* suffered too, a victim of the vagaries of Hollywood finance. Despite a string of critical and financial successes in the 1980s, the releasing studio, Orion, fell into bankruptcy as the production got under way. Completed in 1991, the film was shelved for three years while the studio struggled to get its books in order.

For Lakeland, Florida, and its surrounding communities, however, *China Moon* was surely an economic blessing. The area had suffered through a decade of depression before Bailey and crew came to town. For decades Lakeland, an established Florida community of about 80,000, had thrived on citrus production and mining operations—it has the world's largest deposits of phosphate—but a downturn in both industries led to unemployment rates nearing 20 percent.[3] The neighboring town of Bartow provided a palatial 1909 residence with a sprawling, white-columned gallery—number 33 on the town's historical walking tour—to serve as the home of Rachel and her husband. The area's unique and idyllic waterways, though, are what made it the perfect location for the film. With more than forty well-maintained lakes to choose from, the location scouts were able to find a site that offered the essential combination of natural beauty and primordial menace for Rachel and Bodine to begin their affair and cover their crime.

In addition to the atmospheric locations, sharp script, and knowledgeable direction, *China Moon* enjoyed strong performances all around. Fragile beauty Stowe and edgy everyman Harris slipped comfortably into their characters and played well against a fine supporting cast. Charles Dance, who created memorable urbane villains in several films, is eminently hatable and threatening as Rachel's husband, and Benicio Del Toro showed his promise in this early portrayal of a shifting, complex character. Despite its many virtues, the film opened to mixed popular reviews, with critics contradicting each other about how original or derivative the film was, how weak or strong the performances were, and how compelling or mundane the plot was. The film floundered at the box office, pulling in a paltry $3 million in ticket sales.[4] Though its March 1994 release date pitted *China Moon* against two blockbuster films from that year—Jim Carrey's *Ace Ventura* (see chapter 7) and Hugh Grant's surprise hit *Four Weddings and a Funeral*—there was precious little else of note in theaters at the time, particularly in the way of adult crime dramas.

THE CREDITS	THE CAST	
Released in 1994 by Orion Pictures	Ed Harris	Kyle Bodine
Produced by Barrie M. Osborne	Madeleine Stowe	Rachel Munro
Directed by John Bailey	Charles Dance	Rupert Munro
Written by Roy Carlson	Patricia Healy	Adele
Cinematography by Willy Kurant	Benicio Del Toro	Lamar Dickey
Production design by Conrad E. Angone	Roger Aaron Brown	Police captain
Music by George Fenton		

A FLASH OF GREEN

There could never be enough green for all the wishes I had.

—Aunt Middie in *A Flash of Green*

THE STORY

When local developers reveal a plan to dredge and fill Grassy Bay, concerned residents of Palm City line up to stop them. County commissioner Elmo Bliss invites reporter Jimmy Wing into the world of dirty politics, promising him a future in Bliss's ever-growing sphere of influence if he will dig up blackmail information against the residents. Jimmy accepts the offer even though it means betraying many longtime friends, including Kat, the widow of his best friend.

THE FILM

John D. MacDonald achieved that most difficult of literary accomplishments, building up a loyal popular readership while garnering warm accolades from the academic critics. MacDonald is generally regarded as the successor—some say surpasser—of founding noir novelists Dashiell Hammett and Raymond Chandler. Like Hammett and Chandler, he started by writing pulp fiction for magazines and cheap paperbacks and began his ascent after moving to a new region and adopting it as the setting for his work. For Hammett and Chandler, the new region was California, where most of the original noir stories took place. For MacDonald it was Florida, and his writing makes up much of the critical mass that established the Sunshine State as the new home of hard-boiled fiction. Like such recent Florida crime writers as Elmore Leonard, he constructed a seamy milieu for his characters based on Florida's ever-shifting population, its ethnic and cultural mix, and the land boom that spawned corruption throughout the state.

MacDonald's best-known works, the twenty-one Travis McGee crime novels published between 1964 and 1985, feature an admirable but imperfect protagonist who champions the helpless victims of cruel and corrupt villains. While McGee is intelligent and capable, he does make mistakes that he and others invariably pay for. His most distinctive trait, however, is a tendency to wax philosophical about societal corruption and decay wherever he sees it—white-collar crime, acid rain, consumerism, cosmetic surgery, and above all environmental degradation.

Published shortly before the first McGee novel, *A Flash of Green* prefigures some of the themes MacDonald would explore through his beloved "knight errant" detective. The story centers around a proposed land development in fictional Palm City that would destroy Grassy Bay. The cadre of local investors behind the plan has the backing of ruthless county commissioner Elmo Bliss, who will publicly oppose the development while privately earning a huge profit to bankroll his bid for the governor's mansion. A small group of residents on the Save Our Bay Committee (S.O.B.) plan to stir up what resistance they can and wear down the investors through court challenges. Teetering between these two factions is local reporter Jimmy Wing, an intelligent but detached figure who finds himself at a crossroads with no moral compass to guide him.

The film adaptation of *A Flash of Green* adheres closely to the original material, presenting a varied collection of imperfect characters shaped and defined by their environment. Chief among them is Jimmy, an isolated, self-described observer whose life plan has been derailed by events beyond his control. His catatonic wife is slowly dying from a degenerative nerve disease, and his best friend was recently killed in an auto accident. Buffering himself from the world, Jimmy finds ways to cling to his lost past. He develops a powerful infatuation for his dead friend's widow, Kat. He also becomes fixated on a snapshot of the two couples enjoying a day at Grassy Bay, an unchanging image of his past life that he can observe over and over again.

For reasons that are never made clear, Jimmy agrees to spy on Kat and his other S.O.B. friends and pass on dirt that Elmo can use to discredit the group. Though he performs the job well, even eagerly, Jimmy is never entirely comfortable in the embrace of the personal, political, and ecological corruption of Elmo and his cronies, and in the end he takes extreme measures to break free.

The film unfolds almost literally through Jimmy's eyes. Time and again we see him observing friends, neighbors, and coworkers as they go about their daily lives. Various settings, such as Kat's house, Elmo's office, or the laboratory of an ecologist working with the S.O.B.s, are shown from Jimmy's perspective, and we frequently see the community's quiet streets and spectacular natural views rolling past Jimmy's car window. In this way the film emphasizes both Jimmy's role as observer and the influence that the setting has over him and all the characters.

This strong connection between character and place has become the hallmark of writer-director Victor Nunez. All five of his films are set in his native Florida, and each features characters and everyday places that slowly unfold together in simple but exquisite visual detail. Nunez shot *A Flash of Green*, his second feature film, in eight different towns along Florida's Gulf coast, including Fort Myers, St. Petersburg, Sarasota, Cortez, and Englewood. He relied on mundane, realistic locations such as Fulford's Fish Company, the Farmer's Market Plaza, and the First Florida Bank of Venice, creating a gritty, palpable Palm City that almost becomes an additional character.

The title of the film refers to a peculiar atmospheric phenomenon in southwestern Florida that Nunez would certainly be familiar with. On days when the air is free of haze, a brilliant green hue sometimes engulfs the sky for the briefest moment just as the setting sun drops from view. Those lucky enough to witness the rare event are said to be granted a wish. Nunez introduces this bit of Florida lore as Jimmy visits with elderly Aunt Middie. Significantly, her personal experiences with the display are recounted in flashback, returning the viewer, like Jimmy with his photograph, to a time in the past. As a young woman in the days before Florida's land boom, Middie eked out a living from the region's natural resources. She recounts the end of a long day of fishing for an insufficient catch. As she watched the brilliant flash from a flat-bottomed skiff in the middle of Grassy Bay, she made a wish that she knew was futile. At the end of the visually elegant scene, she says in voice-over, "There could never be enough green for all the wishes I had."

In this story, green connotes both nature and money, and the fleeting flash of color becomes a metaphor for the irreconcilable and imperfect dreams of the region's inhabitants. The developers, who pursue personal gain but genuinely believe they breathe economic life into the community, undermine their own wishes by degrading the environment. The S.O.B.s naively hope to preserve a natural splendor and self-sustaining bounty that, as we learned from Aunt Middie, never really existed. And Jimmy, lost amid the corruption and fragmented dreams that define Palm City, doesn't even have a wish to call his own. Not surprisingly, he admits to Aunt Middie that he has never seen the flash of green.

THE CREDITS		THE CAST	
Released in 1984		Ed Harris	Jimmy Wing
Produced by Richard Jordan		Blair Brown	Kat Hubble
Directed by Victor Nunez		Richard Jordan	Elmo Bliss
Written by Victor Nunez, from the novel		George Coe	Brian Haas
by John D. MacDonald		Helen Stenborg	Aunt Middie
Cinematography by Victor Nunez		John Glover	Ross Halley
Edited by Victor Nunez		Jean De Baer	Jackie Halley
Art direction by Carlos Asse		Nancy Griggs	Nat Sinnat
Original music by Charles Engstrom		Bob Murch	Dial Sinnat

92 in the Shade

In the same year that *Night Moves* appeared in theaters, United Artists released a quirky drama featuring Peter Fonda and Warren Oates as a pair of fishing guides at odds with each other in the Florida Keys. Though not a true noir, *92 in the Shade* presents an imperfect protagonist on a quest through a dark and strangely sinister world that ultimately proves too much for him.

The film was directed by Thomas McGuane, a young novelist who had gained a reputation as both a genius and a wild hare. Literary critics raved over his flamboyant language and wry satire even as they wagged fingers at his hard drinking and carousing. His association with Hollywood only enhanced that perception, first in his personal friendships with bad boys Fonda, Oates, Harry Dean Stanton, and Sam Peckinpah, and then in his professional efforts as a screenwriter of *Rancho Deluxe* and *The Missouri Breaks*. Through his screenwriting, he made enough connections in the film industry to wangle the job as director for the film adaptation of his third novel, *92 in the Shade*.

It's little surprise that McGuane drew such attention from Hollywood; his noirlike, nihilistic characters had much in common with the celluloid anti-heroes being created by the new generation of American filmmakers such as Peckinpah, Arthur Penn, Francis Coppola, and Martin Scorsese. While he may have been a kindred artistic spirit, McGuane did not have their skill behind the camera. The film suffers from the would-be director's lack of experience, but it does offer interesting performances, McGuane's biting dialogue, and a group of dark characters who could be at home only in the exotic hinterland of the Keys.

Figure 3.5. Lobby card from *92 in the Shade*. (Doll/Morrow Collection)

NIGHT MOVES

"Where were you when Kennedy was shot?"
"Which Kennedy?"
—*Night Moves*

THE STORY

An aging film star hires small-time detective Harry Moseby to find Delly, her free-spirited runaway daughter. Harry follows the wayward teen from the studio back lots of Hollywood to a film set in New Mexico and then to the Florida Keys, where Delly is staying with one of her many stepfathers. He escorts her back to Hollywood, assuming his job is done. But Harry is not a very good detective, and when Delly turns up dead, he realizes too late that the case involved much more than finding a runaway.

THE FILM

A brilliant exploration of the film noir genre by Arthur Penn, *Night Moves* belongs to the second era of noir, which began in the late 1960s and lasted through the early 1980s. This time frame corresponded to a very productive and creative era in American filmmaking that introduced such master directors as Francis Coppola, Martin Scorsese, Robert Altman, and Penn. From Coppola's *Godfather* to Penn's *Little Big Man*, the films of these directors pushed the boundaries of accepted techniques and conventions to critique and examine the issues and problems of our culture.

College educated and film literate, Penn and his contemporaries self-consciously played with the conventions of familiar genres. Film noir especially appealed to them because of its darkly romantic protagonist, beautiful visual style, and criticism of the status quo. In tinkering with the conventions of noir, these directors greatly expanded the genre in tone, characterization, and theme. In effect, *Chinatown*, *The Long Goodbye*, *Farewell, My Lovely*, *The Drowning Pool*, and *Night Moves* became the thinking person's films noirs.

Night Moves is set in California and the Florida Keys, which is appropriate for a film noir released after the classic period of the genre but before the modern era. The film uses the Los Angeles setting so associated with the original hard-boiled detective fiction and classic film noir, yet much of it takes place in Florida, currently the preferred setting for contemporary noir. These locations harken back to *The Maltese Falcon* but look forward to *Body Heat*.

Aside from locations, Penn uses dialogue to deliberately recall the old days of Hollywood and classics such as *The Maltese Falcon* in order to force a comparison between Sam Spade and Harry Moseby, between past and present, between a bygone era of waning ideals and a new era of lost ideals. Characters in the film continually confront Harry with comments about old movie detectives. Arlene Grastner, herself a glamorous relic from the old days of Hollywood, hires Harry to find her runaway daughter Delly, a beautiful but unglamorous teenage hippie who likes to live hard and fast. Arlene asks Harry, "Are you the kind of detective who once he gets on the case won't let go?"—a reference to the detectives of classic noir. In an argument over her infidelity, Harry's estranged wife goads him with "Why don't you take a swing like Sam Spade?" The references to the past remind the viewer that the world portrayed in classic noir might have been corrupt but it was still populated with people who knew the differences between right and wrong. Spade may have been cynical and tainted, but he was still savvy enough to solve the case. Harry lacks those Sam Spade skills.

Penn paints Harry Moseby as an alienated, detached character incapable of actively resolving any "case," or conflict. He follows his unfaithful wife, watching her with her lover, but he fails to confront her directly. This mirrors an earlier event in Harry's life when he spent much time and effort tracking down his long-lost father. When he finally found him, he did little more than sit in his car and watch the old man. Harry watches but does not see; he follows but does not resolve.

Harry eventually finds Delly living in the Florida Keys with her stepfather Tom Iverson, but he does not force her to return home. He hangs around, enjoying the open air and tropical lifestyle of the Keys, as well as the company of Iverson's earthy girlfriend, Paula. It is Delly who decides to go back to L.A. after a drunken Iverson apparently makes a play for her. When Harry deposits Delly at Arlene's door, he assumes the case is over, so he does not heed the frantic message from the distraught girl on his answering machine a few days later. As a matter of fact, he turns it off before he hears the entire message—a foolish act for a detective but also a symbol of the character's inability to communicate with other humans.

Harry's approach to working on a case is to drive around L.A. in his car, parking from time to time to conduct surveillance. Cocooned in his car, he sits alone, isolated from an outside world that he watches from a distance. If the car represents his alienation, then the game of chess suggests his incompetence as a detective. Harry plays the game with himself, but he isn't very good at it. The film's title is a play on the phrase "knight moves," as Harry explains to Paula when describing a well-known chess game involving a famous player of long ago. The player did not make use of "three little knight moves," which would have led him to victory, but played something else instead and lost the

Figure 3.6. Gene Hackman in *Night Moves*.
(Doll/Morrow Collection)

match. "He didn't see it," Harry tells Paula, describing himself without realizing it.

Harry does not see that the runaway girl is not the real mystery to be solved.
He cannot add up the clues to uncover an art-smuggling racket that will eventually lead to Delly's murder. He does not see that corruption and moral decay
have spread from gritty Los Angeles to sunny Florida. The Keys seem like a
tropical paradise to Harry when he first arrives, with dolphins splashing in the
ocean, the sun shining on his face, and a beautiful woman interested in him.
An undeveloped Sanibel Island stands in for the Keys in *Night Moves*, and its
white sands, swaying palms, and hotel-less beaches suggest the seclusion of a
tropical paradise, where a world-weary soul could escape the corruption of
the big city. But things are never as they seem in film noir. The dolphins are
confined to a small pen, the sunny days turn into treacherous nights, and the
woman turns out to be the femme fatale. Not even paradise has been left un-
tainted. Ineffectual to the bitter end, Harry finally figures out the smuggling
scheme in the last few minutes of the film. The only one left alive at the end of
a series of backstabbings and betrayals, he lies wounded and helpless on the
floor of a boat that spins in circles in the middle of the sea—a visual metaphor
that needs little explanation.

The character of Harry Moseby sums up the malaise and disillusionment
of America in the post-Vietnam, post-Watergate era, especially from the perspective from someone like the politically conscious Penn. Despite the intentions of so many to make a better world during the 1960s, they were no

match for the evils of war, the pervasiveness of corruption, or the despair that comes from three major political assassinations in a five-year period. Penn and his generation realized the contemporary world was much bleaker than the slightly tainted environs of the classic noirs of long ago, a point driven home by the film's reference to the assassinations. "Where were you when Kennedy was shot?" asks Paula. "Which Kennedy?" retorts a cynical Harry.

THE CREDITS	THE CAST	
Released in 1975 by Warner Brothers	Gene Hackman	Harry Moseby
Produced by Robert M. Sherman	Susan Clark	Ellen Moseby
Directed by Arthur Penn	Edward Binns	Ziegler
Written by Alan Sharp	Harris Yulin	Marty Heller
Cinematography by Bruce Surtees	Kenneth Mars	Nick
Edited by Dede Allen	Janet Ward	Arlene Grastner
Production design by George Jenkins	James Wood	Quentin
Original music by Michael Small	Melanie Griffith	Delly Grastner
	John Crawford	Tom Iverson
	Jennifer Warren	Paula

OUT OF TIME

Can it be shot in Toronto?
—studio executives to Carl Franklin, DVD commentary

THE STORY

Small-town police chief Matt Whitlock's pending divorce from Alex, a big-city cop in Miami, has made him do things he might not ordinarily do. Matt has drifted into a secret, heated affair with an old friend, Ann Merai Harrison, who is now married. When Ann learns she has a devastating illness, Matt steals drug money from the police safe to help her obtain experimental medical treatment. That night, her house is deliberately destroyed in an explosion, apparently killing both Ann and her husband. Matt quickly realizes he has trapped himself in a web of secrets as he tries to solve the case before the evidence points to him as the murderer.

THE FILM

During the 1990s, tax breaks and an attractive exchange rate, combined with competitive production facilities, made Toronto the locale of choice for shooting Hollywood films. Since that time, Toronto has stood in for nearly every major city in the United States, with filmmakers often sacrificing authentic local color for lower budgets. It is not surprising, then, that studio executives asked director Carl Franklin if he would consider shooting *Out of Time* in Canada. The executives may have been oblivious to the artistic compromise of substituting a city in Canada for a town in Florida, but Franklin knew that shooting in the actual state was absolutely essential.

Out of Time is set in fictional Banyan Key, Florida, a quiet community where police chief Matt Whitlock fishes from the back of his houseboat, knows many residents by their first names, and often works the night patrol himself. The police department is located in a green gabled house with a friendly-looking front porch. This contrasts with the grimy urban streets, high-rise hotels, and fast pace of Miami, where Whitlock's estranged wife prefers to work as a detective on the Miami police force. In the fictional world of the film, Banyan Key is close enough to Miami that Alex Whitlock is assigned to the Harrison investigation but far enough away to be out of the urban milieu. The contrast of small town vs. big city is important because it foregrounds the gap, or "irreconcilable differences," between the Whitlocks.

The main locations that make up Banyan Key are parts of two towns located on Florida's Gulf Coast, Cortez and Boca Grande. The latter substituted for downtown Banyan Key. Particularly fitting was the Temptation Club, which can be seen behind Matt as he walks through the town with Alex—a reminder of the chief's fling with Ann Merai. Cortez provided most of the waterfront lo-

Figure 3.7. *Out of Time* director Carl Franklin.
(Doll/Morrow Collection)

cales used in the film, including Matt's house. Ironically, the Banyan Key police station was located in Miami.

Franklin was not thinking about specific towns and cities when he insisted on shooting in Florida, however; he meant to capture the climate, the atmosphere, and even the colors associated with the tropical locale. To Franklin, these were the ingredients that conveyed the unique ambience of the state, which set the perfect mood for a noir story about a good man caught off guard by temptation, betrayal, and deception. In the director's commentary on the DVD release of *Out of Time*, Franklin told an anecdote to explain the offbeat flavor of Florida. During his stay in one of the small towns used in the film, walking catfish came out of the water each night and crept across the streets and yards of the community, much to the dismay of the cast and crew. A state that could produce walking fish was the perfect setting for the unexpected and the unexplained. As Franklin summed it up, there are "all kinds of wild things in Florida."[5]

Crucial to the film is the climate and weather of Florida. The sensation of heat is inescapable, from the flaming red sunsets to the actual sweat on the actors' foreheads and the way their clothes stick to their bodies. The steamy summer provides a sultry backdrop for the sexual temptation of Matt. In the first sequence he fields a call from Ann, whose husband is away for the night. Making a game of his "official visit" to her, in which they pretend that Ann is the victim of an intruder, Matt and Ann engage in a torrid love scene while bantering in double entendre. As Ann tugs at his pants, she asks, "Is the situation about to blow?" and then later asks, should the need arise, "Can you come?" The heat of passion and the heat of Florida make a good combination, just as they did in *Body Heat*.

Later, in the second act of the film, the heat metaphor shifts in meaning. After Matt steals the money, the mood changes. As it becomes increasingly difficult for him to cover his tracks while simultaneously "uncovering" clues with Alex, the pace quickens. The escalating temperature and the sweat on Matt's brow combine to suggest that "the heat is on" for the beleaguered police chief.

Once the production crew arrived in Florida to shoot, the weather played a second, unexpected role in the film. Franklin was surprised by how often it rained in the Sunshine State during the summer, so he decided to incorporate more rain and storms into his narrative. One of the conventions of film noir is the use of rain and fog, so Franklin's decision was logical. Rain underscores the overall bleak outlook associated with the genre, while fog makes a fitting metaphor for mystery. In addition to the rain-soaked streets, foggy nights, and occasional flashes of lightning, Franklin emphasized the cataclysmic nature of storms to heighten the emotion of the climax. A storm rages in the background as Matt discovers that Ann is not dead and that he has been set up to take the rap for her "murder" and her husband's. Thunder claps as guns fire, adding a catastrophic, end-of-the-world quality to the showdown between Matt, Ann, and Ann's husband. Just as it seems that Matt has met his end, with Ann's gun pointing directly at him, Alex steps in and kills her. In the next scene, the police clean up, Matt is aided by an emergency crew, and the storm has passed literally and figuratively. Alex's saving of her husband results in the saving of her marriage—the couple have weathered their personal storm.

Franklin stated that, given his choice, he would always shoot on location.[6] It adds authenticity to the film, and the cast and crew react to the locations in unforeseen ways that bring life to the story. To Franklin, the rich, sultry environment in *Out of Time* was vital to the drama. In that way, Florida was more than a location, it was a character. Could the film have been shot in Toronto? Absolutely not.

THE CREDITS

Released in 2003 by Metro-Goldwyn-Mayer
Produced by Jesse Beaton (as Jesse B'Franklin), Jon Berg, Alex Gartner, Damien Saccani, Kevin Reidy, Stokely Chaffin, Neal H. Moritz, Dan Genetti, Stephen Traxler, and Gina White
Directed by Carl Franklin
Written by David Collard
Cinematography by Theo van de Sande
Edited by Carole Kravetz
Production design by Paul Peters
Original music by Graeme Revell

THE CAST

Denzel Washington	Matt Lee Whitlock
Dean Cain	Chris Harrison
Eva Mendes	Alex Diaz Whitlock
Sanaa Lathan	Ann Merai Harrison
John Billingsley	Chae
Robert Baker	Tony Dalton
Alex Carter	Cabot
Nora Dunn	Dr. Donovan

Out of Time and *Body Heat*

In *Out of Time*, director Carl Franklin included an homage to *Body Heat* as a way to acknowledge the film's influence on him, a common practice among film-literate Hollywood directors. In the scene in which Alex is rushing to Banyan Key to catch up with Matt, she is delayed at a bridge whose midsection rotates out of the way to allow boats to pass through. As she waits, knowing that crucial minutes are ticking by, she stands outside her car and rests her hands on top of the car's roof. The scene duplicates a moment in *Body Heat* when Oscar, the only honest character in the story, is held up at a drawbridge. In frustration, Oscar stands outside his car and rests his hands on its roof. The homage is at once a tip of the hat to *Body Heat*, which was central to the revival of film noir, and an invitation for the knowledgeable viewer to compare Alex to Oscar. Both are honest cops who strive to restore moral order to a corrupt world.

PALMETTO

A town like Palmetto doesn't exist. The vamp doesn't
exist. And the plots are totally unreal. These are scary
fairy tales for grownups involving sex and money.
—director Volker Schlöndorff, to the
Chicago Sun-Times's Lloyd Sachs

THE STORY

Harry Barber is released from prison after his conviction is overturned in court.
The embittered Harry wants to start a new life in Miami, but his old flame,
Nina, persuades him to return to Palmetto. There he is drawn into a scam by
sexy Rhea Malroux and her precocious stepdaughter, Odette, who have a fast
scheme to make some fast money. After Odette turns up dead, Harry suspects
that Rhea is not on the level and that he is being set up to take the fall.

THE FILM

An ugly brown palmetto bug twitches its antennae and stares intently at Harry
Barber, who sits in prison on a trumped-up charge. In voice-over, Harry defends his six-legged cellmate—otherwise known as a cockroach—claiming
that "they're pretty good company." The filthy bug provides a startling opening
image, especially in close-up, and sets the stage for a down-and-dirty film noir
in which the characters wallow in duplicity, deceit, and double-crosses. The
bug also offers a unique introduction to the film's principal setting, central
Florida, because the Sunshine State is home to an assortment of large cock-
roaches, including the American, the Australian, the brown, the smoky brown,
and the Florida woods roach.

Harry suddenly leaves his creepy cellmate behind when a "good citizen"
comes forward with new evidence that overturns his conviction. A former reporter, Harry has been in jail for two years, railroaded by shady politicians because he tried to expose graft and corruption in the small town of Palmetto.

The Palmetto of the film's title is nothing like the actual Florida town. As a
matter of fact, many of the scenes were shot in Sarasota, Fort Myers, Venice,
Englewood, and Punta Gorda. The real Palmetto, Florida, is located midway
between Tampa to the north and Sarasota to the south. Small and low key, it
began as an agricultural community, noted for its abundant fruit and vegetable
production. For the purposes of the film, the name "Palmetto" is more important than any resemblance to the actual town. The film paints Palmetto in
broad strokes as a typical film noir town with a reputation for corruption and
dirty politicians. The film was released seventeen years after *Body Heat* had es-

Figure 3.8. *Palmetto* star Woody Harrelson.
(Doll/Morrow Collection)

tablished Florida as the favored locale for noir, and by 1998 the Sunshine State
was so associated with the genre that no explanation for rampant corruption
and vice was necessary. In the film, it is simply a given.

While Harry's lawyer is elated that his client can go free, the frustrated
writer is bitter at having wasted two years in jail, where he couldn't even spin
a good yarn about his experiences because he had writer's block. As Harry
says, "Nothing's worse than a writer who doesn't have anything to say." Down
and out, Harry is primed to make all the wrong choices, a frequent hazard for
protagonists in film noir. Determined to relocate to Miami, he walks confi-
dently down a two-lane highway that cuts through a subtropical terrain filled
with palmetto bushes. A familiar sight in central Florida, the saw palmetto is a
six- to nine-foot palm shrub native to the southeastern United States. Though
thickets of palmetto bushes can look exotically beautiful, they provide shelter
for such treacherous and unwanted varmints as lizards, spiders, dusky pygmy
rattlesnakes, and—of course—palmetto bugs.

As Harry walks down the two-lane, an old flame, Nina, drives up behind
him and pleads with him to return to Palmetto. After two years in prison,
Nina's form of physical persuasion is hard to resist. Poor Harry stands unde-
cided as the thick palmetto bushes on either side of the highway seem to visu-

ally trap him. He makes the fateful decision to return to Palmetto, where once again he will be trapped, this time by a sexy woman with a bad plan.

With tongue in cheek, director Volker Schlöndorff has offered three meanings for the film's title in the first few minutes of screen time—the bugs, the town, and the shrubs. All three are images associated with Florida, and all three will signify bad luck for Harry Barber.

Back in Palmetto, Harry sits in a bar searching the classifieds for suitable employment when the sound of clicking high heels draws his attention to curvy Rhea Malroux. She piques Harry's curiosity with the offer of a job. It seems Rhea and her promiscuous stepdaughter, Odette, have devised a plan centered around the fake kidnapping of the wayward teen, so that they can extort money from her frail but tight-fisted father. Though Harry is reluctant, he just can't quite resist those feminine powers of persuasion, and he agrees to the flimsy plan. His duties consist of driving Odette to the bar where she will be "kidnapped," making the ransom call, and then picking up the money from the secluded drop-off spot.

In true noir fashion, the plan starts to unravel but the plot becomes more complicated: Odette turns up dead in Harry's bungalow by the water; Mr. Malroux's male aide, Donnelly, becomes a thorn in Harry's side; and Rhea is nowhere to be found. Harry goes to pick up the ransom money at the designated spot in the middle of the night, right where that two-lane highway cuts through the palmetto bushes. As he reaches for the satchel full of money, a car comes along, and he jumps into those palmettos to hide—a fateful decision that lands him in the middle of a police investigation, since he leaves his shoe print behind.

Harry's troubles escalate after he discovers that nobody is who he (or she) seems to be. Donnelly is not the old man's aide but the real mastermind behind the crime; the young girl introduced to Harry as Odette was an imposter; and Rhea is not the trophy wife of wealthy Felix Malroux but Donnelly's wife, who cooks for the Malroux household. Throughout Harry's ordeals, the film frequently intercuts between Harry and a close-up of a palmetto bug creeping across a piece of furniture or a bustle of bugs scurrying away. The editing is making an unflattering comparison between hapless Harry Barber and the lowly bug. Neither gets any respect, and neither is worthy of it.

The ending unfolds true to noir form as Harry discovers too late that he was the dupe of Donnelly and Rhea. He and Nina find themselves about to be dropped by the treacherous couple into a vat of acid. Fortunately, the police step in just in time to save them, but Harry is convicted for his part in the kidnapping scheme. He returns to prison, where he shares his cell with his only friend—the palmetto bug.

THE CREDITS	THE CAST	
Released in 1998 by Columbia Pictures	Woody Harrelson	Harry Barber
Produced by Al Corley, Bart Rosenblatt, and	Elisabeth Shue	Rhea Malroux
Eugene Musso, with Matthias Wendlandt	Gina Gershon	Nina
Directed by Volker Schlöndorff	Rolf Hoppe	Felix Malroux
Written by E. Max Frye, based on the novel	Michael Rapaport	Donnelly
Just Another Sucker by James Hadley Chase	Chloe Sevigny	Odette
Cinematography by Thomas Kloss	Tom Wright	John Renick
Edited by Peter Przygodda	Marc Macaulay	Miles Meadows
Production design by Claire Jenora Bowin		
Original music by Klaus Doldinger		

WILD THINGS

People aren't always what they appear to be.
—Sergeant Ray Duquette in *Wild Things*

THE STORY

Two rival high school students accuse guidance counselor Sam Lombardo of rape, ruining his life and career. When Suzie, the poor girl from the wrong side of town, admits the charges are false, Sam collects a multimillion-dollar settlement from the other girl's rich and powerful family. Police sergeant Ray Duquette believes that the three are in league and attempts to pressure them into revealing their conspiracy.

THE FILM

As high school graduation approaches in the fictional community of Blue Bay, rich and spoiled schoolgirl Kelly Van Ryan spends much of her day publicly panting after guidance counselor Sam Lombardo. Occasionally she takes a break from her provocative glances and double entendres to exchange profane insults with poor and trashy Suzie Toller. To all eyes, the only thing these two classmates have in common is a sexual knowledge that exceeds their age and experience—until Kelly accuses Sam of rape, and Suzie bolsters the accusation by revealing that the cad assaulted her a year earlier. Kelly's oversexed mother, embittered by her own failed fling with the womanizing Sam, vilifies him throughout the community.

In court, however, the case takes an unexpected turn in Sam's favor. Suzie breaks down on the witness stand and admits that the charges were merely a petulant revenge scheme hatched by Kelly after Sam rebuffed her advances. With his reputation as an educator irrevocably besmirched, Sam walks away with an $8.5–million slander settlement, courtesy of Kelly's trust fund.

Many writers would find this ample material for a script fueled by sex and deception, but for *Wild Thing's* Stephen Peters, this complex chain of events is mere set-up. Peters continues the story through the character of dark-edged cop Ray Duquette, played by Kevin Bacon. Though all of Blue Bay wants the tawdry matter put behind them, Duquette voices suspicions that the relationships between Sam, Kelly, and Suzie are steamier and schemier than anyone realizes. As the abrasive, rule-breaking sergeant pursues his hunch, the audience is treated to a feeding frenzy of surprise alliances, betrayal, murder, and more.

Wild Things opened to favorable audience buzz and bemused popular reviews. Steamy sex and hairpin plot turns combined for a viewing experience generally described as good trashy fun. Surprisingly, the daring sex scenes by the young cast—a ménage à trois, a catfight that turns into lesbian petting, a nude scene sometimes referred to as "full-frontal Bacon"—were met with a wink and a nod rather than a hue and cry. Even more surprising is that, while reviewers invariably took note of the sex, few attempted to analyze the role it played in the film.

Peters and director John McNaughton took great pains to use the risqué acts to define characters, reveal unknown relationships, and depict a nearly universal corruption of values among Blue Bay's inhabitants. For each of the wild things, the various sexual displays and couplings are passionate but emotionless. Sex, power, and greed have melded into interchangeable urges that drive all their interactions. In the end, the last schemer standing is the one with the coldest blood.

Even as the film offers up the sordid sexuality of its characters for eager audience consumption, it repeatedly withholds key scenes and relationships and thereby distances us from everyone in the film. As each plot secret is revealed, we learn that the earlier words and actions of the characters were simply acts staged in the service of various scams and double-crosses. In fact, the full picture of events does not unfold until the closing credits, which are peppered with scenes unveiling the hidden manipulations of the movie's mastermind. Throughout the film, the characters remain ciphers, inaccessible to the audience, even as we gawk at their most intimate sexual escapades. The film, in effect, forces us into the role of voyeur rather than viewer.

The pervasive corruption and danger of Blue Bay become apparent from the film's wordless opening scene. The camera follows an airboat—a fan-

Figure 3.9. The cast of *Wild Things*. (Doll/Morrow Collection)

powered hydroplane common in the swamps of Florida—as it skims over the surface of the forbidding Everglades. The opening credits roll over shots of thick sawgrass, tangled mangroves, and still black waters. Just as the title appears, an alligator rises slowly from the depths, its eyes and snout discreetly breaking the water's surface in search of prey. A large flock of birds suddenly take to the air, and the camera takes flight with them, speeding to the edge of the wilderness and passing over the fringes of civilization—a seedy, low-rent strip mall immediately bordering the swamp. Soaring on at high speed, the camera moves over a dense cluster of middle-income houses, then weaves among the city's downtown office towers, and finally intrudes into the luxurious enclaves of the rich and the superrich.

Few places other than south Florida could provide a backdrop for this opening sequence, where a trip of just a few miles encompasses the darkest of natural environs as well as a full range of human economic conditions. And no other opening would have been as suitable for this noirlike thriller where each character is a predator and danger lurks in every setting, from the Van Ryans' Star Island mansion to Suzie's swamp shack. Making further use of south Florida's natural settings, McNaughton visually reinforces the depiction of his characters as self-serving wild things throughout the film by intercut-

Figure 3.10. *Wild Things* director John McNaughton.
(Doll/Morrow Collection)

ting them with shots of various cold-blooded swamp denizens such as lizards, snakes, and alligators.

Wild Things also featured several south Florida landmarks for location shooting. The prestigious and pricey Ransom Everglades School, with its sprawling tennis courts and its private dock for sailing classes, was used in several key scenes. The film crew descended on the campus while school was in session and spent eight days filming with and around the Ransom student body. The famous Jimbo's Place, an intentionally ramshackle restaurant and bait shop on Virginia Key, served nicely as a dingy backwoods bar and motel the characters use for nefarious rendezvous. In addition, local Florida actors took on several of the film's minor roles, bringing fresh faces to the production. Key among them was Marc Macaulay, who played Suzie's alligator-wrestling brother Walter. Macaulay had actually worked as a gator wrestler before, which allowed the film to include realistic depictions of this unique swamp skill.

On the surface, *Wild Things* appears to be a titillating tour of depravity and deception that offers little more than a string of racy visuals and plot manipulations. On closer inspection, the film proves to be a carefully constructed exercise in defining the viewer as voyeur that leaves the audience feeling both captivated and conned.

THE CREDITS	THE CAST	
Released in 1998 by Columbia Pictures	Matt Dillon	Sam Lombardo
Produced by Steven A. Jones and Rodney M. Liber	Kevin Bacon	Sergeant Ray Duquette
Directed by John McNaughton	Neve Campbell	Suzie Toller
Written by Stephen Peters	Denise Richards	Kelly Van Ryan
Cinematography by Jeffrey L. Kimball	Daphne Rubin-Vega	Detective Gloria Perez
Edited by Elena Maganini	Bill Murray	Kenneth Bowden
Production design by Edward T. McAvoy	Theresa Russell	Sandra Van Ryan
Music by George S. Clinton	Robert Wagner	Tom Baxter
	Carrie Snodgress	Ruby Toller
	Marc Macaulay	Walter Toller

THE MOVIE TOURIST'S GUIDE TO FLORIDA NOIR

Plan a vacation around these locations to get into the noir mood. While most of these cities, towns, and regions lack the sultry, edgy atmosphere of their cinematic depictions, movie tourists will recognize the locations as part of their favorite Florida crime dramas.

BODY HEAT

Hollywood

When Ned met the notorious Matty Walker at an outdoor concert, his fate was sealed. Shot in seaside Hollywood, this key scene took advantage of the Hollywood Beach Theater and Bandshell, located at Johnson Street and the Broadwalk. The theater/bandshell sponsors a range of entertainment, including a Theater Under the Stars series on Monday nights, which features free open-air concerts—just like the one Ned and Matty attended in the film. The theater/bandshell is on the city's famed Broadwalk, a 2½-mile cement promenade along the ocean. Visitors can drive south on Highway 1 from Fort Lauderdale, or take Interstate 75 to reach Hollywood.

CHINA MOON

Lakeland

Midway between Orlando and Tampa Bay in central Florida, Lakeland boasts thirteen pristine lakes for boating, fishing, or water skiing among stands of towering oak trees. Kyle Bodine and Rachel Munro found the lakes secluded enough for staging an intimate rendezvous and for covering up their crime. Lakeland is located southwest of Orlando just off Interstate 4.

Bartow

Established in the mid-1800s, this town was named after Francis S. Bartow, who by some accounts was the first Confederate general to fall in battle during the Civil War.[7] A time capsule of Southern history and architecture, Bartow offers a historic walking tour that includes Windsweep, the house used as the residence of Rachel and Rupert Munro in China Moon. Bartow is a short drive southeast of Lakeland at the intersection of Highways 99 and 17.

CAPE FEAR

Hollywood

Hollywood Boulevard in downtown Hollywood stood in for the fictional town of New Essex in Cape Fear, and the town's storefronts and main streets can be glimpsed in several scenes. Movie tourists should make a point of stopping to eat at the Rainbo Café at 1909 Hollywood Boulevard. In the film, crazed killer Max Cady, played by Robert De Niro, taunts lawyer Sam Bowden while coyly eating an ice cream cone in front of this popular local hangout.

Seminole T Stop.

On their frantic escape from Max Cady, the Bowden family rest and refuel at a truck stop. In this famous scene from the film, the audience learns that the Bowdens' efforts are in vain because Cady has stowed away in their vehicle. The scenes were shot at the Seminole T Stop along Highway 27 in Southwest Ranches, Florida, which is about thirty miles northwest of Miami.

A FLASH OF GREEN

The Gulf Coast of Southwestern Florida

A Flash of Green gets its title from a peculiar meteorological phenomenon unique to Florida's southwestern Gulf Coast. This atmospheric event in which a brilliant green flash ignites at sunset occurs only rarely, under the right combination of natural conditions. Movie tourists visiting this region who are diligent about enjoying the sunset every evening just might see the flash. If you're one of the lucky ones, be sure to make your wish.

NIGHT MOVES

Sanibel Island

Though Night Moves is set in Key West, the Florida scenes were shot along the beachfront of Sanibel Island, located on Florida's Gulf Coast, just west of Fort

Myers. Sanibel Island, and its sister island, Captiva, are accessed by a causeway. When *Night Moves* was shot in the mid-1970s, Sanibel was known as a haven for artists and writers and was less developed than it is now. Despite the increase in hotels and resorts, more than half of Sanibel and Captiva remain preserved in their natural state. Sanibel is famous for being the third best shelling area in the world.

OUT OF TIME

Boca Grande

Tiny Boca Grande, with a population of 800, stood in for much of the fictional town of Banyan Key in *Out of Time*. Director Carl Franklin was fascinated by the "walking fish" of Boca Grande, but the town's claim to fame rests with a much larger fish. Known as the Tarpon Capital of the World, Boca Grande hosts a high-stakes fishing competition every July, where the grand prize winner walks away with $100,000. One of town's main restaurants, the Temptation Club on Park Avenue, was featured in the background of the film as police chief Matt Whitlock, played by Denzel Washington, walks down the street. "Temptation" summed up the police chief's situation in the film, because the temptation to help a beautiful woman led him into trouble.

Boca Grande, which is Spanish for "big mouth," is joined by a causeway to Gasparilla Island, a string of barrier islands located halfway between Fort Myers and Sarasota and accessed by Route 771.

PALMETTO

Sarasota

Often in film noir the protagonist meets the femme fatale for the first time in a local restaurant, bar, or other public place that he frequents. Usually it turns out the meeting was not accidental but was planned all along by the femme fatale. Thus Ned meets Matty along the Broadwalk in *Body Heat*, Kyle meets Rachel in a crab shack in *China Moon*, and hapless Harry Barber meets treacherous Rhea Malroux in a local watering hole in *Palmetto*. The bar where Rhea "runs into" Harry is actually a popular and well-known establishment in Sarasota called the Gator Club. Movie tourists will want to stop in and have a beer at the Gator Club, located at 1490 Main Street in a historic building originally constructed in 1913.

Myakka River State Park

Many of Harry's unfortunate encounters along palmetto-lined roads were shot in Myakka River State Park. A 28,000–acre wildlife sanctuary, the park will not be as hazardous for visitors as it was for Harry. Visitors can take the seven-mile drive through the sanctuary to look for the two hundred species of birds that frequent the park, including bald eagles, great blue herons, sandhill cranes, egrets, and ibises. For those with more time, canoes, bikes, and backpacking trails are also available. The park is fourteen miles east of Sarasota on State Route 72.

WILD THINGS

Virginia Key

Run by Jimbo Luznar, the self-proclaimed "friendliest man on earth," Jimbo's Place on Virginia Key offers cold beer, smoked fish, and nonstop bocce ball. Jimbo's has been a Miami institution since 1954 and is frequently used to film music videos and television shows. The bar served as a meeting place for the shady characters of *Wild Things*, and the rundown motel out back was the site of one of the movie's steamiest sex scenes. Jimbo's Place is at the end of Duck Lake Road on the northern tip of Virginia Key, which can be reached from Miami via the Rickenbacker Causeway.

Bill Baggs Cape Florida State Park

Once voted one of the top ten beaches in the United States, Bill Baggs Park offers breathtaking ocean views and inviting beaches. Located on a barrier island near Miami, the park was used to represent a Caribbean island in the film's climactic sequence. The park entrance is at 1200 S. Crandon Boulevard on Key Biscayne.

Oleta River State Park

This thousand-acre park brings a touch of wilderness to Miami. The largest urban park in the state offers kayaking, swimming, fishing, biking, and camping along Biscayne Bay and the Oleta River, which once fed into the Everglades. It was likely used as a stand-in for Florida's more famous swamp, the Everglades, in *Wild Things*. The park entrance is at 3400 NE 163 Street in North Miami.

Star Island

Perhaps Florida's most exclusive residential area, this gated community is home to some of the city's wealthiest and most famous residents. One of the island's many mansions served as the extravagant home of spoiled young Kelly Van Ryan and her vindictive, tawdry mother. Though no tours of the residences are available, Miami charter companies do offer slow cruises past the island for determined movie tourists and stargazers.

STARRING MIAMI

Miami is vulgar, noisy, ugly and frantic,
and you and I can certainly have more fun
there than in any spot in all the world.
—humorist Heywood Broun, *Vanity Fair*

In *Moon Over Miami*, girls vacation in Miami to look for millionaire husbands; the fabulous Fontainebleau Hotel is the unlikely setting for comic high jinks in *The Bellboy*; cynical private investigator *Tony Rome* finds drugs and crime among seedy motels and bars; and the colorful Art Deco district of South Beach comes alive in *The Birdcage*. While Hollywood films are not by any means a reliable source for Miami history, it is easy to see the city's ups and downs reflected in them.

Miami was little more than a swampland in the 1890s when the first visionaries began to see its potential. Fortunately, many of these "visionaries" were affluent and could afford to develop the area themselves or reach out to those who would. Julia Tuttle, a wealthy widow from Cleveland, moved to Miami around 1891 when there was nothing in the area but the ruins of an army post and a few plantations. When an unexpected frost destroyed much of northern Florida's orange crop, Tuttle coaxed Henry Flagler to extend his railroad to Miami by sending him fresh orange blossoms to suggest that Miami was more suitable for crops and commerce. The railroad came in April 1896, and Miami was incorporated three months later.

Tiny Miami began to grow immediately, with wealthy industrialists from the North building banks and other businesses along Brickell Avenue. Flagler himself built the Royal Palm Hotel, and he donated land for public buildings.

Auto baron Carl Fisher, an early visitor to Florida, agreed to finance the completion of a bridge from one of Miami's barrier islands to the mainland in exchange for part of the island. He dredged Biscayne Bay to build up the strip of land in order to construct golf courses, hotels, and polo fields. With Fisher's ambitions, Miami Beach was born as a winter retreat or resort.

Miami Beach was incorporated in 1915, but it wasn't until the mid-1920s that development really took off in the famous Florida land boom. People from all over the country and from all social strata flocked to Florida to get rich quick by buying and selling real estate. Miami Beach was the center of the boom, in which legitimate developers, land speculators, and hangers-on vied for choice pieces of beachfront at insane prices. Within five years, from 1920 to 1925, Miami Beach's population swelled from 30,000 to 75,000.

Though thousands of tourists rushed to vacation in Miami Beach during the Roaring Twenties, the town became best known as a winter resort for the nouveaux riches. America's commerce kings erected magnificent winter mansions in faux European styles along the oceanfront as well as on Star, Palm, and Hibiscus Islands. A raucous crowd compared to the old monied families, these young millionaires actively pursued "the sporting life," which included real sports by day and gambling by night. Miami Beach earned—and deserved—its nickname as America's Winter Playground.

The land boom ended almost as quickly as it began, with prices falling off and sales dropping by 1926. Economic factors, including tax investigations of real estate deals and a major hurricane, sounded the end of the boom. With the stock market crash of 1929, South Florida entered the Depression along with the rest of the country. Developers went bankrupt, construction halted, and all but the very rich left the playground.

The manufacturing magnates, however, still favored Miami and Miami Beach as a winter retreat because of the tropical climate and also because of the area's lax attitude toward gambling. Once the boom atmosphere had ended, a more refined crowd of wealthy winter residents defined the Miami lifestyle. In the era before World War II, Miami and Miami Beach (synonymous in the minds of most Northerners) became famous for luxury and love, a reference to its population of millionaires and its reputation as the marriage and divorce capital of America. The premise of the musical *Moon Over Miami*—in which two sisters vacation in Miami to search for rich husbands—is entirely based on this reputation.

However, millionaires were not the only people to winter in Miami and Miami Beach during the 1930s. About two hundred small hotels in the Art Deco style—called Modern at the time—were built in South Miami Beach between 1935 and 1941. Many of these modest but stylish hotels hosted Jewish tourists from New York City and the East Coast, who vacationed in Miami Beach every year or relocated there upon retirement. By the late 1930s, 20 to 25 percent of Miami Beach was Jewish. Children who came to Miami Beach with their families before World War II continued to vacation on the Beach decades later, a vacation tradition reflected by the Jewish characters in Elaine May's romantic comedy *The Heartbreak Kid*.

During the 1950s, Miami Beach experienced another building boom, launched by the erection of the Fontainebleau Hotel in 1954. A luxury hotel for the middle class, it was built to be ostentatious and extravagant so that guests could show off their jewelry, their wardrobes, even their tans. The hotel attracted celebrities such as Jackie Gleason, Martin and Lewis, and Frank Sinatra—who made the "Bloo" his home away from home while in town. Part of Sinatra's film *A Hole in the Head* was shot at the Fontainebleau, and in Jerry Lewis's unique comedy *The Bellboy*, the hotel is virtually the star.

Tourism in the Miami area declined in the late 1960s, partly because the Woodstock generation seemed uninterested in their parents' vacation spot. Also, by the 1970s, Miami and Miami Beach were suffering from some of the same problems as other inner cities, including drugs and crime. Frank Sinatra returned to his personal playground during this time to make a pair of tough detective dramas that reflected the new Miami—*Tony Rome* and its sequel, *Lady in Cement*. Though Sinatra still liked to stroll the "Bloo" with his entourage, the times were definitely changing.

In the early 1960s, Miami's population received a major boost when Cuban refugees arrived to escape Castro's socialist society. The Cubans made a major impact on the Miami area, transforming it into a multinational society. They poured money and effort into successful local businesses, including restaurants, cigar factories, banks, and garment plants. In 1980 another large influx of Cubans arrived via the Mariel Boatlift, a flotilla of boats, rafts, and ships that Castro allowed to leave the country from the docks of Mariel. More than 125,000 Cubans arrived in Miami, straining the economic and housing infrastructures. Brian De Palma's 1983 reworking of *Scarface* referenced the boatlift while building a story around the cocaine trade that plagued the city, which had become the major East Coast entry port for drug smugglers.

During the 1980s, Miami's image changed again. The Art Deco district in South Miami Beach was placed on the National Register of Historic Places, and the beach was restored by the Army Corps of Engineers. The Deco buildings along Ocean Drive were renovated into an architectural showpiece, and the television series *Miami Vice* showed off an ultramodern city of glamour and vitality. *The Birdcage* captured the new vigor and energy of Miami by setting the story in colorful South Beach.

Miami has a unique history based on its tropical climate and its original settlers, but it also has a fascinating pop-culture history—one that is clearly reflected in the movies that have been shot there.

ABSENCE OF MALICE

Suppose you picked up this morning's newspaper and your life was a front page headline . . . And everything they said was accurate . . . But none of it was true.
—poster for *Absence of Malice*

THE STORY

Businessman Michael Gallagher, the son of a convicted racketeer, finds himself on the front pages of the *Miami Standard* as the chief suspect in the disappearance of a union leader. The story has been deliberately leaked to reporter Megan Carter by an ambitious federal investigator as a way to squeeze Gallagher into informing on his father's associates. Pushed into a corner, Gallagher uses Carter and her paper to clear his name.

THE FILM

Former journalist Kurt Luedtke was inspired to write his first script, *Absence of Malice*, by the case of a *Washington Post* reporter who had won a Pulitzer Prize for a series of stories that turned out to be fabricated. Director Sydney Pollack piloted Luedtke's script into a film that criticized the methods of contemporary journalists while challenging their ethics.

Luedtke had originally set the story in Detroit, because he had spent much of his career at the *Detroit Free Press*. However, when the studio decided that it was not convenient to shoot in Michigan during the winter months, Pollack selected Miami as the most appropriate alternative. Luedtke had worked at the *Miami Herald* and knew the city from his days as a general assignments reporter. The *Herald* allowed Pollack and his crew to shoot scenes inside its building and offices, though filming was limited to the hours between midnight and dawn when the newspaper was not busy. The scenes with reporter Megan Carter and her editor hashing out the ethics and merits of her stories were shot inside the *Herald* offices, capturing the noisy and cluttered atmosphere of a big city newspaper without glamorizing it.

Other scenes were shot in Miami's parks, downtown buildings, and docks, though there is a noticeable lack of recognizable tourist spots, suggesting that the story could have unfolded in any newsroom of any big-city paper. Despite these efforts to make the story universal, Miami was not an arbitrary choice as the primary setting. The city has a reputation as a newspaper town due to the prominence and standing of one of the best second-tier papers in the country—the *Miami Herald*.[1]

The first edition of the *Herald* was published as the *Miami Evening Record* in 1903, making it South Florida's oldest paper. Seven years later it was renamed the *Miami Herald*. The paper almost folded during the Depression, but it was saved when it was bought by the Knight-Ridder syndicate. The *Herald* won its first Pulitzer in 1951 and has gone on to win seventeen more, including seven from 1980 to 1989.[2] Acclaimed for its columnists and commentators, including Dave Barry, Leonard Pitts Jr., and Carl Hiaasen, the *Herald* is considered a training ground for journalism's "major league," because its reporters often move on to such papers as the *New York Times*, the *Washington Post*, or the *Wall Street Journal*.

Though the *Miami Herald* has not been featured in Hollywood films to the same degree as the *New York Times*, or even the *Washington Post*, it has had an occasional brush with Hollywood. The *Herald* earned its 1951 Pulitzer for reporting on Miami's organized crime syndicate, particularly its gambling operations. During the mid-1950s two low-budget crime dramas, *Miami Story* and *Miami Exposé*, were released with plots that could have been ripped from the *Herald's* headlines. In *Miami Story*, an ex-con with ties to the Chicago mob helps the Miami police put a powerful crime boss with an extensive gambling operation behind bars. Interestingly, the crime boss was played by Luther Adler, who played a similar role in *Absence of Malice*. *Miami Exposé* also targeted the Miami crime syndicate, though with a less complex story line. Both movies were scripted by Robert E. Kent and directed by Fred Sears, film industry journeymen who were adept at crafting B-movie quickies based on trends, news stories, and fads.

Later the actual *Miami Herald* served as a "character," and its offices as a major location, for various Hollywood films including *The Mean Season* (1985, in this chapter), *Big Trouble* (2002), and *Absence of Malice*. Though *Malice* was shot at the *Herald*, the newspaper in the narrative was called the *Miami Standard*, undoubtedly because the newspaper business is heavily criticized in the film.

Despite being played by the highly likable Sally Field, reporter Megan Carter is an unsympathetic character whose compassion and sense of honor have been undermined by her profession. Throughout the film she makes poor moral choices in order to "get the story." She snoops through a file on the desk of a federal investigator who is checking out local businessman Michael Gallagher after the disappearance of a labor leader. There is no evidence pointing to Gallagher, played by Paul Newman, though Gallagher's father was part of the Miami mob. The ambitious investigator knows that Carter will snoop through the file and deliberately leaves the room to let her do it. He also knows she will write a story about Gallagher, and the *Standard* will print it. The investigator hopes that Gallagher will feel pressured to inform on his father's old associates.

The headline on the front page, implying that Gallagher is guilty without saying it, ruins his beer distribution business—a consequence Carter didn't think about when she wrote the story. Later a young woman comes forward to tell Carter that Gallagher is innocent because he was helping her get an abortion on the day of the crime. Despite the woman's pleas not to print her name, Carter and her editor decide that the details of the story are what make it believable (that is, titillating). The editor rationalizes the decision by reiterating the old adage that the public has the right to know. But the young woman lives in a Catholic community, and when her name and the story of her abortion are printed, she kills herself.

Gallagher eventually clears his name through an elaborate scheme that exploits the investigator's ambitions and Carter's attraction to him, but the theme of *Absence of Malice*—as evident from the title—clearly focuses on the consequences of an irresponsible press more interested in a story than in the humans behind it. The phrase "absence of malice" is a legal concept that protects the press so that it is free to criticize government officials. Absence of malice means that, if statements made by the press about an official turn out to be inaccurate, the press cannot be held accountable as long as the inaccuracies were unintentional. Critical stories and commentary by the press are considered to be free speech protected by the First Amendment. The use of the phrase for the

Figure 4.1. *Absence of Malice* director Sydney Pollack.
(Doll/Morrow Collection)

title of the film is pointed; it implies that the press is abusing its right of free speech by failing to consider the consequences its work holds for its subjects.

As might be expected, the press was riled by the way the profession was treated in *Absence of Malice*. Many reviewers and feature writers condemned the film by claiming Megan Carter's tactics were "unrealistic"—though, interestingly, few condemned them for being unethical.[3] The situation was compounded by Field's and Newman's attitude toward interviewers and reviewers when the film was released. Despite the fact that scriptwriter Kurt Luedtke had been a reporter and was in essence betraying his profession, Newman took the brunt of the criticism, primarily because of his well-known antipathy toward the media. When introduced to the *Washington Post*'s Diana Maychick during a press junket, for example, Newman greeted her with "I hate your paper."[4]

While *Absence of Malice* was heavily criticized by reviewers, it was redeemed a few months later when it garnered several Academy Award nominations, including one for Luedtke for best original screenplay. Still, considering the treatment of journalism in the film, the *Herald* must have been relieved that Megan Carter worked for the *Miami Standard*.

THE CREDITS	THE CAST	
Released in 1981 by Columbia Pictures	Paul Newman	Michael Gallagher
Produced by Ronald L. Schwary and Sydney Pollack	Sally Field	Megan Carter
Directed by Sydney Pollack	Melinda Dillon	Teresa Perrone
Written by Kurt Luedtke	Bob Balaban	Elliot Rosen
Cinematography by Owen Roizman	Luther Adler	Uncle Santos Malderone
Edited by Sheldon Kahn	Barry Primus	Bob Waddell
Music by Dave Grusin	Wilford Brimley	James A. Wells
Production design by Terence Marsh		

THE BIRDCAGE

Miami Beach is where neon goes to die.
—Lenny Bruce, quoted in *The Life and Times
of Miami Beach*, by Ann Armbruster

THE STORY

Armand and Albert, a gay couple who have been together for more than twenty years, run a Miami Beach nightclub starring Albert as its top female impersonator. When Val, Armand's grown son from a previous marriage, becomes engaged to the daughter of a right-wing politician, father and son panic over what to do about Albert. The two families meet over dinner, with Albert donning drag to pretend to be Val's mother. Each course of the meal brings a new disaster, and the ruse slowly begins to unravel.

THE FILM

In 1978 the French-Italian farce *La Cage aux Folles* conquered the international box office, inspiring two sequels and a Broadway musical. The story of a gay couple who try to pass as heterosexual for the sake of their son's marital bliss appealed to a wide variety of people, including Hollywood director Mike Nichols. Nichols set out to make an American version of the film, but problems with the rights plagued the project for years. He was finally able to direct his interpretation, retitled *The Birdcage*, in 1996 with Robin Williams and Nathan Lane in the starring roles.

Some reviewers questioned whether the subject matter was still relevant eighteen years after the original film had been released, but Nichols managed to update the material without fundamentally altering it. He did so by focusing

Figure 4.2. Publicity photos from *The Birdcage*. (Doll/Morrow Collection)

on the theme of family values, a front-burner issue in the increasingly conservative climate of the 1990s. In *The Birdcage*, Armand and Albert are depicted as a loving couple who have raised Armand's son, Val, with love, tolerance, and responsibility. They have been together for many years, experiencing the same traumas and frustrations as other parents, and now they fear their child is too young to marry. Nichols tweaked the conservative movement by expanding the definition of family and in doing so made the film more about the responsibilities of marriage and family than about homosexuality.

The film contrasts a typical nuclear family, the Keeleys, with a more contemporary version consisting of Armand, Albert, and Val. Senator Keeley is an ultraconservative politician and cofounder of the Coalition for Moral Order, and his wife is the dutiful homemaker. Armand Goldman owns the hottest drag club in South Beach, and his "wife" is the club's main attraction. Though the two couples at first seem to be complete opposites, they come together in their concern for their children, and they work together to get the senator out of a potentially embarrassing situation with the snooping press.

The sequence that brings them together is the dinner scene, which takes up much of the second half of the film. The sequence is structured like a classic stage farce driven by a series of perfectly timed and well-executed entrances and exits. The comic exaggeration of the characters and their farcical actions prevents any one of them from seeming spiteful or villainous, and by the end it becomes easy to accept that they have tossed aside some of their differences and prejudices.

Nichols also updated the material by setting the film in Miami Beach, in particular South Beach, which was restored and revamped in the 1980s and 1990s. South Beach is now famous for the thriving, colorful Art Deco district that covers one square mile running east-west from the Atlantic Ocean to Lenox Court and north-south from 5th to 23rd Street.

Though hip and vibrant now, during the recession of the 1970s and 1980s South Beach and Miami in general suffered through several bad years. The hotels were originally built during the Depression to accommodate tourists from New York and the East Coast, but in the 1950s these stylish but small hotels were left out of the building boom on the other end of Miami Beach. South Beach still attracted those tourists from the 1930s, but now they were retired and on fixed incomes. Retirees began to settle in the community, and many of the Art Deco hotels turned into retirement homes. By 1970, 80 percent of South Beach was aged sixty-five and over, and the neighborhood was ranked the poorest in the state.[5] A redevelopment project was scheduled, which would have torn down the Art Deco district, but fortunately it stalled because of resistance and was eventually canceled. To compound the decline of the district's buildings, the beach—the original attraction that drew millions to Miami— had virtually disappeared, except for Lummus Park.

Two important events changed the downward spiral of South Beach and saved the Art Deco hotels. In 1979 the district was placed on the National Register of Historic Places, and the beach was restored by the Army Corps of Engineers. Antidevelopment activist Barbara Baer Capitman and interior designer Leonard Horowitz were instrumental in getting the historical designation, and with that accomplished, Capitman actively promoted the Deco district. Miami Beach could boast the world's largest collection of Deco architecture, with more than four hundred buildings exhibiting the characteristics of the style, including the curved corners, portholes, glass blocks, eyebrow ledges cantilevered over windows in horizontal bands, and ziggurats rising over doorways with the name of the building written vertically in neon lighting. The ornamentation of the original buildings featured murals with flamingos, friezes with ocean motifs, and decklike balconies, imparting a distinctive Tropical Deco style that evoked the aura of Florida. A young café society was attracted to the newly restored and refurbished sidewalk restaurants that opened, while Horowitz offered to redecorate the hotels to bring out their stylish splendor. The white buildings with pastel highlights were painted with a brighter palette and decorated in neon by Horowitz as a way to attract attention to the buildings. By the 1980s the rehabilitation of the district was proceeding at a rapid pace.

For the film, the front of the Birdcage nightclub was recreated at a studio, but scenes of Armand and Albert strolling through the neighborhood were shot along Ocean Drive and other South Beach streets. A few scenes were shot at the Carlyle, which stood in for the building that housed the Birdcage and Armand's apartment. In the film, the crowded streets of South Beach are alive with energy and activity, while a warm sun bathes the neighborhood in a golden light.

South Beach is more than just a hip locale for a movie, however; it provides a purposeful contrast to the Keeleys' colorless Midwest home, which is made even less inviting by the snow and cold. The settings associated with the two families offer a clue to their personalties and lifestyles—warm, vibrant, and open versus chilly, repressed, and narrow. From the trendy little cafés to the Art Deco designs to the colorful neon, South Beach couldn't look more inviting.

THE CREW

Released in 1996 by Metro-Goldwyn-Mayer/United Artists
Produced by Neil Machlis, Marcello Danon, and Mike Nichols
Directed by Mike Nichols
Written by Elaine May, from the stage play *La Cage aux Folles* by Jean Poiret and the screenplay by Francis Veber, Edouard Molinaro, Marcello Danon, and Jean Poiret
Cinematography by Emmanuel Lubezki
Edited by Arthur Schmidt
Production design by Bo Welch
Art direction by Tom Duffield, with Sean Haworth and Cheryl Carasik
Music arranged by Jonathan Tunick
Costumes by Ann Roth and Stephen Shubin

THE CAST

Robin Williams	Armand Goldman
Nathan Lane	Albert
Gene Hackman	Senator Keeley
Dianne Wiest	Louise Keeley
Dan Futterman	Val Goldman
Calista Flockhart	Barbara Keeley
Hank Azaria	Agador
Christine Baranski	Katharine

FLIPPER

They call him Flipper, Flipper, faster than lightning,
No one, you see, is smarter than he,
And we know Flipper lives in a world full of wonder,
Flying there under, under the sea!
—theme song to *Flipper*

THE STORY

Twelve-year-old Sandy Ricks lives in the Florida Keys and spends his barefoot summers working with his fisherman father. After finding a dolphin injured by a spearfisher, the resourceful boy nurses it back to health. The two become fast friends and enjoy a series of adventures.

THE FILM

Ivan Tors, Hollywood's most successful producer of animal films, emigrated from Hungary to the United States at the outbreak of World War II. A budding playwright in Europe, he began writing screenplays for Hollywood after the war and was producing science-fiction and aviation pictures by the mid-1950s. In 1958 he created the well-known television adventure series *Sea Hunt*, starring Lloyd Bridges, which frequently filmed in Florida. During the four-year run of this show, Tors gained his first experience working with animals. It was also on this show that he met Ricou Browning, a Florida native and professional swimmer who got his start in the film business portraying *The Creature from the Black Lagoon* (see chapter 9). Browning did stunt work for *Sea Hunt* and often directed the underwater sequences. Within a few years the two men were collaborating on *Flipper*, a highly successful family film that became the foundation of an animal entertainment empire.

Browning and his brother-in-law Jack Cowden had developed a story about a young boy who befriends a dolphin. They hoped to sell the idea as a book, but New York publishers were slow to respond to their proposal. Browning brought the idea to Tors, who immediately recognized it as the kind of wholesome, nonviolent family entertainment he was interested in producing.

The first obstacle the filmmakers faced was finding a dolphin suitable for the film. Though marine parks had been popular for some time and trained dolphins were typically their main attractions, the film required a level of interaction with humans that most captive dolphins were not accustomed to. While driving down Highway One through Grassy Key, Tors and Browning noticed a sign for Santini's Porpoise School and stopped to investigate. The owners,

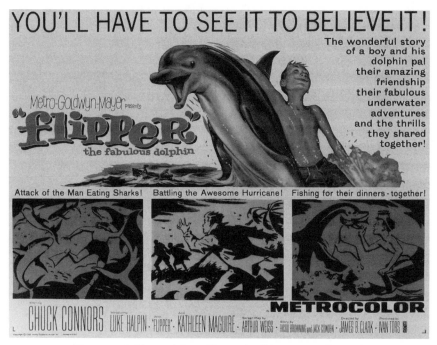

Figure 4.3. Lobby card from *Flipper*. (Doll/Morrow Collection)

Milton and Virginia Santini, captured dolphins and sold them to researchers and aquariums. They kept a female dolphin named Mitzie on the premises permanently, having found that newly captured dolphins became calm and trusting more quickly when kept with another dolphin already accustomed to captivity. After spending a short time visiting Mitzie in her lagoon, Tors and Browning decided they had found their star.

Though comfortable with humans, Mitzie still needed a significant amount of training to prepare for the film. At that time, the standard approach to working with dolphins involved trainers standing outside the pool and issuing commands and rewards. Browning felt Mitzie was tame enough for him to enter the water with her, and he found that this practice stimulated the dolphin and dramatically reduced the time she needed to learn routines. The film required that she allow actor Luke Halpin, who played young Sandy Porter, to hang on to her back and ride along with her as she swam. Knowing that Mitzie was comfortable with the task of retrieving objects, Browning had his son jump into the water and then gave her the signal to fetch. The dolphin picked up on the idea quickly, grabbing the boy by his belt loop and towing him back to Browning. After a few more tries, the dolphin allowed the boy to cling to her back as she swam and even seemed pleased to give him a ride.

Browning, who had no experience working with dolphins or even training animals, consulted Dr. John C. Lilly to develop Mitzie's training program. Lilly had worked as a government scientist in a variety of disciplines, including the study of human consciousness and dolphin intelligence. His Communications Research Institute, founded in Miami and later moved to the Caribbean, focused on breaking the communication barrier between humans and dolphins, which he regarded as sentient creatures. Lilly also invented the sensory deprivation tank and experimented with LSD in attempts to expand the human consciousness. Though much of his later work has been dismissed by the mainstream scientific community, he did develop a number of influential theories on the nature of intelligence in both humans and animals early in his career. Two feature films, *The Day of the Dolphin* and *Altered States,* are loosely based on his research.

Much of the location shooting for *Flipper* took place in the Bahamas, but scenes were also filmed in Everglades City and at the Miami Seaquarium, including the climactic underwater sequence in which Flipper saves Sandy by fighting off a pack of hungry sharks. The soundstage work was done at Greenwich Studios, Tor's production facility in north Miami.

The highly successful 1963 film led to a sequel, *Flipper's New Adventure,* and a popular television show that enjoyed a three-year run. Mitzie appeared in the two films but not the television show. Two other dolphins from the Miami Seaquarium, Suzy and Cathy, were used in the series. For Tors, *Flipper* was the first of many family films and shows to feature animals. He went on to produce the African adventure show *Daktari* and *Gentle Ben,* which chronicled the friendship of a young boy and a 350-pound bear. Tors built a small animal park in Palm Beach Gardens, Florida, where he trained and kept the creatures that appeared in his productions. He also established a sprawling 260-acre park in California that became one of Hollywood's primary sources of animal actors. Browning remained a principal creator of the 1960s *Flipper* stories, working as a writer, director, producer, and stuntman, and eventually became president of Tors's Florida studio. He even appeared occasionally as an actor and later took a regular role in a new *Flipper* series developed for cable in the 1990s. The film was remade for theaters in 1996 with Elijah Wood, Paul Hogan, and an animatronic dolphin, but this updated version failed to make the splash that the original had.

Released in 1963 by Metro-Goldwyn-Mayer	Mitzie — Flipper
Produced by Ivan Tors	Luke Halpin — Sandy Ricks
Directed by James B. Clark	Chuck Connors — Porter Ricks
Written by Arthur Weiss, based on a story by Ricou Browning and Jack Cowden	Connie Scott — Kim Parker
Cinematography by Lamar Boren and Joseph C. Brun	Kathleen Maguire — Martha Ricks
Edited by Warren Adams	
Music by Henry Vars; "Flipper" by By Dunham and Henry Vars	

THE HEARTBREAK KID

I'm gonna give you everything. I'm gonna give you the car . . . all the luggage . . . all the wedding presents. For a marriage that's not a week old, that's pretty good. Some people don't get that after forty years.

—Lenny Cantrow, asking his bride for a divorce in
The Heartbreak Kid

THE STORY

Jewish newlyweds Lenny and Lila Cantrow head from New York to Miami Beach on their honeymoon. Within days, the shallow, egocentric Lenny has grown tired of his clingy bride and fallen for Kelly, a blonde Midwestern coed he meets on the beach. Lenny breaks the union with Lila and moves to Minneapolis to pursue his dream girl over strong opposition from her father.

THE FILM

Neil Simon is undoubtedly one of the most popular and successful American playwrights of the twentieth century. He began his career as a television writer in the 1950s as part of the highly acclaimed writing crew on Sid Caesar's *Your Show of Shows*. He went on to create many of Broadway's top comedies in the 1960s and 1970s, including *Barefoot in the Park*, *The Odd Couple*, *Plaza Suite*, and *The Sunshine Boys*, and he successfully adapted many of his works to the silver screen. Born and raised in the Bronx, Simon brought a decidedly New York sensibility to his work, which illuminates the humor and pathos found in the struggles of everyday big-city life. In adapting *The Heartbreak Kid* from a

Figure 4.4. Publicity photo from *The Heartbreak Kid*. (Doll/Morrow Collection)

short story by Bruce Jay Friedman, Simon delved into a darker and more cynical world than is typical for his writing.

The film was directed by Elaine May, another leading light of New York theater in the 1960s. A brilliant comic writer and performer, May is best remembered for her witty Broadway collaborations with Mike Nichols. *The Heartbreak Kid* was her second directorial effort, after the subtle comedy *A New Leaf*, which she had written and starred in. May directed only two other films, the last of which, *Ishtar*, is considered one of the great financial disasters in the history of Hollywood. In *The Heartbreak Kid*, however, she revealed an authentic talent, anchoring the film on the excellent performances of the cast and skillfully using the camera to reveal the main character's shallow nature and misguided worldview.

Portrayed by Charles Grodin, Lenny Cantrow is a young Jewish professional from New York with no notion of how to go about living a meaningful life. He has a pointless but successful career as a sporting goods salesman, because one is expected to work, and has just tied the knot with Jewish princess Lila, because one is expected to marry. As the newlyweds drive to Florida on their honeymoon, however, Lenny becomes increasingly horrified over the major life decision he has just made. He projects his angst onto a variety of Lila's personal habits, from her messy table manners to her poor singing voice to her requests for reassurance during sex. The camera reveals his exaggerated concerns, lingering on the egg salad smeared on Lila's chin or watching Lenny as he watches her with an unmistakable look of deadpan dread on his face.

On their first day in Miami, Lenny encounters Kelly, a stunning Midwestern WASP who approaches him on the beach. Looking up from his spot in the sand, he strains against the Florida glare to catch a glimpse of her unearthly figure haloed in sunlight. He immediately falls in love with this blonde vision, who could not be more different from his bride. Over several scenes, he spins a shamelessly detailed string of lies to Lila in order to sneak away with Kelly. Each time, the camera fixes on him, revealing his deceitfulness through its unblinking lens. Similarly, when he meets Kelly's parents and simultaneously professes his love and confesses his marital status, the speech is presented in a single, unedited shot that captures the character's remarkable ability to be honest and insincere in a single moment.

Kelly, the beautiful but vacuous object of Lenny's obsession, serves to further emphasize his shallowness. Lenny finds her charming and refreshing, but her witless sardonic jokes reveal a spoiled, immature nature. To her, the relationship with Lenny is at first a simple Florida fling, a vain exercise in flirtation to see just how far she can entice a married man to go. Whatever Lila's faults, she offers a greater emotional maturity and depth than the comely coed, but that gift is entirely lost on Lenny.

The film's Miami Beach setting serves to heighten the anxieties that Lenny has come to feel about his life. For countless middle- and upper-class Easterners of that era, the Florida beachfront resort was the ideal vacation and retirement spot, an indulgent reward after a year or a lifetime of hard work. As a young man lucky enough to venture there with a loving new bride, Lenny surely feels this three-day visit is a glimpse of the best his life will have to offer, and he does not like what he sees. Turning his back on his wife and on the pleasures of Miami Beach, he ventures to the frozen, provincial Midwest to lay claim to

Kelly. Despite his determination and newfound freedom, the callow Lenny is sure to remain unfulfilled no matter where he settles or whom he settles with.

On its release, *The Heartbreak Kid* was frequently but inappropriately compared to *The Graduate*. Grodin, coincidentally, had been considered for the role so memorably played by Dustin Hoffman in that 1967 film, which was directed by May's former partner Nichols. Though both stories center around young men casting about for direction, the messages and sensibilities of the two films differ greatly. *The Graduate* is a sharp social satire with a character who gradually becomes fed up with the emptiness and hypocrisy of the world around him, while *The Heartbreak Kid* focuses more on the emotional and psychological shortcomings of its protagonist. Unable to penetrate the veneer of modern American life, Lenny is in many ways the antithesis of *The Graduate*'s rebellious Benjamin Braddock.

THE CREDITS	THE CAST	
Released in 1972 by Twentieth Century–Fox	Charles Grodin	Lenny Cantrow
Produced by Edgar J. Scherick	Cybill Shepherd	Kelly Corcoran
Directed by Elaine May	Jeannie Berlin	Lila Cantrow
Written by Neil Simon	Audra Lindley	Mrs. Corcoran
Cinematography by Enrique Bravo and	Eddie Albert	Mr. Corcoran
Owen Roizman		
Edited by John Carter		
Music by Garry Sherman		
Production design by Richard Sylbert		

A HOLE IN THE HEAD

A very fresh, very funny, very Frank . . . Capra look at life.
—theatrical trailer for *A Hole in the Head*

THE STORY

Lovable loser Tony Manetta dreams of turning his second-tier hotel into Miami's biggest business empire, but his schemes never seem to materialize. A widower with an adoring twelve-year-old son, he hopes to raise millions for his latest big idea even as the bank threatens foreclosure on the hotel. Caught between a footloose girlfriend and a straitlaced older brother, Tony reconsiders his priorities when financial troubles mean he might lose custody of his son.

The 1959 release of *A Hole in the Head* represents a union of two giants of American film and popular culture. Director Frank Capra and star Frank Sinatra formed a short-lived company, SinCap Productions, to get the film made. Sinatra had bought the rights to the moderately successful Broadway play, drawn to the complex leading character of Tony Manetta, a big-time dreamer and small-time achiever whose admirable confidence and ambition are constantly undercut by an impractical nature.

Sinatra's many screen performances can be categorized by changes in his star image. In the 1940s and early 1950s, he tended to play naive young men in musicals, trading on his bobby-soxer image as a pop singer. In the late 1960s and 1970s, the more mature star played the world-weary detective in a series of crime dramas. The late 1950s and early 1960s saw him favoring flawed characters who were unable to rise above their lot in life or their own weaknesses, in films such as *The Man with the Golden Arm*, *Some Came Running*, and *The Manchurian Candidate*. Though *A Hole in the Head* is decidedly brighter and more upbeat than these films, the role does fit in with Sinatra's other efforts from the period, which many consider to be his finest work.

For Capra, *A Hole in the Head* was a return to feature films after an eight-year hiatus. The director first made a name for himself in the 1920s collaborating with the legendary silent comedian Harry Langdon. He then signed with a struggling new studio, Columbia Pictures, where he fostered the careers of several young stars including Barbara Stanwyck and proved himself a master of the industry's latest technological development, sound. But it was his efforts in the mid- and late 1930s that would help turn Columbia into a major studio and establish Capra as one of the most successful and recognized directors in Hollywood. In films such as *It Happened One Night*, *Mr. Deeds Goes to Town*, and *Mr. Smith Goes to Washington*, Capra developed a definitive directorial voice that resonated with a nation enduring economic hardship and established him as one of the first true auteurs of American film. His tales of plucky idealism overcoming wrongheadedness or corruption in the halls of power earned numerous Academy Awards and made him one of the first directors whose name appeared above the title of his films.

The 1946 release of *It's a Wonderful Life*, however, was the start of a long slide for Capra. Though the film is now one of his best-known works and an icon of American culture, it failed on its release, as did his next three films. Matured by the experiences of World War II and emboldened by the country's new role as a world leader, American critics and audiences rejected Capra's vision as simplistic and old-fashioned. Devastated, the once-renowned director remained idle for much of the 1950s, with the exception of a few science

Figure 4.5. *A Hole in the Head* star Frank Sinatra. (Doll/Morrow Collection)

documentaries he collaborated on for television. Sinatra, who had always been an admirer of Capra's work, lured him back to the big screen for *A Hole in the Head,* which would be the director's first effort in color.

While critics tend to interpret Capra's films as naive political statements celebrating the triumph of moral goodness over corruption, Capra himself claimed his work was always about "the freedom of each individual and the equal importance of each individual."[6] *A Hole in the Head* seems to fit better with Capra's notion than with that of the critics. Much of the story takes place in the Garden of Eden Hotel, a failing enterprise in south Miami owned by Sinatra's character. As Tony fights off an eviction notice from the bank, he struggles to raise his beloved son and put together an ambitious deal to build a Disney-like amusement park in Florida. (The character's foresight was remarkable, as this was ten years before Disney announced its own plans to do just that.) Tony turns to his older brother Mario for help with the mortgage, but Mario and his wife unexpectedly fly down from New York with an alternate proposal. They will set up the widowed Tony in a small retail store if he agrees to abandon his dreams of overnight success and settle down with a nice woman. The proposal does not go over well with Tony's current girlfriend, a free spirit memorably played by Carolyn Jones, who hopes he'll turn custody of his son over to Mario so that she and Tony can live a footloose life on the road. When Tony's eleventh-hour shot at the amusement park deal falls through, he temporarily loses faith in himself. In the end, though, he refuses to give up his dreams, his son, or his identity, and his unquenchable optimism finally wins over his uptight brother.

The film used an Art Deco landmark, the Cardozo Hotel in South Beach, as Tony's faltering business. During filming on Ocean Drive, the neighboring Carlyle Hotel filed a lawsuit against SinCap, claiming that the location shooting interfered with its business. Another suit was brought by the West Flagler Kennel Club. The famous dog track was used in the film for a meeting between Tony and a potential backer, in exchange for a promised appearance by Sinatra, but the star claimed ill health and failed to show. Despite the minor real-life legal trouble, the optimistic film paints an alluring portrait of Miami as a vibrant, free-wheeling town where anyone can make dreams come true—even a guy with a hole in the head.

THE CREDITS

Released in 1959 by United Artists
Produced by Frank Capra and Frank Sinatra
Directed by Frank Capra
Screenplay by Arnold Schulman
Cinematography by William H. Daniels
Edited by William Hornbeck
Music by Nelson Riddle; "High Hopes" by Sammy
    Cahn and Jimmy Van Heusen
Art direction by Eddie Imazu
Set decoration by Fred M. MacLean
Costume design by Edith Head

THE CAST

Frank Sinatra	Tony Manetta
Edward G. Robinson	Mario Manetta
Eleanor Parker	Eloise Rogers
Carolyn Jones	Shirl
Thelma Ritter	Sophie Manetta
Eddie Hodges	Alvin "Ally" Manetta
Keenan Wynn	Jerry Marks
Dub Taylor	Fred (the clerk)

THE MEAN SEASON

The news gets made somewhere else. We just sell it.
—newspaper editor Bill Nolan in *The Mean Season*

THE STORY

Miami crime reporter Malcolm Anderson plans to leave his big-city job for a quiet life managing a small-town newspaper. But when a serial killer contacts him to speak about his ongoing crimes, Anderson decides to stay on and see the story through.

THE FILM

The Mean Season is a compelling but convoluted thriller that offers a harsh look at the ethics of journalism and the price exacted for ambition, celebrity, and success. Kurt Russell stars as Malcolm Anderson, a jaded Miami crime reporter who's covered one too many murders. As he tells his editor, "I don't want to see my name in the paper next to pictures of dead bodies anymore." His plans to give up his high-profile career for a quieter life on a small-town newspaper, however, are interrupted when a publicity-hungry serial killer creates a media sensation by revealing information about his crimes to Anderson.

The film is most effective in the smart way it entwines the ambitions of Anderson and Alan Delour, the killer. Delour's hunger for attention prompts him to contact Anderson in the first place, knowing that a direct link to the media guarantees that his crimes will become front-page news. Later it's revealed that he is actually recreating a series of murders he had committed in the Midwest. Though he confessed to those crimes, the police dismissed him as a crackpot, robbing him of the acclaim he desperately sought. By repeating his spree in Miami, he hopes to reclaim the attention that eluded him before.

Over the protests of his girlfriend, Anderson agrees to stay on and cover the story. He is legitimately able to claim that his communication with the killer offers the police the best hope of catching him, and also that he has an obligation as a reporter to see the story through. At the same time, however, the story is a once-in-a-lifetime opportunity that will lead to celebrity and professional success. Whatever good or harm comes of the situation, it is clear to his family, his coworkers, and even to himself that his interests and those of the killer coincide.

Anderson's ambitions are reflected throughout his workplace. The newsroom is a perpetually clattering nexus of activity where editors and writers constantly work the phones and pound the keys to provide each day's news

Figure 4.6 *The Mean Season* star Kurt Russell. (Doll/Morrow Collection)

fix. His colleagues egg him on, overtly in their advice and more subtly in their keen, jealous interest in his work. Key scenes are intercut with shots of the presses stamping out headlines and rolling out neat bundles of newspapers for the trucks, creating the impression of a ravenous, relentless machine that sweeps Anderson along with it.

Though the character works for the fictional *Miami Journal*, much of the film was shot on the premises of the city's main newspaper, the *Miami Herald*. The film crew descended on the *Herald*'s newsroom in the quiet evening hours and left as much intact as possible for shooting, down to the clutter on the desks of the reporters. Photographers snapped pictures of the staff during the day, and the stills were used in selecting wardrobe for the main characters as well as for extras. Sound engineers recorded the ambient noise of the office during peak working hours and incorporated it into the film's soundtrack.

Russell and Joe Pantoliano, who plays photographer Andy Porter, spent time being tutored by a pair of *Herald* staffers and went on assignment with them to cover a drug-related murder. The actors watched as Tim Chapman, a *Herald* photojournalist, pushed to the front of a crowd to photograph a screaming child being removed from the crime scene. Though unsettling, the experience proved useful in an early scene in the film. Anderson and Porter interview the mother of the killer's first victim as she waits at home while her husband identifies the body at the morgue. Porter pushes the bounds of decorum to get his photographs, while Russell's character displays the doubt that's prompted him to consider leaving Miami.

The film was based on the novel *In the Heat of the Summer* by former *Miami Herald* reporter John Katzenbach. The film's title comes from a passage early in the book describing the oppressive and threatening weather typical at the onset of a Miami summer. According to Katzenbach, the phrase was coined by his wife and is not widely used among Floridians. The climate is a key element of the film's setting, however. Scenes are frequently separated by shots of ominous clouds quickly building under the glaring tropical sun, offering a portent of the danger that lies in store for the city and the film's characters.

The Mean Season fared poorly at the box office, grossing under $5 million, despite its energetic pacing and acclaimed performances by Russell, Richard Masur as his editor, and Richard Jordan as the killer Delour. The film does suffer from a few clichés and late action sequences that seem out of step with its more subtle beginnings. In the end, though, it remains an effective and thought-provoking study of the ambiguous ethics of professional journalism.

THE CREDITS	THE CAST	
Released in 1985 by Orion Pictures	Kurt Russell	Malcolm Anderson
Produced by David Foster and Lawrence Turman	Mariel Hemingway	Christine Connelly
Directed by Phillip Borsos	Richard Jordan	Alan Delour
Written by Leon Piedmont	Richard Masur	Bill Nolan
Cinematography by Frank Tidy	Andy Garcia	Ray Martinez
Edited by Duwayne Dunham	Joe Pantoliano	Andy Porter
Production design by Philip M. Jefferies		
Music by Lalo Schifrin		

MIAMI BLUES

I had to give him the benefit of the doubt because
he had some good qualities. He always et everything I cooked for him, and he never hit me.
—Susie Waggoner, describing her dedication to
sociopath Junior Frenger

THE STORY

Junior Frenger moves to Miami from California intent on building a new
life for himself. A sociopath and career criminal, he sweet-talks naive young
hooker Susie into setting up house with him. Unbeknownst to the girl, Junior
uses a stolen badge to pose as a cop so he can roust and rob Miami's criminal
class. Haggard homicide detective Hoke Moseley, owner of the stolen badge,
relentlessly pursues the charming but brutal criminal.

THE FILM

Charles Willeford was an amiable, soft-spoken man who returned from World
War II a hero and went on to teach college literature and write book reviews
for the *Miami Herald*. He also published two dozen books, dabbling in poetry, short stories, Westerns, and autobiography. For all his accomplishments,
though, he is best remembered as a dean of Florida crime fiction for the series
of four Hoke Moseley novels he produced in the 1980s.

In Moseley, Willeford created a truly memorable character—a rumpled, aging, once-tough homicide cop who relies on dogged determination to stamp
out the seamy but seasoned parasites of Miami's vast and absurd underbelly.
Divorced, broke, and flopping at a run-down hotel, Moseley, who sports a full
set of false upper teeth and isn't shy about taking them out, has little in his life
other than the job. A description by Willeford in the fourth novel, *The Way We
Die Now*, says it all: "Hoke was forty-three and looked every single day of it."[7]

Shortly after the first Moseley novel, *Miami Blues*, appeared in 1984, gruff
character actor Fred Ward bought the movie rights to the story. Within a few
years, he and producers Jonathan Demme and Gary Goetzman had pulled
together a deal with Orion Pictures, and the project was under way with Ward
cast as Moseley.

Demme was a graduate of the Roger Corman finishing school for filmmakers. Known as the king of B movies throughout the 1960s and 1970s, Corman
produced more than 350 films through his various production companies and
gave starts to a string of Hollywood heavyweights including Jack Nicholson,

Francis Coppola, Martin Scorsese, James Cameron, Peter Bogdanovich, Ron Howard, and Joe Dante. Demme had met George Armitage when they both worked for Corman and brought him on board to write and direct the Willeford novel.

Alec Baldwin, cast as Hoke's nemesis Junior Frenger, had worked with Demme two years earlier on *Married to the Mob*. At the time of *Miami Blues*, Baldwin was just establishing himself as a box-office draw, coming off a lauded performance in *The Hunt for Red October*. Jennifer Jason Leigh took the role of Susie Waggoner, a dim but earnest prostitute studying business at Miami-Dade Community College who falls for Junior, unaware of his murderous tendencies.

The film begins with Junior's noteworthy arrival in Miami. Immediately on disembarking from his plane, he walks off with a suitcase belonging to a mother and small child. As he makes his way out of the airport, he encounters a proselytizing Hare Krishna who introduces himself as Ravindra and earnestly asks, "What's your name?" Without breaking stride, Junior reaches over and snaps the man's fingers as he growls his obviously accurate answer, "Trouble."

Checking into a nearby hotel, Junior orders up a prostitute, Susie, who quickly succumbs to his unexpected charm and sensitivity. He then spends the morning at the mall, where he brutally beats a pickpocket and uses the spoils to buy a toy Uzi. With the machine gun, he holds up a corner drug dealer and carjacks a getaway vehicle, then meets Susie for lunch.

That evening at Susie's apartment, she introduces Junior to Japanese poetry as they work together on her English homework. Later, while Susie takes a bath, Junior composes an extemporaneous haiku as he burgles her neighbor's apartment.

> Breaking, entering
> The dark and lonely places
> Finding a big gun

He returns with the big gun, a coin collection, and a package of pork chops he's lifted from the refrigerator, hiding all but the pilfered meat from Susie.

Unfortunately for Junior, the victim of his airport assault has died of shock, and Moseley is put on the case. After a bit of legwork, he connects Junior to Susie and arrives at her apartment just in time for the pork chop dinner, beginning a witty, engrossing cat-and-mouse game between the two men that quickly turns personal. The next day, Junior shows up at Moseley's apartment, coldcocks him, and steals the detective's badge, gun, handcuffs, and false teeth.

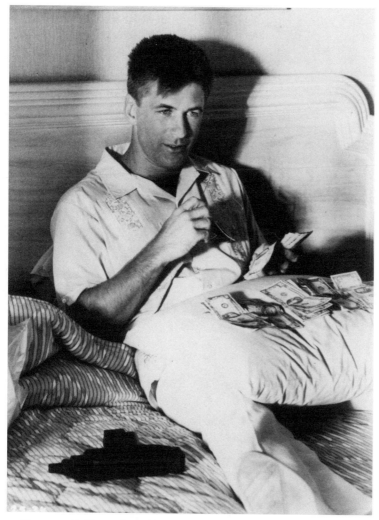

Figure 4.7. Publicity photo from *Miami Blues*. (Doll/Morrow Collection)

In a skewed version of the American dream, Junior and Susie set up house in a Coral Gables postcard cottage, complete with a white picket fence, red tiled roof, and flamingo pink columns on the front porch. There Junior lays out his vision of their life together: "I want to go to work every morning—sometimes at night—and come home to a clean house and a hot meal and a loving wife just like you." He does indeed leave the house each day, posing as a cop to more easily rob and brutalize his fellow petty criminals, and returns home to his loving woman, who bakes him vinegar pie and struggles mightily to believe his claim of being an investment counselor.

Figure 4.8. Publicity photo from *Miami Blues*. (Doll/Morrow Collection)

The film owes its success largely to its perfect assemblage of personnel, with spot-on performances from the major and supporting characters, a writer-director who truly grasped the soul of the genre, and strong work by cinematographer Tak Fujimoto, who brought a dark edge to the carefree pastels of Miami. Quirky, unpredictable, and rich in dark humor, *Miami Blues* perfectly captures the absurd and twisted characters, the wrenching violence, the pointed psychological insights, and the relentless social satire that make modern Florida crime writing so distinctive.

THE CREDITS

Released in 1990 by Orion Pictures
Produced by Jonathan Demme and Gary Goetzman
Directed by George Armitage
Screenplay by George Armitage
Cinematography by Tak Fujimoto
Edited by Craig McKay
Production design by Maher Ahmad
Music by Gary Chang
Set decoration by Don K. Ivey

THE CAST

Alec Baldwin	Frederick J. Frenger Jr.
Jennifer Jason Leigh	Susie Waggoner
Fred Ward	Sgt. Hoke Moseley
Obba Babatundé	Blink Willie
Charles Napier	Sgt. Bill Henderson
Nora Dunn	Ellita Sanchez
Bobo Lewis	Edna Damrosch
Edward Saxon	Ravindra

MOON OVER MIAMI

Miami: Where rich men are as plentiful as grapefruit and
millionaires hang from every palm tree.

—husband hunter Kay Latimer in *Moon Over Miami*

THE STORY

Kay and Barbara, two sisters from Texas, travel to Florida with their aunt, Susie,
who has just come into a small inheritance. The three use the money to stay at
the lavish Flamingo Hotel, where they hope to find millionaire husbands. Kay
masquerades as a wealthy heiress, with Barbara pretending to be her secretary
and Aunt Susie the maid. The ruse quickly attracts the attentions of a wealthy
playboy and his cynical pal.

THE FILM

Moon Over Miami captures a specific moment in Miami's history while at the
same time romanticizing it. A breezy musical in glossy Technicolor, the film
epitomizes the kind of romantic fantasy associated with this genre during the
Golden Age. Yet its story line derives from the real-life image that defined
Miami just before World War II. Viewing *Moon Over Miami* now is like a walk
back in time in more ways than one.

Released in June 1941, the film was a major musical for Twentieth Century–
Fox, as evidenced by the top-end cast, set design, costuming, and location
shooting. It starred Betty Grable in her first film with top billing. Fox was
grooming Grable to be its biggest female star because the studio's reigning
box-office queen, Alice Faye, was talking about retirement.

Grable had previously costarred in *Tin Pan Alley* with Faye and in *Down
Argentine Way* with Don Ameche, who was reteamed with her for *Moon Over
Miami*. The rest of the sparkling cast included Carole Landis as Grable's serious-
minded sister and a young Robert Cummings as the handsome second male
lead. Typical for major musicals of the era, character actors were cast in scene-
stealing roles that provided offbeat comedy and novelty. Charlotte Greenwood
costarred as down-to-earth Aunt Susie, Jack Haley played a worldly-wise bell
captain at the Flamingo Hotel, and a specialty act called the Condos Brothers
danced with incredible vigor and precision.

Fox musicals, which were generally shot in Technicolor, featured a palette of
bright secondary and tertiary colors, such as deep pinks, sky blues, sea greens,
and soft lavenders. The eye-catching candy colors created an optimistic fantasy
world where even night scenes were free of gloomy hues and gray shadows.

Figure 4.9. Poster for *Moon Over Miami*. (Doll/Morrow Collection)

Moon Over Miami was no exception. Costume designer Travis Banton worked closely with art directors Richard Day and Wiard Ihnen to create a Florida that exceeded every moviegoer's dream. As Betty Grable strolled into her hotel bungalow, her sky blue dress trimmed in white fur harmonized with the pale, smoky blue walls decorated with white bas-reliefs. And Carole Landis in her pale green dress provided just the right accent.

The girls' luxurious bungalow recalled Art Deco without exactly replicating it. The spacious rooms were furnished with white chairs and beds, with the windows dressed in rattan blinds. The bathroom featured a curved glass-brick wall, and a private patio was located just outside the bedroom. All of the bungalows encircled a terrace, where the men sang "You've Started Something" to the ladies as they danced around the reflecting pool or the sunken garden. The Flamingo Hotel seemed filled with beautiful women and handsome men who met each evening for cocktails and romance amid exotic tropical foliage under the bright Miami moon.

While the hotel in the film is largely a product of movie magic on a Hollywood soundstage, there actually was a Flamingo Hotel in Miami Beach. A montage of Miami locations near the beginning of the film includes a long shot of the real Flamingo and a close-up of its neon sign. Miami Beach's first grand hotel, the Flamingo was built in 1921 by Carl Fisher, who is credited with turning the mosquito-infested barrier island into one of America's premier winter resorts. Fisher, who was enchanted by flamingos, painted his grand hotel pink and decorated it with flamingo murals, but the hotel was most famous for its dome, which was illuminated at night with red, green, and gold lights. However unique and grand the actual Flamingo was, its rooms and suites looked nothing like their movie counterparts.

The studio sent a second unit to South Florida to shoot background footage for several scenes, though their goal was not authenticity or realism. Instead, the studio sought to evoke the image of Miami and Miami Beach (there's no distinction between them in the film) when it was considered a haven for the rich and elegant. The montage near the beginning includes not only the famous Flamingo Hotel but also shots of yachts and boats on Biscayne Bay, the beautiful hotels along the beachfront, and the Hialeah Park racetrack. Other scenes used background footage of water skiing and boat racing shot at Cypress Gardens, Rainbow Springs, and Silver Springs to depict South Florida as a rich playboy's playground.

Finding the perfect husband in Miami may have been a movie musical fantasy, but the notion of searching South Florida for millionaires to marry was certainly not far-fetched. The lifestyles of Miami and Miami Beach during the mid-1930s reflected a stateliness and romance that had replaced the crazy boom atmosphere of the 1920s, as the wealthy crowd continued to winter there. More than six hundred millionaires spent January through April in Miami Beach during the Depression, including the cream of the self-made industry barons—Elmer Maytag (washing machines), Mark Honeywell (thermometers), Leonard Florsheim (shoes), Warren Wright (Calumet baking soda). Old money also wintered in the area, including a few Vanderbilts and a couple of Astors.[8] The tropical atmosphere and elegant trappings gave Miami and Miami Beach the image of the perfect place for romance—an image propagated by the big magazines of the era, including *Life* and *Time*. Not surprisingly, Miami became the marriage and divorce capital of America by 1940.

Moon Over Miami captures a pre-WWII moment in American popular culture, presenting not only an example of a popular genre of the period but also an enhanced depiction of Miami's romantic image. At the end of the film, the characters express their joy at finding a new love and a new life by singing "Miami (Oh Me, Oh Mi-ami)," an ode to the town as America's Winter Playground. The film does not offer an accurate portrait of Miami, but instead paints the town the way moviegoers and prospective visitors imagined it to be.

THE CREDITS

Released in 1941 by Twentieth Century–Fox

Produced by Harry Joe Brown

Directed by Walter Lang

Written by George Seaton, Lynn Starling, Vincent Lawrence, and Brown Holmes, from the play *Three Blind Mice* by Stephen Powys.

Cinematography by Allen M. Davey, J. Peverell Marley, and Leon Shamroy

Edited by Walter Thompson

Art direction by Richard Day and Wiard Ihnen

Costume design by Travis Banton

Original music by Ralph Rainger; "Moon Over Miami" by Joseph Burke (uncredited)

THE CAST

Betty Grable	Kay Latimer
Don Ameche	Phil "Mac" McNeil
Robert Cummings	Jeff Boulton
Carole Landis	Barbara Latimer
Jack Haley	Jack O'Hara
Charlotte Greenwood	Aunt Susie Latimer
Cobina Wright	Connie Fentress

"Seminole"

Moon Over Miami is the kind of musical that fans of Hollywood's Golden Age feel nostalgic for because of its naïveté and innocence in comparison to today's grittier depictions of sex and violence. However, one song-and-dance number, titled "Seminole," reveals that the dark side of naïveté is ignorance. For this production number, a group of white dancers are dressed in colorful shirts and skirts that are exaggerated versions of garb associated with the Seminole Indians of the past. The male dancers also wear pageboy wigs with bangs to approximate the stereotype of a Native American haircut. The talented Condos Brothers come to the foreground and put on an amazing display of tap dancing in their fast, vigorous style—which, of course, has nothing to do with Seminole culture. The lyrics of the song "Seminole" include lines like "Heap big pow-wow" and "Hear that tom-tom talking" and other insulting clichés. The production number is a painful reminder of the Golden Age's abysmal record in depicting minorities and ethnic cultures.

SCARFACE

Nothing exceeds like excess.
—Elvira Montana in *Scarface*

THE STORY

Cuban thug Tony Montana arrives in the United States as part of the 1980 Freedom Flotilla and goes to work for a Miami drug kingpin. Obsessed with power and unburdened by compassion, Tony quickly rises in the organization and eventually takes his boss's business, his girlfriend, and his life. In the end, however, the brutal gangster's unquenchable ambition destroys his family and leads to his own violent death.

THE FILM

The closing credits of *Scarface* offer a dedication to Howard Hawks and Ben Hecht, director and writer of the original 1932 version of the film starring Paul Muni. Popular critics of the day universally despised the remake for its extreme violence and over-the-top performances, and many took particular umbrage at the nod given to the classic early gangster film. One reviewer called the dedication the most specious gesture in film history.

In many ways, however, the dedication could not have been more appropriate. The 1983 morality tale of the rise and fall of a vicious gangster parallels the original film on a number of levels. The plots are virtually identical, with each telling the story of a brutal immigrant criminal with an obsessive lust for power, a proclivity for violence, and an unnatural affection for his sister. The character's drive propels him to the top of the illicit substance trade but ultimately leads to his downfall. Both films feature a riveting but monstrous protagonist that broke ground as a brutal and sobering portrait of a contemporary gangster. Both films faced significant censorship battles that held up their release, and both were harshly criticized for their extreme depictions of violence. Finally, both films were created through close collaboration between writer, director, and producer, who based their vision on accounts of the underworld provided by criminals and law enforcement personnel of the day.

The two films also share a thematic caution against letting ambition override ethics and the social order, but the remake more overtly sends that message as a critique of American capitalism. The new Scarface, Cuban immigrant Tony Montana, is as much a businessman as a thug. In setting aside any notion of morality or humanity in his furious rise to the top of the cocaine trade, he sets himself up to be isolated and unfulfilled once his goal is attained.

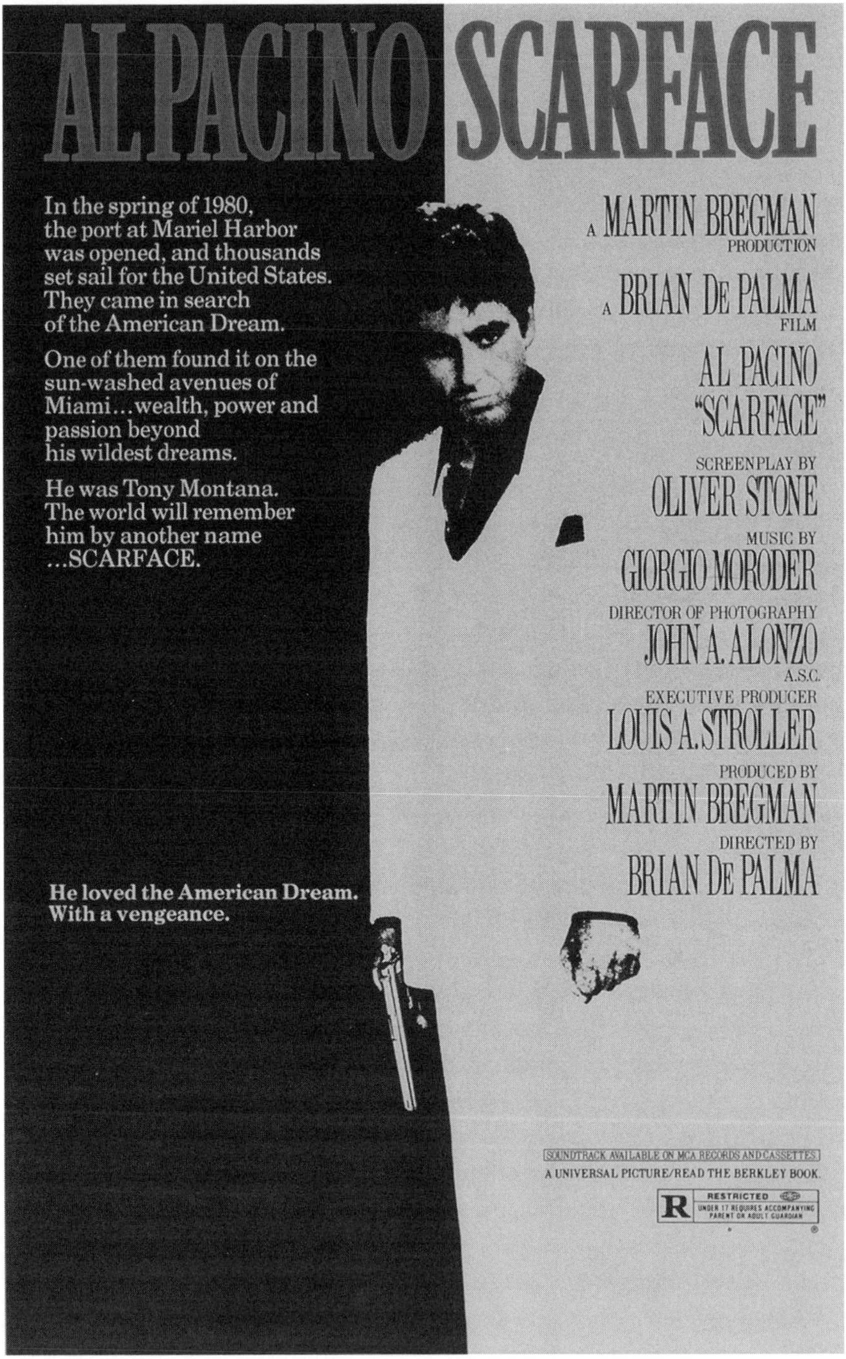

Figure 4.10. Poster for *Scarface*. (Doll/Morrow Collection)

Figure 4.11. *Scarface* director Brian De Palma. (Doll/Morrow Collection)

Tony's success seems to occur almost instantaneously, with very little shown of the day-to-day operations of his business. It takes only a few scenes for him to go from wearing a dishwasher's apron in a sandwich shop to wearing five-hundred-dollar suits in a chic Miami nightclub. After he eliminates his boss, a brief montage sequence shows him consolidating his empire, gathering almost unimaginable amounts of money, and squandering it all on a lavish lifestyle. In the film, cocaine becomes a sort of alchemist's dream, a corrupting philosopher's stone that magically transforms what Tony has—nothing—into what he desires—everything. For Tony, power equals money, which equals cocaine, which equals power. It's no surprise, then, that he violates one of the primary rules of his business: "Don't get high on your own supply." Given his mindless addiction to power, he could do nothing other than become addicted to cocaine, and in the end his addictions lead to his downfall as surely as they led to his success.

Over the course of his rise and fall, Tony debases the dream of capitalism by making it an end in itself. In the film, Miami comes to represent an equally debased land of opportunity, where the drug dealers' conquest of the city and its riches renders them both meaningless. This notion is reinforced visually by the film's depictions of the cityscape. An early scene opens with a breathtaking view of the Miami skyline, but the camera pulls back to reveal that the image is simply a tourism ad on a billboard. Similarly, Tony's boss has a garish mural of the Miami beachfront in his office. A silhouette of tropical foliage against a shrieking sunset of red and orange, the mural simultaneously renders the tropical paradise unattractive and turns it into a possession that can be mounted on a wall. Such scenes represent the characters' attempts to objectify and commodify the city itself. This idea is expressed more obviously early in the film when Tony crudely equates Miami to an attractive woman waiting to be sexually conquered.

Though the Miami setting is prominent and critical to the film's story line, very little of *Scarface* was actually shot in Florida. When the filmmakers arrived in Miami in the fall of 1982, they were greeted with stiff opposition from the city's influential Cuban community. Concerned over the film's negative depiction of Cuban immigrants, they used political and business connections to impede the production and pressured the filmmakers to make changes to the script.[9] The crew quickly retreated to California and filmed most of the movie in Los Angeles and Santa Barbara. They returned to Florida for two weeks in the spring of 1983 to shoot exteriors and a handful of key scenes. Among them was one of the most notorious moments in the film, a harrowing chainsaw murder set in Miami's Art Deco district at the Sunray Motel on Ocean Drive. The bloody scene was commonly cited by detractors as an example of the film's excessive violence.

Such criticisms were nothing new to director Brian De Palma, who had weathered storms over *Carrie* and *Dressed to Kill* and would face even greater controversy over the highly sexualized violence in his next film, *Body Double*. Though known for pushing the limits of decorum in his films, De Palma may have outdone himself with the almost operatic scope of *Scarface*. But the excesses of the film—the sets, the performances, the language, the violence—are clearly not without purpose. They serve as a reflection of Tony's own excesses and thereby reinforce the themes of the film.

THE CREDITS

Released in 1983 by Universal Pictures
Produced by Martin Bregman
Directed by Brian De Palma
Written by Oliver Stone
Cinematography by John A. Alonzo
Edited by Gerald B. Greenburg and David Ray
Production design by Ferdinando Scarfiotti

THE CAST

Al Pacino	Tony Montana
Steven Bauer	Manny
Michelle Pfeiffer	Elvira
Mary Elizabeth Mastrantonio	Gina
Robert Loggia	Frank Lopez
Miriam Colon	Mama Montana
F. Murray Abraham	Omar

Any Given Sunday

Three of the key contributors to *Scarface*—Oliver Stone, Al Pacino, and the city of Miami—reunited in the late 1990s for a behind-the-scenes tale of professional football. Stone, who scripted *Scarface* and collaborated on the set with director Brian De Palma, cowrote and directed *Any Given Sunday*, which chronicles an intense, high-stakes half season of the fictional Miami Sharks football team. As with all of Stone's films, *Any Given Sunday* offers a biting commentary on modern America, addressing such topics as celebrity, the media, big business, and the erosion of idealism. Pacino stars as the veteran Sharks coach, a believer in teamwork and winning or losing with honor, who finds himself fighting a losing battle against a dollar-focused new owner and a hotshot young quarterback more concerned with his own rising star than with the fortunes of the team. Scenes were shot in a number of Florida locations, including the Orange Bowl and Pro Player Stadium.

TONY ROME

Sinatra went all rugged and pessimistic for *Tony Rome* . . . and a sequel, *Lady in Cement,* both of which benefitted from Sinatra's world-weary cynicism. He didn't have to persuade us that he'd seen too much. We knew it.

—Jay Stone, *Ottawa Citizen*

THE STORY

Private detective Tony Rome is drawn into a case revolving around the nouveau riche Kosterman family. Rudy Kosterman hires Rome to uncover why his spoiled daughter, Diana, was found drunk in a seedy hotel; Diana wants Tony to find her missing diamond pin; and Mrs. Kosterman pays him to tell her everything first.

THE FILM

Tony Rome and its sequel, *Lady in Cement,* originated as vehicles for star Frank Sinatra. Taking advantage of Sinatra's ultrahip Rat Pack persona, the filmmakers shaped the character into a cool but cynical private eye. In the tradition of other hard-boiled detectives such as Sam Spade and Mike Hammer, Tony Rome is a weary loner who freely moves through all strata of society when working a case. This narrative strategy generally reveals that the members of the upper crust are just as immoral, indecent, and greedy as the criminal low-lifes. In *Tony Rome*, the wealthy and their criminal counterparts are more sordid and brutal than their 1940s predecessors, prompting many reviewers to protest the crudeness of the dissolute characters. Repeated comparisons to Bogart and his film noir classics did little to elevate the reviewers' opinions of either Tony Rome film.

While the character Tony Rome owes something to the hard-boiled detective of pulp fiction and film noir, the movie lacks the dark visual style that defines the noir genre. Director Gordon Douglas, who had been in the movie business since childhood, was known for his technical proficiency but was not interested in expressing any personal style or vision. Hired to direct quickly and efficiently, Douglas understood the film was a Sinatra vehicle and little more. As such, *Tony Rome* is full of in-jokes, Sinatra cronies, and sixties-era beauties.

Though the film did not feature the Rat Pack's A-list, a few of Sinatra's close friends and members of his entourage do appear. Richard Conte, a well-respected character actor who had also been in *Ocean's 11*, costars as Lt. Dave Santini; former boxer Rocky Graziano, who was part of Sinatra's entourage in the 1960s, has a bit role as Packy the necktie vendor; and longtime friend Jilly Rizzo, who served as a sort of majordomo for the singer, pops up in one scene as a card player. Tiffany Bolling, who began dating Sinatra during the film's production, appears in a bit role as a nightclub photo girl. And, in an in-joke funny only to Hollywood insiders, Michael "Princey" Romanoff plays Sal, the maitre d' of a high-class restaurant. During Hollywood's Golden Age, Romanoff had run a restaurant in Los Angeles where the biggest movie stars regularly dined. Finally, Frank's daughter Nancy Sinatra sings the film's pop-flavored title tune.

Perhaps Sinatra's most effective costar in *Tony Rome* was the city of Miami, which was his kind of town during the 1960s. Sinatra often retreated to Miami to relax and recoup from his turbulent private life, and it seemed convenient and natural to shoot the film there in the spring of 1967. The location shooting proved to be the film's greatest strength, offering a perfect blend of material and milieu to make up for the lack of visual style and depth of character. In the film, shady characters blend into the shadows of seedy hotels while the city's nouveaux riches flaunt their wealth in the sunny mansions of Miami. The two sides of the social spectrum meet in the fast lane of drugs, sex, and parties.

A variety of actual Miami locales illustrate the different rungs of the social ladder—from the magnificence of Vizcaya, the mansion once owned by robber baron James Deering, to the run-down motels of Miami Beach, which was ex-

Figure 4.12. *Tony Rome* star Frank Sinatra with his daughter Nancy, who sang the title song. (Doll/Morrow Collection)

periencing a decline during the late 1960s. As the case unfolds, characters meet at the Sip 'n Sup on the 79th Street Causeway, the famed Fontainebleau Hotel, the Double Deck Turf Bar at the intersection of NW 79th and 7th Avenue, and the old Hotel Dolphin. Throughout the course of his investigation, Tony Rome remains above it all, deliberately eschewing any permanent ties to a specific social class, group, or family. His outsider status is underscored by his choice of residence—a boat called the *Straight Pass* anchored at the Crandon Park Marina on Key Biscayne.

Tony Rome may have called the *Straight Pass* home, but whenever Frank Sinatra was in Miami he was a virtual fixture at the Fontainebleau Hotel. The Fontainebleau, which opened in 1954, was the first big hotel to be built on Collins Avenue in Miami Beach. It had been designed by New York architect Morris Lapidus to represent the opulence and decadence of the 1950s (see *The Bellboy*, chapter 7). Though still in fine shape, the Fontainebleau had lost its allure by the late 1960s as the times changed and tourists flocked to other parts of Florida. While Sinatra was shooting both *Tony Rome* and *Lady in Cement*, he and his entire entourage stayed at the "Bloo," as he called it, and in the evenings he performed in the hotel's Club Tropigala. Sinatra felt so at home at the Bloo that he sometimes cooked pasta and marinara sauce in the hotel's kitchen after hours.

The familiarity of the Bloo must have seemed like a retreat for Sinatra, who was experiencing a low point in his life and career. His marriage to Mia Farrow broke up during the production of *Tony Rome*, and his acting career had grown stale. As a new era of directors began using cinema as a medium of personal expression and new actors emerged to play in those films, Sinatra was stuck in the past, preferring to appear in vehicles tailored to his image. On the surface, *Tony Rome* seems to reflect the swinging 1960s, with its pop sound track and references to drugs, free love, and homosexuality, but other films released that year, such as *Bonnie and Clyde*, *Cool Hand Luke*, and *The Graduate*, clearly reveal the hand of new talents taking American cinema in new directions. When viewed today, those classics are timeless, while *Tony Rome* is dated and even crass.

Like Sinatra, Miami was going out of style by the late 1960s. The year *Tony Rome* was shot, the last new luxury hotel, a Hilton, was built on Miami Beach. The area had ruined itself by overbuilding, making the key attraction—the beachfront—impassible. Also, the opulent, materialistic lifestyle signified by hotel life on Miami Beach had gone out of fashion. During the 1970s, tourism declined steadily, and the run-down South Beach area was inhabited by retirees on fixed incomes.

Luckily, the fortunes of both Frank Sinatra and Miami Beach changed. By the 1990s, Sinatra had become a living legend, and Miami Beach had been revitalized by the restoration of South Beach's Art Deco district. But back in 1967, *Tony Rome*'s depiction of decay and decline in Miami and Miami Beach was authentic, and the world-weary look on Sinatra's face was much more than acting.

THE CREDITS	THE CAST	
Released in 1967 by Twentieth Century–Fox	Frank Sinatra	Tony Rome
Produced by Aaron Rosenberg	Jill St. John	Ann Archer
Directed by Gordon Douglas	Richard Conte	Lt. Dave Santini
Written by Richard Breen, from the novel by	Simon Oakland	Rudy Kosterman
Marvin H. Albert	Gena Rowlands	Rita Kosterman
Cinematography by Joseph Biroc	Sue Lyon	Diana
Edited by Robert Simpson	Shecky Greene	Catleg
Music by Billy May; title song by Lee Hazlewood,		
sung by Nancy Sinatra		

THE MOVIE TOURIST'S GUIDE TO STARRING MIAMI

Miami has been synonymous with glamour and glitz since the 1920s when America's nouveaux riches first settled there. Over the years, the face of the city has changed but its lively beat has not. Many Hollywood films have been set in Miami, capturing the city's unique flavor at different points in time.

THE BIRDCAGE

South Beach

Tourists should explore the now-famous Art Deco district of Miami Beach by walking in order to get a true appreciation for the details that make this architectural style distinctive. The district includes more than four hundred buildings in the Deco style and covers about one square mile, from the Atlantic Ocean westward to Lenox Court and from 5th Street down to 23rd. The Miami Design Preservation League offers guided walking tours twice a week for those interested in more than just a casual glance.

Movie tourists will want to linger at the Carlyle on Ocean Drive, a hotel-turned-condo where scenes from *The Birdcage* were shot, as were two episodes of *Miami Vice*. In 1959 the hotel sued the production company responsible for *A Hole in the Head*, claiming that the film's shooting next door at the Cardozo (see below) interfered with its business.

FLIPPER

The Dolphin Research Center

Santini's Porpoise School has long been closed, but the site is now part of the Dolphin Research Center, a nonprofit organization devoted to education and research. Located on Grassy Key along U.S. Highway 1, the Center offers tours and a variety of dolphin encounters. The original Flipper, Mitzie the dolphin, is buried on the grounds and commemorated with a statue and a marker.

A HOLE IN THE HEAD

The Cardozo Hotel

The Cardozo Hotel in Miami stood in for Tony Manetti's failing Garden of Eden Hotel in *A Hole in the Head*. Today the Cardozo is owned and operated by Latin pop star Gloria Estefan and her husband. Located on 13th Street off Collins Avenue in the heart of the South Beach Art Deco district, the Cardozo offers forty-three rooms and convenient access to the beach and Miami's nightlife. The hotel restaurant is also one of the neighborhood's more popular eateries.

Flagler Dog Track and Entertainment Center

Racing fans have been laying down bets for decades at the Flagler Dog Track, one of Florida's best-known greyhound venues. The dogs run from June through November, and Flagler also offers a casino-style poker room in its sprawling facility just off the Miami Airport Expressway between 37th and 42nd Avenues. The track proved unlucky for Frank Sinatra's character; trying to impress a prospective investor, he bets and loses the $5,000 he needs to stave off a bank foreclosure, only to have the moneyman scoff at his business proposal.

MIAMI BLUES

Big Fish Restaurant

Shortly after stealing Hoke Moseley's badge, Junior Frenger witnesses a knife-point holdup on the patio of a waterfront restaurant. After pumping a slug into the perpetrator's knee, he shouts out, "Police! Stop or I'll shoot!" and then bolts from the scene, much to the amazement of the patrons and staff. The scene was shot at Big Fish Restaurant, located on the south shore of the Miami River at SE 5th Street, just off South Miami Avenue. Known for its simple seafood menu, large portions, and distinctive ambience, Big Fish is a favorite of locals and the occasional visiting celebrity.

SCARFACE

Johnny Rockets

The infamous chainsaw murder in *Scarface* was set in the Sun Ray Apartments at 728 Ocean Drive. The building has since been converted to office space, with a Johnny Rockets diner on the ground floor. Visitors can enjoy the chain's famous burgers and tabletop jukeboxes just steps away from one of the most controversial scenes in film history.

TONY ROME

Vizcaya

This beautiful mansion was the winter residence of industrialist James Deering from 1916 to 1925. Deering was vice president of International Harvester and quite wealthy. Vizcaya consisted of a thirty-four-room Italianate mansion, a series of beautiful gardens, livestock, and a variety of service facilities. It was designed to allow the free flow of breezes through the courtyard into the open house. Today Vizcaya is a museum filled with art and furnishings, plus ten acres of well-tended gardens and a historic village that the museum is in the process of restoring. Though it is no longer an open-air structure, the house and grounds are open to the public. Vizcaya is located on South Miami Avenue along Biscayne Bay.

FLORIDA BUST

While the show may be lousy, the story of the
show, and why it flopped, is always compelling.
—critic Michael Riedel, quoted by *Slate*'s Dana Stevens

All studios, all directors, all actors suffer through their share of unsuccessful films. Some flops are well-intentioned artistic efforts that fail to reach their potential or find an audience. Others are victims of timing, and still others are slapdash efforts meant to fulfill a contract or make a quick buck. A glance at Florida films reveals that this unpleasant reality of the movie business extends to film locations as well.

While a great many Florida films are stellar examples of financial and artistic accomplishment, the state has served as a backdrop for a number of undeniable failures. Some of these are poor-quality films designed to draw audiences through prurient, lurid subject matter, or genre pieces that banked on the steady viewing habits of fans. Others are sequels conceived and led by studio executives who believed that the title would guarantee a return regardless of how ill-conceived or ill-executed the actual film was. A few are legitimate efforts by talented filmmakers and performers that fell short of their potential for one reason or another.

All these films, however, reveal the peculiar relationship between finance and art that drives the American film industry. One primary rule of this relationship is that cost and artistic accomplishment are not necessarily related. Compare, for example, the meager six-figure budget of *Ruby in Paradise* (see chapter 8) to the $23 million spent on *Bad Boys* (see chapter 7).[1] *Ruby* was generally touted as a thoughtful, expressive work of art, while *Bad Boys* was widely derided for its pointless violence, inane story, and choppy direction and editing. While both films eventually turned a profit, *Bad Boys* was declared a major hit since its box-office returns were more than double the cost of the film. As a result, stars Will Smith and Martin Lawrence and first-time director Michael Bay instantly gained heavyweight status in the industry. Victor Nunez, writer and director of *Ruby*, went on to make several other successful films, but each of his independent productions required extensive wheeling and dealing to scrape together adequate funding. As these two examples demonstrate, a film's ability to influence both audiences and filmmakers is often determined by its financial success, at least in the short term, and not by its artistic accomplishment—or lack thereof. In Hollywood, as in all businesses, the accountant's balance sheet ultimately rules.

This chapter presents a collection of Florida films that in one way or another touch on the tension between business and artistry. Some of the films are clearly regarded as flops. Robert Altman's *Health*, for example, involved a talented ensemble cast and a respected director combining to create a flawed but distinctive film with a clear point of view. Studio politics led to the film being shelved and finally given a limited release, where it performed poorly and then slipped into obscurity. *Brenda Starr* was a big-budget vanity project financed by an Arabian sheik whose primary interest was in capturing a personal whim on film. The result was an imaginative but uneven effort tangled in a web of legal issues that ultimately cast an insurmountable pall over it in the press.

Smokey and the Bandit, Part 3 provides an example of filmmakers attempting to wring one too many titles out of a successful concept. While the original *Smokey* was a sharply directed, pulse-quickening romp, the final sequel assembled an inferior cast and creative team and stretched a thin premise beyond believability. With only $5.5 million in ticket sales,[2] the film likely didn't even recoup the costs of its derivative stunt sequences.

Other Florida failures include *The Cape Canaveral Monsters* and *The Fat Spy.* These obscure low-budget productions represent amateurish efforts to capitalize on established movie genres and pop culture phenomena. Such films typically relied on aggressive, sensationalized marketing campaigns to draw a targeted, often youthful audience into the theaters and drive-ins just long enough to turn a profit.

Not all the films included here were failures, however. The independent production *Blood Feast* generated a whopping $4 million on a budget of less than $25,000, an almost unheard-of return of 16,000 percent.[3] It also created an entire genre, the gore film, and influenced the depiction of violence in more mainstream movies. All this from a film that was thrown together in a few weeks with complete disregard for any technical or artistic sensibility whatsoever.

Taken together, these films illustrate that no movie endeavor is immune from either success or failure and that no industry executive, no matter how experienced or shrewd, can predict what combination of talent, timing, marketing, and luck will produce the next major hit or the next colossal flop.

BLOOD FEAST

Two words you'd never hear on our set were "Take two."
—goremeister Herschell Gordon Lewis to
interviewer Sandra Bernhard

THE STORY

As a small Florida town reels from a series of mutilation murders, Dorothy Fremont plans a birthday celebration for her daughter Suzette. Indulging Suzette's interest in Egyptology, she hires caterer Fuad Ramses to prepare an Egyptian feast. Fuad, however, turns out to be the fiend, and he plans to make Suzette the final victim in a cannibalistic ritual that will resurrect an ancient evil goddess. Suzette's suitor, detective Pete Thornton, finally connects Fuad to the killings on the night of the party.

THE FILM

The early 1960s brought tremendous change to the American film industry. The machinelike studio system, where industry bigwigs determined every aspect of a film from the script, costumes, and stars to the promotion and distribution, was all but over. With its demise went the studios' iron grip over content. The system began to weaken in 1948 when the U.S. Supreme Court ruled that the major Hollywood studios constituted a monopoly and ordered them to divest ownership of their theaters. With exhibition no longer controlled by the big studios, anyone with a print had a shot at getting their title on a marquee. Some well-financed, well-connected independents like Burt Lancaster's production company were able to muscle their way into the market with quality offerings such as *Marty* and *The Sweet Smell of Success*. However, a great many would-be filmmakers had neither the resources nor the talent to go toe-to-toe with slick Hollywood offerings.

It took a second Supreme Court ruling—a 1952 case that formally extended the constitutional right of free speech to films—to open the floodgates. With prior censorship of film content all but ended, many independent production companies found their niche by embracing taboo subject matter that the studios would never touch and exhibiting at drive-ins and other second-tier theaters. The exploitation film was born.

Pioneers like low-budget legend Ed Wood churned out genre hybrids (combining horror with sci-fi, for example) and the occasional drama on a titillating topic, such as the anguished transvestite's tale *Glen or Glenda*. Soon, bolder exploiters were releasing "documentaries" that explored the many facets of life in nudist colonies, and then came the overtly contrived flesh flicks such as Russ Meyer's *The Immoral Mr. Teas* and Doris Wishman's *Nude on the Moon* (shot partly in Coral Gables, Florida).

Herschell Gordon Lewis dabbled in similar "nudie cuties" for his first films, but in 1963 this former literature professor and part-time advertising executive changed the face of American film when he decided that the key to success lay in a four-letter word—gore. In Miami after finishing a work-for-hire film, Lewis and his partner David Friedman were brainstorming at the Suez Hotel while the crew waited for them to finalize the details of their next venture. Inspired by the Egyptian décor of the hotel, where much of the shooting was to take place, they concocted *Blood Feast*, the story of crazed caterer and cultic cannibal Fuad Ramses.

Completed on a budget of $25,000, the film suffered from the lowest of production values, with poor acting, uneven lighting, and cheap sets. But it also had gore such as had never been seen in American theaters before, and, as Lewis predicted, that was enough. Previous films had taken American audiences to the edge of propriety—the lurid offerings of Britain's Hammer Studios, the rotting corpses of Italian director Mario Bava, and even Hollywood's own *Psycho*. The graphic mutilations of *Blood Feast*, however, went far beyond the pale—a crudely hacked limb, a brain removed, a tongue ripped out, and, per-

Figure 5.1. *Blood Feast* producer David Friedman *(right)*. (Doll/Morrow Collection)

haps worst of all, Fuad greedily handling his prized morsels. Theater owners balked, community groups picketed, Hollywood clucked and scolded, but a youthful audience streamed to the drive-ins and provided a colossal seven-figure return on the struggling company's meager investment.

The following year, Lewis and Friedman completed their next shocker, inspired by, of all things, the fantasy musical *Brigadoon*. Filmed in St. Cloud, Florida, which ironically would be annexed by the Disney company in a few years as the site of its fabled family theme park, *Two Thousand Maniacs!* features a phantom Southern town that reappears after a hundred years to exact gruesome vengeance for a Civil War atrocity on a group of vacationing Yankees. Between them, these two films presented what would become staple elements of later slasher films: a rural or isolated setting and nubile female victims engaged in promiscuous or provocative behavior. Lewis completed what is now sometimes called the *Blood Trilogy* with 1965's *Color Me Blood Red*. Shot in Sarasota, this film follows the crimes of a tortured painter who decides to work in a more visceral medium.

Lewis's successes spawned a host of gory imitators. Audiences grew, budgets increased, and production values improved, and an indirect path can be traced from his work to *Night of the Living Dead*, *The Texas Chainsaw Massacre*, *Halloween*, *Friday the 13th*, and *Nightmare on Elm Street*. Along the way, mainstream films gradually ratcheted up their level of graphic violence—*Bonnie and Clyde*, *The Wild Bunch*, *The Godfather*, *The Exorcist*, and the recent films *Seven* and even *The Passion of the Christ*. No one will argue that Lewis made any artistic or technical contributions to cinema, but today he is universally acknowledged for having shattered a barrier that mainstream audiences and filmmakers cautiously, tentatively followed him across.

Lewis continued making films through the early 1970s, alternating between sexploitation, gore, and raucous moonshiner tales. Recognizing that Hollywood's embrace of more graphic content had atrophied the exploitation market, he turned his full attention to the advertising game and became a pioneer of direct marketing. Well respected in this industry, he wrote two dozen books and became a must-read author for all serious students of business and marketing. If not for the *Blood Trilogy*, his work as a filmmaker might well have been forgotten. Over time, though, cult movie fans and magazines adopted him as a favorite son, and his name began to appear regularly in scholarly film journals. Eventually the increasing recognition lured him back behind the camera in 2002 to create *Blood Feast 2: All U Can Eat* for DVD release, a tongue-in-cheek homage to his earlier work.

THE CREDITS	THE CAST	
Released in 1963	William Kerwin	Detective Pete Thornton
Produced by Herschell Gordon Lewis,	Mal Arnold	Fuad Ramses
David F. Friedman, and Stanford S. Kohlberg	Connie Mason	Suzette Fremont
Directed by Herschell Gordon Lewis	Lyn Bolton	Mrs. Dorothy Fremont
Written by Allison Louise Downe	Scott H. Hall	Frank, police captain
Story by Herschell Gordon Lewis and	Toni Calvert	Trudy Sanders
David F. Friedman	Ashlyn Martin	Marcy, girl on beach
Cinematography by Herschell Gordon Lewis	Astrid Olson	Motel victim
Edited by Frank Romolo and Robert Sinise	Sandra Sinclair	Pat Tracey
Original music by Herschell Gordon Lewis	David F. Friedman	Drunken husband
Sound recording by David F. Friedman	(uncredited)	
Special effects by Herschell Gordon Lewis	Herschell Gordon Lewis	Radio announcer
	(uncredited voice-over)	

BRENDA STARR

[The sheik] is prepared to keep the film on the shelf and watch it in the desert on Saturday nights if he doesn't get the distribution deal he wants.
—spokesperson for Abdul Aziz al-Ibrahim, to the *Sunday Mail*'s Gordon G

Who in their right mind would hire attorneys to battle over this?
—critic David Kronke, *Atlanta Journal and Constitution*

THE STORY

Ace reporter Brenda Starr, of comic strip fame, sets off on a whirlwind global adventure to track down a secret fuel formula and save her faltering newspaper with the scoop. To complicate matters, she has a falling-out with the artist who draws her, and he pens himself into the strip hoping to patch things up.

THE FILM

Brenda Starr has brought intrigue, excitement, and romance to America's funny papers since 1940. Along the way, the comely red-headed reporter has squared off against villains ranging from underworld bosses and shady businessmen to crooked politicians and international spies. Along with this fanciful entertainment, creator Dalia Messick, who adopted the pen name Dale to hide her gender, delivered a smart, professional, and idealistic female protagonist to generations of Americans. Though publisher Joseph M. Patterson had reservations about the concept, *Brenda Starr, Reporter* quickly became one of the Chicago Tribune Syndicate's most popular comics. Just two years after the strip's debut, tales of Brenda's exploits were eagerly sought by American servicemen overseas during the war. One report claimed that in the midst of the bloody campaign on Guadalcanal, news that the saucy journalist might wed caused a minor uproar among American soldiers on the South Pacific island.[4] At the peak of its popularity, the strip appeared in 250 papers with an estimated readership of 60 million.

Over the years, Brenda has stepped out of the newspapers and into other media several times. A few stand-alone comic books of her adventures have been produced, as was a series of collectible dolls, and her visage appeared on a commemorative postage stamp in 1995. The character also appeared in a 1945 movie serial and in a 1976 made-for-television film with Jill St. John. But Brenda's most infamous incarnation was undoubtedly in the feature film starring Brooke Shields in the title role with Timothy Dalton as her mysterious

Figure 5.2. DVD case from *Brenda Starr*.
(Doll/Morrow Collection)

one-eyed paramour, Basil St. John. The story of the film's production contains elements so outlandish they might have come from Messick's strip itself: an infatuated Arabian financier, contentious legal battles over distribution rights, and the largest criminal fraud scandal of the twentieth century.

The tale begins with Shields aggressively pursuing the role with producer Myron Hyman, in the hope that it would transform her image from the provocative Lolita established in Calvin Klein ads and the film *Pretty Baby* to that of a capable adult leading lady. The media ingenue had at the same time caught the interest of billionaire businessman Sheik Abdul Aziz al-Ibrahim, brother-in-law of King Fahd of Saudi Arabia. The sheik had established residence in the United States and pursued a lavish personal and professional lifestyle, renting entire floors of hotels and engaging in multimillion-dollar real estate deals that frequently ended up in contentious litigation. After several attempts, the infatuated sheik arranged a meeting with Shields in Las Vegas, reportedly mediated by singer Paul Anka. Shortly thereafter she was able to finalize a deal with Hyman by bringing the sheik in as the sole funder of the film.[5]

Shooting began in the summer of 1986 in Florida, with Jacksonville and its environs standing in for New York City and the Amazon jungle, and a distribution deal was arranged with New World Pictures. However, as preparations proceeded for the film's debut the following year, various legal difficulties kept pushing the date back. Shields's representatives took issue with the billing and felt the film needed another round of editing before release. New World learned that Mystery Man Productions, a corporation formed by the sheik for the sole purpose of funding the film, had failed to secure television rights from the strip's copyright holders; for New World, this was a key part of the deal, as it hedged their bet against a poor performance in theaters. Suits and counter-suits followed, and then New World was sold, further complicating the tangled legal situation. Somewhere along the line, the film received an overseas release in countries such as Zambia, Norway, and Colombia, where it did well at the box office. By 1991 the rights issues were finally resolved to all parties' satisfaction, and an American release was planned. Then the international criminal investigation began.

Abdul Aziz al-Ibrahim had financed the film through a partnership with the Bank of Credit and Commerce International (BCCI), a well-connected but secretive financial institution that operated in some seventy-five countries. The sheik had previous ties to the bank through other business interests, and a significant portion of the film's estimated $20-million budget came from BCCI. In 1990 one of the bank's many accounting firms reported a nine-figure discrepancy in its books, and ongoing business deals involving the bank—including *Brenda Starr*—were frozen. Ensuing investigations by governments and auditing firms around the world revealed that BCCI had been involved in fraudulent purchases of businesses and properties, illegal immigration, money laundering for drug traffickers and terrorists, bribery, and the illicit sale of arms and nuclear technology. Much of its $25 billion in paper assets was simply unaccounted for. In the end, BCCI was labeled a bewilderingly corrupt operation and was closed, leaving behind numerous unanswered questions. The investment in the film was ultimately deemed legitimate, however, and *Brenda Starr* was finally given a limited West Coast release in April 1992. Box office statistics indicate the film drew about forty patrons per theater per day, or fewer than ten viewers per showing. [6]

Critically, the film fared no better than it did financially. It was panned for having a ludicrous story, uninspired performances, flat direction, and shoddy production values. While *Brenda Starr* is flawed, this criticism seems overly harsh and was probably prompted by the taint of the film's bizarre behind-the-scenes machinations and by a general disdain for the notion of Shields as a serious actress. In fact, Shields's performance showed glimpses of the comic wit that would blossom in her 1990s sitcom *Suddenly Susan*. The script deserves credit for the clever ways it reflects the story's origins, such as having the strip's artist jump into the action, having Brenda use her purse as a grappling hook, or having her make good an escape with the aid of her cosmetics kit. The set design and special effects do an admirable job of creating a comic strip feel as well, especially in the opening scenes. Also noteworthy are the 1940s-era costumes designed for Shields by Bob Mackie, a visual treat that honors the signature fashions penned by Messick in the strip for four decades.

THE CREDITS	THE CAST	
Released in 1992 by Triumph Releasing Corporation	Brooke Shields	Brenda Starr
Produced by Myron A. Hyman	Timothy Dalton	Basil St. John
Directed by Robert Ellis Miller	Tony Peck	Mike Randall
Written by Noreen Stone and James D. Buchanan	Diana Scarwid	Libby "Lips" Lipscomb
Music by Johnny Mandel	Nestor Serrano	Jose
Cinematography by Freddie Francis	Jeffrey Tambor	Vladimir
Edited by Mark Melnick	June Gable	Luba
Production Design by John J. Lloyd	Charles Durning	Francis I. Livright
Costumes for Brooke Shields by Bob Mackie	Kathleen Wilhoite	Hank O'Hare
	Eddie Albert	Police Chief Maloney
	Henry Gibson	Professor Gerhardt Von Kreutzer
	Ed Nelson	President Harry S. Truman

THE CAPE CANAVERAL MONSTERS

Fizzles out on the launch pad.
—John Stanley, *The Creature Features Movie Guide*

THE STORY

A pair of aliens in human form impede America's budding space program by shooting down rockets as they are launched from Cape Canaveral. NASA's leaders attribute the failures to mechanical error or design flaws, but one young scientist remains suspicious. He and his girlfriend uncover and foil the saboteurs, who teleport back to their own planet. In a surprisingly dark final twist, the last moments of the film show the aliens returning and apparently inhabiting the bodies of the heroes.

The 1950s launched a boom in independent filmmaking in America, largely as a result of court rulings that loosened the major studios' stranglehold over the industry (see *Blood Feast*, above). Many creative and technical film professionals took advantage of this opportunity to form independent production companies that produced films on a par with Hollywood's best fare. The changes in the industry also opened the door to a spate of film entrepreneurs who were less artistic, less skilled, and less solidly funded. Undoubtedly the best known of these latter figures was Ed Wood, the writer, director, and producer of such universally derided films as *Necromania: A Tale of Weird Love* and *Plan 9 from Outer Space*. While Wood's films are maligned for their poor production values and unprofessional acting, he eventually earned posthumous respect for his determination and his sincere love of moviemaking, a notion greatly fostered by director Tim Burton's homage film *Ed Wood*, starring Johnny Depp.

Phil Tucker was a contemporary of Wood who suffered equally scathing criticism for his films but enjoyed no subsequent redemption. His career began in 1953 when he directed *Dance Hall Racket*, a burlesque film written by and starring a then-unknown comic named Lenny Bruce. Tucker is best remembered, however, for his grand "disasterpiece" *Robot Monster*, an absurd sci-fi invasion tale that often comes up in esoteric debates about the worst film ever made. *The Cape Canaveral Monsters*, a largely forgotten science fiction allegory from 1960, was Tucker's final directorial effort.

Canaveral begins with a pair of alien agents who appear as glowing balls of light and take over the bodies of two lovers as they drive away from a secluded Florida beach. The human hosts are badly injured in an ensuing car crash, but the interlopers patch up their new bodies and establish headquarters in a secluded cave near the Cape Canaveral launch center. Using superior technology and weapons, they secretly thwart America's efforts to reach space by destroying various experimental rockets as they are launched.

The movie falls into a subgenre of 1950s science fiction films in which alien invaders take over the bodies of humans, often as part of an invasion plan. The best-known examples, such as *Invaders from Mars*, *Invasion of the Body Snatchers*, and *It Conquered the World*, are commonly interpreted as reflecting America's Cold War fears of communist infiltration. Though poorly crafted, *Canaveral* does add to the subgenre by incorporating a world-gripping event from the day's headlines that represented the pinnacle of the era's technology-inspired fears—the space race.

The American military began launching test rockets in the desert of New Mexico after World War II, with the assistance of former German scientists who had headed up that country's V-2 program during the war. As the range

Figure 5.3. Rocket launch at Cape Canaveral, 1959. (State Archives of Florida)

and effectiveness of these test rockets improved, it became necessary to find a new launch site further removed from populated areas. This need was driven home in 1947 when an experimental rocket went off course and crashed on foreign soil—in a cemetery south of Juárez, Mexico. Several sites were explored, but a tiny spit of land jutting out from Florida's southeast coast quickly became the obvious choice. Cape Canaveral was sparsely populated and provided the entire Atlantic Ocean as a safe proving ground. Its geography was ideal for security purposes, and the region's reliably fair weather promised that most days of the year would be favorable for launches. Nearby islands were also available to set up the tracking systems essential for monitoring rocket flights. The first launch from the cape occurred on July 24, 1950, and soon afterward the army, navy, and air force were each running separate testing programs from the area.

Though some work was being done on rockets capable of reaching space, most of these early efforts focused on developing ballistic missiles with offensive military capabilities. In 1957, however, the Soviet Union famously became the first nation to reach outer space with its Sputnik satellite, inspiring fear and doubt in Americans and kicking the space race into high gear. The National Aeronautics and Space Administration (NASA) was formed in 1958, and the United States committed to an aggressive effort to reach outer space. During the last years of the decade, almost all of the available land on the cape was dotted with launchpads and research facilities, and highly publicized test launches were occurring several times a month.

For both the government and the citizens of the United States, these programs came to be as much about national pride as they were about military security and scientific exploration. With the Soviets consistently achieving technological firsts in space and expertly propagandizing their accomplishments, America's image as a superpower and technological leader was at stake. This may in part account for the seemingly peculiar decision by the United States to grant close media access to its most sensitive and sophisticated technological research programs. Almost weekly, the front pages of American newspapers featured stories filed from Cape Canaveral and accompanied by photographs and surprisingly detailed maps and diagrams of the facility, the launchpads, and the rockets themselves. Television news crews were even allowed to film actual launches. Unfortunately, a great many of these news reports from the 1950s ran under headlines such as "Missile Blows Up in Florida Test" alongside photos of rockets bursting into flame before clearing the launchpad.[7] While the American public was certainly assured that the government was making its best effort to develop missile technology, the discouraging images of countless rockets engulfed in flame became indelibly marked on the American psyche.

For Phil Tucker, though, those same images proved inspirational—or at least economical. In several scenes in *The Cape Canaveral Monsters*, he intercuts footage of his aliens aiming their ray guns from behind rocks with film of actual launch preparations and rocket explosions. By using stock footage of NASA's launch failures, he added a visual punch and authenticity to the film that he could never have achieved on his limited special-effects budget. While all original footage for the film was shot in California, those intercut stock images were filmed at Cape Canaveral itself. Despite the many flaws of the film and its poor reception, *The Cape Canaveral Monsters* remains an intriguing piece of Americana where the popular entertainment and political fears of an era met.

THE CREDITS

Released in 1960
Produced by Lionel Dichter and Richard Greer
Directed by Phil Tucker
Written by Phil Tucker
Cinematography by W. Merle Connell
Edited by Richard Greer
Makeup by Phillip Scheer
Production design by Ken Letvin
Original music by Guenther Kauer

THE CAST

Scott Peters	Tom Wright
Linda Connell	Sally Markham
Jason Johnson	Hauron
Katherine Victor	Nadja
Billy Greene	Dr. Heinrich von Hoften
Chuck Howard	Maj. Gen. Hollister

THE FAT SPY

It's a killer . . . a Diller . . . a blast of laffs!
—tagline for *The Fat Spy*

THE STORY

A cosmetics tycoon has employed a bumbling scientist to find Ponce de Leon's famous Fountain of Youth on a remote island, while a rival cosmetics manufacturer engages in industrial espionage to steal the secret away. In the meantime, a gang of teenagers hit the island looking for an old Spanish galleon. Eventually they all run across the Fountain of Youth, with unexpected results.

THE FILM

Because film is a popular art, it is said that every film—no matter how poorly crafted or ridiculously plotted—will have some fans who like it. *The Fat Spy* sorely tests this assumption.

Spy is a spoof of several movie fads popular in the mid-1960s, particularly beach movies and spy adventures. The nonsensical story line involves a group of teenagers who look for an old Spanish galleon on an island off the coast of Florida, an island that happens to be inhabited by a horticulturalist named Irving who is searching for Ponce de Leon's Fountain of Youth. Irving is played

Figure 5.4. Lobby card from *The Fat Spy*. (Doll/Morrow Collection)

by 1960s stand-up comic Jack E. Leonard, who plays a dual role, also costarring as Irving's ruthless twin brother, Herman. Both Irving and Herman work for a cosmetics tycoon named Wellington, played by Golden Age leading man Brian Donlevy. But Herman is in love with rival cosmetics mogul Camille Salamander, and the two scheme to find the Fountain for themselves. The role of Camille, who is also called Rapunzel Fingernail for reasons never explained, is not performed so much as "inhabited" by comedienne Phyllis Diller. As an additional complication, Irving is in love with Wellington's daughter, Junior, played by the only movie star in the film, Jayne Mansfield.

The Fountain of Youth quest is an attempt to spoof James Bond and other spy adventures. The addition of references to current fads in pop culture and the absurd plot are reminiscent of the intentional campiness of the popular spy spoof *What's New, Pussycat?*. But *Spy* is so poorly conceived, directed, and acted that it misses the mark by a wide margin. The teenagers' slight story line is heavily padded by forgettable pop songs. Indeed, *The Fat Spy*, which has a seventy-eight-minute running time, averages a song every four minutes. The central teenage couple are named Frankie and Nanette, which is supposed to be a joke on the Frankie Avalon and Annette Funicello *Beach Party* movies, but it is a one-note joke stretched over seventy-eight minutes.

Joseph Cates directed the film with the same exaggeration and superficial tone of the television variety specials that were his bread and butter. Diller and Leonard perform in the broad manner of TV comedy sketches, while Mansfield falls back on a parody of her characters from earlier comedies. The appearance of Mansfield in the film is particularly sad, because it reveals the decline of her career. Though she was a gifted comedienne, her range was limited by her star image as a sex goddess and her unique physical appearance. Bad management and an addiction to publicity combined to push her career into a series of too-similar roles in increasingly poor films. In *The Fat Spy*, Mansfield, who was pregnant at the time, looked tired and bloated.

Cates's directorial skills were so poor that he could not handle so basic a technique as matching eyelines from shot to shot during a conversation. In their close-ups or medium shots, the characters rarely look directly at the person speaking to them, but rather stare off into space or in a completely different direction. In an early conversation between Mansfield and Donlevy, for example, the two seem to be standing across the desk from each other. As the conversation progresses, they appear to address someone at the far side of the office. A cut to the master shot reveals that they are actually standing next to each other and there is no one else in the room.

The Fountain of Youth ties the film to its Florida locale, though screenwriter Matthew Andrews changes the legend completely to suit the ridiculous plot. In *The Fat Spy*, the Fountain of Youth is not the legendary water source sought by explorer Ponce de Leon. As a matter of fact, it is not water at all but twin black roses that, when consumed, turn the characters into younger versions of themselves.

If *The Fat Spy* has one redeeming feature, it's that it was shot entirely in Cape Coral, Florida, in 1966, when the community was small and fairly new. The island where the teens search for the galleon is one of the barrier islands near Cape Coral, which was relatively untouched at the time. Long shots reveal strips of scraggly land not yet landscaped or developed, while the Wellington cosmetics headquarters is a generic glass-and-steel office building that looks recently erected. The film is thus a kind of record of a young community in the process of development.

The growth of Cape Coral began about 1957 when Leonard and Julius Rosen purchased 103 square miles of land along the north shore of the Caloosahatchee River, across from Fort Myers. Two years later the Rosens bought 15,000 additional acres at Redfish Point, intending to plan a modern city that would attract people from all over the world. They dug more than four hundred canals, laid out streets, and developed plans for shopping areas and other commercial enterprises. They even built an airfield to be the primary access to the city they dubbed Cape Coral—an airstrip seen in *The Fat Spy* in several scenes. The tiny community grew comparatively quickly, incorporating in 1970. By the 2000 census, its population had swelled to 102,000.[8]

Ironically, the rapid growth of Cape Coral caused the demise of one of the original attractions that the Rosens had built to entice people to their community. In 1964, the grandly named Cape Coral Gardens at Rose Gardens opened to draw tourists and potential residents. The landscaped areas included the promised rose gardens and an array of tropical plants, a replica of a Spanish galleon, a porpoise show, and the Waltzing Waters fountain display. A copy of the famous Iwo Jima statue in Washington, D.C., was one of the landmarks in the gardens that delighted tourists. By the 1970s, the property that encompassed the gardens had become too valuable for developers to consider keeping the attraction intact, and Cape Coral Gardens was closed. The enterprise was typical of those small-scale, offbeat attractions of the 1950s and 1960s that visitors could see in a day—unlike the mega–theme parks of contemporary Florida. Sadly, these kitschy but colorful tourist spots are rapidly disappearing.

For those who find the "lost attractions" of Florida an enticing bit of pop culture, *The Fat Spy* offers an opportunity to see one of those attractions in its heyday, because the final sequence was shot in Cape Coral Gardens at Rose Gardens. At the end, the various plots and subplots collide at the gardens as the teenagers discover their Spanish galleon, Herman and Camille find one of the twin black roses, and Junior and Irving stumble upon the other. The gardens' key attractions are on display, including the roses, the dolphin show, the Iwo Jima replica, and the Spanish galleon.

THE CREDITS

Released in 1966 by Magna Pictures
Produced by Everett Rosenthal and Rick Pleven
Directed by Joseph Cates
Written by Matthew Andrews
Cinematography by Joseph Brun
Music by Joel Hirschhorn, Al Kasha,
    and Hank Hunter

THE CAST

Phyllis Diller	Camille Salamander/
	Rapunzel Fingernail
Jack E. Leonard	Irving/Herman
Brian Donlevy	Wellington
Jayne Mansfield	Junior
Jordan Christopher	Frankie
Lauree Berger	Nanette
Johnny Tillotson	Dodo

HEALTH

Hollywood doesn't want to make the same pictures I do.
—Robert Altman, quoted in *The Film Encyclopedia*,
by Ephraim Katz

THE STORY

The delegates of H.E.A.L.T.H., a high-profile fitness organization, hold a convention at a Florida hotel to elect a new president. The favorite to win is Esther Brill, an octogenarian fitness expert who attributes her good health to her virginity. Opposing Esther is Isabella Garnell, a strong-willed, humorless candidate who preaches against the commercializing of physical fitness.

THE FILM

Robert Altman, one of America's most original and creative filmmakers, cowrote and directed the political satire *Health* (aka *H.E.A.L.T.H.*) in 1979–80. He intended the film to be released in the spring of 1980 to coincide with the primaries for that year's presidential election. Unfortunately, studio executives devised another plan for marketing and distributing the film that relegated it to obscurity.

Rarely seen and never available for home viewing on video or DVD, *Health* is sometimes misidentified as an Altman misfire. That reputation grew from Twentieth Century–Fox's decision to shelve the film for more than a year after it was completed. Typically, when the press hears rumors of a studio's dissatisfaction with a film, the assumption is that it is an artistic flop. When *Health* was finally released, it was a case of far too little, far too late. Its theatrical run consisted of two weeks at a theater in New York and two weeks at a theater in Los Angeles in April 1982. By that time the presidential election was long over, and its effectiveness as a satire on the political process was diminished.

Health features a large ensemble cast in an episodic narrative that unfolds in one primary setting—all hallmarks of Altman's signature style. The story centers around the national convention of a fitness organization called H.E.A.L.T.H., or Happiness, Energy, and Longevity Through Health. The delegates have convened to elect a new president from a field of two—Esther Brill and Isabella Garnell. Lauren Bacall, who was in her mid-fifties at the time, stars as eighty-three-year-old Esther, who declares that her good health and great looks are the result of her virginity. According to clean-living Esther, every orgasm takes twenty-eight days off a woman's life. Glenda Jackson costars as Esther's rival, a cigar-smoking, no-nonsense health aficionada who is fond of taping her conversations.

Figure 5.5. *Health* director Robert Altman. (Doll/Morrow Collection)

The diverse cast also includes Carol Burnett, an advisor to the president of the United States, who wants to curry favor with the members of this large grass-roots organization. James Garner appears as Brill's weary campaign manager, and Alfre Woodard makes her big-screen debut as the manager of the grand hotel where the convention takes place. Altman favorite Henry Gibson plays Bobby Hammer, a dirty trickster for the health food set, who eavesdrops around the hotel while dressed in drag to collect inflammatory information on the candidates.

References to the political events and scandals of the era are clearly recognizable throughout the film. Isabella's humorless demeanor and obsession with taping conversations is reminiscent of Richard Nixon, while Gibson's dirty trickster is certainly a reference to Nixon's tactics. Esther, the vigorous virgin who nonetheless dozes off when tired or bored, seems a jab at Ronald Reagan, though some of her platitudes vaguely recall the words of Jimmy Carter. The political referencing in a fictional format prefigured Altman's groundbreaking television series called *Tanner '88*, which followed a fictional candidate for president through the actual 1988 primary season and, in the process, showcased the modern political process, warts and all.

Health's story unfolds loosely in a series of scenes often improvised by the impressive ensemble of actors, a favored technique of Altman's. For this director, the joy of filmmaking lies in the process the actors engage in as they invent and exchange ideas as well as in the collaboration between director and actors as they work out the blocking of key scenes. The improvisational approach works well with other techniques favored by Altman, such as the use of overlapping dialogue in which the actors speak on top of each other's lines. He also uses the zoom lens and a wandering camera to capture conversations or interactions that are essential to understanding the story or that add texture to the film. In *Health*, for example, the hotel is crawling with strange guests, including people dressed in vegetable costumes, health-food nuts who want autographs from the candidates, and clueless television crews. When a person in a huge tomato costume jumps into the pool to save someone from drowning and then proceeds to sink to the bottom, the incident is funny but not out of place in this film. Altman's moving camera objectively takes in everything— the comic set pieces, the key conversations, the throwaway lines, and the bits of business—to depict the bizarre atmosphere.

Altman's methods have created such masterpieces as *M.A.S.H.* and *Nashville*, but they don't always come together so successfully. While *Health* was not the disaster presumed by the press after the studio shelved it, the film does reveal the weaknesses of Altman's style. Even supporters of the film have observed that Altman got carried away with his process, resulting in "a mess" but "a glorious one."[9]

However, even a lesser film by a master director has much to offer, and the question remains why the studio did not support the film. Fox experienced a change of command during preproduction of the film when Altman supporter Alan Ladd Jr. was replaced by a new studio boss, Sherry Lansing. Despite Lansing's lofty position, she apparently carried less authority than Ladd had. Instead Norman Levy, a sales executive in the distribution and marketing department, gained power within the studio when he became head of distribution. Levy was not an Altman admirer and he disliked *Health*, so it was shelved.[10]

The timing of the film is also significant because 1980 was the year of one of Hollywood's costliest flops, *Heaven's Gate*, which ran over budget as a result of director Michael Cimino's hubris. His heavy expenditures and on-the-set whims were chronicled throughout the film's production by the press, who seemed almost eager for him to fail. His lengthy version of the film was edited down by the studio and released to scathing reviews. The experience served as a wake-up call to all the studios to regain control over production, ending a decade of deference to directors. Members of the so-called film school generation—of which Altman was a part—had used commercial film as a medium of personal expression during the late 1960s and 1970s and were not inclined to care about the business of budgets. The *Heaven's Gate* fiasco might have accounted, at least in part, for Fox's decision not to release so quirky a film as *Health*.

The film's connection to Florida is its principal location, the Don Cesar Beach Resort and Spa in St. Petersburg. The Don Cesar, a grand hotel overlooking the Gulf of Mexico and Boca Ciega Bay, opened in 1928 with 345 rooms, suites, and guesthouses. Dubbed the Pink Palace because of its color, the Don Cesar was the perfect colorful location for the oddball members of H.E.A.L.T.H. to hold their offbeat convention. Shooting in Florida also allowed Altman to stay clear of the studio politics swarming around him—at least temporarily.

THE CREDITS

Released in 1981 by Twentieth Century–Fox
Produced by Robert Altman, Scott Bushnell, Wolf Kroeger, and Tommy Thompson
Directed by Robert Altman
Written by Robert Altman, Paul Dooley, and Frank Barhydt
Cinematography by Edmond L. Koons
Edited by Tom Benko, Dennis M. Hill, and Tony Lombardo
Art direction by Robert Quinn
Music by Joseph Byrd and Allan Nicholls

THE CAST

Carol Burnett	Gloria Burbank
Glenda Jackson	Isabella Garnell
James Garner	Harry Wolff
Lauren Bacall	Esther Brill
Paul Dooley	Dr. Gil Gainey
Donald Moffat	Colonel Cody
Henry Gibson	Bobby Hammer
Diane Stilwell	Willow Wertz
Alfre Woodard	Sally Benbow
Dick Cavett	Himself
Dinah Shore	Herself

JAWS 3-D

A rubber shark in 3-D still looks like a rubber shark, only worse.
—Ziggy's Video Realm

THE STORY

As children, Michael and Sean Brody saw their island community terrorized by a killer shark, which their father ultimately dispatched. Now Michael designs marine park attractions for Sea World owner Calvin Bouchard. When two great white sharks enter the marine park's newest attraction, the Brodys must contend with Bouchard and his glory-seeking underwater photographer Philip FitzRoyce to ensure public safety.

THE FILM

In 1975 Steven Spielberg was a little-known director with some well-received television work and a single theatrical release under his belt. That—and many other things—changed with the release of his phenomenally successful film *Jaws*. The box-office smash about a relentless great white shark established Spielberg as a master behind the camera and became the first of many films in which he earned the love and loyalty of audiences, critics, and studio bean counters alike—a triple-crown feat few directors can consistently achieve.

More significantly, the film also changed the way Hollywood looked at the summer release season. Prior to *Jaws*, summertime had been the domain of exploitation flicks and small, low-budget films, a seasonal doldrums generally dreaded by studio executives. The success of *Jaws* introduced a new term into the film marketers' lexicon—the summer blockbuster—and within a few years summer became the time for studios to unveil their big-budget, high-profile projects. By the mid-1990s, the industry was earning as much as half of its revenue from summer releases.[11]

Jaws also became a ubiquitous reference in American popular culture. Copy-cat films featuring killer eels, octopi, and other denizens of the deep popped up in theaters for the next several years. Documentaries on sharks were common fodder for television and cable, and real shark attacks were much more likely to make the nightly news. Perhaps most pervasive of all was the film's score by John Williams; two simple notes played on the cello became a universally recognized harbinger of encroaching danger.

Eager to capitalize on the film's prominence, Universal Pictures released three sequels over the next dozen years. *Jaws 2*, which featured Roy Scheider and several supporting cast members from the original, was competently done but far from spectacular. The film's most memorable element may have been its clever and effective tagline, "Just when you thought it was safe to go back in the water . . ." Still, like the original, it pulled in more than $100 million at the box office.[12] By the time of the fourth film in 1987, *Jaws: The Revenge*, both the concept and the public's interest had been wrung dry, and the film lost about $2 million in the theaters.

The first two films were shot in the area around Martha's Vineyard, though a portion of *Jaws 2* was filmed in Florida, near Navarre Beach and Gulf Islands National Seashore. For the third film, *Jaws 3-D*, the setting was moved to a prominent Florida tourist attraction, and the novelty of 3-D was added.

The addition of 3-D aside, the third film represented a major shift for the *Jaws* franchise. The story was moved from the fictional resort island of Amity, New York, to a very real and well-known Florida marine park, Sea World, and the main characters shifted from Amity sheriff Martin Brody to his now-grown sons. Michael, the elder Brody boy, is a marine engineer who has just completed work on a new attraction at the park, a sprawling lagoon with a network of underwater viewing tunnels that allow visitors an up-close view of

Figure 5.6. Lobby card from *Jaws 2*, also filmed in Florida. (Doll/Morrow Collection)

the marine life. A pair of sharks enter the lagoon through a sea-gate and begin dining on the park's maintenance workers and water skiers before moving on to threaten the guests.

Florida has been famous for its marine parks for decades. Opened in 1973, Sea World is the best known of the state's many aquatic attractions, but it was not the first. Florida's Marineland, opened in 1938 under the name Marine Studios, was actually the world's first modern oceanarium—a facility that duplicates large-scale natural marine habitats. Located a few miles south of St. Augustine, Marineland was intended as a public attraction, research facility, and underwater film studio. In fact, the park's founder, W. Douglas Burden, anticipated that the film industry would be the facility's primary source of revenue and that any funds generated by public attendance would be incidental. The park operators were famously surprised when some twenty thousand visitors showed up for opening day on June 23, clogging traffic for miles on Route A1A for the entire day. The park quickly shifted its revenue focus to the eager spectators. Marineland was the first facility to train dolphins for performance, and its animal shows were famous the world over. The facility was used to shoot the occasional documentary or feature film, but for the next three decades it would remain Florida's most visited tourist attraction.

The creators of *Jaws 3-D* may have been clever in capitalizing on the popularity of marine parks for the setting of the story. Though it was a poorly made film with a weak story line, it still managed to generate a $20-million profit at the box office.[13]

THE CREDITS	THE CAST	
Released in 1983 by Universal Pictures	Dennis Quaid	Mike Brody
Produced by Rupert Hitzig	Bess Armstrong	Kathryn Morgan
Directed by Joe Alves	Simon MacCorkindale	Philip FitzRoyce
Written by Carl Gottlieb, Michael Kane,	Louis Gossett Jr.	Calvin Bouchard
and Richard Matheson	John Putch	Sean Brody
Music by Alan Parker	Lea Thompson	Kelly Ann Bukowski
Cinematography by Chris Condon		
and James A. Contner		
Edited by Corky Elhers and Randy Roberts		

3-D Technology

The technology for 3-D motion pictures has been around in essentially the same form since the early twentieth century. Several silent 3-D films known as Plasticons were released in the 1920s. While audiences expressed some interest in these novelties, the process had little impact on the industry overall. In the 1950s, when Hollywood was looking to revitalize its offerings in response to competition from the new medium of television, the 3-D process enjoyed its brief but memorable heyday, beginning with the 1952 release of *Bwana Devil*. Though crudely made, this low-budget African adventure film caused a box-office sensation with its innovative special effects, and by the next year almost all of the major studios were working on 3-D projects.

The craze proved short-lived, however, with only about seventy 3-D films released by Hollywood during this period.[14] By 1954, audiences had become put off by the eyestrain and headaches that often accompanied 3-D viewing, and studios had found that the added expense of the process could not be supported by the waning revenues. Since then, the technology has sporadically resurfaced in a handful of films every ten or fifteen years. *Jaws 3-D* was part of a limited resurgence between 1981 and 1983, along with such forgettable films as *Comin' At Ya!* and *Metalstorm: The Destruction of Jared-Syn*.

SMOKEY AND THE BANDIT, PART 3

> In everything [Reynolds] accomplished, he always en-
> deavored to bring Hollywood back home . . . to Florida.
> —Burt Reynolds & Friends Museum Web site

THE STORY

Texas county sheriff Buford T. Justice retires to Florida after a long and pride-
ful career, regretting only that he never captured the elusive road rebel called
the Bandit. The father-and-son duo of Big and Little Enos goad Justice into
a long-distance driving challenge by betting $250,000 against the sheriff's
badge. The scheming Enoses plan to win the wager by distracting Justice with
a Bandit impersonator.

THE FILM

In the mid-1970s, Burt Reynolds was approached by stuntman friend Hal
Needham with a script scrawled in longhand on a yellow legal pad. Needham
intended to use the property to break into directing and realized his chances
would be greatly increased if his well-known friend fronted the project.
Reynolds told him the script was terrible but agreed to do the film if Needham
could secure studio backing. After several rewrites and personal efforts by
Reynolds to lure Sally Field and Jackie Gleason into the project, a deal for the
picture was finally pulled together.

A raucous tribute to the South's rebel mentality and good ol' boy culture,
Smokey and the Bandit made an unexpected bundle of money for Universal
Pictures in 1977 and began a five-year run for Reynolds as America's top box-
office draw. Though generally sneered at by critics as lowbrow, backwoods fare,
the original *Smokey* resonated with audiences across the world. It also began a
successful franchise, with two theatrical sequels and four made-for-TV movies to follow. The film is often credited with spurring the CB radio craze of
the late 1970s and spawning a minor genre of television entertainment that
included *B.J. and the Bear* and *The Dukes of Hazzard*.

Imaginative and action-packed, the film is primarily a skillfully directed
extravaganza of stunts. Its popularity was no doubt boosted by the undeniable
charisma of its stars and the genuine chemistry between Reynolds and Field,
who began a long-term relationship during filming. The movie's true success,
however, lies in its masterful editing, which earned an Academy Award nomi-
nation. The expert cutting was essential not only in the elaborate chases and
crashes that punctuate the film but also in establishing definitive connections

Figure 5.7. *Smokey and the Bandit, Part 3* star Jackie Gleason. (Doll/Morrow Collection)

among the major characters. The story takes place on the roads of the Sun Belt, with Field and Reynolds tearing up the blacktop in a Trans Am in order to draw Gleason's character Sheriff Buford T. Justice and his patrol car away from a third vehicle, a semitrailer piloted by Jerry Reed, who is bootlegging a load of Coors beer from Texas to Georgia on a bet. For much of the film, the occupants of the three vehicles never appear in the frame together, but the smart editing, along with the conceit of the CB radio that allows them to communicate, leaves the audience with the impression that clear and definitive relationships have developed among them.

The cast was brought back together for *Smokey and the Bandit II*, a weaker but still successful effort that revisited the premise of the original. When talk of the third installment began, however, many of the principals stayed away.

The filmmakers were left to construct a story around the characters played by Jackie Gleason and Jerry Reed. Gleason's bombastic redneck sheriff, who spent almost every scene in the series either barely containing his anger or explosively releasing it, had become an iconic nemesis in the first two films, best remembered for his perfectly delivered trademark line, "Sumbitch!" To retain the standard three-part structure, the story brought to the fore a pair of secondary characters, the wealthy father-and-son gamblers Big and Little Enos, played by Pat McCormick and Paul Williams. The Enoses entice Justice, recently retired to Florida, into another cross-country contest and then persuade Jerry Reed's character to impersonate the Bandit in order to sidetrack the sheriff along the route. Aside from this lackluster story, the film suffers greatly from timid direction and weak editing, which only highlight the strengths of the original film.

Figure 5.8. Lobby card from *Smokey and the Bandit, Part 3*. (Doll/Morrow Collection)

Needham and Field had declined *Smokey 3*, but Burt Reynolds agreed to contribute a cameo at the film's end, perhaps out of respect and gratitude to Gleason, whom he much admired. He was also likely supportive of the film because it was shot, in part, in Florida.

Reynolds had moved to Florida at age ten and grew up in Riviera Beach under the strict hand of his police chief father. Rebellious as a teen, he found an outlet on the football field and proved good enough to earn a scholarship to Florida State University. When a knee injury ended his athletic career, he took up acting, moving back and forth between films and television until his portrayal of machismo personified in *Deliverance* turned him into a household name.

He regularly used his star power to bring film work to his home state. He pushed hard for his 1974 film *The Longest Yard* to be filmed there, but state authorities proved uncooperative. The edgy film about a penitentiary football game between prisoners and guards was set in Florida but shot in Georgia. Both *Smokey* sequels included location work in Florida, however, as did later Reynolds films such as *Cop and a Half* and *The Crew*.

Using the proceeds of his 1970s box-office success, Reynolds established the Burt Reynolds Institute of Theater Training and the Burt Reynolds Dinner Theater in Jupiter, Florida, where he still maintains a home. Both ventures were sold in the 1990s, after he fell into financial trouble as a result of his much-publicized divorce from television star Loni Anderson. In 2003, however, Reynolds reestablished his dream of enhancing culture and arts education in Jupiter when he opened the Burt Reynolds & Friends Museum.

THE CREDITS	THE CAST	
Released in 1983 by Universal Pictures	Jackie Gleason	Buford T. Justice
Produced by Mort Engleberg	Jerry Reed	Cledus Snow/"the Bandit"
Directed by Dick Lowry	Paul Williams	Little Enos
Written by Stuart Birnbaum and David Dashev	Pat McCormick	Big Enos
Cinematography by James Pergola	Mike Henry	Junior
Edited by Byron Brandt, David Blewitt,	Colleen Camp	Dusty Trails
and Christopher Greenbury	Burt Reynolds	Real "Bandit"
Art direction by Ron Hobbs		
Original music by Larry Cansler		
Stunts coordinated by David Cass		

THE MOVIE TOURIST'S GUIDE TO FLORIDA BUST

The films in this chapter may have been disappointing to the studios that produced them, or to the viewers that took the time to watch them. However, the locations where they were shot remain just as stimulating or intriguing as they ever were. Movie tourists in particular will want to see the places where these disasters struck!

BLOOD FEAST

Miami

The Suez Hotel, where director Herschell Gordon Lewis and his partner David Friedman filmed parts of *Blood Feast*, is now the Suez Oceanfront Resort, located on Collins Avenue in North Miami Beach. Ownership of the Suez has changed hands several times, and the decor has also been revamped. The pyramid and a vaguely Egyptian statue out front are about all that is left of the Egyptian decor that inspired Lewis while writing the film. Now that the Suez houses the Oasis Restaurant, a tropical look dominates. Still, movie tourists might want to stay in this moderately priced motel, which has been around since the 1950s.

CAPE CANAVERAL MONSTERS

Cape Canaveral

The Kennedy Space Center is the only place in the Western Hemisphere where humans are launched into space. Located within the Merritt Island National Wildlife Refuge on Cape Canaveral, the center is the launching and landing area for the NASA space shuttle. Cape Canaveral Air Station, east of the KSC, was where the Mercury and Gemini flights were launched. Unmanned rockets are still launched from Cape Canaveral.

The Visitor Complex features a wide array of displays, interactive exhibits, and films about the history of America's space program. Astronauts are sometimes on the premises, and behind-the-scenes tours are also available. The Visitor Complex is located eleven miles east of I-95 on State Route 405.

THE FAT SPY

Cape Coral

Situated on the north shore of the Caloosahatchee River, across from Fort Myers, Cape Coral is one of the fastest-growing areas in Florida. Much of the town consists of waterfront property on canals, lakes, or basins, and there is direct access to Pine Island Sound or the Caloosahatchee River, where fishing is a key activity.

Though Cape Coral Gardens at Rose Gardens no longer exists, movie tourists can still see some of the key attractions. The Waltzing Waters was a dancing fountain show set to music, which was invented by Otto Przystawik in Germany during the 1920s. In 1965 Otto's son Günter moved to Florida to create his own, more sophisticated version in Cape Coral. There Günter Przystawik opened the Waltzing Waters industrial plant to produce installations of various sizes for theme parks, tourist attractions, and shopping centers. Currently, a Waltzing Waters outdoor show can be seen at the Shell Factory on N. Tamiami Trail four miles north of Fort Myers.

The Iwo Jima statue, located in Eco Park, is visible from Veteran's Memorial Bridge crossing the Caloosahatchee River from Fort Myers.

HEALTH

St. Petersburg

Health was shot almost entirely at the Don Cesar Beach Resort, dubbed the Pink Palace because of its exterior color. A grand hotel built by millionaire Thomas Rowe, the Don Ce-Sar (as it was known then) opened in January 1928. At a cost of $1.2 million, the hotel was nearly 300 percent over budget, but Rowe was obsessed with building the finest hotel on Florida's West Coast, where wealthy businessmen could find solitude and relaxation.

The hotel has gone through its ups and downs, almost closing during the Depression. Colonel Jacob Ruppert of the New York Yankees came to the rescue and signed a three-year contract to house his team there during spring training. The team attracted sportswriters and family members, which kept the hotel near full. Decades later, after years of neglect, the Don Ce-sar fell on hard times and was abandoned. Vandalism and graffiti took their toll, and the hotel was scheduled for demolition in 1969. A local group of preservationists banded together to save The Don, which was eventually purchased by William Bowman Jr., who brought the hotel back to life.

The Don Cesar (without the hyphen) reopened in 1973 as a luxury resort, and two years later it was placed on the National Register of Historic Places. Though there have been several additions and renovations through the years, it has retained its signature pink color. The Don Cesar is located on Gulf Boulevard in St. Petersburg Beach.

Orlando

While you won't run into any rogue great whites, there are indeed sharks at SeaWorld, where the third *Jaws* film was shot. The marine park features Shark Encounter, in which visitors can view a variety of sharks underwater by walking through an acrylic tunnel inside an aquarium. Those who want their shark encounters up close and personal can snorkel or scuba dive in a protective cage in Sharks Deep Dive. However, SeaWorld's key attraction is the Shamu show, in which several orca whales perform a series of feats and tricks. There are also three major outdoor habitats, two of which allow you to feed and pet marine life, including dolphins and stingrays. There are water ski shows and an amusement park as well.

The serious side of the park is the Hubbs-SeaWorld Research Institute, where research, rescue, and rehabilitation occur. SeaWorld has been responsible for rescuing thousands of whales, dolphins, turtles, and manatees.

SeaWorld is located at I-4 and State Route 528 in Orlando.

SMOKEY AND THE BANDIT, PART 3

Jupiter

Burt Reynolds's collection of awards, merit citations, movie memorabilia, and personal gifts were put on public display in 2002 at the Burt Reynolds & Friends Museum at 100 N. U.S. Highway 1 in Jupiter. Also included is the car used in the *Smokey and the Bandit* series. The town provided the museum with a lease on an unoccupied bank building that the town owned, and a group of volunteers transformed the bank into a museum. In 2006, however, the town announced plans to turn the building over to a nonprofit research group. Current information about the collection's status can be found at http://burt reynoldsmuseum.org.

FLORI-DRAMA

Drama is life with the dull bits cut out.
—Alfred Hitchcock

The broadest of all genres, drama is difficult to define or narrow down into a specific set of conventions. It encompasses a diversity of stories, tones, and themes. Taken together, the various types of drama—romantic, historical, crime, biographical, melodrama—explore the full spectrum of issues related to the events and institutions of our lives, from birth to marriage to death. Likewise, drama can explore a range of intense human emotions, from love to greed to anger to revenge. The history, culture, social structure, and even geography of Florida easily lend themselves to this most comprehensive of genres.

The films *Monster* and *Rosewood* recreate actual events that occurred in Florida, both of them horrific. *Monster* is a biographical drama, or biopic, of

Florida's notorious female serial killer Aileen Wournos; *Rosewood* dramatizes the story of a prosperous African-American town of the 1920s that was destroyed by the racism of the day. In both instances, the filmmakers took liberties with the historical facts of their tales to express their personal views, but because each was based on a true event, it was natural to use the actual locations for the primary settings.

Other dramas make use of Florida in more subtle ways. In *Just Cause*, a law professor who crusades against the death penalty seeks justice for a Florida inmate on death row who claims he is innocent. Widely recognized as a ready enforcer of the death penalty, Florida is a logical choice for the primary setting. The film is also strengthened by a clever use of the state's topography. The lawyer, who begins the story unwavering in his opposition to the death penalty, finds himself willingly acting as executioner in the film's climax in order to protect his family. His final confrontation with the killer occurs in a dense Florida swamp, and the setting serves to represent his descent into his own primal urges as well as the murky complexity of the capital punishment issue.

As light in tone as *Just Cause* is dark, the story in *Cocoon* is also closely tied to its setting. The film follows a group of senior citizens from a retirement community who experience their own private "fountain of youth" through an alien encounter. Not only is Florida the location of the famous Ponce de Leon legend, but it has long been known as the retirement capital of America, making it the obvious choice for this comedy-drama that offers insights into aging and mortality.

Other "Flori-dramas" that focus on serious personal issues include *CrissCross* and *Ulee's Gold*, both of which explore the relationship and responsibility of parents to their children. For these films, Florida again provides an important element to the story. In *CrissCross*, a young mother living in Key West—a mecca for nonconformists and a decadent party town—finds herself blinded to conventional moral norms by her environment. She fails to see the adverse effects that the community and her lifestyle have on her impressionable son. In *Ulee's Gold*, a beekeeper from northern Florida who produces a local specialty, tupelo honey, maintains his hives using age-old methods handed down through his family just as he protects his children by adhering to traditional values and old-fashioned virtues.

Conflicts of class and other social forces are explored in both *Blood and Wine* and *Sunshine State*. In *Blood and Wine*, Miami's diverse elements of old money, nouveaux riches, and Cuban immigrants clash in a tale of crime, greed, and betrayal. *Sunshine State* tackles the ramifications of land development, a continuing problem in Florida. In detailing the consequences of rampant development on established communities, the film makes reference to the unique Florida sites and symbols of the past—everything from gators to mermaid shows—that will soon be replaced by bland gated communities and still more golf courses.

On the surface, the films in "Flori-Drama" seem to have little in common save for their primary setting. Together, however, they demonstrate the great range of expression, technique, and form that can be achieved in dramatic film and at the same time prove that Florida offers a distinctive and appropriate backdrop for thoughtful exploration of the human condition.

BLOOD AND WINE

In a bad crime movie, people do what they do
to fit the plot. In a good crime movie, people
are who they are and that determines the plot.
—Roger Ebert review

THE STORY

Alex Gates sells and distributes wine to Miami's wealthiest citizens, but his taste for elegance and luxury has left him financially strained. He teams with veteran jewel thief Victor Spansky to steal a diamond necklace from one of his clients. Alex's scheme becomes compromised by his dysfunctional family and his Cuban mistress.

THE FILM

With its serious, critical tone, *Blood and Wine* falls neatly in line with other films of director Bob Rafelson. A member of the film school generation—who would use film to criticize and comment on social issues—Rafelson has often examined the nuclear family, marriage, and the success myth, finding them stifling, empty, or corrupt. The film marked the sixth collaboration between Rafelson and actor Jack Nicholson, who first worked together in 1969 on *Head*, a psychedelic oddity designed as a vehicle for the made-for-TV rock group the Monkees. Nicholson did not appear in *Head*, but he coproduced and co-wrote it. The acclaimed actor's stardom had always rested on his ability to por-tray sympathetic cads or complex rogues, and Rafelson's films offered him the most challenging versions of these character types. They next worked together on *Five Easy Pieces*, Rafelson's masterpiece, which established the director's

Figure 6.1. *Blood and Wine* director Bob Rafelson. (Doll/Morrow Collection)

reputation and added to Nicholson's standing as a leading actor of his generation. Over the next two decades, the actor and director teamed for *The King of Marvin Gardens*, *The Postman Always Rings Twice*, and *Man Trouble*. At the time of its release in 1996, Nicholson touted *Blood and Wine* as the completion of a loose trilogy that had begun with *Five Easy Pieces* and *The King of Marvin Gardens*, because each focused on the destructive nature of a dysfunctional family.

In *Blood and Wine*, Nicholson portrays Alex Gates, a man willing to pay any price to live a life of luxury and advantage. Alex's version of the American Dream is the personal comfort and status that come from the superficial accoutrements of the privileged—fine wine, a beautiful mistress, nice clothes. "Put on a shirt," Alex tells his T-shirted stepson Jason before they visit a client; Alex himself wears a crisp dress shirt and matching silk tie. In the service of his selfish ambitions, Alex has used his wife's money to purchase his wine shop, then squandered all the profits on the good life. Now his family is not only broke but broken. Conventionally, the pursuit of a better life through hard work is supposed to strengthen the family, not splinter it, but Rafelson offers a much darker take on the American Dream through the character of Alex.

Among Alex's wealthy clients are the Reeces, who own a valuable diamond necklace that Alex plans to steal to resolve his financial problems and to take his mistress to Paris. Secluded in their gated neighborhood, the Reeces exhibit the worst traits of the nouveaux riches. In his only scene, Frank Reece reveals his weak nature when he tries to master the art of throwing a fishing net for an upcoming vacation. Failing, he glibly remarks, "Why can't you just buy bait and then fish?"—suggesting that his usual approach to resolving a problem is to buy his way out of it. Likewise, his wife Dina flaunts her wealth and position over her Cuban nanny, Gabriela, by making her perform fruitless tasks while complaining about the young woman's "Cubano" temperament. She later fires Gabriela just before the family's vacation cruise, opting to take an American-born nanny instead. If the pursuit of personal success and a better life has led to the materialism and corrupted values of the Reeces, then that American ideal is surely a flawed one.

Michael Caine costars as Alex's partner in crime, jewel thief Victor Spansky, whose Cockney background, consumptive condition, and demeanor of doom exclude him from participation in the American Dream. Victor's reason for teaming up for the heist is the opposite of Alex's: whereas Alex wants the money to pursue the good life, Victor wants to finance a more comfortable death. With illness ravaging his body, he seeks to die comfortably in a tropical paradise, not in a county hospital.

Gabriela, who is not only the Reeces' nanny but also Alex's mistress, provides the most compelling character study in this exploration of the American Dream. She has entered the country illegally on a tiny boat with fourteen other escapees from Castro's Cuba. She literally risked her life to pursue the dream, giving her actions a validity that cannot be claimed by Alex, the Reeces, or any other character. Gabriela seems to pursue the dream in the purest sense, in that she works hard, takes classes to improve herself, and remains close to her relatives. Part of her plan is to bring the rest of her family from Cuba even if she has to do it one at a time. These selfless motives contrast severely with Alex's desire for luxury at the expense of his family.

But the character of Gabriela is more than just the cliché of the hardworking immigrant who deserves to achieve the dream. As the plot unfolds, we begin to first suspect and then expect that her interactions and relationships with Alex, the Reeces, and Jason will change, or even taint, her. Her relationship with Alex has given her a taste of the good life, and she likes it. She allows him to indulge her with fine wine and lingerie. Later, when Alex's wife dies in an accident, Gabriela moves into Alex's home sooner than would be appropriate, because she wants to get out of the small, crowded house where she lives with too many relatives.

Gabriela and Alex's stepson are attracted to each other, and she is torn between the promise of security and luxury that Alex offers and the prospect of passion and love with Jason. Ultimately she chooses the former, betraying the younger man who has incited Alex's wrath after inadvertently gaining possession of the valuable necklace.

The necklace becomes a motif that symbolizes the American Dream: the Reeces buy it; Victor steals it but never really possesses it; Alex takes possession of it but doesn't have the wherewithal to hang on to it; and Jason rejects it for a simpler life. Interestingly, Gabriela returns the necklace twice after Jason gives it to her. The first time, he merely places it around her neck after she confesses that, when she used to help Mrs. Reece put it on, she always wondered what it would feel like to wear it. She then remarks that if the authorities found her with it, they'd blame her for the theft. As she hands it back to Jason—who in any case did not intend for her to keep it at that point—the exchange is lent meaning by the symbolic significance of the necklace. Still thinking from the perspective of an illegal immigrant, Gabriela at first believes that the necklace is out of her reach.

During the final confrontation between Jason and Alex, Jason grabs the necklace and thrusts it in Gabriela's hand, and she speeds away in his truck. Several miles down the road, she changes her mind, turns around, and returns the necklace to a critically wounded Alex. "I thought I wanted it but I didn't," she explains, seeming to reject the greed or materialism associated with the necklace. Yet the gesture is not as noble as it appears. Unbeknownst to either man, Gabriela has palmed one of the diamonds from the necklace. Like Alex and then Jason, she has learned another path to the American Dream—one considerably shorter and more self-serving.

Much of *Blood and Wine* takes place in Miami, though the turning point of the story occurs in Key Largo. The Miami locale is important not so much for its geography as for the makeup of its population. The contrast between the wealthy Reeces in their exclusive neighborhood and Gabriela in Little Havana defines Miami as much as the Art Deco district of Miami Beach.

Miami has been associated with millionaires—especially the nouveaux riches—since the 1920s, when several members of the wealthy class carved out a part of Miami near the water to live the high life. The Cuban population is much more recent, with the first major influx arriving in 1960–61 after Fidel Castro's revolutionaries seized power. Early immigrants tended to be from the wealthy and then the middle classes, but later waves grew increasingly poor. Another wave of immigration occurred from 1965 to 1971, when "Freedom Flights" were arranged from the Varadero airport in Matanzas, Cuba, to carry relatives of Cubans living in the United States to Miami. Finally, the Mariel Boatlift brought 125,000 Cubans to the United States in 1980. In addition to these high-profile migrations, Cuban families desperate to escape the shortages and problems of their country sometimes made their own flights to freedom aboard small boats or rafts, as Gabriela did in the film.

Miami currently holds the greatest concentration of Cuban immigrants in the United States. The influx of 600,000 Cubans has greatly affected the city, transforming Miami from a resort of millionaires and retirees to a thriving modern city with a Latin beat.[1]

THE CREDITS	THE CAST	
Released in 1996 by Paramount Pictures	Jack Nicholson	Alex Gates
Produced by Chris Auty, Hercules Bellville, Kathleen	Stephen Dorff	Jason
M. Courtney, Noah Golden, Terry Miller, Jeremy	Jennifer Lopez	Gabriela
Thomas, and Bernard Williams	Judy Davis	Suzanne
Directed by Bob Rafelson	Michael Caine	Victor "Vic" Spansky
Written by Bob Rafelson, Nick Villiers, and Alison	Harold Perrineau Jr.	Henry
Cross	Robyn Peterson	Dina Reese
Cinematography by Newton Thomas Sigel	Mike Starr	Mike
Edited by Steven Cohen	John Seitz	Frank Reese
Production design by Richard Sylbert	Thom Christopher	Jeweler #1

COCOON

We seniors are a big group and a lot of us have time and
money to spend on movies. But usually they don't make
anything we want to see.
—Helen Schultz, 63, quoted in *Washington Post* review

THE STORY

Aliens come to earth to retrieve several colleagues who are lying dormant in underwater cocoons off the coast of Florida. They store the cocoons in a swimming pool while waiting to leave, and the life force of the aliens transforms the water into a fountain of youth. When a group of senior citizens from a retirement home discover the secret of the pool, they revel in its rejuvenating effects and struggle with unexpected consequences of their newfound vigor.

THE FILM

A surprise box-office success from 1985, *Cocoon* captivated audiences of all ages with its skillful juxtapositions of fantasy and drama, comedy and poi-

Figure 6.2. Advertisement for *Cocoon*. (Doll/Morrow Colelction)

gnancy. The film also provided a high-profile boost to the twilight careers of some of America's leading actors and helped nudge young Ron Howard into the ranks of Hollywood's top directors. In addition, the thoughtful story provided glimpses into the complex psychological and emotional repercussions of aging in America, a subject rarely explored in modern films, which are so heavily oriented toward youthful audiences.

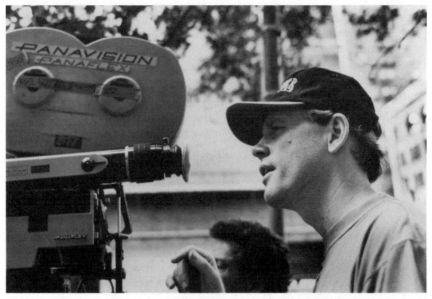
Figure 6.3. *Cocoon* director Ron Howard. (Doll/Morrow Collection)

The film features an ensemble of grand old thespians—Don Ameche, Wilford Brimley, Hume Cronyn, Jack Gilford, Maureen Stapleton, Jessica Tandy, and Gwen Verdon—supported by fresh faces including Brian Dennehy, Steve Guttenburg, and Tahnee Welch. With their varied backgrounds and accomplishments, the elder performers represented a cross-section of twentieth-century popular entertainment. Ameche was a product of Hollywood's Golden Age studio system who had been a smooth, urbane leading man for Twentieth Century–Fox in the 1930s and 1940s. Cronyn, Tandy, and Stapleton were considered among the finest dramatic actors in American theater; Cronyn and Tandy, who were married, frequently worked together and came to be known as Broadway's leading couple for their interpretations of such classic plays as *The Fourposter* and *The Gin Game*. Verdon also came from Broadway, where she reigned as the undisputed queen of dance musicals for two decades; she collaborated with husband and famed choreographer Bob Fosse on such smash hits as *Damn Yankees*, *Sweet Charity*, and *Chicago*. Jack Gilford's roots stretched all the way back to vaudeville. He served his apprenticeship on the borscht belt as a mousy comic foil to the boisterous Milton Berle and went on to become one of the pioneers of monologue comedy. He too became a fixture on Broadway in both dramatic and comic roles. Well-known character actor Wilford Brimley, the youngster of the group, came from a later generation of improvisational performers and was well known for both his television and film work.

UNIVERSITY PRESS OF *Florida*

15 NW 15th Street
Gainesville, FL 32611-2079
(352) 392-1351/www.upf.com

Dear Book Reviewer:

Thank you for supporting University Press of Florida and our titles. We hope you enjoy our books and should you decide to publish a review, we would greatly appreciate receiving (2) tearsheets, sample issues, or an email link to the review. These may be sent to:

University Press of Florida
15 NW 15th Street
Gainesville, FL
32611-2079

or

rg@upf.com.

Once again, thank you.

Kind regards,

Romi Gutierrez
Publicity & Promotions Manager
rg@upf.com

~ Discover the World with Florida Books ~

The story focuses on the male characters, particularly Cronyn, Ameche, and Brimley as the three scrappy seniors who first discover that the pool on the estate next to their retirement community has rejuvenating effects, thanks to the alien cocoons that are being stored in it. The physically demanding roles required them to perform lively dance routines and a fight scene, and Brimley and Cronyn even learned to scuba dive for the film. The most impressive sequence, however, is the pool scene when they first experience the powers of the water. The three actors cavort like schoolboys and perform a series of dives and backflips into the pool. Their acrobatics are captured in slow motion, which emphasizes their grace and agility and lets the audience know that the actors were doing the stunts themselves. The three female leads also have some memorable moments, including a sly breakfast scene in which they wordlessly let each other know that they've all just enjoyed a night of romance thanks to the pool's effect on their partners.

The success of *Cocoon* brought renewed attention to the veteran group, including a Best Supporting Actor Oscar for Ameche. For Ron Howard, the

Figure 6.4. *Cocoon* stars Don Ameche and Gwen Verdon.
(Doll/Morrow Collection)

film provided a major boost to his career behind the camera. He had already proven himself a competent director with a handful of earlier films, and his reputation benefited from the major box-office success of *Splash* the previous year. When *Cocoon* became the second-highest-grossing film of 1985, however, he finally escaped his image as a former child star. Howard brought a number of subtle touches to the film that became significant factors in its success. Drawing on the expertise of his wife, a geriatric psychologist, he reworked the script to bring psychological depth to the characters by introducing negative side effects to their reclaimed vigor. For example, most of the characters experience a renewed sexual interest that is played for both humor and sentiment. One couple, however, face trouble when this increased sexual appetite leads to a resurgence of the husband's philandering ways. Between scenes, Howard also encouraged the actors to share their own thoughts on aging and mortality. These lively philosophical discussions were brought to bear on their characterizations in the film, adding thought-provoking undercurrents to the story as the characters weighed the merits of a natural life cycle against the prospect of eternal youth.

Florida was a natural choice of setting for the film, because of its large population of retirees as well as its association with the legend of Ponce de Leon and the Fountain of Youth. While the ocean scenes in the film were shot in the Bahamas, everything else was done at locations in St. Petersburg, where the film is set. Two retirement communities, Suncoast Manor and Sunny Shores Villas, served as the homes of the senior characters, and many actual residents appeared as extras throughout the film. When the group go out for a night of dancing, they head to the historic Coliseum Ballroom for a spin on its famous oak dance floor. Built in 1924, the Moorish-style hall remains one of the city's great landmarks. An early scene occurs at one of the city's most peculiar attractions, the St. Petersburg Shuffleboard Club. In its heyday from the 1930s to the 1950s, the athletic arena was known as the world's largest shuffleboard club, with 110 courts and five thousand members, and the facility became a social hub of the community, offering such additional activities as card tournaments, dances, and concerts. Other historic sites such as the Snell Arcade and the old Woolworth's store also appeared in the film.

An inevitable sequel was produced in 1988. The entire primary cast returned, although Ron Howard declined to direct. The production was moved to Miami for financial reasons; the city offered a large pool of film professionals, so that a full crew did not have to be brought in from the West Coast. Many of the scenes were shot on sets constructed in a rented Miami warehouse. For outdoor sequences, the backgrounds were gimmicked to retain the St. Petersburg setting; crews changed the signs on buildings, for instance, or added a *St. Petersburg Times* vending machine to the background. Despite these efforts, *Cocoon: The Return* proved disappointing, as it failed to capture the subtlety and freshness of the original.

THE CREDITS	THE CAST	
Released in 1985 by Twentieth Century–Fox	Don Ameche	Arthur Selwyn
Produced by Lili Fini Zanuck and Richard D. Zanuck	Wilford Brimley	Benjamin Luckett
Directed by Ron Howard	Hume Cronyn	Joseph Finley
Written by Tom Benedek, from the novel by David	Brian Dennehy	Walter
Saperstein	Jack Gilford	Bernard Lefkowitz
Cinematography by Donald Peterman	Steve Guttenberg	Jack Bonner
Edited by Daniel P. Hanley and Mike Hill	Maureen Stapleton	Marilyn Luckett
Production design by Jack T. Collis	Jessica Tandy	Alma Finley
Set decoration by Jim Duffy	Gwen Verdon	Bess McCarthy
	Herta Ware	Rosie Lefkowitz
	Tahnee Welch	Kitty
	Tyrone Power Jr.	Pillsbury

CRISSCROSS

In the 60s and 70s, smuggling was a major industry in the Keys and the somewhat secret fortunes of many of the city's most successful businessmen were made as bales of marijuana were openly unloaded on the city docks.
—Alan Maltz, *Key West Color*

THE STORY

Single mother Tracy Cross tries to bring up her son, Chris, in the uninhibited Key West of the 1960s. She works many hours to make ends meet, including a night job as a stripper, which leaves her little time to supervise her adolescent son.

THE FILM

Goldie Hawn starred in this small drama about a working-class single mother who struggles to raise her child alone in Key West during the 1960s. With no skills or education, Tracy Cross works on the fringes of the mainstream world: she dances at a local strip club and waits tables at a boarding house for drifters and tourists. The film unfolds through the perspective of her son Chris, who narrates the story in a voice-over, which allows the viewer to understand the consequences of Tracy's actions on the boy. Tracy believes she has a good reason for taking a job as a stripper: she needs the money to support herself and her son. But compromising her morals for money is the wrong message to send. Using a similar rationalization, Chris decides to steal cocaine from a local drug dealer and sell it himself—because they need the money, and he does not want his mother to strip for it. Both take the wrong course of action for the right reason.

CrissCross differs from Goldie Hawn's usual fare. Famed for her dizzy comic persona, the star typically appears in romantic comedies or other genres that take advantage of her comedic skills. *CrissCross* was one of several films developed and produced by Hawn's production company with Anthea Sylbert. Recognizing that commercial Hollywood rarely offers juicy parts to middle-aged women, Hawn established her first production company in 1980. While she occasionally produced films that did not feature her in starring roles, such

Figure 6.5. *CrissCross* star Goldie Hawn.
(Doll/Morrow Collection)

as *My Blue Heaven* with Steve Martin, most of the Hawn-Sylbert projects were developed especially for the highly regarded actress.

Throughout the 1980s and 1990s, Hawn costarred with Hollywood's best comic actors in such popular comedies as *Private Benjamin, The Out-of-Towners, Overboard*, and *The First Wives Club*. Some of her films touched on women's issues or were written from a female perspective, though they never hit the viewer hard with a message or social agenda. As a producer, Hawn occasionally clashed with directors whose visions for the material were grittier or edgier than hers, most notably with Jonathan Demme on *Swing Shift*, but her commercial instincts were generally on target.

Hawn and Sylbert experienced less luck with their handful of dramas. *Swing Shift, Deceived*, and *CrissCross* were critical and box-office disappointments, perhaps because fans were reluctant to accept Hawn in a dramatic role, or because reviewers were too eager to find fault with her for reaching beyond her star image. *CrissCross* does suffer from a weakly structured plot and a one-note performance by David Arnott as Hawn's son. Yet these weaknesses do not

Figure 6.6. *CrissCross* director Chris Menges.
(Doll/Morrow Collection)

seem to warrant the many harsh reviews and mean-spirited comments, mostly aimed at Hawn's decision to strip for the film.

CrissCross is actually a poignant drama set in a turbulent era when families were ripped apart by generational conflict, social issues, and historical events, just as Chris's family is destroyed when his father is emotionally shattered by his tour of duty in Vietnam. The character of Tracy Cross offered Hawn the opportunity to shed light on single, working-class mothers who survive despite their limited choices. Such women are often sentimentalized on film as sainted, one-dimensional characters who sacrifice all for their offspring. In contrast, Tracy is a flawed character who struggles to figure out the best choices for herself and her son. And she doesn't always foresee the ramifications of her decisions.

Because this is Chris's story, not Tracy's, the narrative perspective provides some distance between Tracy Cross and the audience. As a result, the audience is less likely to identify with her and excuse her misguided choices, poor decisions, and tendency to neglect Chris. Her obliviousness to Chris's daily routine and troubled feelings is suggested by the many times she passes Chris in her car on the streets of Key West without recognizing him. He waves to her, or calls out her name, but she drives by on her way to her own destination, blind to what he is doing or where he is going. Though Tracy loves Chris and worries about their future, she can't quite find a balance between her own needs and her responsibilities as a mother.

Tracy freely befriends and parties with the hippies and transients who live in the Eden Hotel with her and Chris, not realizing that they make poor role models for her son. When she learns that Chris has been selling cocaine to undercover drug enforcement agents, she is shocked into the realization that her lifestyle, friends, and choice of job have had negative consequences. She and Chris move out of the Eden in the hope of finding a better life. The ending is not quite a happy one, at least by Hollywood standards, because Tracy and Chris relocate to a rundown trailer park that is seedier than the Eden. Their moral standards are restored but their fortunes are unimproved. While not a complicated character, Tracy Cross is a complex role, and Hawn offers an effective portrait of female struggle and hardship.

Key West in the 1960s provides an appropriate backdrop for a story about an ordinary woman who loses her moral compass. During that era, hippies and dropouts flocked to the city in their vans and psychedelic buses to take advantage of the Keys' tolerance for freewheeling, unconventional lifestyles. As writer and Key West resident James Leo Herlihy recalled, "the marginal people to whom I'd always been drawn all through my life were suddenly having a heyday."[2] Recreational drugs became prevalent as boatloads of marijuana and other illegal substances landed in town via the Gulf of Mexico. Bales of marijuana were unloaded on the city docks right out in the open.[3]

Key West's lax attitude toward the drug culture was reminiscent of its dismissal of Prohibition forty years earlier. The island simply did not recognize Prohibition, and rumrunners and bootleggers thrived throughout the 1920s—a bit of history briefly referred to in the film when Emmett, the owner of the Eden Hotel, tells Chris that his "old man" was a rumrunner back in the 1920s. Though Emmett warns Chris about the evils of cocaine, his tolerance of the hippies and their drug use at his establishment makes a parallel between the Keys of the 1920s and the Keys of the 1960s. Key West has always welcomed those trying to escape the rigid rules and numbing norms of mainstream society, and the counterculture with its alienated, marginalized youth flourished—an atmosphere well captured by director Chris Menges in *CrissCross*. To the disillusioned and disaffected, such an atmosphere is exotic and intoxicating; for Tracy and Chris, who long to reestablish a normal life, Key West in the 1960s was the wrong place at the wrong time.

In 1982, long after the counterculture lifestyle had disappeared in the rest of the country, the U.S. Border Patrol established a roadblock and inspection points along U.S. 1 to stop traffic headed back to the mainland so that they could search for drugs and illegal immigrants. The roadblocks were a sore point with the Key West City Council, which felt they hurt the Keys' tourism industry. After unsuccessful legal attempts to end the roadblocks, Mayor Dennis Wardlow and the city council opted for a publicity stunt in which Wardlow announced that Key West was seceding from the mainland to become the Conch Republic. With tongue in cheek, the Conch Republic declared war on the United States, then promptly surrendered and requested $1 million in foreign aid. Every February, Key West celebrates the anniversary of the Conch Republic with nonstop parties and festivities—a reminder of the island's freewheeling, uninhibited passion for nonconformity.

THE CREDITS	THE CAST	
Released by Metro-Goldwyn-Mayer in 1992	Goldie Hawn	Tracy Cross
Produced by Anthea Sylbert, Bill Finnegan,	Arliss Howard	Joe
and Robin Forman	James Gammon	Emmett
Directed by Chris Menges	David Arnott	Chris Cross
Written by Scott Sommer	Keith Carradine	John Cross
Cinematography by Ivan Strasburg	J. C. Quinn	Jetty
Edited by Tony Lawson	Steve Buscemi	Louis
Art direction by Dayna Lee		

CROSS CREEK

I do not understand how any one can live without
some small place of enchantment to turn to.
—Marjorie Kinnan Rawlings, *Cross Creek*

THE STORY

Marjorie Kinnan Rawlings moves to rural Florida seeking a quiet atmosphere in which she can develop as a writer. Her observation of the rustic lives of her Cross Creek neighbors inspire her to write a series of critically acclaimed novels.

THE FILM

Of all Florida literary figures, no name is so deeply associated with the Sunshine State as Marjorie Kinnan Rawlings. Born and raised in the North, Rawlings struggled to find her voice as a writer until 1928, when she moved to the rural community of Cross Creek in northeast Florida just outside Gainesville. There she came into her own as a chronicler of Florida's Cracker culture, a waning way of life that had evolved from the original American settlers of the region in the 1820s. Though the term Cracker developed a negative racial connotation during the twentieth century, its origins lie in Florida's hardscrabble communities of black and white settlers who drew their living from the land and who prized their communities and their independence equally.

Rawlings and her husband were both moderately successful journalists and writers who stumbled onto Cross Creek while on vacation. Rawlings immediately felt at home in the tiny community of a few dozen families and the surrounding semitropical scrublands. She believed the isolation of Cross Creek would be ideal for their writing and that the change from a harried urban existence would help their struggling marriage. The couple bought a small Cracker-style house on seventy-two acres with a three-thousand-tree orange grove. Over the next several years, Rawlings became an intense observer of the land, the people, and the way of life along the half-mile creek that connects Orange Lake and Lochloosa Lake. She published a series of short stories in *Scribner's* magazine about the region and its inhabitants in 1931, drawing the attention of famed editor Maxwell Perkins. With encouragement from Perkins, she set out to capture the distinctive setting and lifestyle of rural Florida in her fiction, publishing her first novel in 1933. Her marriage ended that same year, but Rawlings chose to stay on in Cross Creek to pursue her writing.

On two occasions she stayed for long periods with a Cracker family living

Figure 6.7. Publicity photo from *Cross Creek*. (Doll/Morrow Collection)

in the remote woodlands. From them she learned to catch frogs, hunt duck, press cane syrup, and distill moonshine. The experiences left her with a deeply rooted understanding of their traditional way of life, which she translated into her writing. In 1938 she published her Pulitzer Prize novel *The Yearling*, a coming-of-age story about a Florida boy who adopts a deer in the years after the Civil War. Four years later she produced *Cross Creek*, a loosely organized collection of nonfiction essays laced with humor and pathos that captured the spirit of her adopted community.

Throughout the 1930s and 1940s her work was beloved by both critics and popular audiences. After her death in 1953, however, she was remembered largely as the author of a classic children's tale. Critics developed a renewed interest in her complete body of work in the 1980s, and she has since become recognized as a significant American author noted for her sharp prose and detailed reporting of a unique way of life.

The 1983 film *Cross Creek* draws its events from her well-known memoir but focuses more on Rawlings herself than on the culture she set out to capture. Portrayed by Mary Steenburgen, Rawlings is depicted as a passive, intent observer who quietly assimilates the subtleties of her surroundings and then furiously translates them into words during marathon sessions at her typewriter. Though Steenburgen's low-key performance was not generally applauded, the supporting work of Rip Torn, Alfre Woodard, and Peter Coyote as locals who develop close relationships with the author makes the film notable. Director Martin Ritt was well known for projects that focused on the rural South, including *The Sound and the Fury, Hud, Sounder,* and *Norma Rae.* In *Cross Creek,* he focused on the stunning natural beauty of the South as it worked its way into the heart of an outsider.

The film was shot entirely on location in northeastern Florida just a few miles from Cross Creek. There the filmmakers met Norton Baskin, a local hotel owner who had married Rawlings in the 1940s. Portrayed in the film by Peter Coyote, Baskins consulted on the script and frequently visited the set as an advisor during filming. He also appears briefly in the film as one of the Cross Creek residents.

Production designer Walter Scott Herndon oversaw the construction of period buildings for the sets, including a detailed replica of the Rawlings home. Shortly after filming began, a record-breaking storm dumped eighteen inches of rain in a single day, flooding the area and delaying production. One of the key sets, a ramshackle home set back from a river, was completely surrounded by water. When the floodwaters failed to recede, the crew raised the cabin onto stilts and added a broad porch and several walkways so that work could continue.

Rawlings was known to her neighbors as a hard-drinking, heavy-smoking woman who could cuss with the crudest of backwoods moonshiners. Though the film clearly captures her innate strength and independence, it presents her as a more genteel and refined character than the earthy, hard-living woman who once shot and ate a neighbor's pig that had been rooting in her petunias. Still, *Cross Creek* fully captures the intense passion and inspiration Rawlings derived from the distinctly Floridian culture and land that she thought of as home.

THE CREDITS		THE CAST	
Released in 1983 by MCA/Universal Pictures		Mary Steenburgen	Marjorie Kinnan Rawlings
Produced by Robert B. Radnitz and Martin Ritt		Rip Torn	Marsh Turner
Directed by Martin Ritt		Peter Coyote	Norton Baskin
Written by Dalene Young, from the book by		Dana Hill	Ellie Turner
Marjorie Kinnan Rawlings		Alfre Woodard	Geechee
Cinematography by John A. Alonzo		Joanna Miles	Mrs. Turner
Edited by Sidney Levin		Jay O. Sanders	Charles Rawlings
Music by Leonard Rosenman		Norton Baskin	Man in rocking chair
Production design by Walter Scott Herndon		Malcolm McDowell	Max Perkins
Set decoration by Gregory Garrison			
Costumes by Joe I. Thompkins			

DAYS OF THUNDER

A-plus.

—stock car mechanic Waddell Wilson on the film,
as quoted by James Walsh in *Films in Review*

THE STORY

Sports car racer Cole Trickle agrees to race stock cars on the NASCAR circuit for auto dealer Tim Daland. Daland coaxes mechanic Harry Hogge out of retirement to build Trickle's car and train the hardheaded young man for NASCAR racing.

THE FILM

The 1990 film *Days of Thunder* was conceived and constructed around Tom Cruise's star image. After a string of box-office hits in the late 1980s, including *Top Gun*, *The Color of Money*, and *Cocktail*, Cruise had become associated with action-oriented dramas in which a hotheaded young man in a heavily male-dominated profession succeeds because of the tutelage of a father figure. *Days of Thunder* reunited Cruise with director Tony Scott and producers Jerry

Bruckheimer and Don Simpson, who had been responsible for Cruise's blockbuster *Top Gun*.

Director Scott rendered *Days of Thunder* in his trademark slick visual style, with romantic lighting and energetic handheld camerawork. The similarities in style and narrative between *Days* and *Top Gun* did not escape the reviewers or the audiences. The film grossed $84 million—a modest success, but not the blockbuster Paramount had hoped it would be.[4] In retrospect, *Days of Thunder* is remembered as the film on which Cruise met Nicole Kidman, for whom he eventually left wife Mimi Rogers.

In the story, Cole Trickle trains to race and win the Daytona 500, so much of the action was shot in and around this Florida city. Daytona eagerly played

Figure 6.8. Publicity photo from *Days of Thunder*.
(Doll/Morrow Collection)

Figure 6.9. Publicity photo from *Days of Thunder*. (Doll/Morrow Collection)

host to the Bruckheimer-Simpson production team, even closing off a stretch of its famous beach for a scene in which Cole races on the sand. NASCAR also cooperated with the filmmakers, hoping that the film would increase the popularity of stock car racing among the general public. The organization allowed the film crew to outfit two cars from Hendricks Motorparts with cameras, which were turned on for the first forty laps of the actual Daytona 500. The "car cam" footage was edited into the racing sequences to offer the audience the illusion that they were in Cole's car.

For NASCAR fans, *Days of Thunder* was more than a well-crafted film about their favorite sport. The script also contained in-jokes and allusions to NASCAR drivers and insiders. Cole Trickle was supposedly a fictionalized representation of ace driver Tom Richmond, while Robert Duvall's Harry Hogge was based on real-life mechanic Harry Hyde. Car dealer Tim Daland, played by character actor Randy Quaid, was a thinly disguised version of car kingpin Rick Hendricks.[5] Other drivers in the film were based on real-life racers such as Darrell Waltrip and Rusty Wallace, while Hyde advised screenwriter Robert Towne during the film's production. Despite these inside references, the film did contain anomalies obvious to even a casual NASCAR fan. Chief among them is that Daytona is depicted as a culminating event to the racing season when it is actually the first race on the circuit.

The NASCAR heritage was the most unique element to the film, and the filmmakers would have done well to exploit it further. Long associated with the South, stock car racing can claim to be America's most colorful sport largely because of its historical origins. A few of the sport's earliest drivers—including the legendary Junior Johnson—had been bootleggers who honed their driving skills on winding mountain roads in souped-up cars. The drivers generally carried (or "ran") liquor for moonshiners who distilled it in the hills of Appalachia to sell illegally in large towns. The liquor cars were stripped down and revamped with large engines so the drivers could outrun the federal revenue agents.

As bootlegging boomed during Prohibition, some of the drivers began to race among themselves, and locals gathered to watch. In 1938, William H. G. "Bill" France organized a big race on the beach in Daytona, Florida, which prompted other, similar events over the next few years. In 1948, Bill France formed the National Association of Stock Car Racing (NASCAR) to formalize the interest in racing stock cars. The term "stock cars" derived from the idea that they were modified versions of vehicles that everyday people could find in stock at car dealerships. In the 1950s, several bootleggers turned to organized racing to supplement their income or to get away from the dangers and uncertainties of running liquor for a living. These drivers were among the best on the tracks; they were authentic in a way later generations of drivers were not, because they had depended on their automotive knowledge and skills for their livelihoods and their very lives. They became legends through their amazing feats of driving—and also through the tall tales they told to eager reporters.

The first Daytona 500 was held in 1959, and the following year Junior Johnson, one of the original bootleggers-turned-drivers, won. Stock car racing became the South's most popular sport, and the Daytona 500 quickly grew into the most important race on the NASCAR circuit.

Days of Thunder, with its glamorized depiction of the sport and its enthusiasts, makes little use of this history. The South is merely a backdrop in the film, not a force that propels the action or defines the characters. Few characters speak with Southern accents, and only Michael Rooker, as Cole's rival Rowdy Burns, and Robert Duvall, as Harry Hogge, portray Southerners. Aside from Harry's expressed distaste for Cole as a Yankee, the uniqueness of the region and its culture have been omitted or sanitized to appeal to the broadest audience possible. The sport's past link to Appalachian moonshiners and bootleggers is only indirectly referred to in a scene in which Cole's racing team relax with a few jars of moonshine, courtesy of Harry, whose accent, personality, and mechanical skills recall the drivers of the past. The scene concludes with a practical joke in which some phony state troopers "arrest" the team for transporting moonshine across the state line. Only the most diehard of racing fans will understand the significance of this scene—and the differences between Harry's generation and Cole's.

THE CREDITS

Released in 1990 by Paramount Pictures
Produced by Jerry Bruckheimer and Don Simpson
   and Gerald R. Molen
Directed by Tony Scott
Written by Robert Towne, from a story by Tom Cruise
Cinematography by Ward Russell
Edited by Robert C. Jones, Chris Lebenzon, Bert
   Lovitt, Michael Tronick, Stuart Waks, and Billy
   Weber
Music by Hans Zimmer
Art direction by Benjamin Fernandez and Thomas
   E. Sanders

THE CAST

Tom Cruise	Cole Trickle
Robert Duvall	Harry Hogge
Nicole Kidman	Dr. Claire Lewicki
Randy Quaid	Tim Daland
Cary Elwes	Russ Wheeler
Michael Rooker	Rowdy Burns
Fred Dalton Thompson	Big John
John C. Reilly	Buck Bretherton
J. C. Quinn	Waddell
Don Simpson	Aldo Bennedetti

JUST CAUSE

Every once in a while, you've got to get
a little bloody. It's good for the soul.
—Laurie Armstrong in *Just Cause*

THE STORY

A black man on Florida's death row for the rape and murder of a young white girl appeals to Harvard law professor Paul Armstrong to investigate his case. A vocal opponent of the death penalty, Armstrong finds his own convictions tested when he immerses himself in a world of duplicitous murderers, hardheaded cops, and a small town eager for its vengeance.

THE FILM

Just Cause is a twisting crime thriller that explores the murky topic of capital punishment in America. Based on a popular novel by former *Miami Herald* reporter John Katzenbach, the film touches on police brutality, race in the penal system, and the urge for vengeance that often plays a role in the prosecution of particularly heinous crimes. While the story begins with a clearly liberal perspective on these issues, its many turns of plot throw all the characters and their beliefs into an entirely different light.

The film opens with the arrest of a young black man, Bobby Earl, at the home of his grandmother in the backwaters of southern Florida. During a twenty-two-hour interrogation, he confesses to the murder and rape of an eleven-year-old white girl in a swamp near the fictional town of Ochopee. Eight years later, while awaiting execution on death row, he contacts famed Harvard law professor Paul Armstrong, who has built his academic career on his opposition to the death penalty. At first reluctant to get involved, Armstrong is urged to look into the case by his young wife, who believes that an excursion from his ivory tower into the real world will be a useful learning experience.

Armstrong arrives in Ochopee and quickly earns the ire of the small community for reopening the old wounds of the brutal crime. His chief nemesis becomes Sheriff Tanny Brown, the black officer who headed the investigation of the girl's murder. Brown is both feared and respected in the community, and Bobby Earl claims the belligerent lawman coerced his confession through a severe beating and a round of Russian roulette. When Armstrong finds there is little evidence beyond the confession to support the guilt of the educated and articulate Bobby Earl, his investigations lead to another death row inmate, a frightening, egomaniacal serial killer named Blair Sullivan who hints that he may have committed the crime. With the reluctant assistance of Sheriff Brown, Armstrong uncovers evidence that points to Blair as the killer and secures the release of Bobby Earl.

In the film's final act, however, Armstrong learns that he has been nothing more than a pawn in a complex manipulation by the real killer and that many of the allies and enemies he's made are not what they first appeared to be. A final confrontation with the killer in the swamps of Florida forces Armstrong into the role of executioner and leaves his long-held convictions shaken.

Just Cause enjoyed moderate success at the box office despite mixed reviews in the popular press. The most common criticism of the film is that its elaborate plot twists strain credulity, but these shifts are handled skillfully for the most part and they serve a clear function, allowing the film to explore both sides of a murky, emotionally charged issue. The strong performances by Sean Connery as the Harvard professor and Laurence Fishburne as the Southern sheriff also make the manipulative nature of the story more palatable. Connery, who is best known for playing swaggering men of action, ably executes this atypical role of an ineffective man whose vast knowledge is undermined by his real-world naïveté. Fishburne is remarkably enigmatic as the lawman who seems alternately noble and sinister. The film also benefits from skillful choices by director Arne Glimcher, who effectively uses visual and aural flashbacks to manipulate the story line and bring emotional peaks to the tale.

Setting was also crucial to the effectiveness of *Just Cause* in several ways. Placing the story of a violent black-on-white crime in the rural South brought

Figure 6.10. Publicity photo from *Just Cause*. (Doll/Morrow Collection)

the issue of race to the fore and strengthened the film's frequent references to the role that race can play in the outcome of capital cases. Florida in particular made an appropriate backdrop because of the state's leading position in the debate over capital punishment in America. In 1972 the U.S. Supreme Court ruled that the death penalty statutes of forty states including Florida were unconstitutionally arbitrary, effectively banning all executions in the United States. Florida rewrote its statutes within five months to address the flaws cited by the Court and acted as a plaintiff in one of several cases that resulted in a new Supreme Court ruling four years later reinstating capital punishment by states. Since then Florida has been one of the leading states in number of executions and has also had the highest number of wrongful death-row convictions in the nation. Numerous protests and legal challenges have targeted Florida's revised death penalty statutes, but none has been successful.

In addition to these historical and social implications of the Florida setting, the state's natural environment adds several metaphorical layers to the story. The violent acts in the film occur in the swamps of southern Florida, and the preternatural black waters serve to represent the primal urges that lurk in all of us, even in enlightened professors from Harvard University. The swamps also represent the quagmire that Armstrong finds himself in when he steps out from behind his lectern into the real world. When Tanny Brown brings

Armstrong to the scene of the young girl's death, he repeatedly tells him to look around at the dangerous world he's ventured into, clearly telling him that he's wandered into a place more treacherous and complex than he imagined. In a more subtle way, the Florida backwater setting also conveys the idea that the film's topic of capital punishment is murkier than those on either side of the argument may realize.

THE CREDITS

Released in 1995 by Warner Brothers
Produced by Arne Glimcher, Steve Perry,
    and Lee Rich
Directed by Arne Glimcher
Written by Jeb Stuart and Peter Stone, from
    the novel by John Katzenbach
Cinematography by Lajos Koltai
Edited by William Anderson and Armen Minasian
Music by James Newton Howard
Production design by Patrizia von Brandenstein
Art direction by Dennis Bradford

THE CAST

Sean Connery	Paul Armstrong
Laurence Fishburne	Sheriff Tanny Brown
Kate Capshaw	Laurie Armstrong
Blair Underwood	Bobby Earl
Ed Harris	Blair Sullivan
Christopher Murray	Detective T. J. Wilcox
Ruby Dee	Evangeline
Scarlett Johansson	Kate Armstrong

MONSTER

[Director Patty Jenkins] shot it where it happened, so
we have extras on the set every day that were there.
—actor Bruce Dern, in "Based on a True Story,"
by Gabriel London

THE STORY

After a childhood of abuse and neglect in the Midwest, Aileen Wuornos heads to Florida and becomes a roadside prostitute. Now in her mid-thirties, she contemplates suicide until a chance meeting with a confused young lesbian named Selby renews her hope for a normal life. The two run off, but Aileen's attempts to find a job to support them prove fruitless. After returning to prostitution, she kills and robs a client who brutally raped her, and the incident leads her to commit a string of similar murders. When captured by the police, she confesses to the crimes and accepts a death sentence in order to protect Selby.

Figure 6.11. Publicity photo from *Monster*. (Doll/Morrow Collection)

THE FILM

Between December 1989 and November 1990, prostitute Aileen Wuornos shot and killed seven men in central and northern Florida, according to the confession she provided police after her arrest. She claimed all the killings were in self-defense, but prosecutors labeled her a remorseless and dangerous serial killer. A jury found her guilty after a two-week trial in 1992. She ultimately received six death sentences—one body was never found—and the state executed her on October 9, 2002. At the AFI film festival fifty-three weeks later, writer-director Patty Jenkins debuted her first feature film, *Monster*, a fictionalized account of Wuornos's story.

Jenkins did extensive research into Wuornos's life before beginning the film. She contacted Dawn Botkins, a childhood friend of Wuornos who corresponded regularly with the convicted killer during the ten years she spent on death row. Botkins allowed Jenkins to read the letters she had received from Wournos. The filmmaker came away touched by the fact that, despite a horrific childhood of abuse, neglect, and abandonment and twenty years as a low-end prostitute, Wournos could still tenderly express the love and hope she drew from her relationship with Tyria Moore, even after Moore testified against her at her trial. Building on this genuine sentiment, Jenkins crafted a moving story about a woman forced into a hopeless, hellish life who grasps at one last chance for happiness, not realizing she has been damaged beyond all hope of repair.

To prepare for portraying this complex, twisted figure, Charlize Theron read the Botkins letters and watched hours of documentaries and news footage taken after Wuornos's arrest. The beautiful South African actress also gained thirty pounds and subjected herself to an extensive regimen of makeup, hair treatment, and prosthetics that transformed her into a haggard, haunted drifter. The demanding role required her to express a range of emotions both excessive and subtle, from despair and elation to indifference and intense rage. The effort earned Theron rave reviews and an Academy Award.

To bring greater authenticity to the movie, *Monster* was filmed entirely on location in central and northern Florida, where Wuornos lived and perpetrated her crimes. The area is depicted as a blighted urban desert of strip malls, seedy motels, and roadside bars, void of hope or opportunity and surrounded by the wild, imposing woodlands where Wuornos dispatched her victims. As Jenkins put it, "It's not sweeping, lush Florida."[6] The Last Resort, a biker bar in Port Orange, Florida, was used to shoot a number of key scenes in the film. Wuornos was a regular at the Last Resort, and her arrest on January 9, 1991, actually occurred as she was leaving the establishment. The club's owner and one of its bartenders, who both knew Wuornos well, portray themselves in the film.

Despite the realism that the research and use of locations brought to the movie, *Monster* remains a highly fictionalized account of Wuornos's life. In the film, her lover Selby is portrayed by Christina Ricci as a vulnerable, fragile youth confused over her sexuality, but the character is not actually based on Wuornos's real lover Tyria Moore. The film also created a secondary character played by Bruce Dern, a Vietnam vet named Thomas who looks out for Wuornos and offers her brotherly advice. Also, the first killing in the film is in response to a brutal attempted rape, which makes at least this one murder appear justified. Though no one really knows what happened between the killer and any of her victims, Wuornos did later recant her claims of self-defense. All these fictionalized elements in *Monster* serve Jenkins's theme, the oppression of women in a man's world. Still, the movie does not whitewash Wuornos's crimes or depict her as an innocent. The character portrayed by Theron is clearly disturbed, and several of the murders are decidedly cold, brutal, and unjustifiable. Through this combination of events, characters, and images, Jenkins managed the remarkably difficult feat of presenting a sympathetic sociopath who is at once frightening and pitiable.

THE CREDITS

Released in 2003 by Newmarket Films
Produced by Mark Damon, Donald Kushner, Clark Peterson, Charlize Theron, and Brad Wyman
Directed by Patty Jenkins
Written by Patty Jenkins
Cinematography by Steven Bernstein
Edited by Arthur Coburn and Jane Kurson
Production design by Edward T. McAvoy
Art direction by Orvis Rigsby
Music by BT

THE CAST

Charlize Theron	Aileen
Christina Ricci	Selby
Bruce Dern	Thomas
Lee Tergesen	Vincent Corey
Annie Corley	Donna
Pruitt Taylor Vince	Gene/stuttering john
Marco St. John	Evan/undercover john
Marc Macaulay	Will/"daddy" john
Scott Wilson	Horton/last john
Kaitlin Riley	Teenage Aileen
Cree Ivey	Seven-year-old Aileen

Selling Aileen Wuornos

Almost from the day of her arrest, Aileen Wuornos was at the center of an intense media frenzy. The story of "America's first female serial killer" was reported by journalists across the country right up until her death. Her former lover Tyria Moore and others close to Wuornos attempted to negotiate book and movie deals after her arrest, and her own lawyer was reprimanded for charging thousands of dollars for interviews with his client. Two Florida police officers were forced to resign when it was learned they too were attempting to negotiate a movie deal while they were investigating Wuornos's case. Over the years, several documentary films about Wuornos's original trial and her execution have been produced, and several books chronicling her life and crimes have also been written. Composer Carla Lucero wrote an opera titled *Wuornos* that debuted in 2001, and a made-for-television movie titled *Overkill: The Aileen Wournos Story*—also filmed in Florida—aired in 1992.

ROSEWOOD

Rosewood seemed like a ripe subject to
paint a very provocative portrait of the
America people rarely want to talk about.
—director John Singleton,
in "*Rosewood*: Production Notes"

THE STORY

Racial tensions simmer between two communities in 1920s Florida, one prosperous and black, the other struggling and white. When a white woman falsely
claims to have been assaulted by a black man, the tension erupts into several days of violence that end in the complete destruction of the black town.
During the tragedy, two men on opposite sides of the confrontation learn to
work together to save as many lives as they can.

THE FILM

In 1982 journalist Gary Moore was writing a story on western Florida's Levy
County. While investigating the area's history, he uncovered press clippings
describing a horrific crime that resulted in the destruction of an entire Levy
community in 1923. Like most Floridians, Moore had never heard this story
before, and he began to piece together the long-forgotten episode through
old documents and interviews with survivors and their descendants that he
managed to track down. On July 25 he published a lengthy article in the *St.
Petersburg Times* that retold the incident in shocking detail for the first time in
sixty years. National media coverage based on Moore's work caught the attention of producer Jon Peters, who set to work on *Rosewood*, a disturbing depiction of this dark moment in Florida's history.

The town of Rosewood was established in 1845 and originally comprised
only a handful of white homesteaders. The abundant red cedar in the region
soon resulted in a small logging and milling industry that warranted a railroad line and depot. During Reconstruction, the isolated area began attracting
black families who came to work timber, process turpentine, or draw a living
from the land by trapping or farming. Over the next fifty years, blacks became an increasingly large percentage of Rosewood's population. By 1920 the
small town included only a handful of whites among some two hundred black
residents who had built comfortable homes, stable businesses, and an active
community life. The neighboring white settlement of Sumner was by and large
a company town whose simple homes and stores were owned by a local mill.

Figure 6.12. *Rosewood* star Ving Rhames.
(Doll/Morrow Collection)

Little tension seemed to exist between the two communities despite their dif-
fering racial makeup and economic status, and people moved freely back and
forth between the towns without incident or care. Somehow the area seemed
to have escaped the specter of lynchings and race riots that had become epi-
demic throughout the United States in the years following World War I.

On New Year's Day in 1923, however, a Sumner woman named Fanny Taylor
claimed that she had been assaulted by an unknown black man in her home.
Some witnesses later claimed that Fanny had entertained a white visitor that
morning, presumably a lover with whom she quarreled, and that she concocted
her assault story to explain away her bruises to her husband. The residents of
Sumner accepted her story, though, after news arrived that a black convict had
recently escaped from a chain gang in the area. A deputized posse scoured
the woods for the perpetrator and were eventually led by their bloodhounds
to the Rosewood residence of Sam Carter. The interrogation of Carter turned
first into torture and then into murder, and his bullet riddled body was hung

Figure 6.13. Jon Voight *(left)*, John Singleton *(center)*,
and Ving Rhames of *Rosewood*. (Doll/Morrow Collection)

from a tree. The search continued for two more days without success, and Rosewood residents grew increasingly fearful of their neighbors from Sumner. One Rosewood man, Sylvester Carrier, gathered up his extended family and a supply of weapons and barricaded them in his house. The Sumner posse gathered outside the Carrier home, and a gun battle ensued with several deaths on both sides. News of this incident spread rapidly through the state, and armed whites from several parts of Florida descended on Rosewood. Over the next several days the town was burned to the ground, and its terrified residents fled to the surrounding woods and swamps for safety.

Though public officials decried the mob violence that took hold in Levy County, a grand jury investigation later that year failed to find sufficient evidence to press charges against anyone involved in the incident. The little that is known about the destruction of the town after the Carrier shootout has been gleaned from the few remaining official records and from often conflicting eyewitness accounts. A 1993 investigation by the state of Florida confirmed only eight deaths, but some survivors of the incident claim to have seen mass graves holding dozens of burned and brutalized bodies.

The harrowing story of this forgotten community is retold in the 1997 film *Rosewood*. The film was shot entirely on location in Levy County a short distance from the actual site of the town. Few photos or physical descriptions of Rosewood were available, so production designer Paul Sylbert relied on the recollections of survivor Minnie Lee Langley to envision the town. More than thirty period buildings from other parts of central Florida were transported to the site, and the film crew built an additional fifteen homes and laid a railroad line down the center of town.

Given the varying accounts of that week in Rosewood, writer Gregory Poirier and director John Singleton felt free to add embellishments and select those versions of the history that best fit their theme for the film. Early scenes emphasize Rosewood as a strong, stable, and close-knit community, while Sumner is inhabited by stereotypically racist and vile white trash. The film includes invented characters, such as a World War I vet named Mann, played by Ving Rhames, who uses his skills as a soldier to inflict damage on the mob. It also alters the personalities of some of the historical figures, such as Rosewood's white storekeeper John Wright, played by Jon Voight. The real Wright arranged for a train to carry many of Rosewood's women and children to safety during the violence and is generally remembered as a hero who had nothing but respect for his black neighbors. In the film, the character exploits Rosewood's residents both economically and sexually and is initially reluctant to aid them, though he does arrange for the train at the urging of Mann. Many survivors and their descendants took issue with *Rosewood's* accuracy, but the alterations to the story serve to make an effective film that explores the complexities and horrors of racism in American history.

THE CREDITS	THE CAST	
Released in 1997 by Warner Brothers	Jon Voight	John Wright
Produced by Jon Peters	Ving Rhames	Mann
Directed by John Singleton	Don Cheadle	Sylvester Carrier
Written by Gregory Poirier	Bruce McGill	Duke Purdy
Cinematography by Johnny E. Jensen	Loren Dean	James Taylor
Edited by Bruce Cannon	Esther Rolle	Aunt Sarah
Music by John Williams	Elise Neal	Beulah (Scrappie)
Production design by Paul Sylbert	Robert Patrick	Fanny's lover
Art direction by Chris Gorak	Michael Rooker	Sheriff Walker
	Catherine Kellner	Fanny Taylor

STICK

The one thing he couldn't do was stick to the rules.

—poster for Stick

THE STORY

After his release from prison for armed robbery, Ernest Stickley accompanies an old friend to a drug deal only to see him murdered. As determined to seek revenge as he is to go straight, Stickley eases his way into the circle of a wealthy Florida businessman who has ties to the drug dealer responsible for his friend's death.

THE FILM

Throughout the 1970s, Burt Reynolds built a solid career around his roguish, charming, masculine image in films such as *Gator, Rough Cut, Semi-Tough,* and *Smokey and the Bandit.* Through this persona, he established himself as America's undisputed box-office leader by the end of the decade. But he interspersed these films with more thoughtful, complex characters that stretched his skills as an actor in films such as *The End* and *Starting Over.* Beginning with *Gator* in 1976, he proved himself capable as a director as well. His success collapsed in the early 1980s, however, with a string of box-office disappointments. The 1985 film *Stick,* based on the novel by acclaimed writer Elmore Leonard, offered the potential for Reynolds to climb back to the top and bring the varied facets of his career together in one production. Unfortunately, studio interference and poor timing conspired against him, and the film became just another of the many failed attempts to adapt Leonard's complex work to the big screen.

Stick, like many of Leonard's novels, is set in Florida. The main character, car thief Ernest Stickley, first appeared in an earlier Leonard novel titled *Swag,* in which he joined a used-car salesman to go into the armed-robbery business. *Stick* picks up seven years later after the title character gets out of prison, determined to go straight for the sake of his teenaged daughter. When an old friend is callously betrayed and murdered by a drug dealer, Stickley struggles to balance his urge for vengeance with his yearning for a normal life. He walks both sides of the line by finding a straight job as the chauffeur of a flamboyant businessman who likes to socialize with known criminals, including the drug dealer responsible for the death of Stickley's friend. Though he's just the hired help living on a $3-million estate, he develops a romance with his employer's jet-setting financial advisor as he works toward a showdown with the story's villain.

Figure 6.14. *Stick* star and director Burt Reynolds. (Doll/Morrow Collection)

In many ways, *Stick* seemed the perfect vehicle for Reynolds. Stickley is a psychologically complex character who faces difficult choices in an unfamiliar world but remains a rugged, capable man of action who ultimately uses physical force to attain his goals. The film offered Reynolds the prospect of bringing together the two disparate aspects of his acting career that he had been pursuing for a decade.

Reynolds the movie star has always overshadowed Reynolds the director. While none of his directorial efforts brought him high-profile awards, some of them, including *The End* and *Hooper*, were critically acclaimed box-office successes. The films he directed share a number of characteristics, including a savvy use of his own star image. He also proved himself adept at combining action and comedy to create a spirit of conviviality and good times that lights up the screen. Often using the same character actors from film to film, Reynolds built an easy camaraderie among his casts that carried over to their performances. Because many of the films centered on characters who belonged to a clique—stuntmen in *Hooper* or cross-country racers in *The Cannonball Run*—the chemistry created among the performers made the final films better than the scripts they were taken from. Reynolds also drew on his Florida heritage to create a genuine feel for the South in his films, rather than broadly depicting the region in negative stereotypes as is so often done. From the backwoods color of *Gator* to the roguish mix of Miami lowlifes in *Stick*, Reynolds's films offer authentic snapshots of Southern culture.

The script for *Stick*, penned by Elmore Leonard, provided a faithful adaptation of the story, but when Reynolds presented his cut to Universal Pictures, it was rejected. The studio brought in another writer to prepare additional action scenes and sent Reynolds back to Florida for reshoots. While the final version of *Stick* exhibits some of the elements favored by Reynolds as a director, it lacks the light touch that is one of his strengths. It also suffers from an inconsistent tone, likely due to the added scenes. Leonard was bitterly disappointed with the result. In his den he hung a poster bearing the film's tagline, "The one thing he couldn't do was stick to the rules," but altered it by replacing the word "rules" with "script."

While the film proved less than successful for Universal, Reynolds, and Leonard, it did represent a high point in the career of another film professional. Throughout the 1970s and 1980s, Dar Robinson was widely acclaimed as the best stuntman in the world. While crashing motorcycles, setting himself on fire, and being thrown through windows, he managed to set more than twenty world records. But his specialty, which he demonstrated in his first professional stunt for the film *Papillon*, was the high fall. Two of his best-known achievements were a nine-hundred-foot plunge from the Canadian National Tower in Toronto and a spectacular feat in which he drove a convertible over the rim of the Grand Canyon, leapt from the car, and parachuted to safety. Known as a meticulous planner who constantly recalculated the physics of his gags, Robinson also developed revolutionary equipment that is still used by stuntmen today. One of those inventions, a slow-braking mechanism that allowed him to safely free-fall great distances while rigged to a single steel safety cable, was integral to the most memorable scene in *Stick*.

Robinson had played minor parts in a few films before, but Reynolds—a great supporter of stuntmen and their talents—gave him the opportunity to portray a high-profile secondary character in *Stick*. As a menacing albino hitman named Moke, he pursues Stickley through much of the film. Their final confrontation occurs on the balcony of a Coconut Grove high-rise and ends with Moke plummeting twenty stories to his death. Using the slow-braking mechanism on a cable attached to his ankle, Robinson made the jump with nothing but the concrete pavement below him. The camera looks down from the balcony as he falls seemingly all the way to the ground. Making the stunt even more dramatic and difficult, Robinson falls with his back to the ground and his face to the camera the entire time, and he aims and fires a weapon repeatedly as he goes. Even for modern audiences accustomed to computer-generated effects, the scene still provides a heart-stopping thrill in an otherwise uneven film.

THE CREDITS

Released in 1985 by Universal Pictures
Produced by Robert Daley and Jennings Lang
Directed by Burt Reynolds
Written by Elmore Leonard and Joseph Stinson,
    from the novel by Elmore Leonard
Cinematography by Nick McLean
Edited by William Gordean
Music by Joseph Conlan and Barry De Vorzon
Production design by James Shanahan
Art direction by Ed Richardson

THE CAST

Burt Reynolds	Ernest "Stick" Stickley
Candice Bergen	Kyle
George Segal	Barry Braham
Charles Durning	Chucky
Castulo Guerra	Nestor
José Pérez	Rainy
Dar Robinson	Moke

Elmore Goes to Hollywood

Elmore Leonard began writing in the 1950s, penning Westerns for the pulp market and the occasional screenplay while holding down a steady job in advertising. In 1967 he sold the rights to his novel *Hombre* to Twentieth Century–Fox, which turned the story into a well-regarded revisionist Western starring Paul Newman. That sale allowed Leonard to devote his full efforts to writing. Over the next fifteen years he moved away from the Western genre and developed a unique brand of modern thriller that eventually caught the attention of readers, literary critics, and Hollywood. A typical Leonard novel presents a dangerous and colorful cast who operate around the fringes of normal urban life. His stories often involve a complex get-rich-quick caper but focus strongly on the development and interactions of the characters. Leonard's terse, economical prose, rhythmic dialogue, and harshly realistic settings carry the reader through a long setup to a surprisingly brief conclusion.

More than a dozen of Leonard's novels have been adapted to the big screen, but, more often than not, the impact and artistry of his writing fails to survive the transition, which happened to *The Big Bounce* not once but twice. It wasn't until 1995 when John Travolta portrayed Chili Palmer, a Miami loan shark who moves to Hollywood and muscles his way into the movie business in *Get Shorty*, that an effective film was made from a Leonard novel. Even that movie's success was tainted by a baffling and meandering sequel in 2005, *Be Cool*. The two films that best capture the spirit of Leonard's work are *Jackie Brown* and *Out of Sight*. Adapted by Quentin Tarantino in 1997, *Jackie Brown* tells the story of a flight attendant and part-time smuggler who outwits a brutal arms dealer and the federal agents who are out to catch him. In Steven Soderbergh's *Out of Sight*, a roguish bank robber initiates a relationship with a female federal marshal after kidnapping her during his escape from a Florida prison. In both cases, it took a strong, talented director to bring out the best of Leonard's dark, unpleasant world.

SUNSHINE STATE

Almost overnight, out of the muck and the mangroves,
we created this. . . . Nature on a leash.
    —real estate mogul Murray Silver in *Sunshine State*

THE STORY

A huge real estate group arrives at a small island off the coast of Florida with plans for redevelopment. The residents become divided over the future of the community and struggle with their mixed feelings for the land, for each other, and for the area's history and its future.

THE FILM

Some critics claim that it takes less time to watch a John Sayles movie than to explain one. While that may be an exaggeration, *Sunshine State* comes close to proving it true. This epic character study about the effects of real-estate developers on a small Florida island follows an array of intertwined characters over several days as they look inward at themselves and outward at their community, struggling to come to terms with their past so that they can chart a course for the future. The subject matter and episodic structure of the film is typical of Sayles's style.

Sayles's artistic career began in the 1970s when he published a number of critically acclaimed novels and short stories. Through the connections of his literary agent, he secured several screenwriting assignments with B-movie king Roger Corman, including *Piranha* and *The Howling*. He used the script fees to fund his first directorial effort, *The Return of the Secaucus Seven*, about a group of 1960s radicals who come together for a reunion in their hometown. The film was well received, and he went on to create a string of admired films that made him a successful independent filmmaker long before the current independent film movement was launched. As such, he represents an early model for today's independents who seek creative control and freedom from the studios in their filmmaking.

At first, Sayles's films seem most notable for their diversity—a struggling Irish family saved by the mythic beliefs of their heritage in *The Secret of Roan Inish*, America's great baseball scandal of 1919 in *Eight Men Out*, striking West Virginia coal miners in *Matewan*, an extraterrestrial runaway trying to make a new home in Harlem in *Brother from Another Planet*. But acting as writer, director, and editor, Sayles has infused all his films with a consistent narrative and visual style and a clear sociopolitical perspective. Heavy with dialogue and

Figure 6.15. *Sunshine State* director John Sayles. (Doll/Morrow Collection)

monologue, a Sayles film weaves dozens of characters into a complex story structure where the setting or geographic locale weighs importantly on the narrative, often determining the events of the story. His films also echo his liberal views on economics, race, and social justice as they explore his favored themes of community, history, and change.

Sunshine State offers one of the most consistent and thorough expressions of these Sayles trademarks. Following some two dozen characters, the film provides a remarkably detailed portrait of two neighboring communities—white Delrona and black Lincoln Beach—threatened by change in the form of real estate development. The residents sift through their shared histories, struggling to determine which aspects of their heritage are worth preserving, which can be let go, and how far they should carry the fight. Though their attentions are focused on these external questions, each character's motivations come from within. The questions are worth asking because the answers are integral to their personal identities. Only by defining and valuing the past can the characters understand first themselves and then their families and neighbors, so that they can forge and manage relationships with each other.

The film's two most prominent characters are women in their forties who appear not to know each other. Marly of Delrona grudgingly manages the family motel and restaurant in order to preserve the long-held dreams of her ailing father. Desiree is returning to Lincoln Beach for the first time in twenty-five years. Having left town as a teenager, pregnant and disgraced, she's now bringing a new Northern husband to meet her estranged mother. For both women, the burdens of heritage and personal history have hobbled their journeys toward complete and satisfying lives. Over the course of the film, Marly explores her past and her identity through a budding relationship with Jack Meadows, a landscape architect who works for the encroaching developers. Though outwardly railing against the interlopers, Marly has a buried wish that the family sell the business, and her dalliance with Jack represents a flirtation with that wish. Desiree struggles to begin a dialogue with her prim mother, whose middle-class values and concern for appearances drove Desiree away as a youth. In the end, neither Marly nor Desiree has fully shed her burden, but each has begun to understand that she can bear the load and even be grateful to have it.

In addition to Marly and Desiree, the film presents a host of residents who flow naturally in and out of each other's lives. Francine Pinkney, a civic booster from Delrona, struggles to initiate the town's Buccaneer Days festivities, lamenting that no one understands just how hard it is to "invent a tradition." The festival, which presents a trite and sanitized interpretation of the island's violent past as a pirate base, is as meaningless as Francine's hollow marriage. Her husband, an embezzling bank officer, has managed for years to hide his crimes, his desperate gambling problem, and his repeated suicide attempts from her. Francine understands her own life no better than she understands the town's history. Dr. Lloyd, a distinguished elderly neighbor of Desiree's mother, puts up a fierce fight to preserve Lincoln Beach, which he sees as an important landmark of African-American history. During segregation, it provided blacks with their own beachfront resort, and he sorely resents the loss of the united black community that once thrived there. At the same time, Lloyd is shrewd enough to understand that the successes of the civil rights movement led to the town's social and economic demise; without segregation to rally against, Lincoln Beach had nothing left to hold it together. These and all the remaining characters each have their own perspectives on the community's history and their own strategies for incorporating it into their lives.

The Florida setting draws on the very real struggles the state has had with these same issues of preservation-versus-development over the last hundred years. The film offers numerous references to elements of Florida's culture, natural splendor, and history that have been plowed under by bulldozers and built over with strip malls. Marly fondly remembers her brief stint as a performing mermaid at Weeki Wachee, for instance. Though the famed attraction still exists, it lives in the shadow of Florida's many corporate theme parks, and its days are likely numbered. An alligator wrangler displays one of his swamp denizens for Buccaneer Days, touting it as a fearsome reptile from the untamed wilds of the state. However, the caged creature is so sedentary, bored, and nonthreatening that a small child asks if it is dead. And in the end, the developers are ironically foiled by the very history that they so callously dismiss. While breaking ground on their project, they unearth a Native American burial ground that will preclude them from building on the site.

The film is bookended by scenes of a foursome of golfers. These high-powered businessmen pontificate endlessly as they play, reinforcing each other's beliefs in the benefits of capitalism and congratulating each other on having built a civilization out of Florida's wilderness. Almost godlike, they exist in a world outside of both Delrona and Lincoln Beach, but together they manipulate the fates of both communities. For them, the only history is what they create with their business deals and bulldozers, however contrived and inorganic that might be.

THE CREDITS

Released in 2002 by Sony Pictures Classics
Produced by Maggie Renzi
Directed by John Sayles
Written by John Sayles
Cinematography by Patrick Cady
Edited by John Sayles
Music by Mason Daring
Production design by Mark Ricker
Art direction by Shawn Carroll

THE CAST

Alex Lewis	Terrell Wilkins
Alan King	Murray Silver
James McDaniel	Reggie Perry
Angela Bassett	Desiree Stokes Perry
Edie Falco	Marly Temple
Timothy Hutton	Jack Meadows
Miguel Ferrer	Lester
Gordon Clapp	Earl Pinkney
Mary Steenburgen	Francine Pinkney
Bill Cobbs	Dr. Elton Lloyd
Mary Alice	Mrs. Eunice Stokes
Michael Greyeyes	Billy Trucks
Tom Wright	Lee "Flash" Phillips
Sam McMurray	Todd Northrup
Marc Blucas	Scotty Duval
Ralph Waite	Furman Temple
Richard Edson	Steve Tregaskis
Jane Alexander	Delia Temple

ULEE'S GOLD

A lot of people connect to this story. It's not because
they're beekeepers. They've all been in families.
—Victor Nunez, to the *Tampa Tribune*'s Bob Ross

THE STORY

Florida widower Ulee Jackson raises two grandchildren and nurses a drug-
addicted daughter-in-law while his son serves a prison sentence for robbery.
Relying on the steadfast values of his rural heritage, Ulee heals himself and his
family, maintains his beekeeping business, and contends with two of his son's
violent associates.

THE FILM

In some ways, *Ulee's Gold* represented a departure for writer-director Victor
Nunez. The film had a budget of $2.7 million, small by Hollywood standards
but at least three times the funding he had worked with on previous projects. It
also featured Peter Fonda, a major star of an earlier generation who has become
a respected character actor. Nunez typically worked with talented unknowns
or actors whose stars were just beginning to rise. Despite these changes, *Ulee's
Gold* retains the hallmarks of all Nunez films—a Florida setting with a strong
sense of place, a focus on intriguing characters, and a slow dramatic pace that
captures complex aspects of life by concentrating on small moments.

The film tells the story of a taciturn third-generation beekeeper in northern
Florida named Ulee Jackson. The sole survivor of his platoon in Vietnam, he
bears both physical and emotional scars from his wartime experience. In more
recent years he has seen his wife die, his son go to prison for robbery, and his
daughter-in-law run off to lose herself in drug addiction. Battered into a shell
by the events of his life, Ulee struggles to raise his two granddaughters but
is emotionally unable to connect with the needy young girls. Instead he immerses himself in his work, steadfastly facing endless obstacles and long hours
day after day. The solitary, meticulous work of tending his hives requires patience, persistence, and self-reliance—qualities that he's learned from his fore-
bears and that he's obviously clung to all his life. Those same traditional traits
have been abandoned by his son and daughter-in-law, who were seduced into
trouble by a fast and easy modern culture. The oldest granddaughter, a rebellious teen in short skirts and heavy eye makeup who prefers the company of
high school boys to that of her family, seems headed in the same direction. The

Figure 6.16. Publicity photo from *Ulee's Gold*. (Doll/Morrow Collection)

younger girl, just entering adolescence, clings to her innocence by a thread. For Ulee, the apiary seems the only place his philosophy of life can survive.

At the request of his son, Ulee reluctantly tracks down his wayward daughter-in-law only to run into a pair of his son's criminal associates intent on finding the loot from the trio's last robbery. Ulee brings the woman home and forces her through a painful withdrawal while contending with the two threatening criminals. Drawing on the traditional values that had seemed to fail him, he leads the family through its darkest crisis and in doing so rekindles their hope and renews their faith in the family heritage.

These events distract Ulee from his business at a critical time—the few weeks during April and May when the tupelo gum trees blossom along the banks of Florida's Apalachicola River. The bees ignore all other blooms in favor of the trees' pale green flowers and use the nectar to produce one of the finest honeys in the world, with a delicate, flowery taste and a pale amber color slightly tinged with green. Timing is critical to a pure tupelo harvest. Beekeepers must clean their hives out as the blooming season begins and collect the honey just as it ends. Nunez filmed *Ulee's Gold* during tupelo season on the land of the Lanier family, third-generation beekeepers who served as consultants on the film.

The role of beekeeper Ulee Jackson was a major departure for actor Peter Fonda, who is best known as an icon of the hippie generation. He had broken into films in the early 1960s in one of the light *Tammy* comedies starring Sandra Dee. Within a few years he moved away from such Hollywood studio fare to star in a pair of Roger Corman exploitation films about bikers and drugs. Through these films he began to work with Jack Nicholson, Bruce Dern, and Dennis Hopper, who soon came to represent a new Hollywood—edgy, hip filmmakers who embraced the youth movement of the period and turned their backs on the studio-driven movie industry of the preceding three decades. In 1969 Fonda produced, cowrote, and starred in one of the most prominent, influential films of the era, *Easy Rider*. A low-budget independent effort released through Columbia Pictures, *Easy Rider* codified the ideals, disillusionment, and rebellion of America's disaffected youth to a driving rock 'n' roll soundtrack. Fonda's role as the drug-smuggling biker ironically nicknamed Captain America became an icon of the counterculture movement, and the film's success induced many studio executives to embrace this new generation of filmmakers. Fonda steadily appeared in one or two films a year over the next three decades, usually in parts that played off his seemingly indelible image as a counterculture warrior. The 1997 role of Ulee Jackson was the absolute antithesis of this well-established image. Critics heaped praise on Fonda's subtle but expressive performance, frequently comparing it to the work of his well-known father, Henry.

Ulee's Gold ends with a scene of the Jackson family reunited, with all five of them gathered around a table in the prison visiting room. Despite the dire setting, the family is whole, happy, and optimistic about their future together. When Ulee's son asks him how the bees are faring, his stoic response parallels both the plight and the salvation of his family—and of all families: "The mites are choking them. The insecticide's killing them. The drought's starving them. They're fine."

THE CREDITS	THE CAST	
Released in 1997 by Orion Pictures	Peter Fonda	Ulysses "Ulee" Jackson
Produced by Peter Saraf and Sam Gowan	Patricia Richardson	Connie Hope
Directed by Victor Nunez	Christine Dunford	Helen Jackson
Written by Victor Nunez	Tom Wood	Jimmy Jackson
Cinematography by Virgil Mirano	Jessica Biel	Casey Jackson
Edited by Victor Nunez	Vanessa Zima	Penny Jackson
Music by Charles Engstrom	Steven Flynn	Eddie Flowers
Production design by Pat Garner	Dewey Weber	Ferris Dooley
Art direction by Debbie DeVilla	J. Kenneth Campbell	Sheriff Bill Floyd

THE MOVIE TOURIST'S GUIDE TO FLORI-DRAMA

The films in this chapter are serious dramas that address many of the challenging, sobering aspects of life. While movie tourists might reflect on the same mysteries, struggles, and heartaches as the characters in these films, they can also find plenty of life's lighter and more enjoyable moments when visiting these locations.

BLOOD AND WINE

Little Havana, in Miami

The section of Miami now called Little Havana grew into a distinctly Cuban neighborhood after the Mariel Boatlift. It is located approximately between SW 3rd and SW 13th Streets, and from SW 3rd Avenue westward to SW 37th Avenue. The heart of the neighborhood is Calle Ocho, or SW 8th Street.

The area's landmark Cuban restaurant, La Esquina de Tejas, appears in a scene in which Gabriela, played by Jennifer Lopez, has lunch with one of her suitors. Though now under Honduran ownership and called La Esquina de Tejas Hondureña, the restaurant still serves Cuban food along with some Honduran dishes. Located at the corner of SW 1st Street and 12th Avenue, the Esquina was founded in 1965, but the building is much older. Built in the 1920s, it was once the Riverside Tea Garden, and in the 1940s it became the Farmhouse Restaurant with Southern-style cooking.

Key Largo

The plot of *Blood and Wine* thickens at the Caribbean Club, located at mile marker 104 bayside on Key Largo. With its typical tropical decor, the bar fits in with the atmosphere of the Keys. Movie tourists who have seen this sordid crime drama will want to stop in for a beer.

COCOON

St. Petersburg

The St. Petersburg Shuffleboard Club is housed in the Mirror Lake Historic Recreation Complex on Mirror Lake Drive. Founded in the 1920s, it was at one time the largest shuffleboard club in the world, with five thousand members, and it hosted numerous state and national tournaments in addition to offering other forms of entertainment to the community. The club's membership has dwindled, but the historic playing fields are still in operation today. Classes are available for beginners, and the courts are open to the public for play year-round.

The Coliseum Ballroom where the newly invigorated elderly couples in *Cocoon* danced the night away to Big Band music is located on Fourth Street in St. Petersburg. The glittering dance hall has been a town hot spot since 1924 and today hosts a variety of events, from fund raisers and art shows to sock hops and concerts.

CRISSCROSS

Key West

The small hotel where Goldie Hawn's character lives in the film is the Eden House, an Art Deco–era establishment located at 1015 Fleming on Key West. Though the "Edens Hotel" is a haven for hippies and transients in the film, the Eden House is actually a respectable establishment rich in the laid-back atmosphere of the Keys. Movie tourists who stay at the Eden House will want to lounge amid tropical plants in the hammock area called the library, where no music and only soft talking is allowed, which will help "facilitate the shedding of earthly cares," according to the Eden's staff.

CROSS CREEK

Cross Creek

Author Marjorie Kinnan Rawlings's home southeast of Gainesville has been preserved as a state historic site. Visitors can stroll the citrus groves and natural woods on the grounds and tour the house as guides in period clothing tell stories of the Cracker community that Rawlings preserved through her writings. The grounds are open year-round from Thursday to Sunday, but the house itself is closed for cleaning and restoration during the months of August and September.

Just up the road from the Rawlings home, the Yearling Restaurant offers diners an array of authentic Cracker fare including hush puppies, alligator bits, frog's legs, and cooter, a type of soft-shelled turtle native to the area. The restaurant opened in 1952 and became heralded as one of the state's top eateries in the 1970s. It closed in the early 1990s but has since reopened under new management. Chef J. R. Jenkins, whose creations drawn from Rawlings's book *Cross Creek Cooking* earned the restaurant its acclaim in the 1970s, returned to work for the new owners. Five minutes away, in the tiny town of Island Grove, Rawlings's gravesite can be found in the Antioch Cemetery.

DAYS OF THUNDER

Daytona Beach

More than eight million visitors from around the world flock to the Daytona area each year, and while the main attraction is the beach, NASCAR fans come for the racing. Daytona Beach is home to the corporate headquarters of NASCAR.

Daytona International Speedway, located at 1801 W. International Speedway Boulevard in Daytona Beach, is host to eight weekends of racing each year, including NASCAR stock car, sports car, motorcycle, and go-kart races. Just outside the Speedway's fourth turn is Daytona USA, where guests can enjoy a variety of games and activities related to car racing.

Sophie Kay's Waterfall Restaurant

Featured in a prominent scene in the film, the Waterfall Restaurant is owned by local personality Sophie Kay, who has hosted more than 3,500 cooking episodes on television. Movie tourists will want to enjoy the cuisine and check out the famous waterfall after a day at the races. Sophie Kay's is located at 3516 S. Atlantic Avenue along Daytona Beach Shores.

MONSTER

Port Orange

Al Bulling, owner of the Last Resort biker bar, remembers Aileen Wuornos as one of his regulars before her arrest in front of the establishment in January 1991. Located at 5812 S. Ridgewood Avenue, the unpretentious watering hole has capitalized on its association with Florida's famous serial killer, selling T-shirts with her likeness and adopting the slogan "Home of Cold Beer and Killer Women."

ROSEWOOD

Rosewood

The only remaining structure from the Rosewood of the 1920s is a white frame house that belonged to town merchant John Wright, who is portrayed in the film by Jon Voight. In front of the Wright home on State Road 24 about forty miles southwest of Gainesville, a historic marker dedicated in 2004 by Governor Jeb Bush describes the harrowing events of the town's destruction.

STICK

Coconut Grove

Much of *Stick* was shot on location in Fort Lauderdale and Miami. Dar Robinson's spectacular twenty-story free-fall took place in the bohemian but exclusive Miami neighborhood of Coconut Grove. The building from which he plunged, Grove Towers on south Bayshore Drive, offers spectacular views of Biscayne Bay from its high-priced condominiums.

American Beach

John Sayles's *Sunshine State* was shot primarily on Amelia Island, off the northeast coast of Florida. The communities there are remarkably similar to those depicted in the movie and today face the same threat from developers that provided the dramatic impetus of the story. Fictional Lincoln Beach was based on Amelia Island's American Beach. This black resort community was established in the 1930s by A. L. Lewis as a recreational area for the employees of his Afro-American Insurance Company in Jacksonville during the era of segregation. The area quickly became a social and economic hub for blacks throughout Florida and the eastern United States. American Beach's vital role faded along with segregation, but the site remains a major stop on Florida's Black Heritage Trail. Just outside Jacksonville, Amelia Island can be reached via causeway extensions off Highway A1A or First Coast Highway.

ULEE'S GOLD

Wewahitchka

Northeastern Florida along the Apalachicola River is a major center for commercial honey harvesting. The area is known especially for the prized tupelo honey its bees produce in the spring from the blossoms of the tupelo gum trees that line the river. L. L. Lanier and Sons Tupelo Honey, the firm whose lands and bees were used in *Ulee's Gold*, has been in continuous operation since 1890 and is today run by the son and grandsons of founder Lavernor Laveon Lanier. Those interested in a taste of the sweet labors of their bees can visit their operation in Wewahitchka in the Florida Panhandle or order a jar over the Internet.

1

FUN IN THE SUN

[The human] race, in its poverty, has unquestion-
ably one really effective weapon—laughter. . . .
Against the assault of laughter, nothing can stand.
—Mark Twain, "The Mysterious Stranger"

As a popular vacation destination, Florida is naturally associated with fun. In addition to its beaches, oceans, and golf courses, the Sunshine State is home to some of the country's most famous theme parks, including Disney World, Universal Studios, and SeaWorld.

Florida also enjoys a reputation for oddball attractions, which have lured tourists off the beaten path for decades. The mermaid show at Weeki Wachee Springs, the giant gator jaws at Gatorland, and the dancing water fountain in Fort Myers are among the amusing ventures that appeal to the tourist who has seen everything—or wants to.

Oddly enough, while the zany comedies and noisy action films in this chapter are set in Florida, most have little to do with the state's fun-filled attractions, famous or otherwise. Instead, "Fun in the Sun" showcases the breadth and variety of American humor. Even the action films, with their witty one-liners, comic banter, and larger-than-life adventures, offer breezy or lighthearted escape.

Different eras of cinema history are duly represented in this chapter, beginning in 1930 with an early sound film from the Marx Brothers titled *The Cocoanuts*. In their comedy, Groucho, Harpo, Chico, and Zeppo ingeniously combined physical humor and verbal wordplay, making it perfectly suited to the then-new medium of sound film. Groucho's comic persona combined puns, word associations, and doublespeak to con, cajole, or confuse the other characters, revealing his sly superiority over them. He was thus a natural for the role of a land speculator who tries to sell swampland to wealthy tourists in *The Cocoanuts*. Chico, who spoke with a heavy accent of indeterminate origin, used distorted English and malapropisms to habitually misinterpret what other characters were trying to say to him. His comic persona was built on deliberate miscommunication, which frustrated others. Handsome, sporty Zeppo was the consummate straight man for his brothers, amiably tossing verbal cues to Groucho or Chico so they could steal the scene. And finally Harpo, who never spoke, used sound effects to communicate and harp solos to express his inner emotion, making his personal humor as dependent on synchronized sound as the verbal sparring of his brothers.

The Marx Brothers had tapped into a long tradition of physical comedy when they created the unique comic personas they maintained from performance to performance. The creation of a specific character who remained constant was the norm in vaudeville, and this tradition passed into cinema through the films of Mack Sennett during the silent era, then carried through to the sound films of W. C. Fields, the Marx Brothers, Hope and Crosby, Abbott and Costello, and on to Jerry Lewis. Lewis excelled at creating physical comedy, and he proved to be at the peak of his talents when he directed *The Bellboy* in 1959. Portraying his typical naive goof, Lewis wreaks havoc as a bellboy at the Fontainebleau Hotel. The comedian, who is often unfairly maligned for a lowbrow humor, turned Miami's legendary hotel into his own personal theme park as he expertly exploited the comic possibilities of the locale.

Picking up where Lewis left off, contemporary comedian Jim Carrey has also created a comic persona that is consistent from film to film. While Carrey sometimes appears in roles in which he is cast against type, he is firmly identified with the obnoxious title character in *Ace Ventura: Pet Detective*. In this vehicle built around his considerable comic talents, Carrey steals every scene with his distorted facial expressions and loud, exaggerated comic bits.

Other film comedies are not star vehicles constructed around the antics of specific comedians but instead are situational comedies dependent on setup and dialogue. Using legitimate actors in the key roles, these comedies rely much more on the scripted material. In "Fun in the Sun," situational comedies run the gamut from the timeless *Some Like It Hot* to the time-bound *Hello, Down There*. The former, starring Marilyn Monroe, Jack Lemmon, and Tony Curtis, makes clever use of the old Florida cliché about gold diggers looking for millionaires in Miami, while the latter is a 1960s family comedy too heavily tied to dated pop music and technology. *Some Like It Hot* is Billy Wilder's clever satire on American sexual mores and customs; *Hello, Down There* is a bit of fluff starring Tony Randall that attempted to spoof modern domestic science.

The action genre frequently uses—and sometimes misuses—humor to soften scenes of violence. Explosions, car crashes, and a high body count follow the adventures of two Miami cops, played by Martin Lawrence and Will Smith, in *Bad Boys*, but their entertaining banter defuses the grim proceedings. *True Lies* combines a romantic comedy premise with over-the-top action scenes to offer a lighthearted action film that is appealingly far-fetched. Arnold Schwarzenegger plays a spy whose wife thinks he is an ordinary businessman who just happens to go out of town a lot. *Licence to Kill* stars Timothy Dalton as James Bond, who thwarts an array of worldly women and vile villains—all in a day's work for the screen's larger-than-life secret agent. While the Bond films are not intended to be laugh-aloud comedies, their tongue-in-cheek depiction of sex lends a light tone to the films.

The films in this chapter are quite diverse, but they share two characteristics. All of them are escapist or humorous in content, style, or tone, and all of them take place in Florida. Often the films make use of their locales in a comic way; at the least, they reference their uniquely Floridian properties. And while the locations may not be fun-filled theme parks or offbeat attractions, the films themselves are certainly fun to watch.

ACE VENTURA: PET DETECTIVE

See, in '82, we just choked. We had a chance to win it and we didn't.
—quarterback Dan Marino in *Ace Ventura: Pet Detective*

THE STORY

Pet detective Ace Ventura is hired when the Miami Dolphins' mascot, Snow-flake, is kidnapped two weeks before the team's Superbowl game with the Philadelphia Eagles. The plot thickens when Dolphins quarterback Dan Marino is also snatched just before the big game.

THE FILM

Comedian Jim Carrey became a major box-office star in 1994 after *Ace Ventura: Pet Detective* grossed blockbuster numbers on a budget of about $12 million.[1] The lunatic comedy was an immediate hit with young males—the target audience for studios in the contemporary era. Carrey's first big break came when he was cast as a regular on Keenan Ivory Wayans's television series *In Living Color*, where he excelled in sketch comedy and created such memorably outrageous characters as Fire Marshal Bill and body builder Vera de Milo. The series gave him the opportunity to evolve his unique brand of comedy that is larger than life on every scale.

Ace Ventura embodies all of the properties associated with Carrey's roles and could be considered the comedian's signature character. Obtuse and just on the verge of being annoying, Ace sports an exaggerated ducktail haircut, a big overbite, and loud, mismatched outfits but has no awareness of his lack of decorum. Carrey's undeniable talents for exaggerated facial expressions and broad physical comedy are exploited throughout the film, as in the scene where he parodies a grimacing athlete caught in slow motion, then repeats the same action in reverse. The fact that he is dressed in a tutu for the entire gag adds a ludicrous quality that is also part of his style.

Carrey's humor draws attention to the body. The rubber-faced expressions and exaggerated gestures are distorted to such a degree that viewers are in awe of Carrey's physical capabilities, speed, and even grace. He has a unique ability to cavort with complete abandon but control his movements to give shape to the gag or stunt. Another way that his comedy focuses on the body is the penchant for gags that deal with distortion or mutilation. Fire Marshal Bill, whose body is severely scarred from his pyromaniac adventures, offers an obvious example, but even Ace Ventura's extended overbite qualifies. The focus on the body also comes through in the jokes dealing with bodily functions,

Figure 7.1. *Ace Ventura* star Jim Carrey. (Doll/Morrow Collection)

most notably when a frustrated Ace bends over and makes his buttocks appear to talk when his friend stalls with some much needed information. While this joke was a big hit among the adolescent crowd, countless reviewers cited it as an example of the low brow nature of Carrey's humor.

Ace Ventura: Pet Detective was shot in Miami, and the film makes good use of its locale by incorporating the city's football team into the plot. Ace must find Snowflake, the Dolphins' mascot, before their Superbowl game, because the players are too superstitious to think they can win without their good-luck charm. The situation moves from bad to worse when Dolphins quarterback Dan Marino is also kidnapped by a crazed ex-player named Ray Finkle. Not only does Dan Marino play himself, but the film incorporates Dolphins lore and legend into the plot.

Miami was awarded an expansion franchise in 1965, with Minneapolis lawyer Joseph Robbie and entertainer Danny Thomas listed as owners. A contest was held to name the new team, and almost 20,000 entries were submitted by an eager public. Among the names suggested were Mariners, Marauders, Missiles, Moons, Sharks, and Suns, but the committee consisting of seven members of the local media selected "Dolphins." At a public announcement in October 1965, Robbie suggested the suitability of the name when he stated, "The dolphin is one of the fastest and smartest creatures of the sea."[2] The new team quickly advanced from a losing expansion team to a Superbowl participant. The Dolphins played a dismal first season in 1967, but six years later they enjoyed a perfect, undefeated season, going on to win two playoff games and then beat the Washington Redskins 14–7 in Superbowl VII. Since that time the team has participated in five Superbowls and is often a playoff contender; indeed, "since the AFL-NFL merger in 1970, the Miami Dolphins have compiled the best winning percentage of any team in the league."[3]

While George Wilson was the team's first head coach, it is Don Shula who is best remembered as the Dolphins' leader. The record he built up during his tenure included breaking the record for total wins as a coach, with 324 victories. Shula retired after the 1995 season, but he took a job in the front office to remain close to the team that he made famous. Arguably the Dolphins' most revered player is quarterback Dan Marino, who first played for the team in 1983 as a rookie. During the mid-1980s Marino produced an impressive list of NFL statistics, and ten years later he broke the career passing records of Fran Tarkenton for most yards (48,841), touchdowns (352), and completions (3,913).[4] He officially retired in 2000.

The plot makes reference to the Dolphins' real-life Superbowl loss at the end of the 1982 season. In spite of leading with only ten minutes left to play, they lost 27–17 to the Washington Redskins. In the film, blame for the loss is laid literally at the feet of fictional player Ray Finkle, who supposedly missed an all-important field goal. Finkle is ostracized by virtually every football fan in Florida, and the strain drives him insane. He is committed to an asylum by his family, and there he stews over his plight, blaming his holder Dan Marino for not positioning the ball with the laces out. Finkle escapes and steals another person's identity to wreak havoc on the Dolphins by kidnapping Snowflake and Marino so the team will not succeed in their latest bid for a Superbowl championship. Ace Ventura tracks the missing Dolphins through a key clue—the stone from a 1982 AFL championship ring that was left behind when Snowflake was taken. He finds Marino and Snowflake in time to get them both to the big game.

Marino scores a lot of screen time in the film and receives fifth billing. Not surprisingly, his acting is stiff and superficial, but he has one repeated "schtick" that redeems his appearance in the film. In each of his scenes, Marino is compelled to rationalize the Dolphins' loss in the 1982 season. He whines to a police detective, "We just choked in '82. We had a chance to win and we didn't. But nobody's gonna choke this time. If they do, I'll kill 'em," which is an excuse he repeats to anyone in earshot throughout the film. The fact that Marino was not yet a member of the team when the big loss occurred is glossed over in the film.

The weaving of real-life sports trivia and zany comic fiction was never mentioned in any of the reviews of Ace Ventura: Pet Detective. The reviews were brutal, though some critics did single out Jim Carrey's amazing physical talents. The scatalogical humor and gross-out jokes tended to overshadow the film's few redeeming qualities. Ironically, while those aspects appalled most critics, they attracted the intended adolescent audience to make the film a blockbuster hit, spawning a sequel and two animated cartoons.

THE CREDITS

Released in 1994 by Morgan Creek Productions
and Warner Brothers
Produced by Gary Barber, Peter Bogart, Bob Israel,
and James G. Robinson
Directed by Tom Shadyac
Written by Jack Bernstein, Tom Shadyac, and
Jim Carrey
Cinematography by Julio Macat
Edited by Don Zimmerman
Production design by William A. Elliott
Costumes by Bobbie Read

THE CAST

Jim Carrey	Ace Ventura
Courteney Cox	Melissa Robinson
Sean Young	Lt. Lois Einhorn/Ray Finkle
Tone Loc	Emilio
Dan Marino	Himself
Noble Willingham	Riddle
Troy Evans	Roger Podacter
Udo Kier	Ronald "Ron" Camp

The Truman Show

In 1998, Jim Carrey made a bold break from his comfortable comedic milieu to star in director Peter Weir's dramatic satire *The Truman Show*. His touching performance as a man who learns that his entire life has been staged as the subject of a television show earned him critical praise as well as a Golden Globe. The film, which presaged the reality TV craze, also received three Oscar nominations in major categories, though Carrey's work was passed over by the Academy. In the film, Truman is legally adopted as an infant by a television network, which constructs an entire community enclosed in a sphere. All the people in his life, family and friends included, are actually actors who manipulate the character according to the whims of the hit show's producer.

The filmmakers selected the planned community of Seaside, Florida, to serve as Truman's idyllic hometown. Built in the 1980s by Robert Davis, Seaside spawned the New Urbanism movement, a philosophy of city planning that strives to strengthen community through its mixed-income, mixed-use buildings densely packed in a small, pedestrian-friendly space. The two Miami architects who worked with Davis developed a distinctively quaint style for all of Seaside's homes and businesses by studying various small towns across the South. Though New Urbanism has its critics, the creation of Seaside has been one of the most talked-about events in urban planning of the last twenty years, and the town proved to be the perfect setting for a story about a man whose life was too good to be true.

BAD BOYS

Miami is actually a beautiful place to shoot.
—Michael Bay, "Director's Commentary"

THE STORY

Miami police detectives Mike Lowrey and Marcus Burnett must track down the European drug lord who stole $100 million in heroin from the basement of the police station. Their only lead in the case comes from Julie Mott, who witnessed the kingpin brutally murder her close friend because she knew too much.

THE FILM

Bad Boys epitomizes what went wrong with the action film during the 1990s: it is hackneyed, superficial, and over the top. The story of two cops who are after a ruthless drug lord is beyond formulaic—it's derivative. The film cuts and pastes key bits from such action classics as *48 Hrs.*, *Lethal Weapon*, and *Beverly Hills Cop*—though it is doubtful that the target audience of adolescent males minded. Indeed, according to veteran film reviewers and such trade publications as *Variety*, this young target audience prizes the familiar over the new. Likewise, this same audience would not have minded the assault-style editing, which is kinetic and energetic but also incoherent and exhausting to watch. The action genre has been adversely affected by the mainstream film industry's decision to aim action films at the young male audience accustomed to video games and music-video stylistics. The long-term effect of the industry's pandering to a young, undiscerning audience is a hot-button topic among studio executives, filmmakers, critics, and other industry pundits. *Bad Boys* provides ammunition for those arguing against this trend.

Bad Boys exploits two elements that make it tolerable viewing for true fans of the action genre. The best characteristic of the film is the chemistry between the two male leads, Will Smith and Martin Lawrence. Both are solid comic actors who use their skills at ad libbing and improvisation to invigorate the lackluster material, exhibiting a familiarity and ease with each other that is infectious. Most of their banter revolves around a situation in which they are required to switch identities, so that Lawrence's character, Marcus Burnett, pretends to be Will Smith's character, Mike Lowrey, and vice versa. This is supposedly for the benefit of the girl they are assigned to protect, Julie Mott, but there is really no logical narrative reason to keep the ruse going; it exists only to facilitate the repartee between Lawrence and Smith. Buddy-cop films are

Figure 7.2. Publicity photos from *Bad Boys*. (Doll/Morrow Collection)

driven by the relationship between the protagonists, not the plot, so formulaic stories and situations are to be expected. Unfortunately, the narrative of *Bad Boys* is so badly thrown together that Smith and Lawrence's verbal riffs and stream-of-conscious dialogues actually get in the way of the plot. Viewers who try to follow the story will be confused, because there is no direction to the drug investigation, no explanation of character motivation, and no attempt to tie the slight plot threads together.

The film's other high point is its use of Miami as a principal location. Depicted in long shots saturated in oranges and yellows, the city looks modern and sleek. Often the two protagonists are captured in a low angle in front of palm trees or some other iconic motif, suggesting a hip and edgy urban milieu. In the opening sequence, a nicely rendered shot announces this aura of fashion-magazine hipness. As the sun sets in an orange sky, a plane flies above a large sign that reads Miami. The image is shot from a very low angle, so that the underbelly of the plane looms large just above the sign, narrowly missing it. The plane's silhouette against the fiery sky gives the film a graphic, almost abstract design. The effect is one of glamour with just a hint of danger.

Another notable Miami moment occurs in a scene that was shot in the Biltmore Hotel in Coral Gables. The scene depicts the murder of Julie's friend in a luxurious two-story suite that, according to one of the drug lord's henchmen, is known as the Al Capone Suite. A classic hotel from the 1920s, the Biltmore was indeed a favorite of the notorious gangster, who also liked to frequent the hotel's speakeasy on the thirteenth floor. In the DVD commentary for the film, director Michael Bay claims that Capone dispatched several cronies in the suite, and the rooms are haunted by the victims.[5] Bay's version of the Capone folklore is likely untrue, but referencing it in the film makes a playful connection between the fictional gangster in *Bad Boys* and the real-life Capone.

Bay may have liked Miami for its visual potential, but he was otherwise not too pleased with filming in Florida. His directing experience was in music videos, and *Bad Boys* was his first feature film. In his commentary for the DVD, Bay criticizes the abilities of his Florida-based film crews in a series of statements that are unusually tactless and ungracious for such a public forum. During the scenes that take place in Mike Lowrey's apartment, he complains, the Miami-based physical effects crew used too much smoke to create atmosphere in the rooms. He also sneers at the mechanical effect used to destroy the door of the apartment in one of the action scenes, claiming it wasn't realistic—as though realism were a desired effect in a genre known for being over the top.[6] Bay fails to acknowledge his own role in these so-called blunders although, as the director, he is ultimately responsible for the outcome of every scene in the film.

Bay's most telling remarks offer insight into why *Bad Boys* is so poorly edited. In describing the scene in which the drugs are stolen via conveyer belt from the basement of police headquarters, he complains that the crew fought him about the way it was shot, telling him, "This isn't going to cut." They were trying to explain that he wasn't getting the shots necessary to depict the scene with clarity and fluidity. But he did not take their advice, rationalizing that he was shooting in a "nontraditional manner" and that "there are no rules to film."[7]

Bay's "nontraditional manner" resulted in the hyperkinetic editing style that rendered the action scenes incoherent. In this style, a series of brief shots of movement are edited together to create an illusion of speed or ferocity. Sometimes called vertical editing, it is actually a version of Russian montage, and it is frequently exploited in music videos or television commercials. This technique is the opposite of conventional continuity editing, which is linear, offering the illusion that one shot picks up where the last shot left off, so that the action in a scene seems to progress logically and the space is clearly laid out. Vertical editing adds a short-term visceral charge to a scene, but it doesn't always service the story. Vertical editing might be effective in commercials and videos, and even in experimental approaches to narrative films, but its frenetic pace and kinetic style render the car chases, gunfights, and other mainstays of the action film incomprehensible. If every action scene is cut in this style, the film's narrative and themes are obscured, and the scenes become monotonous. In short, Bay should have listened to his Florida crew, because there are indeed rules to film.

THE CREDITS

Released in 1995 by Columbia Tristar
Produced by Don Simpson and Jerry Bruckheimer,
   with Lucas Foster and Bruce S. Pustin
Directed by Michael Bay
Written by George Gallo, Michael Barrie,
   Jim Mulholland, and Doug Richardson
Cinematography by Howard Atherton
Edited by Christian Wagner
Stunts coordinated by Kenny Bates

THE CAST

Martin Lawrence	Marcus Burnett
Will Smith	Mike Lowrey
Tea Leoni	Julie Mott
Tcheky Karyo	Fouchet
Joe Pantoliano	Captain C. Howard
Theresa Randle	Theresa Burnett
Marg Helgenberger	Captain Alison Sinclair

2 Fast 2 Furious

Another action film shot in Florida, *2 Fast 2 Furious*, exploits the same film-making techniques, targets the same youth audience, and suffers from some of the same shortcomings as *Bad Boys*. Yet *Furious* is better crafted, primarily because director John Singleton has a firm grasp of the editing techniques he employs to thrill the audience. Shot in South Florida from Miami to the Keys, the film continues the adventures of the central character from the original film, *The Fast and the Furious*. This time, he and a childhood friend are tapped by a drug lord to use high-powered cars to carry money to a drop-off point before the police can catch them. The film is in effect one long chase, with the plot subordinate to it.

"Fast and furious" could also describe the pace of the editing, as the film pounds on to its major climax, which is a *Dukes of Hazzard*–like stunt in which a car jumps hundreds of feet to land on a speeding boat. Each stunt is captured in dozens of brief shots that propel the action at breakneck speed. However, Singleton, a USC film-school grad, uses a linear editing style that is clear and logical. The screen direction and principal action is matched from shot to shot so that viewers always know who is chasing whom, and the event unfolds with logic, clarity, and fluidity. Space is clearly delineated so the viewer is never confused as to where the police are in relation to the protagonist, making the sequences tense to watch. The solid editing, along with the vivid use of primary colors in the art direction, helped this mediocre action sequel rise above the material.

THE BELLBOY

Because I chose to do *The Bellboy* as a pantomime [Paramount was] frightened . . . so I put up all my own money.
    —Jerry Lewis, "Dialogue on Film"

The picture was made for $900,000. To date, it's grossed $8 million. Isn't that a pussycat?!
    —Lewis's publicist Jerry Keller, in *Who the Hell's In It*, by Peter Bogdanovich

THE STORY

Stanley works as a bellboy at the Fontainebleau Hotel in Miami, where he creates havoc with the guests, who in turn drive Stanley to new heights of frustration.

THE FILM

Jerry Lewis had just completed *Cinderfella* for Paramount Pictures in early 1960 when he learned the studio was planning to release the film in July. Lewis insisted that the material was more suitable for a Christmas audience. However, that would leave Paramount without a Jerry Lewis film for the summer. For some time the studio had released one Lewis film in July to take advantage of kids' summer vacation and another in December for the holidays. To secure a December release for *Cinderfella*, Lewis promised studio executive Barney Balaban another film for July.

In February the comedian headed to Florida, where he was engaged to appear at the Fontainebleau Hotel. While there, he wrote, directed, and starred in *The Bellboy*, which he shot entirely at the famed Miami hotel, cleverly integrating aspects of the location into the content. The film had a small budget, a short shooting schedule, and no stars save Lewis. It also had no linear plot and little meaningful dialogue. The comedy is dependent on the art of pantomime, and Lewis's character Stanley does not speak until the very last joke in the film. The concept was daring and original, and after the completion of *The Bellboy*, Lewis's standing as a master comedian could not be denied.

One of the strengths of *The Bellboy* is that it harkens back to the silent era while embracing a modern sensibility. Structured as a series of comic blackouts, the film recalls the silent-era practice of exploiting the comic possibilities of a particular locale rather than relying on plot to drive the film. At the same time, *The Bellboy* seems quite modern in its lack of sentiment and in its sense of self-awareness as a film, now known as self-reflexivity. Many of the comic

Figure 7.3. Publicity photo from *The Bellboy*.
(Doll/Morrow Collection)

bits emphasize the idea that we are watching a film: Walter Winchell explains in voice-over in the beginning that we are about to see a motion picture with no plot; Lewis lampoons himself as a celebrity by appearing as himself in a second role; and some of the big laughs depend on a trick of editing rather than on a joke or a pratfall.

Jerry Lewis may have been the star and driving force behind *The Bellboy*, but the Fontainebleau was his second banana, so integral was it to the comedy. In 1960 the hotel was still considered the epitome of luxury for celebrities, the newly rich, and the middle class who aspired to be either. The film captured the Fontainebleau in all its extravagance and gaudy idiosyncracies in an era when men had to dress in jackets to linger in the lobby, and the air-conditioning was cranked high so women could wear their fur stoles. Opened in 1954, the mammoth 920-room Fontainebleau initiated the era of architectural eccentricity in Miami Beach—a style known as MiMo, or Miami Modern.[8] The hotel was owned by Ben Novack, who is played by Alex Gerry in several of *The Bellboy*'s scenes, and designed by Morris Lapidus, who went on to design other hotels in the MiMo style, including the Fontainebleau's neighbor, the Eden Roc. The hotel was named after the sixteenth-century palace of Fontainebleau, which Novack and his wife had seen in France, and which prompted the fleur-de-lis motifs in the hotel as well as the murals of well-known French sites.

All of the hotel's trademark components were used in the film, from the famous curved front to the black bow-tie marble pattern in the floor of the main lobby. Several comic bits feature characters pulling up to the front of the hotel, including the one in which Lewis, playing himself as a spoiled celebrity, arrives with a huge entourage. The whole group pours out of a single vehicle until the joke reveals itself—obviously, they could not all have fit. The hotel's long, curved entrance looks sleek and modern, making it a perfect destination for a celebrity of the magnitude of Jerry Lewis—Lewis the movie character, not Lewis the real director.

One of the distinctive details of the hotel's interior was the "stairway to nowhere." Lapidus liked to declare he had designed the hotel for those who had struck it big and wanted to show off, and the stairway to nowhere was an example of that. At the top of the stairs was a small mezzanine where the elevators stopped. In the evenings, couples would descend on the elevators to the mezzanine, where the women would get off while the men continued to the lobby. The men waited at the bottom of the staircase while their elegantly dressed partners would walk down the stairs to the delight of their admirers. In *The Bellboy*, Stanley encounters an odd stranger on the stairway. The stranger, played by Larry Best, pantomimes the act of eating an apple while providing an elaborate crunching sound effect. Though incredulous at first, Stanley is eventually caught up in the man's enthusiasm for his tasty treat and takes a bite of the nonexistent apple himself.

A couple of comic bits are staged in the hotel's dining areas. In the first, Stanley takes a break for lunch, but the three-thousand-seat main dining room is packed with guests and tourists. Stanley spots the very long counter, where, fortunately, every stool is empty. The camera tracks with him as he walks to the nearby buffet to grab a quick lunch; when he turns back to the counter a split second later, it is completely filled with noisy, hungry customers, leaving Stanley perplexed and without a seat. Later in the film, Stanley takes another lunch break, this time at the far end of the Poodle Lounge, where a window looks into the pool—not onto the pool but into the pool. The Fontainebleau's huge pool, which was 60 feet by 120 feet, had windows at either end below the waterline so guests in the lobby or in the lounge could watch the swimmers. For poor Stanley, however, the roles are reversed as the swimmers gather round the window and relentlessly stare at the solitary eater, intimidating him. The payoff comes when a swimmer who looks remarkably like Stan Laurel of Laurel-and-Hardy fame walks along the bottom of the pool and tips his hat to

Stanley. The Laurel look-alike is a recurring presence in the film, popping up to pester Stanley when least expected. The running gag is an homage to the great comedian, who was a major influence on Lewis.

One of the public rooms in the hotel features a huge piano and hundreds of rows of chairs. Upon entering the room, Stanley takes the opportunity to conduct an orchestra that is not there, though we can hear his efforts. The scene is interesting because Stanley is in complete control as he conducts a symphony for his own pleasure, much as Jerry Lewis is in complete control of his personal vision as he directs a film that allows him to explore the medium he loves.

Not only was Lewis innovative in his comedy, he also pioneered a technological tool that has become standard in the contemporary era. He innovated the video assist, in which a video camera records the action at the same time as the film camera. The director can play back the video immediately after the scene, or even watch the scene as it is performed if a monitor is hooked up. Lewis patented the Closed Circuit Television Applied to Motion Pictures in 1956, but did not get a chance to use it until his first directorial effort, *The Bellboy*. There was no video in 1960, but Lewis attached a TV camera with a zoom lens to his film camera. The setup allowed Lewis to watch the action on a TV monitor as the film camera was moved around during blocking and rehearsal. He used this system to fine-tune camera moves, improve the timing of entrances and exits, and block his actors.

Lewis had a month to shoot *The Bellboy* at the Fontainebleau, and he made the most of his time there. He edited the film quickly and handed it over to Paramount in time for the promised July release. *The Bellboy*, which was budgeted at $900,000, grossed $8 million by 1962, returning a major profit on the investment.[9] More important, it established Lewis as a director-comedian in the tradition of Chaplin and Keaton, who not only created comedy but also knew how to use the medium of film to get it across.

THE CREDITS	THE CAST	
Released in 1960 by Paramount Pictures	Jerry Lewis	Stanley/Jerry Lewis
Produced by Ernest D. Glucksman and Jerry Lewis	Alex Gerry	Manager
Directed by Jerry Lewis	Bob Clayton	Bell captain
Written by Jerry Lewis	Sonnie Sands	Sonnie, bellboy
Cinematography by Haskell B. Boggs	Eddie Schaeffer	Eddie, bellboy
Edited by Stanley E. Johnson	Herkie Styles	Herkie, bellboy
Art direction by Henry Bumstead and Hal Pereira	David Landfield	David, bellboy
Music by Walter Scharf	Bill Richmond	Stan Laurel
	Larry Best	Apple man
	Milton Berle	Bellboy/himself
	Walter Winchell	Narrator

THE COCOANUTS

Let's step up for the big swindle!
—Groucho Marx in *The Cocoanuts*

THE STORY

The disreputable manager of the Hotel de Cocoanut in sunny Florida tries to auction off the lots next door to the hotel to get rich quick during the Florida land boom. Meanwhile, hotel thieves prey on wealthy Mrs. Potter, who is distracted by her love-struck daughter.

THE FILM

The Florida land boom of the mid-1920s provided the perfect subject matter for the Marx Brothers' second Broadway comedy. *The Cocoanuts* was written by the great George S. Kaufman in 1925, the peak year of the boom. The basic story line of the play lampooned not only the frenzy surrounding the boom but also the notorious practices of the real estate agents and land speculators involved. The play became a smash hit on Broadway and ran for more than a year. Later Kaufman revamped *The Cocoanuts* for a special summer edition of the play, before the original was taken on the road for two seasons.

The success of the play did not escape the notice of the Hollywood studios, who were mining Broadway and vaudeville at the time for successful talent and material to turn into talking films. *The Cocoanuts* was adapted into the Marx Brothers' first feature film by Paramount Pictures.

Though the story line stayed the same, the film version differed from the stage play. During the run of the play, the Marx Brothers often ad-libbed much of their performance, adding physical bits as well as dialogue to the show nightly. Some claim that the brothers rarely performed *The Cocoanuts* the same way twice. For the film production, both the Marx Brothers and codirector Robert Florey changed and added bits to the original stage play. Still, plenty remains of the Florida material to get an idea of Kaufman's topical satire.

The Florida land boom began in the early 1920s in Miami and South Florida and then spread across the state. The population of Florida and the development of property escalated at a rapid rate as thousands of people from around the country came to buy. Cars jammed bumper to bumper on the highway to Miami, and trains and buses to Florida were filled to capacity. Famous orators, such as William Jennings Bryan, were hired to lure crowds to real estate offices and land auctions.

Figure 7.4. Poster for *The Cocoanuts*. (Doll/Morrow Collection)

Land speculators and promoters took advantage of the most naive buyers. While brochures and travel guides promoted the eternal sunshine and excellent climate, they failed to mention mosquito infestations and the hurricane season. Unscrupulous brokers sold lots on property that was more or less under water, where artificial islands or draining were planned for the future. However, these brokers didn't bother to tell the buyers that their lots were still a bit soggy. Such chicanery gave rise to the standard joke about buying swampland in Florida as a measure of naïveté.

The Cocoanuts stretches the joke into an entire film by adding a clichéd romantic subplot and several laborious musical numbers. While much of the film is bogged down with subplots unrelated to the Marx Brothers, the Florida material rests on the considerable talents of Groucho Marx. Groucho's comic persona as the keen-witted, wisecracking hustler is perfectly suited to his character, Hammer, who is the shifty manager of the Hotel de Cocoanut. Hammer also owns Cocoanut Manor, an undeveloped tract of land next door to the hotel. Despite the lofty name, Cocoanut Manor consists of palm groves, tree stumps, and subtropical undergrowth. Throughout the film, Hammer tries to sell part of Cocoanut Manor to wealthy widow Mrs. Potter, who is played by the indomitable Margaret Dumont, Groucho's favorite female foil. At one point he tries to sell her a piece of property by showing her only a short section of the sewer pipe that will eventually go beneath the lot—not the lot itself—which was not that far removed from the tactics of some of the real brokers and speculators at the time.

Hammer harangues Mrs. Potter with the hard sell: "I'm going to tell you about Florida real estate. It's the first time it's ever been mentioned around here . . . today. Do you know property values increased 1929 since a thousand percent? [sic] Do you know this is the biggest development since Sophie Tucker?"

Near the end of the film, Hammer plays the auctioneer at a real estate sale, which is a perfect setup for Groucho's verbal prowess with allusions, puns, and wordplay. He primes the crowd with the promise that there are big plans for eight hundred residences in Cocoanut Manor . . . and at this point that's all there is—big plans. He tells them they can get any type of home they want. "You can even get stucco. Boy, can you get stuck-o."

Hammer knows from personal experience that the hype, promotion, and promises of the Florida land boom are phoney, and he knows that the potential property buyers are doomed. He tells his staff, who are impatient to get paid, "Think of the opportunities here in Florida. Three years ago I came to Florida without a nickel in my pocket. Now I got a nickel in my pocket."

The Cocoanuts is not only an exaggerated account of a unique event in Florida history, it is also a reflection of an interesting moment in film history—the early sound era. The film is a prime example of the problems that plagued early talkies, and the comedy suffers as a result. The primitive, cumbersome recording technology and the limited experience of sound engineers and editors made it difficult to smoothly marry sound to image in the editing phase. For this reason, scenes with music and complex dialogue were generally shot without interruption. Thus, if a director wanted to cut to a close-up during a musical number, he would have to shoot the scene with two cameras—one positioned for close-up shots and one for long shots—so the soundtrack could be recorded intact. That meant the cinematographer faced the difficult task of lighting the set for a close-up and a long shot simultaneously. In general, the cumbersome nature of the new sound recording equipment made it difficult for directors to cope with many aspects of filmmaking. For the sake of convenience, most directors opted to limit the number of shots per scene or per musical number, which is true in The Cocoanuts. The lack of editing and the lack of close-ups make the mediocre musical numbers seem slower and longer while taking the spice out of the Marx Brothers' fast-paced verbal style.

In those days, there was no multitrack system like the setup that Hollywood uses today; all sound was recorded on one track. Sound effects and dialogue were recorded at the same level, so incidental noises often drowned out dialogue. In The Cocoanuts, this caused problems with several scenes when rustling notes, paper, and maps obscured the actors' voices. Someone on the crew finally figured out that if the paper was wet, the rustling sound could be avoided. Thus characters unfold limp-looking notes and maps very delicately, with no explanation as to why.

The Marx Brothers had little patience for the slow pace of shooting, often disappearing while scenes were set up or when the sound equipment broke down, which was often. The tedious production process was antithetical to their ad libs, verbal sparring, and spontaneous approach to comedy. In one key scene, Chico either forgot or didn't bother to learn his lines, and his costar filled in the dialogue for him; elsewhere the brothers trample on other actors' lines, or deliver their jokes with no punch, as though they were overrehearsed.

Despite these shortcomings, The Cocoanuts was a hit at the box office on its initial release and launched the Marx Brothers into a successful series of film comedies. Quite quickly the film industry ironed out the problems with the sound technology, and just as quickly the brothers adjusted their comedy to the film format. The result was a comic style that perfectly suited the new sound medium.

The Credits	The Cast	
Released in 1929 by Paramount Pictures	Groucho Marx	Hammer
Produced by Monta Bell and James R. Cowan	Zeppo Marx	Jamison
Directed by Robert Florey and Joseph Santley	Harpo Marx	Harpo
Written by Morrie Ryskind and George S. Kaufman,	Chico Marx	Chico
based on the play by Kaufman	Oscar Shaw	Bob
Cinematography by George J. Folsey	Mary Eaton	Polly Potter
Edited by Barney Rogan	Margaret Dumont	Mrs. Potter
Music by Irving Berlin	Kay Francis	Penelope
	Cyril Ring	Yates

HELLO DOWN THERE

A combo of scuba dupes rock up a storm in a mad pad under the surf!
—tagline for *Hello Down There*

THE STORY

Research scientist Fred Miller has designed an underwater house as an answer to the population explosion. When his boss dismisses the idea as impractical, Miller vows to prove him wrong by moving his family to a home ninety feet below the ocean off Florida's coast. The family contend with a variety of sea life, Fred's conniving colleague, a hurricane, and the U.S. Navy, while figuring out how to get their two teenage children to an important audition for their rock band.

THE FILM

In the early 1950s Ricou Browning worked as a producer and performer at Florida's legendary Weeki Wachee Springs. When director Jack Arnold arrived in the area to scout locations for a film, Browning volunteered to serve as a guide. In addition to looking for locations, Arnold hoped to find some local talent to perform in the underwater sequences of his upcoming science-fiction film, and Browning got the job. Within a short time, the athletic young swimmer found himself working on what would become a sci-fi classic, *The Creature from the Black Lagoon* (see chapter 9). Browning played the creature in underwater scenes in the original film and its two sequels. This experience led to work as a stuntman and underwater director for the popular television show *Sea Hunt*, where he met producer Ivan Tors.

Tors had the dream of producing wholesome family entertainment from his studio in Miami, and within a few years he and Browning had created the classic family film *Flipper* (see chapter 4). The highly successful movie spawned a popular television series and led to many collaborations between Tors and Browning during the 1960s and 1970s. One of those efforts, *Hello Down There*, united Tors, Browning, and *Creature* director Jack Arnold for the first and only time.

Hello Down There was exactly the sort of film Tors set out to make—a fanciful adventure that offered something for viewers of all ages. The story features the Miller family living in an underwater habitat, nicknamed the Green Onion, off the coast of Florida for one month. While there, the family face a dizzying series of adventures. They befriend a sea lion and a pair of dolphins and fight off a pack of threatening sharks. The mother deals with her fear of water while the father contends with a competitor out to sabotage their stay. The teenage children, who've brought their two bandmates along, compose several ocean-inspired pop songs—"Hey, Goldfish" and "Glub, Glub (Floating on a Sea of Love)"—and devise a way to sneak their recordings to a music producer, who then arranges their debut on *The Merv Griffin Show*. At one point the children are trapped after sneaking out in the family's minisubmarine, and their father

Figure 7.5. Lobby card from *Hello Down There*. (Doll/Morrow Collection)

rescues them with help from the dolphins. Meanwhile the U.S. Navy, unaware that the Green Onion has been built, misinterprets the sonar reading received from the structure and fears the enemy has created a new weapon of some sort. And, of course, there's a hurricane. In the end, the hurricane blows over, the experiment in underwater living is a success, and Merv Griffin decides to do a live broadcast from the Green Onion featuring the teens' band. All appears well—until the clever comic ending, which shows the navy beginning an assault on the Green Onion.

The zany film was ably directed by Browning, who handled the underwater sequences, and Arnold, who did the dry work. Further buoying the effort was a top-notch cast—Tony Randall, Janet Leigh, Roddy McDowell, and Richard Dreyfuss in one of his first roles, with support from Jim Backus and Charlotte Rae and a guest appearance by Merv Griffin.

The set work for *Hello Down There* was filmed at Ivan Tors Studio in Miami. One soundstage on the facility had a large pool, and an elaborate set was constructed over this as the interior of the Green Onion. It looked much like any efficient but comfortable family home of the period, except that the front door was a large hole in the floor that opened into the "ocean." The round windows looked out into the deep blue sea, which was actually a series of large fish tanks set up outside each window. The film included several scenes in which dolphins, a sea lion, and a marauding shark pop up into the family abode. These scenes were shot out of sequence so that all the work with a specific animal could be done at once. The animals, which were provided by the Miami Seaquarium, were kept in an outdoor enclosure while the crew set up each shot, and brought into the pool on the soundstage when all was ready.[10]

Underwater location filming was done over three weeks in the Bahamas. In these open-water scenes, Browning worked with wild animals rather than those provided by the Seaquarium. For each sequence animal wranglers would capture the sharks or dolphins they needed and keep them temporarily in a large containment pen they had constructed in a natural lagoon. The crew would set up for each shot just outside the containment pen and then grab one or two minutes of footage as the animals were released. Most of these scenes had to be shot over and over again to capture the precise animal behavior needed for the film. A fight scene between several dolphins and sharks proved particularly difficult, and Browning resorted to using a combination of real animals and models that were maneuvered by stuntmen.[11]

With its combination of animal antics, underwater adventure, and youth culture, *Hello Down There* was crafted to appeal to the family audience of the late 1960s. Though now a bit dated, the 1969 film remains fun and undeniably unique.

THE CREDITS

Released in 1969 by Paramount Pictures
Produced by George Sherman and Ivan Tors
Directed by Jack Arnold
Underwater sequences directed by Ricou Browning
Written by John McGreevey and Frank Telford, from
   a story by Art Arthur and Ivan Tors
Cinematography by Clifford H. Poland Jr.
Underwater cinematography by Lamar Boren
Edited by Erwin Dumbrille
Original music by Jeff Barry
Songs by Sam Coslow and Arthur Johnson
Art direction by Jack T. Collis
Set decoration by Don K. Ivey

THE CAST

Tony Randall	Fred Miller
Janet Leigh	Vivian Miller
Jim Backus	T. R. Hollister
Ken Berry	Mel Cheever
Roddy McDowall	Nate Ashbury
Charlotte Rae	Myrtle Ruth
Richard Dreyfuss	Harold Webster
Kay Cole	Lorrie Miller
Gary Tigerman	Tommie Miller
Lee Meredith	Dr. Wells
Harvey Lembeck	Sonarman
Merv Griffin	Himself
Henny Backus	Mrs. Webster

LICENCE TO KILL

The sixteenth of the most successful series in motion picture history.
—advertisement for *Licence to Kill*

THE STORY

British superspy James Bond and his friend CIA agent Felix Leiter arrest international drug dealer Franz Sanchez in the Bahamas. Sanchez escapes from custody and exacts revenge on Leiter by killing his bride and leaving Leiter maimed. When Bond hunts down Sanchez to avenge his friend, ignoring orders to let the matter lie, his superiors revoke his legendary license to kill.

THE FILM

James Bond is one of the most enduring characters ever to appear on the silver screen. For more than forty years, fans have flocked to theaters to see the dashing, deadly, devil-may-care agent woo beautiful women and foil the outlandish schemes of supercriminals and megalomaniacs. Whether portrayed by Sean Connery, Roger Moore, or Pierce Brosnan, the character has remained uniquely capable and cool—"always in peril, but never in a hurry."[12]

The Bond filmmakers have tinkered with the character and his universe throughout the series, from the realistic cold warrior of *From Russia with Love* to the campy bon vivant in the sci-fi tale *Moonraker*. Through it all, however,

Figure 7.6. *Licence to Kill* star Timothy Dalton.
(Doll/Morrow Collection)

the producers have retained the basic elements of a Bond tale that keep the theater seats filled—obvious but not explicit sex, clever humor, intriguing villains, hair-raising stunts, and a string of exotic locations.

This last element may be one of the least noticed but most consistent hallmarks of the series. A typical Bond movie involves location shooting in several distant and exciting locales—Cairo, Malta, and Okinawa in *The Spy Who Loved Me*; Hong Kong and Thailand in *The Man with the Golden Gun*; Spain, Finland, and South Korea in *Die Another Day*. Surprisingly, the location most frequently used for Bond's exploits, outside of England where the production company is centered, is Florida. Six different Bond films—almost one-third of the entire series—have involved significant location shooting in the Sunshine State.

Of these six, 1989's *Licence to Kill* makes the most overt and extensive use of the state. The first third of the film is set in the Florida Keys, where Bond is acting as best man at the wedding of CIA agent Felix Leiter, a recurring character in the series. This situation is unusual, as audiences rarely see glimpses of

Bond's personal life when he isn't on active duty. The two agents interrupt the nuptials with a bit of derring-do when they make a spectacular midair arrest of a drug kingpin who has left his South American stronghold to track down an errant girlfriend. After the drug dealer engineers a daring underwater escape and then maims Leiter and murders his new wife, Bond sets out on a dark personal vendetta to kill the villain, despite orders to the contrary from the British government.

Licence proved to be one of most controversial films in the series among Bond fans. Though Timothy Dalton, in his second and final outing as 007, was well liked and well suited to the role, many were displeased with the sharp turn away from the implausible, over-the-top approach of the preceding string of films with Roger Moore. *Licence* instead harkened back to the first several Bond films, which involved fewer gadgets and more realistic story lines. In keeping with this, *Licence* included several references to earlier films—a mention of Bond's wife, who died in *On Her Majesty's Secret Service*, and the return of David Hedison from *Live and Let Die*, making him the only actor to portray the Leiter character more than once.

The first Bond film to use a Florida location was the classic *Goldfinger*, in which 007 is assigned to investigate the title character and learns of his scheme to irradiate the gold in Fort Knox, making it useless and thereby increasing the value of his own hoard. Bond first encounters Goldfinger at Florida's famed Fontainebleau Hotel, where the villain is swindling fellow guests at cards with the aid of Jill Masterson, who spies on his opponents' hands with binoculars. Bond surprises Masterson, orders Goldfinger to lose or be exposed as a cheat, and then proceeds to seduce the girl. He's knocked unconscious by a Goldfinger henchman and wakes to find the girl dead and her body covered in gold paint. The bizarre image of the gilded corpse is at once captivating and horrifying and remains one of the best-known moments in Bond history.

The next film in the series, *Thunderball*, reaches its climax in Florida, where Bond disrupts a diabolical plot of the criminal organization SPECTRE (Special Executor for Counter-Intelligence, Terrorism, Revenge, and Extortion). The group has stolen two atomic bombs and threatens to destroy a major city unless an exorbitant ransom is paid. The target turns out to be Miami, and Bond squares off against the enemy army in the waters off the coast in one of the most complex and ambitious underwater stunt sequences that had ever been filmed at that time.

The series next returned to Florida in 1979 for *Moonraker*. Billionaire industrialist Hugo Drax plans to wipe out life on earth with poison gas, saving only himself and a select contingent of prime human specimens by taking them into space and then returning to create a master race. NASA's space shuttle plays a prominent role in the story, and scenes were shot at the Kennedy Space Center on Cape Canaveral. *Never Say Never Again*, which was essentially a remake of *Thunderball*, came to Silver Springs in 1983. *Tomorrow Never Dies*, in which Pierce Brosnan puts an end to a media mogul's scheme to instigate and then report on global catastrophes, was the most recent Bond film to make use of Florida.

In keeping with the Bond oeuvre, the series uses Florida locations to evoke a sense of exoticism and luxury, just as it does with such far-flung settings as Switzerland, Tokyo, and Malta. In a small way, the state's frequent appearances in the Bond films serve to validate it as a world-class destination.

THE CREDITS

Released in 1989 by United Artists
Produced by Albert R. Broccoli and Michael G. Wilson
Directed by John Glen
Written by Michael G. Wilson and Richard Maibaum
Cinematography by Alec Mills
Edited by John Grover
Original music by Michael Kamen
Production design by Peter Lamont
Art direction by Dennis Bosher and Michael Lamont

THE CAST

Timothy Dalton	James Bond
Carey Lowell	Pam Bouvier
Robert Davi	Franz Sanchez
Talisa Soto	Lupe Lamora
Anthony Zerbe	Milton Krest
Frank McRae	Sharkey
David Hedison	Felix Leiter
Wayne Newton	Professor Joe Butcher
Benicio Del Toro	Dario
Desmond Llewelyn	Q
Robert Brown	M

MATINEE

THEATER MANAGER: The country is on red alert!
WOOLSEY: What a perfect time to open a new horror movie.
—*Matinee*

THE STORY

Outrageous film promoter Lawrence Woolsey arrives in Key West for the grand opening of his latest low-budget sci-fi flick just as the Cuban Missile Crisis begins. A preteen boy who has long admired Woolsey's work befriends the charismatic rake and learns the ins and outs of Hollywood hucksterism.

On October 22, 1962, John F. Kennedy made one of the most significant and disturbing presidential addresses in the history of the United States. In a grave but confident voice, he announced that U.S. intelligence photos taken only days before had documented the construction of offensive nuclear missile sites by the Soviet Union on the island nation of Cuba, just ninety miles from America's southernmost border. For the preceding decade, the human race had lived nervously on the brink of nuclear annihilation, and Kennedy's voice that night became the terrifying sound of the precipice crumbling beneath our feet.

In the six days that followed before the Cuban Missile Crisis was peacefully resolved, everyday life in the United States was transformed.[13] Local civil defense offices were swamped with inquiries, and an estimated ten million urban dwellers fled their homes for the perceived safety of rural areas far from potential targets.

Attendance at religious services jumped 20 percent that week, and air raid drills became daily occurrences in many schools. Television networks interrupted their regular programming with news bulletins and specials more than a hundred times in five days, and crowds routinely gathered around the front windows of electronics stores to get the latest information from the television sets on display. Citizens stockpiled canned goods, bottled water, medical supplies, batteries, transistor radios, and firearms, preparing for survival in the aftermath of nuclear devastation.

No region of the country was more affected by the crisis than southern Florida, especially Key West. The entire area became a vast military staging ground as a naval blockade was deployed in the Caribbean and preparations got under way for a possible invasion of Cuba. Trucks, trains, and planes loaded with military equipment and thousands of troops streamed into the area. Civilian air traffic was restricted, tourist hotels were commandeered to house soldiers, and stunned citizens watched as antiaircraft missile batteries were deployed along public beaches.

In the lighthearted film *Matinee*, set in Key West during the missile crisis, impending nuclear devastation is only one of the troubles on the horizon of teenage protagonist Gene Loomis. Many of his other fears loom larger than the towering ICBMs in Cuba. With his naval-officer father away as part of the blockade, he deals awkwardly with new responsibilities as the man of the house. From the adults in his life, he receives pressure to perform well at school and to live up to their expectations and rules. His peers also prove to be a source of stress, as he struggles to fit in with his friends, contend with antisocial bullies, and, worst of all, face the prospect of his first date.

The one place Gene can find comfort and relief from all these pressures is

Figure 7.7. *Matinee* star John Goodman. (Doll/Morrow Collection)

the Strand Theater on Duval Street, where the Saturday matinees offer escape from both global destruction and next week's math test. When Gene's idol, the bombastic producer/director Lawrence Woolsey, comes to town for the premiere of his latest low-budget sci-fi flick, Gene is beside himself with excitement. The resourceful boy manages to develop a relationship with the huckster and watches hungrily as Woolsey implements one outrageous gimmick after another to promote the film. Through these experiences, Gene learns more than a few lessons about life, the movies, and where the two intersect.

Woolsey's new film, entitled *Mant*, relates the tragic tale of a young man who is transformed into a hideous beast after being bitten by an ant while undergoing an X-ray. To draw audiences into the theaters, Woolsey touts what he calls the next great technological developments in film—Atomo-vision and Rumblerama. The former is a simple gimmick in the film that makes it appear as if the theater screen is disintegrating from a nuclear blast; the latter involves wiring motors beneath the theater seats to shake up patrons at key moments in the film. And to top it off, the master showman hires a local youth to don a Mant costume and run through the theater during the screening to further spook the viewers.

The likable Woolsey character is based loosely on William Castle, a legendary figure from the 1950s era of independent filmmaking. Castle revealed his talent for sly promotion early in his career. As the manager of a Connecticut theater in the late 1930s, he touted the actress starring in his first play as the Girl Who Said "No" to Hitler because she declined an invitation from the German government to attend an arts festival. The publicity generated strong sales for opening night, but Castle took his ploy one step further by vandalizing the theater the night before the premiere, breaking a few windows and painting

Figure 7.8. *Matinee* star Cathy Moriarty. (Doll/Morrow Collection)

swastikas on the building's exterior, and then requesting protection from the National Guard during performances. Ticket sales went through the roof. Castle moved on to Columbia Pictures as a B-movie director and then joined the wave of independent filmmakers in the 1950s. He specialized in horror films but typically put as much effort into developing gimmicks and promotions as into making the films themselves. As ridiculous as *Mant*'s Rumblerama might seem, it is actually based on a gimmick Castle devised for his 1959 film *The Tingler*.

For *Matinee* director Joe Dante, who grew up in the 1960s avidly consuming the horror and sci-fi offerings of Castle and others like him, the film is a loving remembrance of his own childhood. His personal connection to the material shows through in the scenes from *Mant*, which pepper the last half of *Matinee*. Shot in five days with a cast including Robert Cornthwaite, Kevin McCarthy, and William Schallert, who all appeared in B movies from Dante's childhood, the scenes balance hilarious satire with genuine affection for the genre. On a deeper level, by contrasting the real-life terror of the missile crisis with the make-believe horror of *Mant*, Dante and screenwriter Charles Haas use *Matinee* to acknowledge the unique ability of the horror and sci-fi genres to coalesce society's fears into contemporary pop-culture allegories.

THE CREDITS

Released in 1993 by Universal Pictures	Edited by Marshall Harvey
Produced by Michael Finnell and Pat Kehoe	Music by Jerry Goldsmith
Directed by Joe Dante	Production design by Steven Legler
Written by Charles S. Haas	Art direction by Nanci Roberts
Cinematography by John Hora	

John Goodman	Lawrence Woolsey	Robert Picardo	Howard, the theater manager
Cathy Moriarty	Ruth Corday/Carole	Jesse White	Mr. Spector
Simon Fenton	Gene Loomis	Dick Miller	Herb Denning
Omri Katz	Stan	John Sayles	Bob
Lisa Jakub	Sandra	David Clennon	Jack
Kellie Martin	Sherry	Mark McCracken	Mant/Bill
Jesse Lee	Dennis Loomis	Robert Cornthwaite	Dr. Flankon
Lucinda Jenney	Anne Loomis	Kevin McCarthy	General Ankrum
James Villemaire	Harvey Starkweather	William Schallert	Dr. Grabow, DDS

Castle's Gimmicks

Below are some of the more outrageous gimmicks William Castle used to draw audiences into his low-budget films.

Macabre (1958). In his first, simplest, and perhaps most inspired film gimmick, Castle offered patrons a free $1,000 life insurance policy from Lloyds of London that would pay off if a viewer "died from fright" while watching this story of premature burial. No payouts were ever made, of course, but viewers came away with a bona fide insurance agreement as a souvenir.

The Tingler (1959). Vincent Price stars as a scientist who discovers a deadly creature that attaches itself to the spinal cord and feeds on human fear. Castle juiced up the experience for moviegoers with an effect he called Percepto by rigging selected seats in the theater with motors that would send a jolting vibration to viewers at key moments in the film.

Thirteen Ghosts (1960). For this haunted-house tale, patrons were armed with Illusion-O "ghost viewers," similar to the simple cardboard 3-D glasses used in the 1950s. When any ghosts appeared in the film, moviegoers could look through the lenses and see the ghosts or take them off if the terror became too great to bear.

Mr. Sardonicus (1961). This movie relates the diabolical exploits of a sadistic nineteenth-century nobleman. Castle appears in the film before the climax and takes a Punishment Poll, allowing the audience to vote on the villain's fate by raising "thumbs up" or "thumbs down" placards that were distributed before each show. According to Castle, there were two versions of the final reel, one in which Sardonicus dies and another in which he is allowed to live, but it's generally assumed that only the fatal ending was ever filmed.

SOME LIKE IT HOT

> Look at that! Look how she moves. That's just like Jell-O
> on springs. . . . I tell you, it's a whole different sex!
> —Jerry, looking at Sugar Kane in *Some Like It Hot*

THE STORY

Joe and Jerry, two jazz musicians from Chicago, witness the St. Valentine's Day Massacre. To escape the mobsters who are on their trail, Joe and Jerry disguise themselves as women and join an all-girl orchestra on its way to Miami. Once in Florida, they intend to discard their disguises and move on. However, the band's beautiful blonde singer, Sugar Kane, distracts them from their plans.

THE FILM

Some Like It Hot is often discussed as a Marilyn Monroe film; either it is touted as one of her best comedies or it is used to illustrate her increasing struggle with emotional problems, evident in the behind-the-scenes turmoil on the set. Artistically, however, the film belongs to Billy Wilder, and since his death, more critics have pointed to it as one of the high points of his impressive career.

Born in Vienna, Wilder had worked briefly in the German film industry before emigrating to America to be absorbed into the Hollywood system, first as a screenwriter and then as a director. From his vantage point as a foreigner, and thus an outsider, he crafted his films to comment on American manners and mores. In *Some Like It Hot*, Wilder seamlessly combined a variety of comic conceits, situations, and tones to create a classic farce that resonates on several levels.

On the surface, the comedy spoofs the trends, preoccupations, and character types of America in the Roaring Twenties. The title refers to the racy popular music of the 1920s, jazz, and its association with a loose sexual morality. Someone tells flapper Sugar Kane to "goose up" her song "Running Wild," because "some like it hot." Since Sugar is played by Marilyn Monroe, an icon of sexuality, the sexual connotations of her music, lyrics, and singing style are obvious. *Some Like It Hot* also spoofs the gangster film, a movie genre established during Prohibition. Edward G. Robinson, George Raft, and Pat O'Brien, three actors who became famous for their roles in gangster dramas, parody the archetypes they created in *Little Caesar*, *Scarface*, and *Angels With Dirty Faces*.

The old cliché about Miami as the land of millionaire sugar daddies is also burlesqued in the film to great effect. The Miami area had been developed by wealthy auto baron Carl Fisher during the 1910s to attract the leisure class. By the Roaring Twenties, many of America's nouveaux riches had begun to winter in Florida, particularly the manufacturing magnates of the early twentieth century. The privileged crowd spent January through April in their Florida homes or in the grand hotels where they relished their lives of luxury (see introduction to chapter 4). In *Some Like It Hot*, the all-girl orchestra known as Sweet Sue and Her Society Syncopators travels to Florida to play at the Seminole Ritz Hotel, a grand hotel in Miami Beach. (The Florida scenes were actually shot at the Hotel del Coronado at Coronado Beach in California.) Sugar hopes to land a millionaire who will treat her with more respect than the saxophone players she generally ends up with. As the band members enter the hotel, the porch is lined with elderly millionaires sitting in rockers in identical poses. They all sport sunglasses, white panama hats, and canes while reading the *Wall Street Journal*. They greet the girls in unison, suggesting they are as interchangeable as they are plentiful—and just ripe for the plucking.

Oil magnate Osgood Fielding III, played by comic character actor Joe E. Brown, distinguishes himself from the crowd with his persistence in pursuing Jerry, who is in disguise as Daphne. Though likable and good-hearted, Osgood is an exaggerated depiction of the madcap sugar daddy often seen in Hollywood musical comedies—he owns a yacht and chases chorus girls whenever he can sneak out from under the thumb of his domineering dowager mother. Joe, played by a handsome Tony Curtis, dons a disguise that is another version of the movie millionaire. He pretends to be the bespectacled heir to the Shell Oil empire whose life of contemplation and solitude has rendered him incapable of responding to women. The ruse is a ploy to challenge Sugar to try to seduce him. The romantic shenanigans between the millionaires and the gold diggers are well suited to the Miami setting, which was known as a playground for the rich before World War II.

Though a comic reminder of the fads and follies of another time, *Some Like It Hot* does more than just spoof the era. Wilder also delivers a perceptive farce on gender roles and relationships. He uses deception, reversed sex roles, and disguise and masquerade to comment on sexual mores and politics. Because Joe and Jerry are in disguise as women, they can experience "how the other half lives," as Joe says. In their feminine guises as Josephine and Daphne, they are ogled, pinched, and hounded by predatory males not unlike themselves. For example, Joe plays the saxophone and is keen to seduce Sugar, making him the type of uncaring heel Sugar generally falls for. Ironically, when dressed as Josephine, he literally understands male-female interactions from another point of view. After Daphne encounters Osgood in the elevator, he/she fumes, "I just got pinched in the elevator. . . . I'm not even pretty." Joe opines, "They

Figure 7.9. Publicity photo from *Some Like It Hot*. (Doll/Morrow Collection)

don't care. Just as long as you're wearing a skirt. It's like waving a red flag in front of a bull."

Jerry, played by Jack Lemmon in a role that proves his genius for comedy, adopts a more complete female persona than Joe does. Jerry selects an entirely new name, Daphne, rather than merely feminizing his male name. Truly interested in becoming a convincing woman, he picks up beauty tips from Sugar. Gradually he forgets he is male, even agreeing to a date with Osgood. They dance the tango together—that most sexual of dances—and end up engaged by morning. When Joe states the obvious, that Jerry cannot possibly marry Osgood, Jerry is so absorbed by his female persona that he responds, "Why, do you think he's too old for me?"

Joe and Jerry not only learn something about women in their masquerades but they also learn something about themselves. Joe realizes his previous behavior toward women has been hurtful and shameful, while Jerry realizes he longs for the security of marriage and a family. In other films, these revelations might have signaled that the characters have become better people, and they will change their ways for a brighter future. However, Billy Wilder's films seldom have this much faith in humankind, and a more complete look at *Some Like It Hot* suggests he sees little improvement in male-female relationships anytime soon.

Throughout the film, the women, the men, and the men dressed as women play games, conceal their true feelings, and pretend to be what they are not. They manipulate the opposite sex in order to get something from them, whether it is money, sex, or long-term security. In the film's famous conclusion, the two central couples—Joe and Sugar, and Osgood and Daphne—are escaping from the gangsters on Osgood's boat. Joe reveals to Sugar that he is just a saxophone player, but Sugar realizes she loves him anyway despite her bad luck with sax players in the past. The implication is that she is headed down the same destructive path once again. Meanwhile Daphne tries to convince Osgood that she cannot possibly marry him, finally confessing that she is, in fact, Jerry. Osgood, uttering one of the most memorable lines in movie history, replies, "Nobody's perfect!" A brilliant capper to a classic film, the line implies that Osgood, once again blinded by desire, refuses to see the inappropriateness of the relationship, which was the same problem he had in his three previous marriages to chorus girls. Since the long-term prospect of neither relationship is good, it is fitting that the film concludes with both couples running away—but with no clear destination ahead.

THE CREDITS	THE CAST	
Released in 1959 by the Mirisch Company for United Artists	Marilyn Monroe	Sugar Kane
Produced by Billy Wilder, Doane Harrison, and I. A. L. Diamond	Tony Curtis	Joe/Josephine/Junior
	Jack Lemmon	Jerry/Daphne
Directed by Billy Wilder	Joe E. Brown	Osgood Fielding III
Written by Billy Wilder and I. A. L. Diamond	George Raft	Spats Columbo
Cinematography by Charles Lang Jr.	Pat O'Brien	Mulligan
Edited by Arthur P. Schmidt	Nehemiah Persoff	Napoleon
Art direction by Ted Haworth	Mike Mazurki	Spats's henchman
Costume design by Orry-Kelly	Edward G. Robinson	Johnny Paradise
Makeup by Agnes Flanagan, Emile LaVigne, and Alice Monte		

STRIPTEASE

I can't complain. They kept the Vaseline scene, the cockroach scene,
and the snake scene. That's my contribution to culture this year.

  —author Carl Hiaasen to the *New York Times*'s Mireya Navarro

THE STORY

Erin Grant dances at the Eager Beaver strip club hoping to earn enough money
to gain custody of her eight-year-old daughter from her ex-husband, a petty
thief who acts as an informer for Miami's vice squad. Lecherous congressman

Figure 7.10. *Striptease* director Andrew Bergman. (Doll/Morrow Collection)

David Dilbeck's infatuation with Erin leads to blackmail and murder when he's caught on film assaulting a patron at the club just six weeks before his reelection.

THE FILM

Florida native Carl Hiaasen began his writing career in 1976 as a general reporter for the *Miami Herald* and quickly moved up to the paper's investigative team. By 1985 he had earned his own column, which he famously used to expose the bizarre world of crime and graft that had evolved in Florida's largest city. In 1986 he fictionalized that world in his first solo novel, *Tourist Season*, and he went on to publish a dozen titles noted for their dark satire and imaginative violence. In all of his writing, Hiaasen reveals a contempt for hypocrisy, pretention, greed, and corruption in any form and at any level of society. The film *Striptease*, based on his 1993 book, faithfully retains Hiaasen's contempt and humor in its depiction of oily lawyers, corrupt politicians, criminal business practices, and a failed court system.

When the film was released, the attention of the press and public was riveted on star Demi Moore, whose $12.5-million salary made her the highest-paid film actress in Hollywood history.[14] Moore had begun her career on the soap opera *General Hospital*, where her feisty character became a favorite among fans. Her major film break came with 1985's *St. Elmo's Fire*, an ensemble vehicle whose young stars Moore, Rob Lowe, Emilio Estevez, Andrew McCarthy, Mare Winningham, Judd Nelson, and Ally Sheedy were tagged the Brat Pack. Moore surpassed the other Brat Packers to become a box-office draw with her performances in *A Few Good Men*, *Ghost*, and *Indecent Proposal*, but she earned the ire of the press for her quirky lifestyle, headstrong business practices, and penchant for tasteful but shocking displays of her body in calculated feminist ways. *Striptease*, in which she boldly bared her well-sculpted form in addition to serving as a major creative contributor to the film, represented a confluence of all that she was generally criticized for, and the press pounced. Many reviews snidely calculated how much she earned per second of nudity or complained about her aggressive dance style in the film. Others criticized her dramatic performance as out of step with the satiric nature of the story or generally dismissed the film as an uneven, ill-executed mess.

In truth, *Striptease* offers a complex and thoughtful story, consistently offbeat humor, and an impressive array of vividly imagined and unique characters. Ving Rhames portrays a jaded, tough, yet sensitive bouncer with a deadpan sense of humor. Robert Patrick is both hateful and hilarious as Moore's trailer-trash ex who clings to his daughter, Angela, out of spite and employs her in his despicable business of stealing wheelchairs from Don Shula Hospital. Moore's

Figure 7.11. *Striptease* star Demi Morre. (Doll/Morrow Collection)

daughter, Rumer Willis, plays the young girl and provides believable chemistry between mother and daughter. Armand Assante presents a noble cop who lends a much-needed note of hope to Hiaasen's dark and depraved world.

Without doubt, though, the film's most memorable performance is Burt Reynolds's characterization of corrupt congressman David Dilbeck. Reynolds had been the top box-office draw of the late 1970s, but his career had languished in the 1980s and early 1990s. A high-profile divorce from Loni Anderson hurt his popularity, as did a seeming inability to reconcile his manly self-image with his advancing age. The Dilbeck role had originally been offered to Gene Hackman, and the producers reluctantly considered Reynolds only after Hackman declined. An audition quickly won them over, and Reynolds earned accolades for his complex, self-deprecating performance. Thematically, the film rests on the congressman as a focal point of corruption, and Reynolds skillfully crafted a character who was comically debauched yet still presented a very real threat through his far-reaching corruption.

For much of the film, Dilbeck appears to be nothing more than a drunken buffoon and letch, and it seems inconceivable that he could actually hold on to an elected office. Later scenes show that he is a skilled campaigner with a completely different public face, as when he charms the entire population of a Jewish retirement home by glad-handing and dancing with them. His shameless hypocrisy becomes apparent when an aide finds him prancing about in a hotel room smeared in Vaseline and wearing cowboy boots and boxer shorts, just before giving a speech to a conservative Christian youth group. Dilbeck's darkest side is revealed toward the end of the film through his connection to a ruthless family of sugar barons, who fund his campaigns and employ violence to clean up his messes in exchange for political favors for their empire.

The jab at the entwined corruption of politics and business is typical for a Hiaasen story, and the use of the sugar industry provides a clear connection to Florida. Sugarcane, first grown in the state by the Spanish in the 1500s, grew into a small commercial industry in 1767 but collapsed during the American Revolution. It wasn't until the 1920s that Florida became a major producer of sugar, and today it leads all states in the export of the sweet crystals. Centered around the southeastern shore of Lake Okeechobee, the state's sugar industry has long been attacked for the generous federal subsidies it receives, its aggressive and highly funded lobbying efforts, its poor treatment of field workers, and its harmful effect on the environment, particularly the Everglades. For Hiaasen, who frequently incorporates ecological themes into his work, the industry provided a perfect foil.

Striptease performed poorly in the United States, with domestic receipts falling roughly $20 million short of the film's budget. A strong showing overseas, however, allowed it to top $100 million worldwide.[15] Moore's next film, *G.I. Jane*, was also filmed in Florida and also suffered inexplicably severe reviews from the press. Her portrayal of a woman undergoing commando training with the Navy SEALs was a remarkably intense performance that anchored a thoughtful, well-crafted film by stylish director Ridley Scott. Its critical and financial failure led to Moore's withdrawal from high-profile roles, and she has appeared in only a handful of films since. Reynolds, on the other hand, parlayed his success with *Striptease* into even greater acclaim in his next role as a world-weary porn producer in *Boogie Nights*.

THE CREDITS	THE CAST	
Released in 1996 by Columbia Pictures	Demi Moore	Erin Grant
Produced by Andrew Bergman and Mike Lobell	Burt Reynolds	Congressman David Dilbeck
Directed by Andrew Bergman	Armand Assante	Lt. Al Garcia
Written by Andrew Bergman, from the book by Carl	Ving Rhames	Shad
Hiaasen	Robert Patrick	Darrell Grant
Cinematography by Stephen Goldblatt	Paul Guilfoyle	Malcolm Moldovsky
Edited by Anne V. Coates	Rumer Willis	Angela Grant
Production design by Mel Bourne	Robert Stanton	Erb Crandal
Art direction by Elizabeth Lapp	Dina Spybey	Monique Jr.
Original music by Howard Shore	PaSean Wilson	Sabrina Hepburn
	Pandora Peaks	Urbanna Sprawl

Big Trouble

A colleague and friend of Carl Hiaasen's, Dave Barry has become one of America's leading humorists through his columns in the *Miami Herald* that exaggerate the irony in everyday situations. In 1999 he published his first novel, *Big Trouble*, a farcical variation on the Florida crime genre pioneered by writers such as Hiaasen, Elmore Leonard, and Charles Willeford. The 2002 film adaptation of the book embroiled Tim Allen, Rene Russo, Stanley Tucci, Tom Sizemore, Janeane Garofalo, and Dennis Farina in a madcap chase for a stolen atomic bomb involving satiric cops, impatient contract killers, Russian arms dealers, a Frito-loving hippie, and a frog with hallucinogenic saliva. Shot entirely in Miami, the offbeat film offers some truly funny moments, but it failed to connect with audiences and performed dismally at the box office.

TRUE LIES

Nuclear terrorists take on the nuclear family
and live just long enough to rue the day.
—Rita Kempley, review in *Washington Post*

THE STORY

To his family, Harry Tasker appears to be a mild-mannered computer sales-man and a loving if unattentive husband and father. In reality he is a top se-cret agent working for the U.S. government. When his wife becomes bored with their suburban existence and seeks a bit of adventure, the entire Tasker family become embroiled in an international terrorist plot involving nuclear blackmail.

THE FILM

Arnold Schwarzenegger and director James Cameron joined the ranks of Hollywood heavyweights through their collaboration on the surprise hit *The Terminator* and reunited for a sequel noted for innovative, mind-bending spe-cial effects, *Terminator 2: Judgment Day*. Teaming up again to create 1994's *True Lies*, the pair pushed the limits of both movie technology and the action genre to create an immense spectacle that incorporated humor and romance.

Schwarzenegger approached Cameron about the film after seeing the light French farce *La Totale!* in which a timid librarian who yearns for adventure discovers that her apparently mild-mannered husband is actually a secret agent. Cameron at first demurred, as he planned to move on to smaller films and avoid being labeled a mere genre director. Eventually he agreed to con-sider the idea, and after watching the French film, he recognized the potential of the story.

In writing the script, Cameron took steps away from the typical action film by incorporating a consistent streak of broad humor and by bringing the re-lationship of the husband and wife to the fore. Though these efforts did bring additional facets to the movie, they also resulted in depictions of women and Arabs that earned the ire of many.

Schwarzenegger's character, Harry Tasker, learns that his wife Helen is en-gaged in a dalliance with another man. Heartbroken by the news, he uses the resources of his spy agency to investigate his wife and learns that her poten-tial paramour is a weasely used-car salesman who pretends to be a spy to se-duce women. Harry has his wife captured by fellow agents and then electroni-cally disguises his voice as he interrogates her from behind a two-way mirror.

Figure 7.12. Publicity photos from *True Lies*. (Doll/Morrow Collection)

Learning that Helen still loves him and was only seeking a bit of excitement, he decides to give it to her by inventing a covert assignment for her: she must pose as a prostitute and plant a listening device in the hotel room of a notorious arms dealer. When Helen arrives at the hotel, Harry portrays the villain, this time hiding his face in the shadows of the darkened room as she performs a provocative bump and grind for her "customer." According to Cameron, these scenes were meant to comment on the male reluctance to communicate and express emotions, with Harry's attempts to hide his face serving as a metaphor for his suppressed feelings.[16] Many viewers, however, found Harry's actions cruel and even misogynistic, as his wife experiences genuine terror during the ordeal. Cameron's history of creating powerful heroines in films such as *Terminator 2*, *The Abyss*, *Aliens*, and *Titanic* lends credence to his professed intentions, however poorly Helen's transformation from mouse to minx was executed.

The film also earned heavy criticism for the buffoonish, one-dimensional crew of Arab terrorists who serve as the Taskers' enemies in the film. The group has acquired four Soviet nuclear warheads and plans to destroy one American city per week unless the United States withdraws its forces from the Persian Gulf. The ineptitude of the terrorists is a major source of humor in the film, and their leader is simplistically brutal, if more capable. Numerous Arab-American groups protested the film on opening day in cities around the country, and their objections prompted the filmmakers to add a disclaimer in the credits stating that the movie did not "represent the actions or beliefs of a particular culture or religion."

Despite these shortcomings, *True Lies* undeniably offers some of the best-conceived, best-executed action sequences ever captured on film. The most remarkable of these action set pieces occurs in Florida. The terrorists have smuggled their nuclear devices into the Florida Keys and plan to drive them onto the mainland via Highway 1, which connects the archipelago to Miami. This story line leads to a breathtaking confrontation on the Seven-Mile Bridge, the longest and highest part of the causeway that connects Marathon Key and the lower islands. A pair of Marine Corps Harrier jets blast a portion of the bridge ahead of the terrorist convoy with missiles, destroying two of their trucks but leaving Helen trapped in the back of a runaway limo as it careens toward the fatal gap. In a spectacular stunt, Harry reaches down from a helicopter and pulls his wife through the sunroof just as the limo plummets into the placid blue waters below.

The action on the bridge made for a remarkably realistic sequence that left many viewers wondering how it had been accomplished. The bridge's destruction was shot in miniature using a meticulously crafted eighty-foot model built

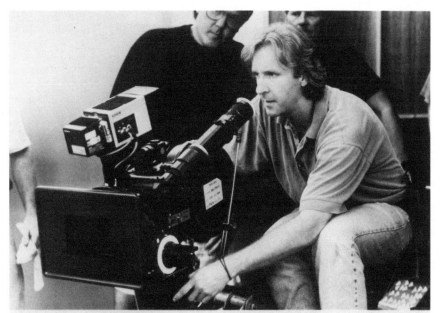

Figure 7.13. Publicity photos from *True Lies*. (Doll/Morrow Collection)

off the coast of Marathon Key. The filmmakers were able to drive real vehicles off a gap in the bridge because there are actually two Seven-Mile Bridges. The original structure was completed in 1912 by Henry Flagler as a part of a railroad line connecting the Keys to the mainland and was considered one of the engineering marvels of its day. When the bridge was damaged in a hurricane in the 1930s, the state rebuilt it for auto traffic, and it served as the primary access route to the lower Keys for forty-five years. In 1982 a new Seven-Mile Bridge was constructed parallel to the original, and much of the old bridge was left standing, although with gaps in it. The footage of vehicles dropping into the water was all filmed on the old bridge.

The climax of the film takes place in downtown Miami, where the terrorists have holed up with their one remaining nuclear device on the top floor of an office building. Harry commandeers one of the Marine Harriers and uses the hovering ability of the jet to execute a lengthy assault on the building. For this sequence, Cameron and his special-effects crew conceived of a simple but daring old-school approach that again achieved a stunning level of authenticity: they suspended an actual Harrier jet from a crane outside the office building. The extended sequence shows views of the jet from both inside and outside the high-rise as it fires on the terrorists and battles with their helicopter. In the end, the confrontation becomes a mano-a-mano affair, with the lead terrorist and Harry's daughter clinging to the outside of the jet as it hovers hundreds of feet above the Miami streets. While the sequence does incorporate computer-generated effects and blue-screen work, its greatest impact comes from the realism achieved through audacious but old-fashioned prop rigging.

Several reviews of the film touted Schwarzenegger and costar Jamie Lee Curtis as the Nick and Nora Charles of the 1990s, an allusion to the Golden Age pairing of William Powell and Myrna Loy in the *Thin Man* detective pictures. Other reviewers made frequent and favorable comparisons to the James Bond series. While familial concerns are never a part of 007's adventures, the multiple exotic locations and the stunning action sequences of *True Lies* hold up against the best that Bond has to offer.

THE CREDITS	THE CAST	
Produced by Stephanie Austin, James Cameron, and Pamela Easley	Arnold Schwarzenegger	Harry Tasker
Directed by James Cameron	Jamie Lee Curtis	Helen Tasker
Written by James Cameron	Tom Arnold	Albert Gibson
Cinematography by Russell Carpenter	Bill Paxton	Simon
Edited by Conrad Buff IV, Mark Goldblatt, and Richard A. Harris	Tia Carrere	Juno Skinner
Original music by Brad Fiedel	Art Malik	Salim Abu Aziz
Production design by Peter Lamont	Eliza Dushku	Dana Tasker
Art direction by Robert W. Laing and Michael Novotny	Grant Heslov	Faisil

THE MOVIE TOURIST'S GUIDE TO
FUN IN THE SUN

On the surface, the locations in this chapter might not seem particularly fun or amusing, but movie tourists will recognize them as the settings for a spree of zany comedies and lighthearted action tales.

ACE VENTURA: PET DETECTIVE

Miami

Though movie tourists are unlikely to run into Dan Marino or Don Shula in Miami, they can at least visit the Pro Player Stadium at 2269 Dan Marino Boulevard. Home to the extremely popular Miami Dolphins, this modern stadium seats 75,000 "Dol-fans," who patiently wait for another perfect season like the one their team pulled off in 1972.

BAD BOYS

Coral Gables

In its heyday, the Biltmore Hotel in Coral Gables hosted European royalty and Hollywood's biggest stars. Completed in 1926, it also became a favorite of gangster Al Capone. In honor of its most notorious guest, the Biltmore currently houses the Al Capone Suite, where one of the key scenes in *Bad Boys* occurs. Director Michael Bay stayed in the Al Capone Suite while he was shooting his film in Miami.

The two-story suite is supposedly haunted, either by the ghosts of Confederate soldiers, by Capone himself, or by people the gangster had eliminated. One of the ghosts is said to be Capone crony Fats Walsh, who was murdered in the hotel on the thirteenth floor of the tower, which featured a speakeasy during Prohibition. The elevator going to that part of the hotel sometimes makes unscheduled stops at the thirteenth floor, and employees believe it to be Fats visiting the speakeasy one more time.

THE BELLBOY

Miami Beach

The Fontainebleau Hotel was the primary location of Jerry Lewis's first directorial effort, and many of the hotel's famous features are included in the film. Opened in 1954, the Fontainebleau was designed by Morris Lapidus, who wanted his hotel to epitomize the luxury associated with conspicuous consumption. The grandiose design was criticized at the time but is now heralded for its uniquely American style. The Fontainebleau introduced certain motifs that would become clichés of kitschy buildings, including "woggles," which are shaped like artists' palettes, "cheese holes," which are amoebalike cutouts in walls, and "beanpoles," or metal rods that support nothing. Located at 4441 Collins Avenue in Miami Beach, the hotel houses the Club Tropigala, a renowned nightclub and restaurant.

In addition to *The Bellboy*, the Fontainebleau also "starred" in *Goldfinger* and *A Hole in the Head*.

LICENCE TO KILL

Key West

Agent 007 gets his famous "license to kill" revoked in a scene shot at the Ernest Hemingway Home on Whitehead Street in Key West. Hemingway lived in this Spanish-colonial-style house from 1931 to 1940, and penned several novels in the room above the carriage house. Built out of coral rock, the house was designed to withstand the mighty hurricanes that have been known to blow through the Keys. Visitors can tour the house to see his library, souvenirs of his legendary travels, and the cigar-maker's chair that he sat upon when he wrote. Descendants of a six-toed cat that was allegedly a Hemingway pet are taken care of by the staff and prowl the grounds at will.

MATINEE

Key West

The Strand Theater at 527 Duval Street opened in the 1920s and served as Key West's grand old movie palace for decades. The Art Deco theater was featured prominently in the film but was converted into a Ripley's Believe It or Not attraction shortly thereafter. The building was sold in 2002 and now houses a Walgreen's. The drug chain has maintained some of the original interior architecture and restored the facade, including the marquee, which now touts the store's weekly specials.

STRIPTEASE

Miami

The Miami Seaquarium, located on the Rickenbacker Causeway on Virginia Key, provided the setting for a clandestine meeting between stripper Erin Grant and protective cop Al Garcia in *Striptease*. The thirty-five-acre attraction specializes in marine mammal exhibits and recently added a Swim With Our Dolphins program in which participants are allowed to romp with the Seaquarium's bottlenose dolphins. There are notable attractions devoted to sharks and manatees, plus a mangrove swamp with pelicans.

The Seaquarium also trained and provided the dolphins used on the *Flipper* television show (see *Flipper*, chapter 4) and for many years touted itself as "the home of Flipper." Today the facility offers the Flipper Dolphin Show in the Flipper Lagoon, which was used for filming the television show.

Lake Okeechobee

Okeechobee is one of the largest freshwater lakes in the United States, covering 750 square miles. In the film, the vast lake served as a dumping ground for the body of a blackmailer foolish enough to tangle with corrupt congressman Dilbeck. While there is not a lot of scenery to take in, those movie tourists who are anglers will be pleased to know the lake is famous for its abundance of fish. The town of Okeechobee, which is located at the crossroads of State Route 70, U.S. 98, and U.S. 441, serves as a center for boating, fishing, and camping.

Clewiston

Tiny Clewiston was developed in the 1920s and incorporated in 1925. It gets its nickname, America's Sweetest Town, from the area's primary industry—the growing of sugarcane. The Clewiston Sugar Festival, sponsored by the town's U.S. Sugar Corporation, is an annual event celebrating the end of the cane harvest. The main events are held in April in Clewiston, Hendry County's largest municipality. Tourists can enjoy old-fashioned sugarcane grinding, musical entertainment, exhibits, arts and crafts, and regional food. The Chamber of Commerce offers heritage and historical tours that visit cane fields and sugar mills. The town is located sixty miles east of Fort Myers and sixty miles west of Palm Beach, along U.S. 27 on the southwest shore of Lake Okeechobee.

TRUE LIES

Overseas Highway

Part of the large-scale climactic sequence of this action film takes place on the Seven Mile Bridge that connects Florida's Middle Keys with the Lower Keys. The bridge is part of the extension of U.S. Highway 1—called the Overseas Highway—which ends in Key West, the southernmost city in the continental United States. The first bridge that spanned that part of the Keys was constructed by Henry Flagler as part of the Florida East Coast Railway in 1912, and it runs parallel to the new highway bridge that was finished in 1982. The old railway bridge was considered an engineering marvel in its day and is now on the National Register of Historic Places. It rested on a record 546 concrete piers. No cars are allowed on the old bridge, but a two-mile section is open for biking and walking with a terminus at historic Pigeon Key. In addition to *True Lies*, this spectacular bridge was used in *2 Fast 2 Furious*, *Licence to Kill*, and *Up Close and Personal*.

FLORIDA AS PARADISE

A treasure—in truth—at the rainbow's end!
—1920s Florida tourism pamphlet

Florida has long enjoyed a reputation as an earthly paradise. For more than a century it has been among the top tourist and retirement destinations in America, for obvious reasons—the inviting tropical climate, the endless sandy beaches, the world-class entertainment and attractions. The state's natural beauty, supplemented by a well-developed tourism industry and some shrewd marketing, has indelibly associated Florida with the notion of fun in the sun.

The image of Florida as "America's sun porch" has its origins in the efforts of two American industrialists of the late 1800s, Henry Flagler and Henry Plant. Both men belonged to that dubious group of business giants known as the robber barons, who amassed enormous wealth with the coming of the Industrial Age. In the mid-nineteenth century, Plant built an express delivery service into one of the largest railroad empires in the South. Flagler, a prominent executive in that monopoly of all monopolies Standard Oil, relinquished his post in the Rockefeller court to create an empire of his own.

During the 1880s and 1890s, these two friends and amiable competitors drained swamps, laid rail lines, and built opulent resorts throughout Florida—Flagler down the east coast and Plant through the central and southwestern parts of the state. With America's nouveaux riches as their market, they made the state easily accessible, provided sumptuous accommodations that set a new standard for luxury hotels, and encouraged the development of local businesses such as river cruises and fishing excursions. They also heavily advertised the sun-drenched wonders of the state and the grand excesses of their hotels through brochures, books, and high-quality postcard sets. One fifty-eight-page pamphlet from 1892 called *Florida, Beauties of the East Coast* provided glowing descriptions of various stops along the Flagler rail line—"There is nothing equal to it on the face of the earth"—accompanied by full-page photographs. Another, *Seven Centers in Paradise*, offered romanticized tales of fictional guests staying at the Flagler resorts, such as the story of a young American woman who falls in love with a prince at the Ponce de Leon Hotel.[1]

Together, Flagler and Plant transformed Florida from a remote, swampy province into the most fashionable vacation destination of the Gilded Age, an American Riviera where the wealthy could show off their wealth. In the early twentieth century, burgeoning automobile ownership brought Florida a whole new breed of vacationer, the "tin can tourist." Lured by the image of an exotic paradise that Flagler and Plant had offered to the upper classes, these middle-income travelers rattled through the state in their tin lizzies, staying at campgrounds or small rental cottages and stretching their budgets by subsisting on canned food. While the grandeur of the posh hotels was not within their reach, they found paradise in the endless sunshine and natural splendor of the state.

In addition to transforming the state's tourism industry, Flagler and Plant built up an infrastructure that allowed agriculture and many other industries to thrive in Florida. The ever-growing economic opportunity combined with the idyllic image of the region that had been crafted to draw vacationers brought an influx of new residents and eventually led to the Florida land boom of the 1920s. A spate of books extolled the healthy climate, natural bounty, and great economic opportunity of the state, creating the impression that new residents could expect to find prosperity without toil, and perfect weather besides. Northerners bought parcels of Florida land, sometimes sight unseen, intending to resettle in a land of economic bounty and natural splendor. Though some would end up with worthless swampland, many moved southward in pursuit of this dream, and communities across the state doubled in size in a matter of a few years.

While immigration to Florida remained strong for decades and surged again in the latter half of the twentieth century, the population never managed to outpace the influx of tourists. In 1940 the state's 1.9 million residents were hosting 2.6 million visitors annually.[2] Today Florida's population is the fourth largest in the country at 15 million, but the state sees well over 70 million tourists a year.[3]

Since the end of World War II, tourism has been far and away the state's largest industry. Slick, successful advertising such as the 1970s "When You Need It Bad" campaign perpetuated the state's image as a place free from the pressures and drudgery of everyday life. In 1971 the opening of Disney World brought a whole new level of fantasy to the state's image, and subsequent mega-theme parks have only added to that.

The perception of Florida as a paradise has always been crucial to the state's development and economy, but it has also had a significant impact on the way the state is depicted on film. *Girl Happy* and *Where the Boys Are*, for example, celebrated the culture of youth through the collegiate version of paradise, spring break in Fort Lauderdale. *Follow That Dream* and *Summer Rental*, on the other hand, traded on Florida's image to reveal the intrinsic value and integrity of the traditional family unit. Other films, such as *Ruby in Paradise* and *Midnight Cowboy*, deconstructed the myth of Florida to present the notion that even in a tropical paradise, true happiness lies within us rather than in the material world. For filmmakers, the established cultural perception of Florida as paradise has provided a ready-made icon that can be honored, alluded to, or subverted to suit the needs and messages of their films.

FOLLOW THAT DREAM

I've never seen a movie filmed here which
showed Florida off to better advantage.
—Wendall Jarrard, Florida Development
Committee, to the *Pensacola Journal*

THE STORY

The nomadic Kwimper family, consisting of Pop, Toby, and several adopted orphans, declare squatter's rights along an unclaimed stretch of beach next to a new Florida highway. There they build a simple home, set up a simple business, and prepare to lead a simple life. However, the modern world, in the form of crooked gamblers, a predatory female psychologist, and petty state officials, are determined to interfere.

Figure 8.1. Publicity photo from *Follow That Dream*. (Sharon Fox Collection)

THE FILM

Intended as vehicles to promote his image as a pop singer, many of the films of Elvis Presley fit a rigid formula dubbed the "Elvis movie." The Elvis movie is a romantic fantasy in which Presley plays a singing race-car driver, airplane pilot, or boat captain who woos the perfect girl with a never-ending supply of pop songs. In biographies and critical examinations of his career, the Elvis movie is generally scorned, particularly by those who prefer their Elvis raw and rockin'.

Actually, Elvis Presley appeared in thirty-three films during his lifetime, and many of them did not follow the rigid formula of the Elvis movie, including *Follow That Dream*. *Dream* showcased Elvis singing six songs, and it was a comedy, but its basis in a satirical novel by Richard Powell makes it a unique entry in the Presley filmography. While Powell's novel did feature a sharper satire and a more complex story line than the film, the script by veteran Hollywood writer Charles Lederer still contained some witty jabs at modern life.

The story follows the adventures of the Kwimper family, who homestead a small strip of beach alongside a new Florida highway, much to the chagrin of local bureaucrats. The Kwimpers, who hail from the backwoods of the South, have a rare, simple outlook on life that many mistake for ignorance or stupidity. Though Presley's character, Toby, is handsome and attractive to women, he is also a naive bumpkin—a far cry from his typical cocky leading man.

The characters and story line are structured around a series of oppositions: country vs. city, common sense vs. a college education, simple values vs. sophisticated lifestyles, regular folks vs. bureaucrats. Toby and his family represent the down-to-earth values of small-town life, which at first seem outdated and unsophisticated. After all, they lack education, direction, and ambition. Their car is old, their clothes are plain, and before staking their claim on the Florida beach, they survived through government assistance. Pop's only accommodation to modern living is to install a commode—the epitome of luxury in his eyes. However, as the story unfolds, the audience learn they have misjudged the Kwimpers, just as the other characters in the film do. The Kwimpers may be simple, but they are unaffected by consumerism, free from the pressure of the rat race, compassionate toward the less fortunate, and motivated by the simple pleasures of family, fun, and fishing.

The modern world intrudes upon the Kwimpers via several characters who try to change them, get rid of them, or con them. Clinical psychologist Alisha Claypoole, a contemporary woman who aggressively comes on to Toby, represents the modern tendency to put faith in "progressive" modes of thought rather than in old-fashioned family values. When Toby rejects her advances, preferring down-home girl Holly Jones, Dr. Claypoole tries to prove that Pop Kwimper is unfit to raise children, using "science" in the form of a word-association test. A low-level bureaucrat assigned to keep Florida's newest highway in top condition joins forces with Dr. Claypoole so he can oust the Kwimpers from their homestead. Their wooden dock, simple beach house, and outdoor "facility" are an eyesore to this petty official who does not want his newly opened highway stained by outdated structures. Finally, two big-city thugs who run a floating gambling operation for an organized crime syndicate try to homestead next to the Kwimpers because their beach is not in the jurisdiction of any law enforcement.

By the end of the film, Toby's honest, straightforward approach to life and Pop's wise understanding of human motivations help them outsmart dishonest gamblers, pushy local bureaucrats, and sophisticated women. Their simple old-fashioned values are proven superior to such modern concepts as psychology, social welfare, the highway beautification projects, and even "living the high life." While most facets of modern life are lampooned in the film, psychiatry and the social welfare system are absolutely skewered. Pop Kwimper insists that his receipt of government benefits such as relief, disability, and child support stems from his sense of patriotism. If the government is so determined to

Figure 8.2. Publicity photo from *Follow That Dream*. (Sharon Fox Collection)

give money away, then it's his duty as a good citizen to take it! Alisha Claypoole is confounded when she gives her word-association test to Toby, who answers "death" to her prompt of "girl," because it reminds him of the folk song "On Top of Old Smokey," in which the girl dies. Toby's obtuse answer reveals the limitations of Alisha's test and, by extension, social "science."

The Kwimpers did find something in Florida that changed them, however. They found a new life and a new home, complete with the luxury of a flush toilet. To the Kwimpers, this was paradise. Their stretch of Florida, with its white sand beaches, palm trees, and blue water, actually looks like the stereotype of paradise. *Follow That Dream* was shot entirely in Florida, and the state's natural beauty was used to good advantage. However, the Kwimpers were smart enough to realize there was more to paradise than palm trees and ocean breezes. The Kwimpers successfully kept their makeshift family together, started their own fishing business, and created a real home on their patch of land. Paradise, as it turns out, is the simple life of old-fashioned family values, self-sufficiency, and compassion for others—in other words, a life unencumbered by the false values of the modern world. As Toby explains to the judge during their custody case, "I thought there was maybe more to living than the way Pop taught me, but I was never dumb enough to go against him. . . . I was glad I didn't."

THE CREDITS

Released in 1962 by United Artists
Produced by David Weisbart
Directed by Gordon Douglas
Written by Charles Lederer, based on the novel
  Pioneer, Go Home! by Richard Powell
Cinematography by Leo Tover
Edited by William B. Murphy
Original music by Hans J. Salter

THE CAST

Elvis Presley	Toby Kwimper
Arthur O'Connell	Pop Kwimper
Anne Helm	Holly Jones
Joanna Moore	Alisha Claypoole
Jack Kruschen	Carmine
Simon Oakland	Nick
Roland Winters	Judge Wardman
Alan Hewitt	H. Arthur King
Howard McNear	George Binkley

GIRL HAPPY

Elvis jumps with the campus crowd
to make the beach "ball" bounce!
—tagline for *Girl Happy*

THE STORY

Rusty Wells and his band are working in Chicago when the club owner coerces them into taking on an extra gig. Knowing that the band has been booked into a Fort Lauderdale hot spot, he asks them to chaperon Valerie, his college-age daughter, over spring break. At first Rusty and the boys think eggheaded Valerie couldn't possibly be much trouble, but one glance at the cute coed in her bikini makes them realize how hard it will be to keep the boys away.

THE FILM

Girl Happy epitomizes the "Elvis movie," in which Presley plays a handsome bachelor who works in a glamorous occupation in an exotic locale or popular vacation spot. During the course of the film, his character sings several songs, usually to the leading lady to whom he is attracted, and vice versa. This formula does not cover all of Elvis's thirty-three films (see *Follow That Dream*, above), but it is the type of musical vehicle most associated with the legendary singer. The Presley vehicles were all financially successful at the time of release, though later they were often maligned, with Elvis himself ridiculing them as "the Presley travelogues."

In *Girl Happy*, Elvis stars as Rusty Wells, a singer with his own band, or, to use the vernacular of 1965, "combo." The musicians tour the country perform-

Figure 8.3. Publicity photo from *Girl Happy*. (Sharon Fox Collection)

ing in nightclubs, and while they struggle financially, their lifestyle is exciting, liberating, and fun. As a special favor to the owner of the 77 Club in Chicago, they agree to look out for his daughter Valerie, who is on spring break in Fort Lauderdale, Florida. The combo has been booked into a hot club there, and they plan to keep an eye on Valerie without her knowing it. Rusty is distracted by other girls, particularly the provocative Deena Shepherd, but he falls in love with Valerie. The ups and downs of their relationship are chronicled through the dozen songs that pepper the film, including "Cross My Heart and Hope to Die" and "Puppet on a String."

The negative criticism of Presley's films is unfair to some degree, because most of them were intended to be nothing more than musical vehicles to showcase his singing talents. Taken out of context by biographers and music historians, who prefer the hard-rocking Elvis of the 1950s, his films are ridiculed as trite, or they are offered as evidence of the decline in Elvis's music during the 1960s.[4] But Elvis's movies are too tightly bound to their era to be considered outside the context of their specific genre, the teen flick.

Presley was not the only rock or pop singing idol to star in film vehicles during the 1960s. Everyone from Frankie Avalon to Herman's Hermits to Nancy

Sinatra appeared in teen comedies and musicals aimed at youthful audiences. The plots focused on problems relevant to young people; the stars were actors or singers popular among the rock 'n' roll set; and the locations were familiar to a generation who were much more mobile than the youth of previous eras. Beach and ski party movies, surfing movies, and the Elvis movies were all part of the teen-flick genre.

Like many films of this genre, *Girl Happy* centers on such anguishing aspects of youthful romance as sex vs. love, predatory males vs. nice guys, bad girls vs. good girls. But it also involves the theme of independence from parental authority and the responsibility that goes with it—a rite of passage that members of the intended audience could relate to. The film featured a cast of familiar faces from other youth-oriented films, including Joby Baker, Jimmy Hawkins, and Gary Crosby as Elvis's musical combo. Crosby, son of legendary singer Bing Crosby, was the only one with any musical ability, but the actors were not cast for their singing talents. Baker had costarred in such teen fare as *Gidget Goes Hawaiian, Hootenanny Hoot,* and *When the Boys Meet the Girls,* while Crosby and Hawkins were recognizable from various television series. Valerie was played by Shelley Fabares, widely known for her role as the teenage daughter on *The Donna Reed Show* and for her number-one hit record, "Johnny Angel," in 1962. Chris Noel, who costarred in the teen comedies *Get Yourself a College Girl, Beach Ball,* and *For Singles Only,* had a small role as Fabares's girlfriend.

Of the dozen songs in *Girl Happy,* one has often been singled out as "evidence" of Elvis's musical decline in the 1960s.[5] "Do the Clam" was written to accompany a dance called the Clam that was specially created for the film by choreographer David Winters. Winters served as the dance director for *Hullabaloo,* a hit television series that featured miniskirted go-go dancers moving to the latest rock music. During the 1960s, several dance crazes swept popular music, including the Monkey, the Pony, and the Swim. Winters and the film's producers hoped the Clam would be the next dance sensation, but it did not catch on. When considered in the context of the times, the song and the dance are not nearly so ridiculous as they might otherwise seem.

Fort Lauderdale had been the most popular destination for college students on spring break since the 1960 film *Where the Boys Are,* so it is not surprising that an Elvis movie would be set there. However, very little of *Girl Happy* was actually shot on location in Florida. Only a pre-credits scene explaining the lure of Lauderdale for the younger set, plus some background footage for the scenes involving rear-screen projection, were shot in the Sunshine State. The beach, the motel and pool, the nightclub, and the Fort Lauderdale jail were recreated on the soundstages and back lots of Hollywood.

For a few weeks every spring, Fort Lauderdale became paradise for thousands of young men and women who were roughly the same age, listened to the same music, spoke the same slang, and reached for the same dreams. In many ways the fictional world created in *Girl Happy*, and in other teen flicks, is similar to the real-life atmosphere of Lauderdale in the spring: young characters populate a world in which their concerns are the main focus. The characters are united by age, music, language, and their dreams and goals. Fort Lauderdale, onscreen and off, was a paradise not because it was a tropical location but because it was a communal experience to be savored.

THE CREDITS		THE CAST	
Released in 1965 by Metro-Goldwin-Mayer		Elvis Presley	Rusty Wells
Produced by Joe Pasternak		Shelley Fabares	Valerie Frank
Directed by Boris Sagal		Harold J. Stone	Mr. Frank
Written by Harvey Bullock and R. S. Allen		Gary Crosby	Andy
Cinematography by Philip H. Lathrop		Joby Baker	Wilbur
Edited by Rita Roland		Nita Talbot	Sunny Daze
Music by George Stoll		Mary Ann Mobley	Deena Shepherd
		Jimmy Hawkins	Doc
		Chris Noel	Betsy

Clambake

Of the thirty-three films that Elvis made during the Hollywood phase of his career, three were set in the Sunshine State—*Follow That Dream*, *Girl Happy*, and *Clambake*. Released in 1967, *Clambake* was one of the worst of the Elvis movies. By this point, the formula for the Elvis movie had run its course, and ticket sales were diminishing with each film. Elvis's manager, Colonel Tom Parker, sought deals with shorter shooting schedules, lower budgets, and fewer cast members, to keep production costs low in order to ensure a profit. Saddled with the same genre over and over, the aging Presley grew bored and disillusioned with his films. The results were often disastrous.

A poorly constructed "Prince and the Pauper" tale, *Clambake* was set in Miami, but it was filmed entirely on Hollywood stages and back lots. Unlike *Girl Happy*, it had almost no background scenery or establishing shots. The few that were used were shot in California, including a scene in which Elvis and another character are driving around the Miami area. One of California's mountain ranges can be clearly seen in the distance!

MIDNIGHT COWBOY

The two basic items necessary to sustain
life are sunshine and coconut milk.
—Ratso Rizzo in *Midnight Cowboy*

THE STORY

A young, alienated Texan, emotionally scarred by a difficult upbringing, rides
a bus to New York City, where he plans to make his fortune providing sexual
services to Park Avenue matrons. When his naive dream fails to materialize,
he forms an intimate bond with a grimy, physically scarred street hustler, and
together they eke out an existence among the affluent, jaded, and disenfran-
chised denizens of Manhattan.

THE FILM

Like all great films, *Midnight Cowboy* represents many things to many people.
For some, it is a landmark of American cinema that signifies the passing of the
old studio system. For others, it offers a metaphor for the disenfranchisement
and loneliness that characterized America's gay subculture in modern times,
or a sharp criticism of media culture and the masculine ideal. Still others cite it
as an unerring snapshot of the decadence, indifference, and grandeur of New
York City in the late 1960s. Universally, however, the film is recognized as a
poignant character study of two pitiful souls who overcome their alienation
through each other.

Released in 1969 just six months after the implementation of the MPAA
rating system, *Midnight Cowboy* was one of the first Hollywood films to receive an X rating and the only such film to earn an Oscar for Best Picture.
Eventually the porn industry would coopt the X rating as a marketing tool
that touted explicit sexual content, but *Midnight Cowboy* represents the rating
as it was intended—as a signifier of serious content directed at mature audiences. By today's standards, in fact, the film appears rather tame, with little
nudity or foul language despite its pervasive sexual themes. Given that the rating system was designed as the industry's new form of self-regulation after the
demise of the studio system and the Production Code, many film historians
see the film's Oscar success to be as much a political as an artistic statement by
the Hollywood establishment.[6] In presenting its highest accolade to *Midnight
Cowboy*, the American film industry openly embraced its new generation of
filmmakers who presented rough antiheroes and frank treatments of sex and
violence for a more sophisticated audience. The Academy also awarded the

Figure 8.4. Publicity photo from *Midnight Cowboy*. (Doll/Morrow Collection)

Best Adapted Screenplay award to *Cowboy*'s Waldo Salt. A veteran screen-writer who began his career in the late 1930s, Salt was one of many Hollywood artists blacklisted for his left-wing political affiliations in the 1950s, and his win only strengthens the notion that the 1969 Academy Awards served as a memo-rial service for the practices and purveyors of the Golden Age.

Director John Schlesinger, a pioneer in Britain's Angry Young Man move-ment of the early 1960s, earned the film's third Oscar. Openly gay, Schlesinger presented a dark and squalid glimpse of the 42nd Street hustlers and their johns, emphasizing the self-loathing and angst many gays suffered as a re-sult of society's ostracism. He also used the film to subvert generally accepted views of American masculinity, contrasting the affected and ineffective cow-boy persona of Texan Joe Buck (Jon Voight) with the source of his redemption, the emotional and frequently tender relationship he develops with tubercular vagrant Ratso Rizzo (Dustin Hoffman). The film includes several references to familiar Western film heroes, including John Wayne and the Paul Newman character Hud, and makes it clear that Joe associates the wild-and-wooly West with his own virility. It's not until Ratso points out that cowboy garb has be-come a recognized uniform among New York's gay hustlers that Joe—and the audience—begins to question his long-established notions of masculinity.

Schlesinger began his career with documentaries and brought an eye well trained in capturing realism to the streets of New York. From the all-night coffee shops to the glitz of Times Square, from condemned tenements to luxurious penthouses, from Manhattan's throngs of working stiffs to its shameless drug addicts, he employed the city as a character of oppression and indifference that served as the film's antagonist. He also made use of some of the city's notorious celebrities—Viva, Ultra Violet, International Velvet, Paul Morrissey, and other creations of Andy Warhol's Factory—in a scene that juxtaposes the peaks of wealth and celebrity with the chasms of poverty and obscurity that exist side by side in urban America.

Though *Midnight Cowboy* is firmly rooted in New York City, the film has several strong connections to Florida. Writer James Leo Herlihy, who published the original novel in 1965, was a longtime resident of Key West, and a number of his works are set there. Though he produced a varied body of work, Herlihy is noted for his depictions of seamy urban life and his ability to produce visceral, realistic dialogue, two prominent features of *Midnight Cowboy*. The film is also well remembered for its music, both the effective soundtrack by John Barry and the theme song "Everybody's Talkin'" that so perfectly captured the defiant loneliness of Joe and Ratso. As performed by Harry Nilsson for the film, the song became an enormous hit that still receives radio play today. Its composer, Fred Neil, was a leader of the folk rock scene of the 1960s, influencing performers from David Crosby and John Sebastian to Roy Orbison and Bob Dylan. Neil is often described as a music purist who shunned celebrity, and the mainstream success of his song prompted the Florida native to abandon the New York music scene and return to Coconut Grove, where on the first Earth Day in 1970 he established the Dolphin Rescue Project, an organization that combats illegal trafficking and exploitation of marine mammals.[7]

The most significant connection, of course, is Ratso's dream of escaping his miserable existence in New York for the sunny climes of Florida where, he believes as naively as Joe, he will find a paradise. Midway through the film, when the pair think that Joe's career as a gigolo is about to take off, Ratso indulges in a whimsical daydream, accompanied on the soundtrack by the breezy "Florida Fantasy." He sees himself outrunning Joe in a friendly beach race beneath the warm Florida sun, having his shoes shined at poolside as he wears a cream-colored suit with an ostentatious RR monogram, and being called after by matronly snowbirds who sport mink stoles over their bathing suits. The fantasy comes to an abrupt end when Joe mishandles the assignation and it becomes clear Ratso will have to settle for the Florida tourism posters that adorn the condemned apartment they share as squatters. Later, with the onset of a New

York winter and a serious decline in Ratso's health, Joe strong-arms a would-be john for enough money to buy two bus tickets to Florida. In the film's final, touching scene, he tenderly administers to his dying friend as they roll past glistening waters and rows of palm trees on the outskirts of Miami.

THE CREDITS

Released in 1969 by United Artists
Produced by Jerome Hellman
Directed by John Schlesinger
Written by Waldo Salt, based on the novel
by James Leo Herlihy
Original Music by John Barry; "Everybody's
Talkin'" by Fred Neil
Cinematography by Adam Holender
Editing by Hugh A. Robertson
Production design by John Robert Lloyd
Costume design by Ann Roth

THE CAST

Dustin Hoffman	Enrico Salvatore "Ratso" Rizzo
Jon Voight	Joe Buck
Sylvia Miles	Cass
John McGiver	Mr. O'Daniel
Brenda Vaccaro	Shirley
Barnard Hughes	Towny
Jennifer Salt	Annie
Bob Balaban	Young student
Viva	Gretel McAlbertson
Gastone Rossilli	Hansel McAlbertson
Ultra Violet	Woman at party
International Velvet	Woman at party
Paul Morrissey	Man at party
Waldo Salt	Joe Pyne on TV show

RUBY IN PARADISE

The answers are probably real simple, real close. Smiling
somewhere quiet-like, waiting for us.
—Ruby Lee Gissing in *Ruby in Paradise*

THE STORY

Just of age, Ruby Lee Gissing flees an oppressive hometown in Tennessee to begin a new life in a Florida resort town. After finding simple work and simple lodgings, she begins an ill-fated affair with the boss's son that wrongly costs her her job. Wounded but not defeated, she perseveres until the situation is rectified. Along the way, she chooses new friends, contemplates a new man, and meticulously thinks through every decision and every experience as a way to understand herself.

Young Ruby Lee Gissing is looking for something. We see that in the first few moments of *Ruby in Paradise* as she speeds down a snaking two-lane, accompanied only by a driving country-rock soundtrack and the image of her small-town life receding in the mirror. She pushes on into the night, relentless, never looking back, until she breezes past a roadside marker that tells her she's arrived: "Welcome to Florida," it reads.

As the film's title implies, Ruby's quest is for nothing less than Paradise, and in her mind Paradise is to be found in Panama City Beach—a prime tourist town on the "redneck Riviera" of Florida's northwestern Panhandle. Writer-director Victor Nunez ensures we see the irony of her choice through a myriad of details that capture the texture, the atmosphere, the very soul of the resort town. This is a place where people come but never stay, a place of sandy beaches and strip malls, of snapshots and service with a smile.

Nunez's Panama City Beach serves as a faux paradise for most of the movie's vacationers. College students have come for the anonymity, which they equate with a license for indulgent spring revelry. Retired Canadians have come to shop all day and debate whether or not the water is too cold to dip a toe. But Ruby has come to find a place where she can make her own decisions, fix her own mistakes, and overcome her own obstacles, a place where the expectations and needs of the people she's known since childhood won't chart the path of her life. Ruby has come to find Paradise. Ruby has come to be Ruby.

Working on a tight $800,000 budget, Nunez happily accepted the cooperation of Panama City Beach residents and businesses while shooting the independent film in 1993. "They only had to look at us in our beat-up old truck to know that we weren't living high on the hog," Nunez reflected. "People were really wonderful. I love Panama City."[8] And he made excellent use of the town's welcome by featuring many local landmarks in key scenes: Thunderbirds nightclub, where Ruby initiates her first romantic liaison in her new town; Sharky's Beach Bar, where she bemusedly circles the fringe of a raucous college party; and St. Andrews Beach, which offers her a haven of salt spray, lapping waves, and bleached scrub grass.

Against such backdrops, Ruby goes about building the exteriors of her new life. She sets up house in a cramped rental and fights to get a job selling retail to the tourists at Chambers Beach Emporium. She gets involved with a man clearly undeserving of her, and pays the price. She finds another, this one genuine and thoughtful, but realizes that for the comfort of a relationship she would have to pay a greater price—her independence.

If it seems that there's not much of a plot to *Ruby in Paradise*, it's because there isn't. But that's not to say that not much happens. And in that seeming

Figure 8.5. *Ruby in Paradise* star Ashley Judd. (Doll/Morrow Collection)

contradiction lies the beauty of this thoughtful, engrossing film. The real action takes place not in the bars or the beaches or the beds of Panama City Beach but in Ruby's head. In a string of everyday small encounters, she works her way through all the great issues of a lifetime—ethics, justice, religion, love, crime, community, violence, friendship, lust, responsibility, fear, hope. She meets each head on, sometimes winning, sometimes flinching, sometimes falling, but always in her own way, on her own terms, with her own courage.

For a male writer, Nunez plumbs the depths of the modern female psyche with remarkable sensitivity and insight. And in her breakout role, Ashley Judd crafts a perfect Ruby, revealing the character's determination, frailty, and growth through a performance built on nuance, subtlety, and gesture. Together, they manage to do for 114 minutes what many talented filmmakers can't always sustain even for a scene: they guide the audience on a journey through the heart and mind of a character in the unlikely town where she has staked out her own little Paradise.

THE CREDITS	THE CAST	
Released in 1993	Ashley Judd	Ruby Lee Gissing
Produced by Sam Gowan with Keith Crofford	Todd Field	Mike McCaslin
Directed by Victor Nunez	Bentley Mitchum	Ricky Chambers
Written by Victor Nunez	Allison Dean	Rochelle Bridges
Cinematography by Alex Vlacos	Dorothy Lyman	Mildred Chambers
Edited by Victor Nunez	Betsy Douds	Debrah Ann
	Donovan Lee Carroll	Tennessee boyfriend

Victor Nunez

With five feature films in twenty-five years, Victor Nunez could hardly be called prolific, but he is unquestionably the preeminent writer-director-editor of movies set in northern Florida. Born in Deland, Florida, and currently residing in Tallahassee, Nunez has used his native region as the centerpiece of every one of his acclaimed films. Many of them, including *Gal Young 'Un* and *A Flash of Green*, were also adapted from literary works by Florida natives.

His films are noted for their insightful character development and strong sense of place and have been universally well received by critics, if not by distributors. Both *Gal Young 'Un* and *Ruby in Paradise* earned the Grand Jury Prize at the Sundance Film Festival—which, incidentally, Nunez helped found. As an independent, Nunez has faced long struggles to get his films made. *Gal Young 'Un*, his first feature, was shot on a minuscule budget of $40,000,[9] and *Ruby* was financed in large part with an inheritance Nunez had recently received.

After studying film at UCLA, Nunez turned from Hollywood and chased the often difficult path of an independent regional filmmaker. Enamored of both Italian neorealist film and Southern literature, he adapted the notion shared by both genres of integrating character, place, and story. "I asked myself, 'Why not make movies that way, and build from a place where one has a beautiful connection?'"[10] For Nunez, that place was the Florida Panhandle.

RUNNING SCARED

These people gotta learn to stop and watch a sunset every now and then.
—Detective Ray Hughes in *Running Scared*, commenting
on Chicago after vacationing in Key West

THE STORY

A pair of wisecracking Chicago cops set their sights on a brutal drug dealer while struggling to maintain their personal lives. When their captain imposes a forced vacation after a bungled raid, the two decide to retire to Florida and buy a bar, but only after bringing their quarry to justice.

THE FILM

In many ways, *Running Scared* is a conventional buddy-cop film, with a pair of seasoned detectives going all out to rid their city of a vicious criminal boss. Populated by recognizable supporting characters and punctuated with over-the-top action, much of the film is predictable and implausible. It's made distinctive, however, by the peculiar casting of the lead characters as well as the smart contrast of its Chicago and Florida locations.

Stars Billy Crystal and Gregory Hines make an unlikely pairing as two of Chicago's finest. Neither performer brought the physical presence or star image normally associated with the action genre. The diminutive Crystal, a gifted mimic and extemporaneous comedian, was best known for his role as network television's first openly gay character on *Soap* and for his stint on *Saturday Night Live*, where he reinvigorated the lagging late-night comedy show and led it to one of its most successful periods. Hines, of course, was recognized primarily for his incredible dance talent, though he had proven himself a capable dramatic actor in earlier films such as *White Nights* and *The Cotton Club*.

Running Scared was originally written with two older, white actors in mind, and the bold casting of Hines and Crystal virtually reinvented the film. Director Peter Hyams pushed for the two performers, hoping to bring some freshness to an otherwise unoriginal story, and the idea succeeded. Concerned about their physical suitability for the roles, Crystal got Hines to join him in a daily weight-lifting regimen under the supervision of a trainer, and they formed an easy friendship during the production. Their rapport both on and off the set allowed the actors to improvise some of the banter between their characters and rework several of the action scenes to add comic touches. Their personal chemistry is evident throughout the film, as they exchange flippant chatter with perfect timing and take turns handing each other straight lines.

Figure 8.6. *Running Scared* director Peter Hyams. (Doll/Morrow Collection)

The likable friendship between their characters becomes the film's most effective emotional hook, whether they're arguing over marksmanship during a gunfight, contemplating the dangers and rewards of their careers, or helping each other dodge subpoenas or win over women.

The other memorable component of the film is its locations. Set in Chicago during one of the city's bitter winters, the film opens with credits rolling over a series of immediately recognizable images—the Picasso sculpture, the Chicago River, Wrigley Field, the world-class skyline. Distinctive Chicago landmarks are also integral to the film's two action set pieces. When the detectives intercept a cocaine shipment at O'Hare Airport, they end up in a hair-raising car chase on the El tracks that quickly becomes a wild roller coaster ride of sharp turns and narrowly dodged trains. The climactic gun battle with the drug lord takes place in the State of Illinois Building and makes effective use of the structure's glass-and-tubular-steel architecture. The city's distinctive feel remains evident all through the film, which depicts Chi-town as a dangerous but exhilarating mix of waterfront hideouts, Gold Coast high rises, tattoo parlors, and neighborhood taverns.

Altogether, 101 minutes of this 108–minute film are set in Chicago. The other seven minutes are reserved for Key West, where the protagonists take a brief vacation at their captain's insistence after one of their escapades goes wrong.

The idyllic Florida location serves as a foil to the mean streets of Chicago in winter, a contrast made clear immediately on their arrival. When the detectives come upon a crowd gathered on the pier at Mallory Square, they assume the group has been drawn by a drowning, a shipwreck, or some other catastrophe, and are baffled when a woman explains that they've all come simply to watch the sunset—an actual daily ritual for many Key West residents and visitors. After that introduction to the famously laid-back Key West lifestyle, the detectives quickly immerse themselves in the island's carefree ambience. In an extended montage set to the Michael McDonald song "Sweet Freedom," the two are shown snorkeling, lounging in hammocks, building bonfires on the beach, deep-sea fishing in the sparkling Gulf waters, cruising on the island's preferred mode of transport, the moped, and roller-skating past bikini-clad women along Duval Street. Before long, they are stopping at the end of each day and watching the sunset on their own. It quickly becomes apparent to both the audience and the characters that Key West is a far more suitable environment than Chicago for the easygoing pair. They decide to retire from the force and buy the Sailfish Bar near Lands End Marina. All that remains is for them to return to the frozen North, turn in their thirty days' notice (while wearing garish Hawaiian shirts), and capture their drug-dealing nemesis.

Though the Key West scenes are presented as a carefree interlude in paradise, they also serve to heighten the dramatic tension of the film by increasing the stakes that the two heroes face. While in Chicago, it's clear that their jobs bear a high cost, demanding personal and emotional sacrifices as well as the prospect of physical danger. Seeing the pair of irreverent, fun-loving men in the indulgent setting of Key West, however, makes both the audience and the characters much more aware of what they risk and what they give up in their role as keepers of the peace.

THE CREDITS	THE CAST	
Released in 1986 by Metro-Goldwin-Mayer	Gregory Hines	Ray Hughes
Produced by David Foster and Lawrence Turman	Billy Crystal	Danny Costanzo
Directed by Peter Hyams	Darlanne Fluegel	Anna Costanzo
Written by Gary DeVore and Jimmy Huston	Joe Pantoliano	Snake
Cinematography by Peter Hyams	Dan Hedaya	Captain Logan
Edited by James Mitchell	Tracy Reed	Maryann
Production design by Albert Brenner	Jimmy Smits	Julio Gonzales
Music by Udi Harpaz		

STRANGER THAN PARADISE

Ya know, it's funny. Ya come someplace new, and everything looks the same.
—Eddie in *Stranger Than Paradise*, commenting on the
American landscape

THE STORY

When Eva arrives in New York from Hungary, her cousin Willie reluctantly agrees to let her stay with him for ten days before she moves on to Cleveland. In that brief time, the taciturn Willie and his friend Eddie develop an attachment to the young girl. A year later, the two drive to Cleveland for a visit and whisk Eva away to Florida, where each hopes to fill the vague isolation in their lives.

THE FILM

Since the release of his 1984 *Stranger than Paradise*, Jim Jarmusch has served as something of an unofficial role model for American independent filmmakers. He has strictly excluded the producers and financiers of the Hollywood establishment from his filmmaking in order to maintain complete creative control over his work, from scripting, casting, and editing down to the soundtracks and his insistence that all home releases be letterboxed only. In doing so, Jarmusch has created a small body of work with a consistent but evolving voice that critiques American culture through the concepts of alienation and failed communication.

While still a student at New York University, Jarmusch served on the crew of the 1980 Wim Wenders–Nicholas Ray film *Lightning Over Water*. Apparently impressed with his talent, Wenders gave Jarmusch enough unexposed film left over from another project to create a thirty-minute film titled *The New World*. Chronicling the developing relationship between young Hungarian immigrant Eva, her cousin Willie, and Willie's friend Eddie in New York, the short would become the first part of *Stranger Than Paradise*. Using the short to entice backers, Jarmusch pulled together the rest of the money he needed to complete an independent feature-length film, and then wrote and shot the remaining two parts. In "One Year Later" Willie and Eddie visit Eva in her new home in Cleveland, and in "Paradise" the trio take an impromptu trip to Florida.

In many ways, the production was defined by the project's limited resources. The film was shot in a matter of weeks with three unknown performers— stage actress and singer Eszter Balint and musicians John Lurie and Richard Edson. Lurie composed the film's soundtrack, and Jarmusch's girlfriend, Sara Driver, managed the production and made a cameo appearance in the Florida sequence.

Figure 8.7. Publicity photo from *Stranger Than Paradise*. (Doll/Morrow Collection)

Jarmusch's parents let the crew bunk in sleeping bags in their Cleveland home while shooting the second segment. In Melbourne, Florida, they slept three to a room in the tiny Surfcaster Motel where most of the sequence took place. To shoot some of the driving scenes, Jarmusch strapped a camera to the hood of the car by tying rope to the bumper and door handles, and then had the actors drive through traffic with the camera turned on. In a typical Hollywood production, such scenes would be done by towing the actors' car on a trailer with a camera operator in the back of the lead vehicle.

Even under these difficult circumstances, Jarmusch managed to create an artful, intelligent film that won universal praise at festivals around the world, including the Cannes award for first-time directors, the Golden Camera. He achieved this, in large part, by carefully structuring the film around his resources and turning many of the production's limitations into artistic strengths.

Each scene of the bare plot was shot as a vignette with no editing, using a single stationary camera that occasionally tracks or pans to follow the actors. This allowed Jarmusch to shoot with one camera and a minimum of film, but it also effectively forces the viewer to become an active participant in the film. Without close-ups or rapid-paced editing to guide the viewer's gaze, the audience is prompted to focus on the characters and the details of the simple sets in order to draw out meaning. The entire film consists of sixty-seven slowly paced shots separated by carefully timed blackouts. Through the limited action and slow pacing, Jarmusch builds anticipation and leads the viewer to contemplate what the characters do during the time we don't see them in addition to the brief moments of their lives shown on the screen. As in a poem or piece of music, the rhythm and the pauses in the film come to convey meaning of their own.

Together, the pacing, performances, and bleak settings work to create a sense of isolation and dissatisfaction among the film's three characters. Eddie and Willie, a pair of cardsharps and racetrack hustlers, live on the undefined margins of society and barely manage to communicate with each other, let alone anyone in the outside world. Though Willie has rejected the cultural heritage of his family for a distinctly American lifestyle, he remains vaguely unfulfilled. Eva, who arrives from Eastern Europe presumably seeking a richer, more satisfying life, is unimpressed with the economic, cultural, and social offerings of America and has no answers for her cousin.

Hoping a change of scenery will make some difference, Eddie and Willie visit Eva in Ohio but find that the hollow, decaying industrial parks of Cleveland offer no more than the hollow, echoing streets of New York. The three set off for Florida, excited and certain that America's vacation paradise will offer something new. Instead, they find ramshackle tourist traps and a windswept beach that's as bleak and barren as the shores of Lake Erie were when they visited in the middle of a blizzard.

Unlike most road movies, where the characters' journey is spiritual and psychological as well as geographical, Eddie, Willie, and Eva carry isolation and find emptiness wherever they go. They remain strangers to each other and to whatever community exists outside the frame of the film. For them, Florida and all of America is a desiccated paradise where even the simplest earthly pleasures of communion, communication, and connection remain forever off-screen.

THE CREDITS	THE CAST	
Released in 1983 by the Samuel Goldwyn Company	John Lurie	Willie
Produced by Sara Driver	Eszter Balint	Eva
Directed by Jim Jarmusch	Richard Edson	Eddie
Written by Jim Jarmusch	Cecillia Stark	Aunt Lotte
Music by John Lurie	Danny Rosen	Billy
Cinematography by Tom DiCillo	Rammellzee	Man with money
Edited by Jim Jarmusch and Melody London	Tom DiCillo	Airline agent
Production design by Matt Buchwald, Guido Chiesa, Sam Edwards, Tom Jarmusch, Una McClure, Louis Tancredi, and Stephen Torton	Sara Driver	Girl with hat

SUMMER RENTAL

Life's a Beach!

—tagline for *Summer Rental*

THE STORY

Overworked air traffic controller Jack Chester takes his wife and three children on a much-needed vacation to Citrus Grove, Florida. The Chester family expect to enjoy a carefree month of fun in the sun in a luxurious beachfront rental unit. But when their luxurious home turns out to be a run-down rattrap along a public beach, the Chesters suspect their vacation will not be the slice of paradise they envisioned.

THE FILM

In the decades following World War II, paradise for many middle-class families came in the form of a vacation to the Sunshine State. Even before the major theme parks were constructed, millions of couples with kids drove south in the family station wagon to enjoy the multiple splendors of Florida. In addition to its sandy beaches and ocean waters, the state offered an array of offbeat restaurants, tourist traps, and colorful local sites to amuse and delight family members of all ages. *Summer Rental* is a valentine to such family outings, gently poking fun at the mishaps and disappointments that often accompany the Florida vacation. At the same time, it is a reminder for those who have taken their own Florida vacations that the paradise found was not a geographical one. Instead, it was in the feelings of closeness that only family members can experience when they embark on an adventure together.

John Candy was perfectly cast as Jack Chester, the father of three who drives his entire family, including Archie the dog, to the fictional beach community of Citrus Grove for a monthlong vacation. Using his star image as the fat, lovable clown to great advantage, Candy portrayed Jack as a hapless, bumbling everyman with a preference for festive Hawaiian shirts and gaudy beach wear. Most of the indignities befall Candy's character as the family experience a series of misfortunes that threaten to ruin their holiday. Their misadventures effectively lampoon "the Florida vacation."

Jack has rented a beachfront home sight unseen, and when the family pull into the driveway, they are thrilled at the modern two-story home that overlooks a serene bay. However, the Chesters soon discover that they have pulled in at 415 Beach Drive, not 415 Beach Lane—a comic jab at the many streets and byways called "Beach" in Florida. Their rented home on Beach Lane turns out

Figure 8.8. Publicity photos from *Summer Rental*. (Doll/Morrow Collection)

to be a small, run-down rental property next to a public beach. Each morning, a parade of people pass by their kitchen window on the way to the beach and peer in as the Chesters have breakfast. Before the first week is over, Jack has been sunburned a bright red, twisted his knee while trying to sail, and been locked out of his beach home during a downpour. Less-than-stellar accommodations, sunburns, accidents, and unexpected rain showers are part of the Florida experience that few tourists anticipate but many go through.

Summer Rental also gently pokes fun at the offbeat theme restaurants and tourist traps associated with Florida. One evening the Chesters opt to dine at the Barnacle, which features a nautical decor and pirate theme. An old man dressed in a pirate costume plays a tiny piano in the corner, while fishing nets, treasure maps, and other clichés festoon the near-empty restaurant. Scully, the owner of the Barnacle, appears at the Chesters' table in full pirate garb, complete with a hook for a hand. The family orders Scully's "special catch of the day," which turns out to be frozen fish sticks from the grocery store.

Despite the trouble in paradise, Jack Chester decides to enter Citrus Grove's annual summer regatta—a sailboat race that has been won by local champ Al Pellet for many years. Jack enlists his family and newfound friend Scully as his crew, and, by working together, they defeat the snobby Pellet. In doing so, the Chesters discover that a vacation in paradise has little to do with where the family goes; instead it has to do with the emotional bond created by experiencing the vacation together. That loving bond is revealed during the closing credits, which are accompanied by photographs that mom Sandy Chester has taken of the family throughout the story. The photos highlight their shared good times and, like vacation photos for any family who has made the trek to Florida, help transform the mishaps and misadventures into fond memories.

Summer Rental was shot on location on the St. Petersburg Beaches, a strip of barrier islands flanking greater St. Petersburg along the Gulf coastline called the Suncoast. Scenes were shot at Madeira Beach, Treasure Island, and St. Pete Beach. Madeira Beach has a laid-back atmosphere with many sailing opportunities, while nearby John's Pass Village offers quirky restaurants not unlike the Barnacle. Like the fictional Citrus Grove, the barrier beaches of the Suncoast are family friendly, waiting for all the real-life Chesters to drive down and make their memories.

THE CREDITS	THE CAST	
Released in 1985 by Paramount Pictures	John Candy	Jack Chester
Produced by Bernie Brillstein, Mark Reisman,	Karen Austin	Sandy Chester
George Shapiro, and Jeremy Stevens	Kerri Green	Jennifer Chester
Directed by Carl Reiner	Joey Lawrence	Bobby Chester
Written by Mark Reisman and Jeremy Stevens	Aubrey Jene	Laurie Chester
Cinematography by Ric Waite	Richard Crenna	Al Pellet
Edited by Bud Molin	Rip Torn	Scully
Production design by Peter Wooley	John Larroquette	Don Moore
Music by Alan Silvestri		

WHERE THE BOYS ARE

It looks and sounds like a chummy dramatization of the Kinsey reports.
—Bosley Crowther, review in *New York Times*

THE STORY

Four Midwestern coeds head to Fort Lauderdale over spring break in search of sun, fun, and romance. As they frolic on the beaches and in the bars, each finds a prospective beau and faces the bliss and heartache of young love.

THE FILM

For decades, throngs of students have set aside books, parental expectations, and social conventions during March and April to attend a hedonistic gathering centered on parties, alcohol, and sex in Fort Lauderdale and Daytona Beach. Today the most familiar images of this event come from the slick, corporate-sponsored specials on MTV or the jittery, exploitive *Girls Gone Wild* videos, but for many, the first and most indelible image of this yearly youthful spree in paradise came from the 1960 film *Where the Boys Are*.

In the decade leading up to the release of *Where the Boys Are*, teenagers had emerged as a distinct demographic group with disposable income, and one of their primary leisure-time activities was going to the movies. Producers took note of the impressive box-office numbers generated by the youth-oriented science-fiction films of the period, as well as the success of a new movie venue that had become the domain of the teen audience, the drive-in. Eager to capitalize on this growing market, Hollywood producers and studios were seeking new ways of representing teens on film.[11]

Publicity over the increasing independence of teens, for example, prompted a spate of social-issue films addressing juvenile delinquency. These ranged from low-budget exploitation flicks such as *Juvenile Jungle* to major releases like *Rebel Without a Cause*. As the decade continued, teen films grew in number and diversity, so that by 1958 the studios were investing and earning more on the teen audience, whether their films featured the dangerous, sexually charged Elvis Presley (*Jailhouse Rock* and *King Creole*) or his wholesome pop-music counterpart Pat Boone (*Bernardine* and *April Love*). Films with female teen protagonists, such as *Tammy and the Bachelor* or *Gidget*, were producing handsome returns as well.

As a big-budget studio film in which adults were relegated to inconsequential roles, *Where the Boys Are* expanded the conventions of the teen flick.[12] Unlike many teen-oriented movies where parents, teachers, and other authority figures set expectations and provide guidance for the young protagonists, the main characters in *Where the Boys Are* have only each other when struggling with the film's primary issue, premarital sex. The notion of youthful independence from established norms is announced early in the film when Merritt, played by Dolores Hart, defends the sexual freedom of "today's youth" against a college professor who promotes virtue and old-fashioned values.

The film makes it clear, however, that with autonomy comes responsibility. Three of the four heroines retain their virtue during the Florida bacchanal despite their suitors' best efforts, and the one who does give in is discarded by her lover, then taken advantage of by a second college cad and left to suffer a nervous breakdown. Though the film's marketing alluded to youthful abandon and indulgence, its subtext cleaved to the traditional values of mainstream society.

While other films of the period achieved success with a similar moral bait-and-switch, *Where the Boys Are* became a bona fide phenomenon. Aside from its surface representation of independence, its great appeal came from a decidedly attractive depiction of youth. From music to slang to fashion, the film offered an unabashed celebration of the teen subculture of the day. Whether flirting on the beach, holding philosophical debates in the bars, or engaging in mischievous pranks, the characters in *Where the Boys Are* led decidedly cool lives. To those teens too young to travel on their own or too poor to participate in the Florida pilgrimage, the film's depiction of fun in the sun amid crowds of people their own age represented a paradise of independence and revelry.

The movie's impact spread far beyond its box-office success. Pop idol Connie Francis, somewhat miscast as the unattractive Angie, propelled the title song to the top of the charts, and the title itself soon became a familiar expression in America's cultural lexicon. Attributing some of the film's success to the chemistry between stars Jim Hutton and Paula Prentiss, MGM cast the pair in three more romantic comedies in the next two years. Direct variations on *Where the Boys Are* followed. *Palm Springs Weekend* chronicled spring break in California, while *Ski Party* depicted winter break on the ski slopes. Such was the success of the film that some erroneously attributed the spring break phenomenon itself to the movie. The origins of the annual ritual are unclear, but college revelers had been visiting Fort Lauderdale for years prior to 1960. One plausible account holds that wealthy Ivy Leaguers who regularly sought the sun in the Caribbean discovered Fort Lauderdale in the early 1940s when there were wartime restrictions on travel.[13] The postwar rise of the middle class and the increased spending power of youth made the trip feasible for many more during the next decade.

Fort Lauderdale residents have had mixed reactions to the annual invasion. On the one hand, the college visitors were always a nuisance—they littered, they clogged traffic with their endless cruising on South Atlantic Boulevard,

Figure 8.9. Publicity photo from *Where the Boys Are.*
(Doll/Morrow Collection)

and one outrageous year pranksters dumped a dead shark in a hotel swimming pool. But the money they brought with them more than made up for
such minor inconveniences. By 1960, however, their numbers had swelled to
40,000, and tensions mounted among the city's 100,000 citizens. The following
year, police prohibitions against late-night gatherings on the beach led to a riot
and three hundred arrests. The city responded by arranging athletic competi-
tions and nightly dances for the 1962 crowd, but the incident prompted many
students to try out other Florida locales such as Daytona Beach and Panama
City Beach.[14] For the next two decades, other Florida cities took turns courting the ever-growing spring break crowd for a few years and then shunning
them when locals grew tired of their annual high jinks. By the 1980s, well over
250,000 collegians showed up every year, and their behavior grew increasingly
lewd and destructive, with nudity, public drunkenness, vandalism, and the occasional death. Fort Lauderdale clamped down hard, installing a barrier wall
between the beach and the bars and encouraging family-oriented restaurants
and other businesses to set up along the beachfront. Today, students looking
for a mellower spring break experience go there and share the beach with families and Canadian tourists, while wilder gatherings are held in other Florida
cities and in new sun spots such as South Padre Island, Texas, or Cancún,
Mexico. Regardless of how the locations and decorum of spring break have
changed over the decades, though, Fort Lauderdale will always remain where
the boys are.

THE CREDITS

Released in 1960 by Metro-Goldwin-Mayer

Produced by Joe Pasternak

Directed by Henry Levin

Written by George Wells, from the novel by Glendon Swarthout

Music by Pete Rugolo (dialectic jazz), Neil Sedaka ("Turn on the Sunshine"), George E. Stoll, and Victor Young

Cinematography by Robert J. Bronner

Edited by Fredric Steinkamp

Art direction by E. Preston Ames and George W. Davis

Costume design by Kitty Mager

THE CAST

Dolores Hart	Merritt Andrews
George Hamilton	Ryder Smith
Yvette Mimieux	Melanie Tolman
Jim Hutton	TV Thompson
Barbara Nichols	Lola Fandango
Paula Prentiss	Tuggle
Chill Wills	Police Captain
Frank Gorshin	Basil
Connie Francis	Angie
Paul Frees	Narrator (uncredited)

Teen Paradise in the 1980s

American teenagers were working more, earning more, and spending more in the 1980s than ever before—as much as $45 billion annually, much of it on new products such as portable music systems, designer clothes, and video games. Keeping pace with this growing and malleable market were new and increasingly influential media outlets that directed their attentions to young adults, including cable television and the home video industry. In 1981 teens made up 40 percent of the moviegoing public, and the film industry, like so many other businesses of the period, actively pursued this rich pool of consumers.

While filmmakers such as John Hughes (*Sixteen Candles*, *The Breakfast Club*) and Francis Ford Coppola (*The Outsiders*, *Rumble Fish*) attempted serious treatments of modern teen life, films such as *Spring Break* and *Where the Boys Are '84*—both shot in Florida—presented a youth culture of sexual exhibitionism and conquest that was as unfamiliar as it was titillating to its intended audience. In the original *Where the Boys Are*, the female protagonists had both the freedom to say yes and the power to say no to sex during courtship, and the central conflict was each individual's struggle with this decision and its consequences. In the shameful 1980s remake, sex for its own sake was the primary goal of each character—male or female—and the only conflict occurred when something got in the way of a character's mindless pursuit of it.

The burgeoning independence of American youth in the 1950s had been a strange and intimidating development that the established social order struggled to accept. By the 1980s, the youthful ideal had become one of the driving forces in American culture, and the only ones left struggling with that concept were the youths themselves.

THE MOVIE TOURIST'S GUIDE TO FLORIDA AS PARADISE

Whatever your vision of paradise—youthful revelry, a family excursion, or simply escape from the pressures of everyday life—you'll be able to find a slice of it somewhere in Florida. For more than a century, the state has opened its doors to guests of all sorts and has prided itself on being the perfect host.

FOLLOW THAT DREAM

The Gulf Coast

Boasting a continuous stretch of white, sandy beaches and 361 days of sunshine per year, the Gulf Coast represents the best of what Florida has to offer. In addition to the idyllic climate, the region offers a remarkable combination of big city culture and unspoiled wilderness, along with distinctive Florida attractions such as Spongeorama and Weeki Wachee Springs. The Kwimper family in *Follow That Dream* found their little stretch of paradise near the tiny communities of Inglis and Yankeetown, about 150 miles north of Tampa. The towns are connected by County Road 40, which the residents have renamed Follow That Dream Parkway in honor of the Presley film.

GIRL HAPPY

WHERE THE BOYS ARE

Fort Lauderdale

Located just north of Miami on U.S. 1, Fort Lauderdale has been a prime spring break destination for decades. The city has toned down the annual collegiate celebration since the 1990s, and it's now common for families and retirees to share the beach with a tamer youth crowd in March and April. Whatever your age, no spring break visit would be complete without a pilgrimage to the Elbo Room on South Fort Lauderdale Beach Boulevard, which has been serving beer to spring visitors since the 1940s. For armchair revelers, the Elbo Room offers a live webcam that captures the action in the bar and on the beach across the street year round.

MIDNIGHT COWBOY

Hollywood

Ratso Rizzo's Florida fantasy sequence was shot at the luxurious Diplomat Hotel in Hollywood, just north of Miami. Opened in 1958, the Diplomat was a world-class resort that lavishly catered to the whims of its well-to-do and celebrity guests for decades. Like many of Florida's grand hotels, it eventually suffered financial trouble and shut down in the early 1990s, but a new, equally splendid Diplomat Resort—1,000 rooms with a five-story atrium lobby—opened in 2001 at the same location on South Ocean Drive.

Key West

Midnight Cowboy author James Leo Herlihy was a longtime resident of Key West and is proudly counted as one of the tiny island's many literary stars. The Authors of Key West Guesthouse, a quaint bed-and-breakfast on White Street, offers suites and rooms named after various Key West writers. The James Leo Herlihy room, located near the pool, sleeps three and comes with a private terrace.

RUBY IN PARADISE

Panama City Beach

The largest resort area on the Florida Panhandle, Panama City Beach offers arcades, amusement parks, and hotels along its twenty-seven miles of sandy beaches. Though the area is known as one of the more raucous spring break destinations, it caters primarily to working-class families for most of the year, and thus made a suitable new home for Ruby Lee Gissing as she escaped her small-town existence in *Ruby in Paradise*. The introspective Ruby found solitude on the shores of St. Andrews State Recreation Area, a state park three miles east of Panama City Beach known for its wildlife and unspoiled beaches.

RUNNING SCARED

Key West

The fun-loving lifestyle of Key West depicted in *Running Scared* was no mere movie magic. Conchs, as the residents are known, work hard to preserve their island's laid-back atmosphere and reputation for tolerance and cultural diversity. Visitors and locals alike really do gather in the early evening at Mallory Square to watch the spectacular sunsets across the Gulf.

STRANGER THAN PARADISE

Melbourne

Located along Interstate 95 midway between Miami and Jacksonville, Melbourne is the southern anchor point of Florida's Space Coast. Founded by black freedmen in the 1860s, this town of 75,000 is separated from the Atlantic Ocean by a small barrier island and the Indian River Lagoon. The region is best known for its many nature preserves and its proximity to the Kennedy

Space Center. Melbourne may have been selected as the site for the Florida segment of *Stranger Than Paradise* because, though small, it has an international airport, which was required for the film's conclusion.

SUMMER RENTAL

St. Petersburg Beaches

This strip of barrier islands in the Gulf just outside St. Petersburg has long been a popular destination for families such as the Chesters in *Summer Rental*. The area offers plenty of sunshine and warm, gentle Gulf waters, though crowds are often a drawback. The Chesters' rental cottage was located in Redington Beach, and a Madeira Beach restaurant provided the setting for the first encounter with the film's villain, Al Pellet. The area offers countless family-friendly attractions and restaurants, such as the 1950s-style Starlite Diner or Johnny Leverock's, which has an Old Florida nautical theme.

FLORIDA FACADE

The Sunshine State deserves its reputation as the perfect family
vacation spot, but Florida is much richer in its culture, landscape, and character than its stereotypical image suggests.
—*Eyewitness Travel Guides: Florida*

An isolated highway snakes through rolling meadows and fertile farmland,
leading a young couple to a rendezvous with terror. A B-17 bomber makes
a desperate landing amid enemy fire on a crude airstrip carved from jungle
wilderness. An American family vacationing in Europe get trapped behind
the Iron Curtain when they are mistaken for spies. Through the magic of film,
each of these stories transports its audience on a far-flung adventure in a distant land. Surprisingly, these examples of movie magic were all shot in the state
of Florida.

From the earliest days of cinema, filmmakers have capitalized on Florida's ability to stand in for a range of settings from around the world. From the forested parks of the northern Panhandle to the grasslands of mid-Florida to the tropical paradise around the Keys, the state offers a diversity of geography and environs.

The subtropical climate and lush vegetation of southern Florida make it an obvious substitute for any number of hard-to-reach exotic locations. More than 3,500 species of plants can be found in the state, including orchids, birds-of-paradise, and bougainvillea of countless hues, along with tropical palms, mangroves, and 300 other types of trees. Florida's fauna is equally exotic, from panthers and miniature Key deer to manatees and sea turtles. Because of its location on the main north-south migratory route, the state boasts an enormously varied array of bird life: herons, spoonbills, and other distinctive waterfowl, as well as finches, warblers, woodpeckers, osprey, and the majestic bald eagle. More species of snakes live in Florida than any other state—not to mention alligators, turtles, and lizards.

With this kind of natural panorama, any treacherous jungle, exotic port of call, or tropical paradise can be easily simulated in the Sunshine State. The crew of scientists searching for the mysterious creature in the lost waters of the Amazon's Black Lagoon were actually exploring the "wilds" of Wakulla Springs. The lusty Caribbean pirates who frequented the bawdy tavern in *Hell Harbor* were really cavorting on an outdoor set near Tampa Bay. And the barren South Sea island where JFK led a heroic rescue of his shipmates in *PT 109* was actually a private vacation spot in the Keys.

Everyone associates Florida with subtropical climes, but the northern part of the state has cooler temperatures and less precipitation, supporting pine trees, towering oaks, and other temperate-zone vegetation. While much of the state is remarkably flat and even, the Panhandle is dotted with low hills that spill out into broad, rolling grasslands in the eastern and central part of the state. For filmmakers, this means Florida can stand in for much of middle America. With its prominently featured meadows and farmland, *Jeepers Creepers* appears to be set in America's heartland, though principal shooting was actually done in Marion County, Florida, the self-proclaimed "horse capital of the world." *Parenthood*, a touching comedy about middle-class family values, is likewise set in the Midwest, specifically in the suburbs of St. Louis, even though it was shot on the soundstages of Universal Studios and at various locations around Orlando.

Filmmaking in Florida was also boosted by one of the state's long-term business partners—the U.S. military. Since the late nineteenth century, the federal government has depended on Florida in time of war, and vice versa. Some of the earliest known film footage shot in the state documents federal troops leaving for Cuba in 1898 to fight in the Spanish-American War. Rarely more than a minute long, titles such as *Roosevelt's Rough Riders Embarking for Santiago* and *With the Army at Tampa* and *Col. Terry's Rough Riders and Army Mules* mark the beginning of a decades-long relationship between Florida, the American armed forces, and the mainstream film industry.

Seeking to do their part during national crises and also looking to spur the state's economic development, Florida officials actively courted government contracts during both world wars. Military officials saw the state as a strategic defensive position that also offered a desirable climate and geography for training facilities. Submarine bases, airfields, ports, and other military installations dotted the state during the 1910s and again in the 1940s. During this latter period, the War Department developed a close relationship with the film industry, providing technical advice, personnel, and equipment for war-era films that helped bolster morale on the home front. The existing bases and airfields, plus the subtropical environment, made Florida the ideal location for *Air Force*, *They Were Expendable*, and other war films set in the South Pacific. Long after World War II, continued cooperation from the military made Florida a favored choice for location shooting for war-related films. In 1959, for example, the navy went so far as to allow Universal Pictures to paint one of its submarines pink for *Operation Petticoat*.

By the 1970s, state and various local governments began to see filmmaking as a worthwhile industry to actively court. New legislation, new government agencies, and new marketing efforts became part of an aggressive effort to draw film work to the state. Today, the Governor's Office of Film and Entertainment provides scouting services and research libraries, issues filming permits, and acts as a liaison with local officials and various professional groups. The state also offers generous tax incentives, a relaxed attitude toward union and non-union workers, and more than fifty local film agencies to smooth the way for everything from commercials and music videos to major feature films. All this, along with a variety of distinctive locations, combines to make Florida an appealing state to shoot a film, regardless of where the story is set.

AIR FORCE

I think Warner Brothers produces a better war all around.
—American G.I. in Sicily, quoted in *Projections of War*,
by Thomas Doherty

THE STORY

The nine-man crew of the B-17 bomber *Mary Ann* sets off from San Francisco on December 6, 1941, arriving in Hawaii just in time to witness the aftermath of Pearl Harbor. Flying on to Wake Island and then Manila, the crew relies on teamwork to stay one step away from the devastation wrought by the initial Japanese attacks on American outposts. On their way to Australia, they spot the Japanese fleet and lead a successful open-ocean raid against the huge convoy.

THE FILM

In the early 1940s, Hollywood studios were facing pressure from an increasingly vocal isolationist movement in the federal government. At issue were *A Yank in the RAF*, *Sergeant York*, *Confessions of a Nazi Spy*, and a host of other films criticized for fostering sympathy toward the Allies among the American populace and potentially drawing the nation into war. The issue reached a climax in the fall of 1941 when a Senate committee led by D. Worth Clark and Gerald Nye subpoenaed the major studio heads and threatened new censorship legislation. The studios, represented by former presidential candidate Wendell Willkie, held their ground, and the contentious hearings adjourned temporarily after eighteen days. Just over two months later, the Japanese attack on Pearl Harbor rendered the debate moot, and the hearings never reconvened. Instead, Hollywood and Washington embarked on a whole new relationship that would transform American film into an instrument of war.

The ability of film to influence behavior and shape opinion had been hotly debated for decades. With America's entry in World War II, however, all questioning of this notion seemed to cease, and the nation as a whole embraced Hollywood as a source of information, inspiration, and unity. Studios, eager to do their part—and earn a profit—hurried one war film after another into production. The War Department and the Office of War Information quickly became influential Hollywood players, providing technical advice and materiel, arranging location shoots, collaborating on scripts, and signing off on final prints. Even much of the moviegoing public, shocked and disheartened at the nation's early losses in the conflict, were eager to consume the uplifting if biased messages that awaited them in their neighborhood theaters.

Figure 9.1. Publicity photo from *Air Force*. (Doll/Morrow Collection)

Released early in 1943, Warner Brothers' *Air Force* was among the first of the big-budget World War II films produced as part of the war effort. Along with *Bataan*, also released that year, it served to establish the conventions for war-era combat films that conveyed the essential messages of teamwork, sacrifice, and defense of home and country.

Like so many films of the period, *Air Force* centers on a disparate group of Americans with varied backgrounds and distinct personalities who pull to-gether as a team and rely on training and technology to face the uncertain-ties of war. All the members of the crew, from the pilot, the navigator, and the bombardier to the gunners, radiomen, and mechanics, use their special-ized skills at critical moments to contribute to the ship's success. Emphasizing the importance of the entire crew, director Howard Hawks favored medium shots of multiple characters rather than close-ups. And despite the large cast, *Air Force* featured only one star actor, John Garfield. Establishing a character type that would recur in many war-era films, Garfield played tail gunner Joe Winocki, an embittered flight school washout who plans to leave the service and never look back when his tour is up, but decides to reenlist and continue his thankless role once hostilities begin.

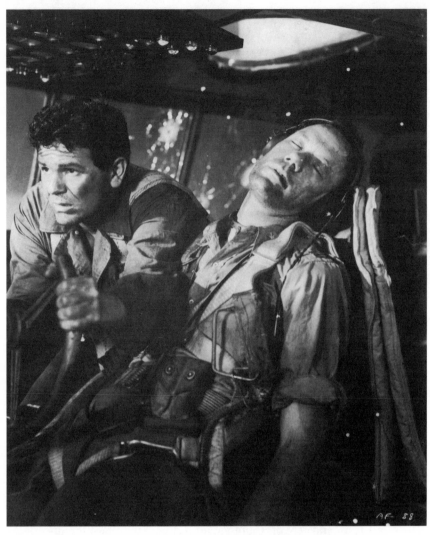

Figure 9.2. Publicity photo from *Air Force*. (Doll/Morrow Collection)

The notion of necessary and willing sacrifice escalates throughout the film. Early on, the crew visits a pilot comrade in the hospital who has lost an arm, and the airman's only regret is that he can fight no more. Later, when the chief mechanic of the *Mary Ann* learns that his fighter-pilot son has been killed in the Philippines, he sheds a tear and then stoically returns to his duties. And finally, when the crew itself suffers the loss of its pilot, his last thoughts are of his role as their leader: with the crew gathered around his hospital bed, he runs through their preflight checklist with them as he prepares to take off on his final journey. The female characters in the film are minor but critical, as they stand for home and hearth. A wife and a mother serve to remind the men of what they are fighting for, and a budding romance between one crewman and a nurse is put on hold as both go off to war.

Hawks was perhaps the perfect choice for crafting this model war film. Though accomplished in virtually every genre from screwball comedy to sci-fi thriller, he has come to be regarded as a true master of the action film for his work on *Red River*, *Rio Bravo*, *Ceiling Zero*, *Dawn Patrol*, and a host of others. While these films range widely in setting and story, Hawks brought a consistent sensibility of stoicism and professionalism to his action heroes, and he excelled at telling stories of a tight-knit group facing overwhelming odds in a confined setting. Working closely with writer Dudley Nichols, Hawks incorporated these favored themes into *Air Force* and delivered exactly the message that wartime America wanted to hear.

Major shooting for *Air Force* began before the script was finished, with a second-unit crew filming the climactic battle scene in miniature off the California coast in May of 1942. Hawks began filming about a month later, shooting hospital sequences and the plane interiors in Hollywood. While California might have been able to provide suitable stand-in locations for American air bases and South Seas islands, wartime invasion fears precluded any notion of having extras in Japanese uniforms and mocked-up Zero fighter planes travers-

Figure 9.3. *Air Force* star John Garfield.
(Doll/Morrow Collection)

ing the West Coast. On July 21 the cast and crew embarked for Tampa, where they spent a grueling thirty-one days at Drew Field capturing all of the film's aerial footage and the exterior scenes set in Hawaii, Wake Island, and the Philippines.

From the start, the location shooting was plagued by difficulty. Tampa was suffering its worst heat wave in three decades, and the filmmakers were required to take daily salt pills and drink lime and quinine water to ward off any ill effects. Despite their best efforts, government liaisons repeatedly fell short of their promised requisitions; electrical equipment, lighting, and precious gasoline were in short supply, and military vehicles were frequently pulled from the set for government use, sometimes prompting changes in the script. Extras of Asian descent were almost impossible to find in Florida, so Cuban-Americans were hired to portray most of the Japanese soldiers. When shooting at night, the crew was mercilessly attacked by insects drawn to the lights. They resorted to setting up extra lights away from the set and turning them on just before shooting, distracting the insects long enough to get one or two minutes of footage.

Over budget and off schedule, Hawks began to take heat from the studio. At one point producer Hal Wallis ordered him to leave Tampa no later than August 26, but Hawks insisted he needed several more days for a critical scene of the *Mary Ann* landing at a bombed-out air base. As they were setting up for the shoot, the generator for the lights failed. Legendary cinematographer James Wong Howe rigged up a lighting system using signal flares and reflectors, and the flickering lights and dense smoke of Howe's improvisation helped create an unexpectedly dramatic depiction of a war zone. In the end Wallis, the studio, the War Department, and all of America were more than satisfied with the results.

THE CREDITS	THE CAST	
Released in 1943 by Warner Brothers	John Ridgely	Capt. Mike "Irish" Quincannon
Produced by Hal B. Wallis	John Garfield	Sgt. Joe Winocki
Directed by Howard Hawks	Harry Carey	Sgt. Robbie White
Written by Dudley Nichols	Gig Young	Lt. Bill Williams
Cinematography by James Wong Howe	Arthur Kennedy	Lt. Tommy McMartin
Aerial photography by Elmer Dyer and Charles	Charles Drake	Lt. "Monk" Munchauser
A. Marshall	George Tobias	Cpl. Weinberg
Edited by George Amy	Robert Wood	Cpl. Peterson
Music by Franz Waxman	Ray Montgomery	Pvt. Chester
Art direction by John Hughes	James Brown	Lt. Tex Rader
Technical advice by Capt. Samuel Triffy		

By 1945 America's attitude toward World War II had shifted considerably from the early days of the conflict, and Hollywood films shifted along with it. Four years of loss and sacrifice, of combat newsreels and letters from the front, helped create a moviegoing audience that was both educated in and weary of modern warfare. With the decisive Allied victories in the last twelve months of the war, Americans were ready to take a hard look at their recent history as they prepared to move on to a new era. *They Were Expendable*, which began filming on February 1, 1945, in Key Biscayne, Florida, grimly recounts the sacrifices of a PT boat squadron operating against a vastly superior Japanese force during the evacuation of the Philippines. In direct contrast to *Air Force*, it tells the story of a well-honed military unit that fractures before the enemy, and it includes characters motivated more by honor and duty than by patriotism and defense of home. Based on the true exploits of Lieutenants John Bulkley and Robert Kelly, the film remains widely praised as a moving and realistic depiction of combat. No doubt, some of this realism stems from the wartime experiences of the cast and crew: director John Ford served briefly with Bulkley, and star Robert Montgomery was a PT boat commander himself.

THE CREATURE FROM
THE BLACK LAGOON

Centuries of passion pent up in his savage heart!
—poster for *The Creature from the Black Lagoon*

THE STORY

Scientists and sweethearts David Reed and Kay Lawrence join benefactor Mark Williams on an expedition down the Amazon in search of an apparent missing link between marine and mammal life. Discord builds as their trek down the forbidding river yields no evidence and Mark reveals an increasingly aggressive interest in Kay. Their search leads to an isolated lagoon where they discover a living Gill-Man who also becomes enamored of Kay and repeatedly attacks the interloping scientists.

The Creature from the Black Lagoon is one of the all-time monster hybrids: part mammal, part amphibian; part sci-fi, part horror; part adventure, part sexual allegory. One of the few memorable movie monsters to come from the 1950s, the creature itself is a striking mix of the familiar and the alien. Though humanoid and somewhat intelligent, he's all scales and gills and seems driven by fear, instinct, and primal urges. Displaced from another time and living in a remote, mysterious wilderness, he's an aberrant species unto himself with no place in the modern world. At the same time, his adolescent sexuality and aggressiveness mirror those found in the film's human characters and in the minds of the audience.

Sexual tension permeates the film, beginning with an unwanted love triangle. Early on, scientist Kay Lawrence finds herself succumbing to the boyish charms of her colleague David Reed. As they head down the Amazon to find evidence of the mysterious Gill-Man's existence, their chaste pairing is threatened by expedition leader Mark Williams, who pursues Kay more and more aggressively as they get further and further from civilization. When they finally arrive at the forbidding Black Lagoon, the creature is added to the mix. The Gill-Man first sees Kay as she swims in his watery lair, and he too becomes captivated by her. In one of the film's many remarkable underwater scenes, he swims in sync beneath her in an elegant water dance that simulates lovemaking. From that point on, the Gill-Man has just one thing on his mind, and his attacks on the expedition seem designed to take Kay for his own. Of course, wanton sexuality of this sort—Mark's or the Gill-Man's—can't be left unchecked. Mark dies at the hands of the creature, the victim of his own unbridled urges, and David fights off the Gill-Man so that he and Kay can return to civilization and their innocent love.

Director Jack Arnold crafted this tight fable of human desire on a modest budget from a conventional script. A prolific director for Universal Studios throughout the 1950s, Arnold tried his hand at everything from melodrama to comedy, but *Creature* was his second foray into the genre for which he would be best remembered. His other sci-fi achievements include *It Came from Outer Space*, *Tarantula!* and, perhaps his best work, *The Incredible Shrinking Man*. In *Creature*, Arnold benefited from a cast of solid B-movie actors, including Richard Carlson, Julie Adams, and Richard Denning as the intrepid scientists. A young Henry Mancini had a hand in composing the film's effective score, memorable for the creature's brassy three-note leitmotif. In addition, the film was originally released in 3-D, a novelty format devised by Hollywood to fend off its own worst nightmare, the new medium of television.

As for the creature, it took two different performers to bring him to life. An imposing six-foot-five Tahitian named Ben Chapman portrayed the Gill-Man

Figure 9.4. Poster for *The Creature from the Black Lagoon*. (Doll/Morrow Collection)

on land during shooting at the Universal lot. Ricou Browning, a professional swimmer from Florida's Weeki Wachee resort, donned his own customized foam and latex suit for the groundbreaking underwater scenes shot in Silver Springs, Wakulla Springs, and other locations in Florida.

These famous freshwater springs are what brought the film to Florida, which boasts one of the largest artesian spring systems in the world. Over millennia, acid rain has percolated through the state's limestone bedrock and carved out a massive network of deep underground channels and caves. Every day, billions of gallons of water filter through this system and emerge, pristine and cool, to refresh the hundreds of springs dotting the central and northern parts of the state. For the filmmakers, these unusually large bodies of crystal-clear water were ideal for shooting the film's complex underwater action scenes. And the springs themselves—isolated, surrounded by exotic vegetation, and riddled with caves—made the perfect home for the Gill-Man.

With its peculiar mix of psuedoscience and bristling sexuality, *The Creature from the Black Lagoon* thrilled and titillated audiences of 1954 like no other film of the period. An effective hybrid of the ubiquitous sci-fi flicks of the 1950s and the classic Universal horror films of two decades earlier, the film prods our deeply rooted desires while providing the delicious distraction of a truly unique movie monster.

Released in 1954 by Universal International Pictures	Richard Carlson — Dr. David Reed
Produced by William Alland	Julie Adams — Kay Lawrence
Directed by Jack Arnold	Richard Denning — Dr. Mark Williams
Written by Harry Essex and Arthur A. Ross	Antonio Moreno — Dr. Carl Maia
Cinematography by William E. Snyder; special	Nestor Paiva — Lucas, captain of the *Rita*
underwater photography by Scotty Welbourne	Whit Bissell — Dr. Edwin Thompson
Edited by Ted J. Kent	Ricou Browning — Gill-Man in water (uncredited)
Art direction by Hilyard M. Brown and Bernard Herzbrun	
Makeup by Bud Westmore	Ben Chapman — Gill-Man out of water (uncredited)
Creature design by Milicent Patrick	

The Sequels from the Black Lagoon

Spurred by *Creature*'s unexpected box-office success, Universal braved the depths of the Amazon to make two more Gill-Man features. In 1955 *Revenge of the Creature* chronicled the indignities suffered by the Gill-Man as he is put on display in Florida's Marineland and introduced to the business end of a cattle prod by scientists Clete Ferguson (John Agar) and Helen Dobson (Lori Nelson), whose interest in behavior modification is surpassed only by their interest in each other. The ill-conceived *The Creature Walks Among Us* from 1956 ended the series with a truly odd twist. Scientists remove the Gill-Man's gills, hoping to acclimatize him to human ways. The wild thing will not be tamed, however, and the film closes with the gill-less, pitiable creature trudging back into the ocean, choosing death in the water over life on the land.

Director Jack Arnold returned for the first sequel but not the second. In both sequels Ricou Browning carried on as the creature in the underwater sequences, but on land the Gill-Man was played by a different—though always tall—actor in each of the three films. This shuffling of cast members has led to squabbling among the performers in recent years, particularly between Chapman and Browning, over who's entitled to the bragging rights—and convention appearances—generated by the role.

CROSSWINDS

It was like a vacation away from Hollywood.
—Rhonda Fleming, on the making of *Crosswinds*

THE STORY

When Steve Singleton sails into Curra Bay, New Guinea, aboard his schooner, he attracts the attention of both Jumbo Johnson, a local scoundrel, and Katherine Shelley, a dispirited war widow. Johnson maneuvers Singleton out of his boat, while Katherine complicates his life. All scramble to retrieve a lost shipment of gold located deep in the jungle, where unfriendly natives, hungry crocodiles, and treacherous animals await them.

THE FILM

Long before *action* films assaulted the senses of audiences with endless explosions and rapid-fire gunplay, *action-adventure* films sparked imaginations with fanciful tales of high adventure in exotic locales. *Crosswinds* provides a perfect example of a genre known primarily to contemporary viewers through Steven Spielberg's updated homage to it, *Raiders of the Lost Ark*.

Taking full advantage of its setting, *Crosswinds* is packed with a variety of exciting adventures. Some are fun and carefree, including a romantic interlude with Steve Singleton and Katherine Shelley as they swim under the deep blue waters to search for pearls, while others are fraught with danger, as when Jumbo Johnson instigates a race to find a lost treasure. He sails Singleton's schooner deep into the jungle to steal a shipment of gold from a downed airplane, while Steve teams with two con men to retrieve both his schooner and Katherine. The jungle seems to come alive with dangers. Angry natives attack the group as they sail up and down the river, while big boas, ferocious felines, and carnivorous crocs lurk along every path.

The outdoor locations in *Crosswinds* captured the atmosphere of a distant foreign land, though the film was not shot in New Guinea. Instead, Florida's Homosassa Springs and Weeki Wachee Springs provided a credible substitute. Much of the film was shot in what is now Homosassa Springs Wildlife State Park, which encompasses some of the state's most beautiful landscape, including wetlands, lagoons, rivers, and tropical foliage. And Weeki Wachee Springs, famous for its crystal-clear waters, was the perfect choice for shooting the underwater footage. The exotic beauty of this part of Florida played a major role in creating the allure of romantic adventure.

The state of Florida was most hospitable to the cast and crew during pro-

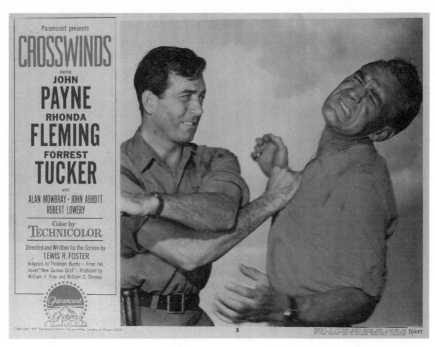

Figure 9.5. Lobby card from *Crosswinds*. (Doll/Morrow Collection)

duction, with Governor Warren Fuller and his wife Barbara inviting the cast to the state capital, Tallahassee, and then entertaining them at a special dinner party. According to star Rhonda Fleming, who played Katherine, the experience of shooting on location was like taking a vacation from Hollywood. Very few feature films had been shot in their entirety in Florida since the 1920s, and the production of *Crosswinds* along the beautiful Gulf Coast was appreciated as a boost for the Sunshine State.

Crosswinds was made by the Pine-Thomas unit, an autonomous production unit under the wing of major studio Paramount Pictures. Producers William H. Pine and William C. Thomas, who had been staff producers at Paramount, formed the unit during the 1940s to make small-budget action adventures. The unit used Paramount's facilities and contract players to make their movies, which were then released through the big studio's distribution channels. During the Golden Age, Pine-Thomas specialized in B movies produced on the tiniest of budgets, which earned the unit's two frugal Williams the nickname Dollar Bills.

In the 1950s the big studios began to farm out more and more films to independent production companies and small production units, because it was financially advantageous for them to do so. The smaller companies produced the films, while the studios acted as financiers and distributors. In this new era Pine-Thomas graduated to bigger budgets, bigger stars, location shooting, and Technicolor. Pine-Thomas's films benefited greatly from location shooting in color because their specialty, the action-adventure genre, thrived on larger-than-life stories in exotic or unusual locales. With its Florida location work and reel-to-reel adventure, *Crosswinds* became the quintessential Pine-Thomas film of the 1950s.

The action-adventure film is a male-dominated genre, and the Pine-Thomas productions were no exception. Most of their films feature several handsome, brawny males struggling against nature and its elements for treasure, love, or redemption. The male stars who became associated with the Pine-Thomas adventures included John Payne, Ronald Reagan, and Richard Arlen. *Crosswinds* stars Payne as Steve Singleton, whose very name signifies his identity as the strong, independent male, while Forrest Tucker plays Jumbo, whose unusual moniker matches his burly physique. With Alan Mowbray costarring as a slippery con artist and Robert Lowery as a suave ladies' man, virtually every male archetype is present in *Crosswinds*.

Balancing this cast of big and beefy boys is the film's only female star, Rhonda Fleming, who was also a Pine-Thomas regular. A star of the 1940s and 1950s, Fleming tended to play sophisticated women who were glamorous yet dignified. In recalling her experience on *Crosswinds*, Fleming wished that she could have had a few more dramatic scenes in the film, lamenting that she may have been "upstaged" a bit by all the men.[1] In retrospect, however, it is Fleming's character that stands out, because Katherine Shelley was not typical for the era. A recovering alcoholic and war widow with inner strength and courage, Katherine does not yearn for a traditional home with a husband, children, and a white picket fence like so many female characters of the 1950s, but seems at home in the exotic locale—as one of the film's most romantic scenes suggests. She and Steve swim together, kissing and holding hands as they explore life beneath the deep blue water. At the end of the film, Katherine and Steve survive to sail off together for parts unknown; she has been, in Fleming's words, "set free on the ocean she loved."[2] The surprisingly modern character of Katherine is thus more memorable than most of the men.

The use of Technicolor also worked in Fleming's favor, helping her hold her own in a male-dominated cast. The auburn-haired actress is often costumed in bright blue or pristine white, a combination even more eye-catching than Payne's shirtless torso.

Like so many films from Hollywood's past, *Crosswinds* has been forgotten, relegated to the late show or the old-movie channels. Yet the tightly structured film features a charismatic cast, beautiful cinematography, and a vivid use of Florida locations. It is a reminder of the solid craftsmanship that marked the Hollywood of another era.

THE CREDITS

Released in 1951 by Paramount Pictures

Produced by William H. Pine and William C. Thomas

Directed by Lewis R. Foster

Written by Lewis R. Foster, based on the novel
  by Thomson Burtis

Cinematography by Loyal Griggs

Edited by Howard Smith

Art direction by Lewis Creber

Costumes by Edith Head

THE CAST

John Payne	Steve Singleton
Rhonda Fleming	Katherine Shelley
Forrest Tucker	Jumbo Johnson
Robert Lowery	Nick Brandon
Alan Mowbray	The Hon. Cecil Daubrey
John Abbott	Sykes
Frank Kumagai	Bumidai

DON'T DRINK THE WATER

When the movie came out, loved ones told me, "Better you don't see it."
—Woody Allen, to Ron Miller of Knight Ridder/Tribune
News Service

THE STORY

New Jersey caterer Walter Hollander reluctantly takes his wife and daughter on a whirlwind tour of Europe in lieu of the family's regular Miami Beach vacation. Their plane is hijacked and taken to the East Bloc country of Vulgaria, where the secret police mistake Hollander for an American spy. When the family takes refuge in the American embassy, the ambassador's son—smitten with Hollander's daughter—only makes matters worse.

THE FILM

Little if anything about *Don't Drink the Water* seems to suggest a connection to Miami, or any other part of Florida. Based on a Broadway play by quintessential New York comedian Woody Allen, the film is set in a fictional country behind the Iron Curtain. The story unfolds almost entirely indoors, and the few exterior scenes require snowy backdrops to simulate an uninviting Eastern European locale. In order to film in Miami, the producers had to provide transportation and ten weeks' lodging for everyone in the cast—everyone, that is, except Jackie Gleason, the film's star and Miami's premiere celebrity-citizen.

Gleason had cut his show business teeth as a nightclub comic and amateur-hour emcee in the second-tier clubs and neighborhood theaters of his native New York City. Building on his rancorous exchanges with nightclub hecklers

Figure 9.6. Publicity photo from *Don't Drink the Water*. (Doll/Morrow Collection)

and his earlier experiences as a boxer, pool hustler, and carnival barker, he developed an exaggerated, highly physical comic persona that would vault him to success in virtually every form of American entertainment—radio, recording, theater, film, and, of course, television. Together with Milton Berle, Sid Caesar, and Lucille Ball, Gleason not only pioneered but virtually defined the first decade of television.

After a limited stint in Hollywood as a contract player for Warner Brothers in the 1940s, Gleason came into his element as the host of the New York–based *Cavalcade of Stars*. This early live-broadcast variety show on the DuMont network allowed him to play the affable raconteur who exchanged ad libs with each week's guests and punctuated the show with signature broad comic vignettes. Though best remembered for the classic sitcom *The Honeymooners*, Gleason spent the bulk of his twenty years in television working in the same comedy-variety format.

By the early 1960s, nearly everything about Gleason's show—from the well-worn characters to Jackie's broad mugging—had become dated, and Gleason cast about for a way to retain his top-twenty ratings. His solution was to pack up the show and move it to Miami, a plan as risky as it was audacious. At the time, every other prime-time television show was shot either in New York or in Los Angeles. Gleason shrewdly realized that he could revitalize the show by bringing it to his fan base of Miami retirees who still associated him with the success of his early years. Even more shrewdly, he realized that the city of Miami would bend over backward to bring a national television show to town. Taking advantage of the publicity hunger of the local government, Gleason's longtime manager Jack Philbin arranged a number of deals that cut the show's production costs and thereby doubled Gleason's income overnight.

In the summer of 1964, a chartered luxury train dubbed the *Great Gleason Express* carted the show's cast, crew, and office staff from New York to Miami. Their arrival was heralded with an enormous parade and reception. Gleason was given a key to the city, and he never looked back. The new locale helped keep his show on the air for another six years, and Gleason immediately embraced his new role as the unofficial master of ceremonies to Miami Beach.

By the late 1960s, however, the television show was flagging once again, and Gleason turned to feature films in hopes of sustaining his career. To date, his greatest successes on the silver screen had come in dramas such as *The Hustler*, *Soldier in the Rain*, and *Requiem for a Heavyweight*, but he decided to bring his TV persona to the movies through a series of broad farces, including *Don't Drink the Water*.

Though they couldn't be further apart in terms of background, comic style, and physical traits, Gleason had long been an admirer of Woody Allen's work. He frequently went to see Allen's famous stand-up routines in the early 1960s and no doubt had kept up with his work when Allen wrote for the competition, Sid Caesar's *Your Show of Shows*. Opening on Broadway on November 17, 1966, *Don't Drink the Water* was Allen's first play. It received warmish reviews from the critics, who approved of its nonstop humor but unanimously frowned on the story's lack of theatrical structure. For audiences, though, the laughs were more than enough, and the show enjoyed an impressive eighteen-month run.

Though credited as writer on the film, Allen actually had no involvement with the production. The script was adapted by R. S. Allen (no relation) and Harvey Bullock, a television writing team with credits on *Gomer Pyle, USMC*, *Hogan's Heroes*, *I Spy*, *The Dick Van Dyke Show*, *The Andy Griffith Show*, and a number of Hanna-Barbera cartoons. Director Howard Morris was also a well-known television veteran who had collaborated with Woody Allen as a writer and performer on *Your Show of Shows*. Much of the cast consisted of familiar TV players as well. Given the television background of so many of the film's principals, it's no surprise that *Don't Drink the Water* has a distinctly small-screen feel, with simple sets, a static camera, and an episodic structure. Most damaging of all was the film's shift from the original setting of a cramped, overcrowded embassy, which allowed for recurring physical gags, to a spacious old-world mansion that served only to dwarf the performers.

Like Gleason's other films from this period, *Don't Drink the Water* offers little to recommend it, but the circumstances of its production remain a testament to the Great One's star power and his love of his adopted second home. Few performers of any era could have mustered the gravity to pull an entire film production to their backyard. But then, few performers ever forged such an indelible link with a city as Gleason did with his beloved Miami.

THE CREDITS

Released in 1969 by AVCO Embassy Pictures
Produced by Charles H. Joffe and Jack Rollins
Directed by Howard Morris
Written by R. S. Allen and Harvey Bullock, from the
  play by Woody Allen
Cinematography by Harvey Genkins
Edited by Ralph Rosenblum
Art direction by Robert Gundlach
Original music by Patrick Williams

THE CAST

Jackie Gleason	Walter Hollander
Estelle Parsons	Marion Hollander
Ted Bessell	Axel Magee
Joan Delaney	Susan Hollander
Michael Constantine	Krojack
Richard Libertini	Drobney
Avery Schreiber	Sultan
Howard Morris	Getaway pilot (uncredited)

HELL HARBOR

It would not have been feasible to make the film in
Hollywood. . . . the general languor of the tropics
could scarcely have been captured in California.
—Henry King, to the *New York Times*

THE STORY

Harry Morgan, a descendent of the notorious pirate Henry Morgan, lives with his spirited daughter, Anita, in Hell Harbor, a hidden cove in the Caribbean. Hell Harbor is home to a variety of scalawags and misfits, including unscrupulous trader Joseph Horngold. After Horngold witnesses Harry stabbing a stranger to death in a seedy cantina, he strikes a deal to marry Anita in exchange for his silence. Anita refuses, hoping that Bob Wade, a dashing American sailor, will rescue her.

THE FILM

Hollywood director Henry King spent much of 1929 traveling across the country looking for a suitable location for his first talkie, a romantic adventure

Figure 9.7. Film crew on the set of *Hell Harbor*.
(State Archives of Florida)

titled *Hell Harbor*. The film was set in the Caribbean, and King was searching for an authentic tropical atmosphere, which he hoped to capture on film. As soon as he saw the shaggy palms of Rocky Point, a tiny peninsula near Tampa, Florida, he knew he had found the ideal location.

Immediately, King sent art director Robert Haas to Rocky Point to plan the primary set for the film, which would be an entire pirate village built from scratch. After sculpting a model out of soap, Haas oversaw the construction of the fictional Hell Harbor on Rocky Point, a secluded area with a sandy beach and a small harbor. Unlike most Hollywood sets, the village was not a collection of false fronts. It was soundly constructed, with complete interiors built inside some of the key buildings. King requested a solid, authentically constructed village so that both exteriors and interiors could be shot on location. He did not want to shoot a single foot of film in Hollywood, least of all on a recreated set on some studio soundstage. The result is a film steeped in a sultry atmosphere, from the opening shots of swaying palms silhouetted against the skyline to the climactic fight scene in the seedy El Marino Café.

Figure 9.8. *Hell Harbor* star Jean Hersholt.
(Doll/Morrow Collection)

Ultimately the well-built sets proved useful for more than their authenticity, because Florida gave King and his crew a slice of tropical life that was not part of the script. During the last Saturday in September, after the film had been in production about four weeks, a messenger from the local weather bureau dropped by to warn the cast and crew of an approaching hurricane. The crew packed up the sound equipment and the lights and raced back to Tampa. Haas and a few men lashed down what they could and then filled and stacked sandbags along the front of the sets. The next day King and Haas returned to Rocky Point as the tides continued to rise. By midnight the waves were beating against the tropical-style shanty that served as Anita's home. Haas and some of the crew stayed throughout the night, rushing sandbags to the shanty to keep the water from claiming it. A shift in the wind around three a.m. signaled a change in direction for the hurricane, and the waters began to subside. By eight on Monday morning, King was setting up his first shot of the day. The stout sets, designed by Haas and built by the carpenters of Tampa, had been strong enough to survive a hurricane.

The authentic tropical flavor was not the only advantage to shooting in Tampa. King also benefited from the goodwill of the Tampa residents, who were eager to appear as extras in the film. A variety of Tampa citizens were selected to fill out crowd scenes or to serve as the residents of Hell Harbor, including many from the Cuban and African-American communities. The diversity of extras helped suggest the mix of ethnic groups that might make up a pirate village. Anita was played by Mexican-born star Lupe Velez, who was a hit with Tampa's Cuban community. Many Cuban-Americans were among the five thousand residents who greeted her when she arrived in town by train on September 24. By the end of the shoot, all of Tampa had embraced the colorful Velez, who was crowned Queen of the Ball at a gala thrown in her honor at the Davis Islands Coliseum.

While Henry King typically shot his films on location for authenticity, *Hell Harbor* proved more difficult than usual because it was a "talkie"—a synch sound film with spoken dialogue. Talkies had been around for only two years when King undertook to shoot his film entirely on location. Conventional wisdom of the sound era maintained that Hollywood soundstages were the only reasonable places to shoot dialogue scenes, because the early recording equipment was too sensitive, cumbersome, and unsophisticated for location work. "Looping," or overdubbing, was not yet possible, so sound and action had to be recorded at the same time on a single track. The difficulties in recording clearly audible dialogue were overwhelming in the early sound era.

King was determined to show the Hollywood studios that shooting sound films on location was indeed possible, so the sensitive RCA Photophone sound equipment and the editing gear were loaded onto seven freight cars bound for Tampa.

Despite the hardships, King used sound intelligently in the film, taking delight in such details as the squeaky shoes of his villain, Joseph Horngold. In a scene in which Harry Morgan is hiding in the dark from Horngold, suspense is created when the telltale squeak of the trader's shoes is heard coming closer and closer, and viewers realize Harry is in grave danger. To add to the tropical atmosphere, King imported a band from Cuba to play authentic Caribbean music. The Sexteto Habañero played in the cantina and also in the background during a love scene aboard Bob Wade's ship. Recording live music and spoken dialogue simultaneously was not easy, and the dialogue is occasionally lost in the sound of a strumming guitar, but the live music added a unique richness to the film.

Of all the scenes in *Hell Harbor*, those shot aboard Wade's boat were the most difficult. While the actors performed in front of the camera, a barge full of recording equipment floated nearby just off-camera. Cables hooked to generators ran from the shoreline over the water to the barge, a distance of a thousand feet. More cables ran from the barge to the cameras on the boat. The actors, the recording equipment, and the cameras had to be in perfect placement in order to capture the dialogue, and any act of nature—a gust of noisy wind, a flock of cackling birds, or a row of crashing waves—meant the shot had to be redone. Shooting was painfully slow. It took some seventeen days to shoot on shipboard for a handful of scenes that amounted to just over fifteen minutes of screen time.

The hard work and long hours were worth it, because *Hell Harbor* is far superior to the majority of early sound films. Intimidated by the sync sound equipment, most Hollywood directors were afraid to leave the soundstages. They essentially sacrificed visual style for sync sound, depending on spoken dialogue to carry their films. The results were several years of static, banal, and unartistic efforts that exploited the novelty of sound instead of mastering it. *Hell Harbor* is a remarkable exception. While most directors avoided camera movements, reduced the number of camera setups, shot inside studios, and refused to work with actors who had accents, King moved the camera extensively in several scenes, used a variety of shots in his film, shot on location thousands of miles from Hollywood, and selected Lupe Velez precisely because of her accent. Unfortunately, King's experiences were not enough to persuade producers and directors that shooting on location was reasonable in the sound era, and studio production remained the norm.

Governor Doyle E. Carlton had hoped that King's experience with *Hell Harbor* would result in the return of film production to Florida, but those hopes were dashed by a Hollywood cowed by the Depression and by its struggles with sound technology. However, this did not dampen the spirits of the sold-out crowd who packed the Victory Theatre in downtown Tampa on January 24, 1930, for the world premiere of *Hell Harbor*.

THE CREDITS	THE CAST	
Released in 1930 by United Artists	Lupe Velez	Anita Morgan
Produced by Henry King for Inspiration Pictures	Jean Hersholt	Joseph Horngold
Directed by Henry King	John Holland	Bob Wade
Written by Clarke Silvernail, from the novel *Out of the Night* by Rida Johnson Young	Gibson Gowland	Harry Morgan
	Al St. John	Bunion
Cinematography by John Fulton and Mack Stengler	Ulysses Williams	Nemo
Edited by Lloyd Nosler	Paul E. Burns	Blinky
Art direction by Robert Haas	Rondo Hatton	Cantina bouncer
Sound engineering by Ernest Rovere		

Rondo Hatton: A Tragic Fate

Reporter Rondo Hatton was sent by a local newspaper to cover the making of *Hell Harbor* in Tampa. As soon as Henry King saw Hatton's striking appearance, he asked the young reporter to appear as an extra in the two cantina scenes. Hatton's astonishingly ugly mug rendered his character a villain, but it also earned him several close-ups—a privilege not afforded most extras.

Hatton's appearance was the result of acromegaly, a rare disease of the pituitary gland that caused his hands, head, and feet to become oversized and distorted. Ironically, he had been a handsome high-school football player in Tampa before joining the National Guard, but exposure to poison gas during World War I may have brought on his disfiguring condition, or at least exacerbated it. Acromegaly is usually caused by a tumor of the pituitary gland, but Hatton was convinced that his misfortune during the war had caused the disease. His worsening disfigurement eventually resulted in divorce from his first wife.

Hatton moved from Tampa to Hollywood in 1934, perhaps because *Hell Harbor* had opened a few doors for him. He scratched out a living by appearing as an extra or in bit parts. During the early 1940s he was cast in a few horror films, which raised his profile in Hollywood and created a fan base. His most famous role was as the Creeper in *The Pearl of Death*, released in 1944. Sadly, he died in 1946 of a heart attack, a complication of his disease, just as he was finally able to use his unusual appearance to best advantage.

JEEPERS CREEPERS

> You know the part in horror movies when somebody does something really stupid, and everybody hates him for it? This is it.
> —Trish in *Jeepers Creepers*

THE STORY

Trish Jenner and her brother Darry decide to drive home from college the long way, using an isolated two-lane highway. While cruising past the pastures and cornfields of farm country, they see a strange, cloaked figure dispose of something in an old, abandoned churchyard. Realizing he has been spotted, the mystery man relentlessly pursues the two teens, who discover they have stumbled across something dark and horrific.

A low-budget horror film needs neither major stars, expensive effects, nor a well-known director to generate interest among fans, who are steadfastly loyal to this underrated genre. Though dismissed and deplored by critics, the low-budget horror film is often a boon to producers and studios, who can make a substantial profit on a small investment. With a budget of less than $25 million, *Jeepers Creepers* made about $38 million for its production company, American Zoetrope, and its distributor, MGM-UA, during its initial theatrical release in 2001.[3]

The key to any successful horror film is the monster, which must both repel and fascinate the audience. For the antagonist in *Jeepers Creepers*, writer-director Victor Salva created a malevolent monster influenced by the famous creatures of classic horror. Instead of a knife-wielding psychopath—the mainstay of the contemporary slasher film—the Creeper is a supernatural fiend who relentlessly stalks his victims across a dark and peculiar landscape, much as in the old Universal films from the Golden Age.

The two protagonists, Trish and Darry, are brother and sister rather than boyfriend and girlfriend. By making the central characters siblings, Salva avoids the contemporary cliché of promiscuous teen characters who meet their demise after engaging in sex or foreplay. He also avoids, with the exception of one line, the recent tendency toward self-reflexivity, in which characters talk or joke about other horror films. The result is a stark, stripped-down theme of good versus evil, which suits the low-budget style of the film.

A great deal of the film takes place at night and makes good use of cinematographer Don E. FauntLeRoy's low-key lighting and shadowy compositions. Aside from creating a foreboding mood, low-key lighting is an age-old strategy to prevent the monster from being seen too early in the film. Just as Trish and Darry are not quite sure what they are dealing with, so the audience is kept in the dark—literally and figuratively—about the nature of the monster. The emphasis on lighting effects in lieu of elaborate makeup, process shots, or computer-generated imagery (CGI) helped keep the budget low.

The director had a three-stage strategy for revealing the nature of the Creeper. In the first stage, Trish and Darry (and the audience) see only his vehicle, which is an old, dark, rusted delivery truck. The 1940s-era flatbed truck was customized by the film's production designers, who outfitted it with a specially made box for the back and a large grille for the front. Early in the film, when the Creeper is chasing Trish and Darry down the highway and the pair look back, the front of the truck with its oversized grille suggests a lurid, grinning face. The vehicle seems to be an extension of the Creeper himself—an outer shell. In the next stage, Trish and Darry see the actual Creeper, but only as a silhouette on top of a police car as he pulls the officers out of the car and kills them. Though no details can be made out, the large, angular figure in its flowing garments suggests a creature that is humanlike but definitely not human. In the next sequence, the Creeper is shown in silhouette once again, this time in a cornfield, where he is mistaken for a scarecrow. At this point the audience begins to understand the nature of this monster, who looks as if he has been carelessly assembled from spare parts. Finally, the Creeper is completely revealed during the climax, where the horror of his deformed face and red, misshapen mouth is depicted in close-up. The only CGI in the film occurs when the Creeper is shown in his full glory, and then again a few seconds later when he flies away with his last victim.

The classic monsters of the past inhabited distinct landscapes that were familiar as actual places but at the same time were strange and eerie, whether it was Dracula's remote castle in Transylvania, the Wolf Man's foggy moors, or the Creature's Black Lagoon. Part of the strategy of the horror film is to make the familiar seem strange or alien, which is disturbing for viewers. The Creeper also inhabits a recognizable landscape. He stalks the meadows and cornfields of the heartland, trolling for victims along the two-lane highway and hiding in old, abandoned buildings. The script describes the story's setting as "Any Rural Place, U.S.A.," but director Salva has referred to the setting in interviews as a "rural Andrew Wyeth–like setting" and "Norman Rockwell land" and the "heartland," suggesting that he sees the setting as America's breadbasket—the Midwest. The association between the Creeper and the Midwest is important because of his connection to scarecrows. Scarecrows are stereotypically found in cornfields, which in turn conjure up images of the heartland. While no detailed explanation for the Creeper's existence is offered, Salva and his team wanted to play off the natural eeriness of scarecrows, an icon or archetype not widely explored in the horror genre. Also, the idea that something wicked is afoot in America's heartland opens *Jeepers Creepers* to an array of sociopolitical interpretations and turns an otherwise quaint setting into something dark and sinister. Like the Creature's lagoon or the Wolf Man's foggy moors, the farmland setting is at once familiar and beautiful but also strange and threatening.

Despite the heartland iconography, *Jeepers Creepers* was actually shot in Marion County, Florida, a choice that astonished the director when it was originally proposed to him. Salva assumed Florida was all palm trees and white sandy beaches, but when he was shown location photos of central Florida, he was convinced that it would all work out.

Dubbed the Horse Capital of the World by the U.S. Department of the Census in 1999, Marion County is home to more horses and ponies than any other county in America. The rich pastures and rolling hills are ideal for rais-

Figure 9.9. Poster for *Jeepers Creepers*. (Doll/Morrow Collection)

ing horses, just as they made an ideal substitute for the Midwest in *Jeepers Creepers*. The area's rural character is enhanced by the old farm buildings and other run-down structures that decorate the landscape, including an abandoned church that Salva used as a key location. In a crucial scene, the Creeper disposes of a victim in a weed-choked cemetery by an empty church. The structure was actually the remnants of an African-American church located just outside Ocala. The film's production designers could not have constructed a more atmospheric or suitable setting.

The Florida location was not without its problems, however. The cast and crew arrived to shoot in July during an unusually hot summer, even for Florida. The heat made the Creeper costume almost unbearable for actor Jonathan Breck, who spent long hours in the latex suit. In addition, a few Florida-style images, such as trees laden with Spanish moss, occasionally crept into the background despite the director's best efforts to depict the heartland.

Though dismissed by reviewers, *Jeepers Creepers* was a cut above most low-budget fare, partly because Salva harkened back to a more classic form of the genre. In many ways the Creeper evokes the Creature from the Black Lagoon, a monster that Salva frequently mentions as an inspiration. Oddly enough, *The Creature from the Black Lagoon* was shot in Wakulla Springs, Florida, just 150 miles from Marion County.

THE CREDITS	THE CAST	
Released in 2001 by Twentieth Century–Fox	Gina Philips	Patricia "Trish" Jenner
Produced by Francis Ford Coppola (executive producer), Tom Luse, and Barry Opper, with J. Todd Harris	Justin Long	Darius "Darry" Jenner
	Jonathan Breck	The Creeper
Directed by Victor Salva	Patricia Belcher	Jezelle Gay Hartman
Written by Victor Salva	Eileen Brennan	The Cat Lady
Cinematography by Don E. FauntLeRoy	Brandon Smith	Sgt. David Tubbs
Edited by Ed Marx	Peggy Sheffield	Waitress Beverly
Production design by Steven Legler		
Art direction by Kevin Egeland, with Barbara Peterson		
Costumes by Emae Villalobos		
Creeper designed by Brad Parker		
Creature and makeup effects by Brian Penikas		
Visual effects by Sonny Kato Chapman		
Sound by Angelo Palazzo		
Original music by Bennett Salvay		

OPERATION PETTICOAT

A woman just shouldn't mess around with a man's machinery.
—Chief Mechanic's Mate Sam Tostin in
Operation Petticoat

THE STORY

Former submarine commander Matt Sherman returns to the *Sea Tiger* one last time before it is decommissioned. The visit prompts him to recall the sub's many misadventures during the early days of World War II, particularly after the addition of clever but conniving Lt. Nick Holden to his staff. Sherman recalls that misadventure turned to calamity after the *Sea Tiger* rescued a group of stranded nurses who made themselves at home aboard the sub.

THE FILM

Operation Petticoat lacks the stellar reputation of many of Cary Grant's other comedies, particularly those of the screwball variety from the 1930s and 1940s. Contemporary critics and historians can't seem to get beyond the surface of the plot, in which the male-dominated world of a military submarine is overrun by attractive army nurses. Viewing the story through twenty-first-century eyes, they find the film sexist and old-fashioned—and leave it at that. Yet when the film was released in 1959, it was a box-office hit, becoming Universal's biggest moneymaker up to that time.[4]

Part of the popular appeal of the film was undoubtedly due to factors modern audiences and reviewers can't relate to, or don't recognize. For example, censorship restrictions were loosening during the 1950s, but visual and verbal references to sex and other controversial topics were still not explicit or obvious. Thus the subtle, well-written one-liners and double entendres in *Operation Petticoat* are tame by today's standards. They go unappreciated and perhaps even unnoticed by moviegoers accustomed to the crude, slam-dunk sexual humor in such hit comedies as the Austin Powers series. In 1959, reviews noticed *Petticoat*'s witty script and dialogue by Stanley Shapiro and Maurice Richlin, who had penned another popular favorite, *Pillow Talk*.

Shapiro and Richlin could ask for no better actor to deliver their lines than Cary Grant, whose ease with keen comic dialogue was as much a part of his star image as his handsome good looks. Audiences went to Grant's comedies expecting to see the much-admired star deftly handle clever dialogue with expert timing, and the actor did not disappoint in *Petticoat*. Grant, as Lt. Cdr. Matt Sherman, argues with his superior officer that the severely battered *Sea*

Tiger should not be destroyed before having a chance at combat, remarking, "That's like a beautiful woman dying an old maid . . . if you know what I mean by old maid!" To today's audience the line seems out-of-date, or inconsequential. But in 1959 it was still uncommon to use the word "virgin" in dialogue, especially in comedies. Shapiro and Richlin get the idea across by emphasizing the phrase "old maid" through repetition. Not only is that approach funnier, but the idea that it is a waste for a beautiful woman to die a virgin is made credible because it is Grant—Hollywood's most handsome, most dashing romantic lead—who says so.

Director Blake Edwards, who made Peter Sellers a major star with the Pink Panther series, had a talent for casting well-known stars based on the nuances of their images. Grant's identity as a master of romantic comedy is widely known today, but during the 1950s he was also well remembered as a submarine captain in the popular war drama *Destination Tokyo*. His association with comedy, plus his role in *Destination Tokyo*, is built into his appearance in *Petticoat*. Tony Curtis was cast as Lt. Nick Holden, the slick junior officer who charms women out of their virtue and cons the supply post out of their goods. Curtis, who was also associated with romantic comedy, had just appeared in *Some Like It Hot*, successfully seducing Marilyn Monroe by doing a killer Cary Grant imitation. These subtleties of casting would have resonated with movie fans in 1959, who were aware of both stars in a way lost to today's audiences.

The third "star" in the cast turned out to be not an actor but a submarine, the *Sea Tiger*, which had a personality all its own. Painted pink during repairs because the standard gray was not available, the sub made quite a sight as it belched billowing clouds of black smoke while chugging through the waters of the South Pacific. At one point a critical mechanism in the engine room was held together by a woman's girdle, in a perfect blend of male and female imagery that serves as a metaphor for the way the sailors and nurses worked out their differences aboard ship. Despite its peculiarities, the *Sea Tiger* never let the men down, so by the end, when it is decommissioned and scheduled to be sunk for target practice, the audience is as sad as Sherman and Holden because the sub was akin to a colorful old war buddy.

The use of submarines in *Operation Petticoat* accounts for its Florida connection. Though the setting was the coast and waters of the Philippines during the opening days of World War II, the film was shot primarily at the Key West Naval Air Station, with additional footage of the sub's ocean voyages shot off the coast of San Diego. The presence of the U.S. Navy in Key West dates back to 1823, when a naval base was built to counter pirates. Designated as a naval air station during World War II, the base became a training facility after the war. Its submarine facilities made it a natural as the primary location for

Figure 9.10. *Operation Petticoat* star Tony Curtis.
(Doll/Morrow Collection)

Operation Petticoat, and the cast and crew were flown to Key West in early 1959 for principal photography. Scenes of sailors handling the sub's lines at pierside featured recruits from the naval air station and from the USN Sonar Operators School.

The *Sea Tiger* was "played" by three subs—the U.S.S. *Balao* (SS-285), the U.S.S. *Archerfish* (SS-311), and the U.S.S. *Queenfish* (SS-393). The *Balao* and the *Archerfish* were docked at Key West, while the *Queenfish* was used for ocean shots near San Diego. The *Balao* is most associated with *Operation Petticoat* because it had the honor of being painted pink for the film—a dubious distinction, considering the *Balao*'s history. The first of the Balao class submarines to be built, the U.S.S. *Balao* saw wartime action from July 1943 through August 1945. The sub completed ten war patrols and sank seven large Japanese ships, plus numerous small craft. It was recommissioned during the Korean War, when it was transited to Key West for training purposes. The sub remained in Florida for the duration of its commission. The *Balao* was repainted grey after the film, but pink paint was still being chipped from some surfaces as late as 1962.

Ultimately, the fate of the *Balao* was not unlike that of the *Sea Tiger* in the film. Decommissioned in the summer of 1963, the *Balao* was sunk as a target that September, but its conning tower fairwater was preserved and put on exhibit at the Washington Navy Yard in the nation's capital. The *Balao*—like the *Sea Tiger* in the film and even the film itself—was renowned in its day; but as time passed, its value was diminished and then lost on subsequent generations who lack the context to fully appreciate its strengths.

THE CREDITS	THE CAST	
Released in 1959 by Universal Pictures	Cary Grant	Lt. Cdr. Matt Sherman
Produced by Robert Arthur	Tony Curtis	Lt. Nick Holden
Directed by Blake Edwards	Joan O'Brien	Dolores Crandall
Written by Stanley Shapiro and Maurice Richlin,	Dina Merrill	Barbara Duran
suggested by a story by Paul King and	Arthur O'Connell	Chief Mechanic's Mate Sam Tostin
Joseph Stone	Gene Evans	Molumphrey
Cinematography by Russell Harlan	Richard Sargent	Ens. Stovall
Edited by Ted J. Kent and Frank Gross	Virginia Gregg	Maj. Edna Howard
Production design by Alexander Golitzen	Gavin MacLeod	Hunkle
and Robert E. Smith	Madlyn Rhue	Lt. Claire Reid
Music by David Rose	Marion Ross	Lt. Ruth Colfax

PARENTHOOD

It could happen to you.
—tagline for *Parenthood*

THE STORY

Four generations of the Buckman family face the ups and downs of raising children in upper middle-class suburbia. Oldest son Gil frets about the emotional health of his kids and sets work aside to tend to family matters. Overwrought divorcee Helen struggles to keep up with her two wild teens, while sister Susan contends with a husband bent on turning their toddler into a supergenius. Complicating matters, a black-sheep younger brother shows up with an illegitimate multiracial child and a destructive gambling habit.

Figure 9.11. Publicity photo from *Parenthood*. (Doll/Morrow Collection)

THE FILM

With the all-powerful Baby Boom generation at the peak of their child-rearing years, issues of parenting became a familiar pop-culture topic in the 1980s. Many Boomers had put off having children in order to pursue their careers, but now, approaching middle age and poised to move into senior positions at work, many decided it was time to raise a family. Parenting became the new hot topic for America's most influential demographic group.

This trend was nowhere more apparent than in Hollywood. Top executives such as Disney's Jeffrey Katzenberg and Columbia Pictures president Dawn Steele were widely known to slip out of the office for time with their children or to show up at industry events with their entire families in tow. Attuned to the ever-shifting interests of their fellow Boomers, these market-savvy professionals saw a bankable audience for quality films about real-world issues that their peers were becoming personally acquainted with—like parenthood. The result was a string of successful, high-profile films—*Three Men and a Baby*, *Overboard*, *Baby Boom*—in which Boomers learned to accept the responsibilities of parenting. A common story line in these earlier films featured successful, carefree, and independent adults unwillingly burdened with a child but learning to appreciate the joys of child rearing by the film's end.

Figure 9.12. Publicity photo from *Parenthood*. (Doll/Morrow Collection)

Parenthood represents an evolution in the theme, in that its characters fully embrace the demands of raising a family from the outset. Throughout the film, they struggle with the consequences of that decision, and occasionally doubt their resolve, but in the end the events of the film always serve to reinforce their original viewpoint. The creative team behind *Parenthood*—director Ron Howard, producer Brian Grazer, and writers Lowell Ganz and Babaloo Mandel—had formed a new production company that was gaining clout in the industry. They also had fifteen children among them. Howard points to a personal experience as the genesis of the film, a nightmarish plane ride during which his bored six-year-old and his screaming two-year-old twins left him and many of his fellow passengers frazzled. This and similar experiences became fodder for the film's planning meetings, which Howard likened to therapy sessions where he and his creative partners shared the anxieties, stresses, and sacrifices that parenthood had brought to their own lives and found ways to translate them into a script.

The film offers far more, though, than platitudes about the joys of family. Abortion, teen pregnancy, addiction, and pornography are just some of the challenges faced by the Buckmans, an extended upper-middle-class family that learns to solve the problems it can and bear the ones it cannot. With its deft blend of humor, angst, insight, and sentimentality, *Parenthood* was well received by critics and audiences alike, earning a $100-million box-office gross and an Academy Award nomination for Dianne Wiest.[5]

It took some effort to convince Ron Howard that Florida was the right location for his ensemble comedy about a Midwestern family. Universal Pictures went so far as to arrange a helicopter flight so the director could scope the terrain around Orlando. In the end, Howard agreed that central Florida could indeed stand in for the anonymous suburb on the outskirts of St. Louis that he wanted to create, and *Parenthood* became the first major theatrical film to be shot at Universal Studios Orlando.

For the studio, *Parenthood* was simply the right film at the right time. The company's famed Florida theme park was slated to open the following year, and an essential component of the marketing plan was to emphasize the facility as a working studio. Universal was banking on this image to help distinguish its park from the just-opened Disney-MGM Studio, which was generally perceived to be more park and less production facility. Indeed, Universal likely considered this image to be a part of their tradition, and rightly so. The studio had begun capitalizing on the public's fascination with moviemaking back in the 1915 by adding bleachers to two outdoor soundstages in California and charging 25 cents to view the making of silent films. The advent of sound made public seating on the set impractical, though, and Universal had to dis-

Figure 9.13. Publicity photo from *Parenthood*. (Doll/Morrow Collection)

continue the practice. In 1964 the company reintroduced limited tours of its back-lot facilities and fourteen soundstages. The tours were wildly popular, and Universal eventually expanded the idea to create the Universal Studios Hollywood theme park.

Despite these successes, setting up shop on Disney's doorstep in Florida was a risky venture. Universal intended to further distinguish itself from the formidable competition by targeting a slightly older market. Its rides were edgier, its stage shows were more sophisticated, and its restaurants offered a more mature atmosphere and bill of fare. The park was still a family destination, but it was designed to appeal to families with teens and tweens rather than toddlers. *Parenthood*, with its sharp wit and frank but tasteful handling of mature subject matter, was an ideal feature for the studio's public christening.

Filming began on January 30, 1989, after two weeks of rehearsal by the principal actors. Much of the shooting took place at the new Universal facilities, but a number of scenes made use of Florida locations. In the opening sequence—a flashback in which Steve Martin's character revisits his unsatisfying childhood trips to the ballpark with gruff father Jason Robards—the University of Florida's football stadium stood in for the St. Louis Cardinals' home field, Busch Stadium. A brief scene in which Martin's son reveals his own emotional instability took place at the Mystery Fun House on International Drive, directly across the street from Universal Studios. Ironically, that family-oriented Orlando landmark, which offered pizza, video games, and miniature golf, shut down twelve years later, no longer able to compete with its wildly successful new neighbor. Finally, the film's coda, a silent sequence in which virtually every Buckman woman of childbearing age totes a new addition to the family, took place in the maternity ward of Orlando General Hospital.

THE CREDITS	THE CAST	
Released in 1989 by Universal Pictures and	Steve Martin	Gil
Imagination Entertainment	Dianne Wiest	Helen
Produced by Brian Grazer	Mary Steenburgen	Karen
Directed by Ron Howard	Paul Linke	George
Written by Lowell Ganz and Babaloo Mandel	Jason Robards	Frank
Cinematography by Donald McAlpine	Rick Moranis	Nathan
Edited by Daniel Hanley and Michael Hill	Tom Hulce	Larry
Production design by Todd Hallowell	Martha Plimpton	Julie
Art direction by Christopher Nowak	Keanu Reeves	Tod
Original music by Randy Newman	Harley Jane Kozak	Susan
	Eileen Ryan	Marilyn
	Joaquin Phoenix	Garry
	Rance Howard	Dean at college

Universal Studios Florida—A Selected Filmography

Universal's Orlando facilities have played an important role in a number of high-profile films and television series. In some films, such as *Van Helsing*, the Florida studio was used only for blue-screen shots and other special effects work.

Van Helsing (2004)
2 Fast 2 Furious (2003)
Minority Report (2002)
Ocean's Eleven (2001)
The Perfect Storm (2000)

Angel (TV series, 1999)
Out of Sight (1998)
Buffy the Vampire Slayer (TV series 1997)
Matinee (1993)
Parenthood (1989)

PT 109

This was the end of the line for *PT 109* and
yet in a way, it was only the beginning . . .
—lobby card for *PT 109*

THE STORY

John F. Kennedy arrives in the South Pacific as a young navy lieutenant in 1943, eager to contribute to the war effort. He assumes command of *PT 109*, showing quiet leadership as he whips the boat and crew into shape and gets his first taste of combat. During a dangerous nighttime mission, his vessel is rammed by a Japanese destroyer. Kennedy and his crew spend seven days stranded on enemy-occupied islands, and the young officer sets an example of determination, courage, and resourcefulness that sees the group through until rescuers arrive.

THE FILM

Lieutenant (j.g.) John F. Kennedy began his eight months of WWII combat service in April 1943. Assigned to the Solomon Islands, he volunteered for Patrol Torpedo (PT) duty, the only way for a young, inexperienced officer to get his own command. At this point in the war, America was still in the process of building up its navy to face the formidable Japanese fleet. The small, wooden-hulled PT boats, which could be quickly and inexpensively mass produced, proved an effective stopgap weapon used to harass enemy shipping, lay mines, gather intelligence, and perform rescue operations. Though the nimble PT boats were most often pitted against barges, tankers, and other less formidable targets, it was their infrequent but much publicized hit-and-run forays against heavily armed and armored warships that earned their crews a roguish, daring image as "hell on keels."

On the night of August 1, 1943, a detachment of American PT boats set out from Rendova Island on such a mission. Prowling the waters of Blackett Strait, the fifteen vessels sought to intercept a small convoy of Japanese destroyers ferrying troops and supplies to positions in the Solomon Islands. The destroyers slipped through and made their deliveries unscathed, but as the PTs lay in wait for a second shot at the returning Japanese convoy, the stage was set for one of the most well-known and influential war stories of the century.

Spotting a group of three PT boats crossing her bow, the Japanese destroyer *Amagiri* bore down on the lead boat, *PT 109*, slicing the plywood craft in two. Two crewmen died in the collision, and eleven others were left floundering

In response to countless inquiries and requests, this theatre is honored to announce a special engagement of **PT 109**

Figure 9.14. Poster for *PT 109*. (Doll/Morrow Collection)

in the water. Over the next seven days, the survivors hid out among enemy-occupied islands, scrounging for food and water and desperately attempting to contact friendly forces. After being picked up by fellow PT boaters, the crew, to a man, cited the leadership, determination, and encouragement of their captain, twenty-six-year-old John Kennedy, as the key to their survival. Kennedy earned the Navy and Marine Corps Medal for his service.

The story of *PT 109* was written up in the *New Yorker* in June 1944 and soon after was reprinted in *Reader's Digest*. As he pursued a political career, Kennedy made hay with the well-known story, using the image it presented of a capable, clear-headed leader to offset voters' concerns over his young age. In fact, he and his staff freely handed out PT-shaped tie clasps as mementos to Kennedy admirers, to the point that the practice became a target of gentle chiding by the media. The war-hero image was given a further boost in 1961 when Robert J. Donovan, a journalist and later presidential historian, published a chronicle of JFK's time in the Solomons titled *PT 109*. The following year, Warner Brothers began shooting a film adaptation of Donovan's story, and country singer Jimmy Dean released a crossover single recounting the ordeal, which made it to the Top Ten on both the country and pop charts.

As with all things Kennedy, wisps of controversy and conspiracy swirled about JFK's service record and the attention it received. Rumors claimed that a lax crew or faulty orders by Kennedy led to *PT 109*'s sinking, though a routine military investigation at the time cleared Kennedy of any wrongdoing. Others noted the unusually long time it took for the navy to award his medal, implying that family influence was used to eventually elicit the decoration. And, of course, there were accusations that the various incarnations of the story were all orchestrated for political gain.

It is remarkable that the film *PT 109* was produced and released to theaters in the middle of Kennedy's term in the White House. Biopics of well-known living individuals are fairly uncommon in any case, but this was the first and only time a major theatrical film focused on the youthful exploits of a sitting president—and only a year before he was to run for reelection. The timing was made more precarious by the changing relationship between Hollywood and the Department of Defense. Going back as far as the silent film epic *Wings*, the American military had generously offered technical advice, equipment, personnel, and access to records and military sites for many a war movie. However, when journalists decided to question the practice in connection with the monumental production of *The Longest Day* in 1961, the Pentagon quickly drafted new guidelines that would limit such assistance. These rules were just going into effect when the *PT 109* project was started, but the president was clearly keen on the film—it's said he assisted Warner Brothers in casting the lead—and so the navy lent out a destroyer and six other vessels to the production.

Studio head Jack Warner, a longtime ally of the Democratic Party, sought a first-rate team for the project, securing veteran producer Bryan Foy and preeminent cinematographer Robert Surtees, winner of three Oscars. The director's chair proved harder to fill. A deal with Raoul Walsh fell through before production began, and his replacement, Lewis Milestone, was fired during filming on account of his frequent complaints about the weakness of the script. Lewis H. Martinson, known primarily as a television director, saw the film through. A strong supporting cast, including Robert Blake, James Gregory, Norman Fell, Robert Culp, and beefy Ty Hardin, buoy the film somewhat, but in the end Milestone's criticisms ring true. Hamstrung by the need for historical accuracy, the script limps along from one wholesome, selfless act to another: Kennedy declines to use family connections to avoid combat duty, Kennedy rolls up his sleeves and works with the enlisted men, Kennedy rushes to the aid of stranded marines. Even after the survival ordeal begins, the pace of the 140-minute film barely picks up.

Historical accuracy notwithstanding, the script emphasizes Kennedy's ability as a leader of men by tacitly contrasting his skills with those of three other officers. Navy veteran C. R. Ritchie (Gregory) is an experienced and determined commander, but his perpetually harsh disposition distances him from those under him and prevents him from offering even a simple "Well done" to reward their efforts. Kennedy's contemporary, Ensign Barney Ross (Culp), is similarly educated and just as at ease with the men, but his lack of resolve surfaces when he recommends to Kennedy that the starving group surrender to the Japanese. Young Ensign Leonard Thom (Hardin) shares Kennedy's dedication and easy nature but lacks the clear, world-wise vision that comes with maturity. Of all the officers, only JFK can offer the compassion, will, and knowledge that the stranded crew need to survive.

Little Munson Island, a five-acre spit of land about an hour north of Key West, stood in well for the South Pacific during the shooting of PT 109. The island, privately owned by county sheriff John Spottswood, had been a favored hideaway for Harry and Bess Truman and other Washington dignitaries in the 1950s. New owners have since rechristened the idyllic spot Little Palm Island and converted it into an exclusive resort. The Florida location also brought another layer of authenticity to the production. Gerard Zinser, a machinist's mate in Kennedy's crew, had settled in the Sunshine State after leaving the military and was invited to appear as an extra in the film. When PT 109 opened in the summer of 1963, Zinser accepted offers from several local theaters and drive-ins to greet moviegoers and sign autographs.

The film was still in theaters on November 22 of that year, having gone through about three-fourths of its scheduled screenings at the time of JFK's assassination. In deference to his memory, Warner Brothers chose to pull PT 109 from circulation. But the studio released it again in March of 1964, beginning with theaters in Dallas.

THE CREDITS	THE CAST	
Released in 1963 by Warner Brothers	Cliff Robertson	Lieutenant John F. Kennedy
Produced by Bryan Foy	Ty Hardin	Ensign Leonard J. Thom
Directed by Leslie H. Martinson	James Gregory	Commander C. R. Ritchie
Written by Richard L. Breen, from the book	Robert Culp	Ensign George "Barney" Ross
by Robert J. Donovan, adapted by Vincent	Robert Blake	Charles "Bucky" Harris
Flaherty and Howard Sheehan	William Douglas	Gerald Zinser
Cinematography by Robert Surtees	Norman Fell	Edmund Drewitch
Edited by Folmar Blangsted	George Takei	Helmsman on Japanese
Art direction by Leo K. Kuter		destroyer
Technical advice by J. E. Gibson		

TARZAN FINDS A SON

Ross Allen would go ahead of us and search the bank for alligators and cottonmouth water moccasins. He found a few too. I remember one time he got a water moccasin on the bank and put it in his mouth and swam back to the boat. A few minutes later Big John [Weissmuller] and I were working right there on the bank where Ross captured the aquatic pit viper.

—Johnny Sheffield, in *Johnny Weissmuller*, by David A. Fury

THE STORY

Tarzan discovers the only survivor of a crashed plane, a tiny infant whom he names Boy. He and Jane decide to keep the child and raise it as their own in their jungle home. Boy enjoys an idyllic existence in an exotic paradise until the child's relatives come looking for him five years later. Tarzan refuses to let Boy go, but the conniving relatives convince Jane that the child should return to grow up in civilization.

THE FILM

Ask anyone of a certain age, "Who played Tarzan?" and the answer will undoubtedly be "Johnny Weissmuller." As a matter of fact, Weissmuller *was* Tarzan for most moviegoers, though he was actually the sixth actor to don a loincloth and play Edgar Rice Burroughs's famous jungle hero.

Weissmuller starred in MGM's highly popular Tarzan film series during the 1930s and 1940s. Though based on Burroughs's *Tarzan, the Ape Man*, the MGM series freely deviated from the source material to create a definitive version of the jungle man still remembered for his athleticism, courage, and simple virtues. A tall, muscular athlete who had won five Olympic gold medals for swimming, Weissmuller perfectly embodied MGM's vision for Tarzan. Maureen O'Sullivan, a cultured and well-educated actress, costarred as Jane, complementing Weissmuller's monosyllabic interpretation of the Ape Man. In addition to the excellent casting, the MGM films benefited from high production values and good scripts, making the series the most memorable of the Tarzan features. Earlier Tarzan films pale in comparison, while later versions lack MGM's attention to character development, script, and casting.

The first two films in the MGM series were produced prior to the enforcement of the Production Code, the censorship code that controlled the content of Hollywood movies during the Golden Age. *Tarzan, the Ape Man* (1932) and *Tarzan Finds a Mate* (1934) featured an undercurrent of eroticism as Tarzan and Jane are depicted in revealing costumes sharing a loving relationship in an Edenic jungle. The Production Code, with its strict guidelines on the depiction of male-female relationships, squelched that element in the Tarzan-Jane pairing. *Tarzan Finds a Son*, the fourth film in the MGM series, pushed the Tarzan legend in a new direction by introducing a pivotal character—Boy, played by Johnny Sheffield. With the introduction of a son to the series, Tarzan assumed the role of the ideal father and provider, while Jane became the dutiful mother. The introduction of family values to the series neutralized any hint of eroticism. Not only were the costumes changed to cover more skin, but Boy had to be *found* by Tarzan, not *conceived* by him and Jane, who had never been married in the traditional sense.

To suggest that Tarzan loved Boy as much as any birth father, and to visually imply the unbreakable bond between them, writer and director Richard Thorpe created a scene with the pair playfully swimming in their jungle paradise. Underwater photography of Tarzan and Boy romping together seemed an ideal way to capture the concept. As the principal photography neared completion, Weissmuller, Sheffield, and a small crew traveled to Silver Springs, Florida, to take advantage of the crystal clear waters to shoot the underwater sequence. O'Sullivan, who was pregnant with her first child, did not go.

Several Hollywood films have been shot in the clear waters of Silver Springs, which are often credited with launching the tourism industry in Florida. A network of springs pumps 800 million gallons of pure water from the ground each day, keeping the lakes, ponds, and waterways clean and clear. Tourists view the springs and the aquatic life by cruising the area aboard the famous glass-bottom boats, first constructed by Phillip Morell in the mid-1870s when he placed a sheet of plate glass in the bottom of a rowboat. Hullam Jones launched his own version of the unique boat shortly thereafter to ferry visitors around the waters. Jones became the registered inventor of the glass-bottom boat in 1878 because he was the first to patent it.

By the time the *Tarzan* cast and crew arrived in Silver Springs in 1939, the springs had become one of Florida's top tourist attractions, thanks in part to an aggressive marketing campaign by owners Carl Ray and W. M. Davidson during the 1920s. Another popular feature of the springs was Ross Allen's Reptile Institute, founded in 1929. Allen was a true Florida original who began his career at Silver Springs by displaying native snakes and alligators alongside a not-too-authentic "Indian village" consisting of Seminoles he recruited from the Everglades. Allen exhibited a particular fondness and understanding of reptiles, and he eventually shifted the emphasis of his Institute to more scientific goals. His studies of the alligator became well known among herpetologists, and his snakes were milked so that their venom could be used in the production of antivenin. Allen accompanied the *Tarzan* cast and crew around Silver Springs and Wakulla Springs to keep the swimming areas free of snakes. Years later, when reminiscing about the shooting of the Tarzan films for a Weissmuller biography, Johnny Sheffield vividly recalled Allen swimming in the springs with a water mocassin in his mouth.

The Silver Springs footage shows Tarzan and Boy cavorting underwater for almost five minutes, playing tag and hide-and-seek. A potential misfortune turned into a stroke of luck when a baby elephant used in the film fell off a raft near the shore. A quick-thinking camera operator, already underwater in the camera bell, started rolling as soon as he saw the elephant slide off the raft. Unexpectedly graceful and coordinated, the elephant swims around a bit, and then is joined by Weissmuller and Sheffield before scurrying up the bank and back to dry land. The sequence concludes with Weissmuller and Sheffield being pulled through the water by a giant tortoise. Weissmuller hangs onto a back flipper, while Sheffield hangs on to the big man's feet, resulting in a remarkable image of synchronous movement between beast, man, and boy. Not only are Tarzan and Boy in harmony with each other, they are in harmony with the jungle as well.

More than sixty years later, the underwater footage is still remarkably fresh and vivid—so vivid and memorable that much misinformation has circulated about it. Tourist brochures and Web sites for Silver Springs often claim that all six Weissmuller Tarzan films were shot "on location" there. In fact, the crew came to the area only once, and they shot footage at both Silver Springs and Wakulla Springs, which was then used sparingly in two of the six films. The majority of the footage focused on Tarzan and Boy, though "Jane" was shot

Figure 9.15. Johnny Weissmuller and Maureen O'Sullivan in *Tarzan, the Ape Man.*
(Doll/Morrow Collection)

swimming with the family at Wakulla Springs. A Florida resident doubled for
Maureen O'Sullivan. This footage was used in *Tarzan's Secret Treasure.* The
principal location for all six MGM films was the Lake Sherwood area, including Sherwood Forest, near Los Angeles. The tree house where the Tarzan family lived was built at Crater Camp in Malibu Creek State Park, then duplicated
on a soundstage at MGM. Interiors were all shot at MGM.

Somehow it is appropriate that Tarzan's jungle is not an actual geographic location but a composite of real places and man-made sets, because his home is mythic—like Mount Olympus. His jungle home is a paradise, a peaceable kingdom without guns, where he and the animals not only coexist but are kindred spirits. In Tarzan's jungle, there is no need for money, jobs, banks, social class, or any other concerns of the civilized world. While a world without the need for money undoubtedly resonated most strongly with Depression-era audiences, the vision of a carefree existence devoid of the rat race has universal appeal.

We envy Boy cavorting in the clearest of water with a loving father and his animal friends—an ideal existence for children of all ages.

THE CREDITS	THE CAST	
Released in 1939 by Metro-Goldwyn-Mayer	Johnny Weissmuller	Tarzan
Produced by Sam Zimbalist	Maureen O'Sullivan	Jane Parker
Directed by Richard Thorpe	Johnny Sheffield	Boy
Written by Cyril Hume	Ian Hunter	Austin Lancing
Cinematography by Leonard Smith	Henry Stephenson	Sir Thomas Lancing
Edited by Frank Sullivan and Gene Ruggiero	Frieda Inescort	Mrs. Austin Lancing
Production design by Cedric Gibbons	Laraine Day	Mrs. Richard Lancing
Special effects by A. Arnold Gillespie, Warren Newcombe, and Max Fabian	Morton Lowry	Richard Lancing
Animals trained by George Emerson and Johnny Kerr	Gavin Muir	Pilot
Special animal handling by Ross Allen		

THE MOVIE TOURIST'S GUIDE TO
FLORIDA FACADE

Can't afford to travel to the South Seas, Eastern Europe, or even St. Louis? Then plan a Florida Facade tour of sites and cities that have stood in for other parts of the country or other parts of the world.

THE CREATURE FROM THE BLACK LAGOON

Wakulla Springs

On the silver screen, the mysterious creature swam freely around his Black Lagoon located deep in the heart of the Amazon. In reality, stunt swimmer Ricou Browning, who played the creature, swam in Wakulla Springs located about fifteen miles south of Tallahassee on State Route 267. Wakulla Springs State Park is a 2,888-acre wildlife sanctuary that includes the world's deepest spring, a large pool in which 600,000 gallons of limestone-filtered water gush forth every minute. Though movie tourists are unlikely to see the creature, or even Ricou Browning, they can enjoy the park's jungle cruises and glass-bottom boat tours. Also of interest is the historic Wakulla Springs Lodge, a Spanish-style inn built in the 1930s, which offers a taste of Florida tourism from another era.

CROSSWINDS

Homosassa Springs

The Homosassa Springs State Wildlife Park is located fifteen miles north of Weeki Wachee Springs on U.S. 19. The park's best attraction is its center for manatees, which includes a permanent home and rehabilitation center for injured manatees, plus a floating underwater observatory where tourists can view them. In addition, the park features nature trails that wind through the habitats of other permanent residents, including owls, otters, and even a black bear.

DON'T DRINK THE WATER

Miami

The suggested sites for this film will separate the true movie tourists from the pretenders, because little exists for visitors to see from *Don't Drink the Water*. However, movie fans will want to pay their respects to Jackie Gleason, who adopted Miami as his hometown.

The Jackie Gleason Theater of the Performing Arts at 1700 Washington

---

Avenue in Miami Beach was the home of Gleason's show and still offers performances by top-flight touring acts. The 2,700-seat theater was renamed for Gleason shortly after his death in 1987. Just outside the box office on the south side of the building, the Miami Walk of Stars features the handprints of celebrities that have contributed to the cultural landscape of Miami Beach, including actress Ann-Margret, actor Andy Garcia, and jazz singer Nancy Wilson.

Those wishing to pay their respects to Gleason can visit Our Lady of Mercy Cemetery in Doral, Florida, at 11411 NW 25th Street, just off State Route 836. His monument, which resembles a small Roman temple with four pillars and two couches resting on a dais, is inscribed with Gleason's trademark line "And Away We Go."

HELL HARBOR

Tampa

Though set in the Virgin Islands, this early sound film was shot completely in Tampa in an area known as Rocky Point. In 1929, Rocky Point looked much like a tropical paradise, with a ring of palm trees lining the shore of Old Tampa Bay—a perfect spot for the pirates' cove that the production crew constructed. Not surprisingly, much has changed through the years, including the expansion of several neighborhoods and the development of the waterfront property. Determined movie tourists might want to visit Rocky Point's Rusty Pelican Restaurant on the Courtney Campbell Causeway, because that marks the closest spot to where *Hell Harbor* was filmed.

Downtown Tampa was not part of the location for the film's story, but it played a crucial role in the offscreen lives of the cast and crew. During filming, they stayed at the legendary Floridan Hotel, built by A.J. Simms in the mid-1920s. The Floridan can still be found at the corner of Florida Avenue and Cass Street, but sadly it lies empty and unused. Across the Hillsborough River, opposite Hyde Park Avenue, is Plant Park, where star Lupe Velez was lauded by the governor of Florida, the mayor of Tampa, and five thousand well-wishers.

JEEPERS CREEPERS

Ocala

Local legend has it that the setting for one of the scenes in this low-budget horror film is actually haunted. Early in the film, the Creeper is spotted dumping a victim on the grounds of an abandoned church, which is actually the St. James Church and Cemetery, a former African-American church located just a few miles west of Ocala on Route 40. Locals claim that at night the cemetery and church grounds are often covered in a light fog, though the rest of the landscape is clear. An eerie light can sometimes be seen emanating from the vicinity of the church. When visitors drive close to the cemetery, car radios and cell phones stop working. Unfortunately, after *Jeepers Creepers* was released, two local teenagers vandalized the church, setting it on fire. What was left of it was torn down in 2003, though the graveyard and church grounds are still accessible.[6]

For the more faint of heart, tours of Marion County's famed horse country are available, including one excursion by horse-drawn trolley. Tours generally begin in Ocala, which is the seat of Marion County.

OPERATION PETTICOAT

Key West

Most of this romantic comedy about the misadventures of a submarine crew was shot at the Key West Naval Air Station, just northeast of Fort Zachary Taylor State Historical Site. Though visitors cannot freely walk around the grounds, they can check out the nearby Harry S. Truman Annex, which used to be the quarters for navy personnel before it was sold for condos. The Little White House, situated in the Annex, was a retreat where Truman and other presidents vacationed. Because it became Truman's favorite getaway, the Little White House tours focus on his presidency and his love of Key West.

PT 109

Key West

Movie tourists and military buffs can take a ride on an authentic WWII-era PT boat. Supposedly the only operating PT boat outfitted to original military specifications, *PT 728* departs daily from Key West's Schooner Wharf at the foot of William Street. Bill Bohmfalk's "Cruise Into History Tours" offers a ninety-minute battle-stations tour that includes a simulated torpedo run and visits to important sites in the area's naval history. *PT 728* was supposedly one of several PT boats used by Warner Brothers in the film.

Little Palm Island

Movie tourists wanting to escape from it all can vacation at exclusive Little Palm Island, formerly Little Munson Island, which doubled for the South Seas island where John Kennedy and his crew were stranded in the film. A private five-acre resort, Little Palm is accessible only by boat or ferry from Little Torch Key. Guests on the island stay in thatched-roof duplexes, surrounded by lush foliage and tropical plants, free from such distractions as telephones, televisions, and alarm clocks.

Universal Studios in Orlando

Except for the opening stadium sequence and a few other brief scenes, the majority of this film was shot at Universal Studios in Orlando. One of the most widely visited tourist spots in Florida, Universal Studios may be the ultimate movie tourism destination. The park is most famous for its rides based on Universal movies, from *Spiderman* and *Back to the Future* to *Jaws*, *Psycho*, and *E.T.* True film fans, however, will be equally thrilled by the park's many shows, which disguise lessons in moviemaking as thrilling entertainment. Audiences learn about the art of animation, the secrets of special effects, and the trademark techniques of master director Alfred Hitchcock. Universal Studios is located in the heart of Florida's theme park region, just outside Orlando off Interstate 4.

TARZAN FINDS A SON

Silver Springs

Famous for its crystal-clear waters, Silver Springs is Florida's oldest tourist attraction and has played host to such notable visitors as Mary Todd Lincoln, Harriet Beecher Stowe, and William Cullen Bryant. When the producers of *Tarzan Finds a Son* needed a clear, natural pool to shoot one underwater sequence with Johnny Weissmuller and his onscreen son, Johnnie Sheffield, they chose Silver Springs, located one mile east of Ocala on State Route 40. A primary attraction is the glass-bottom boats, which enable visitors to see all the way to the bottom of the springs, 120 feet below.

For many years, reptile master Ross Allen operated his Reptile Farm at Silver Springs. It was Allen, a snake enthusiast long before it was popular, who helped keep the pool clear of serpents while Weissmuller and Sheffield shot their swimming scenes. Allen, who died in 1981, worked tirelessly to educate the public about reptiles, and in January 2000 the largest island in Silver Springs was renamed Ross Allen Island in his honor.

NOTES

CHAPTER 1. SILENT FLORIDA

1. Nelson, *Lights! Camera! Florida!* 15.
2. Gauntier, *Blazing the Trail*, pt. 4, 4.
3. Russo, *The Celluloid Closet*, 11–13; Brasell, "A Seed for Change," 3.
4. Brasell, "A Seed for Change," 9.
5. Bowser, Gaines, and Musser, *Oscar Micheaux and His Circle*, 63.
6. Acker, *Reel Women*, 155, 351.
7. Gauntier, *Blazing the Trail*, pt. 2, 3.
8. Ibid., pt. 3, 6–8.
9. Ibid., pt. 4, 6.
10. Bowser, *The Transformation of Cinema, 1907–1915*, 178.
11. Schickel, *D. W. Griffith: An American Life*, 423.
12. Ibid., 424.
13. Brooks, "The Other Face of W. C. Fields," 9.
14. Curtis, 184–86.
15. Brooks, 10–11.
16. "Lost in the Jungle," *Moving Picture World*, October 1911, 109.
17. Accounts vary wildly (see sidebar). Olive Mix's reminiscence in *The Fabulous Tom Mix*, is reprinted at <www.cinemaweb.com/silentfilm/bookshelf/33_mix05.htm>, 2. Tom Mix's version in *Photoplay*, April 1925, and Kathlyn Williams's account to the *New York Clipper*, April 20, 1912, are both reprinted in Bruce Long's *Taylorology*, no. 48 (December 1996), <www.public.asu.edu/~ialong/Taylor48.txt>. The same *Taylorology* issue contains the *Movie Weekly* piece from which this section's epigraph is drawn.
18. See, for example, the entry for "Midnight Faces" on The Missing Link, <www.missing linkclassichorror.co.uk/mar.htm>.
19. Schickel, *D. W. Griffith: An American Life*, 479.
20. Ibid., 481.

CHAPTER 2. THE GOLDEN AGE

1. Briant, "Soak Up Ambience."
2. Haskew, "San Pietro: Capturing the Face of War."
3. Brown and Brown, *Historical Catastrophes*, 42; Longshore, *Encyclopedia of Hurricanes, Typhoons, and Cyclones*, 212.
4. Brown and Brown, *Historical Catastrophes*, 42.
5. Maza, "Preston Sturges: A Screwball Centennial."
6. DeMille, *Autobiography*, 372–75.
7. Ibid, 374.
8. Gleasner and Gleasner, *Florida: Off the Beaten Path*, 165.
9. T. Williams, *A Streetcar Named Desire*.

CHAPTER 3. FLORIDA NOIR

1. Ebert, review of *Palmetto*.
2. Bouzereau, "The Making of *Cape Fear*."
3. Lakeland, "Living in the City of Lakeland!"
4. Internet Movie Database (hereafter IMDb), <www.imdb.com/title/tt0109417/business>.
5. Franklin, "Director's Commentary."
6. Ibid.
7. Bartow Chamber of Commerce, "Historic Bartow."

CHAPTER 4. STARRING MIAMI

1. Villano, "Has Knight-Ridder's Flagship Gone Adrift?" 2. Ibid.
3. Tatara, "*Absence of Malice*."
4. Ibid.
5. Armbruster, *The Life and Times of Miami Beach*, 177–78.
6. Shales, "Appreciation: It Was a Wonderful Life."
7. Wilson, "Willeford, A Pro at the Miami Beat."
8. Armbruster, *The Life and Times of Miami Beach*, 59.
9. Pevere, "Scarface was De Palma's Farewell to Coke."

CHAPTER 5. FLORIDA BUST

1. IMDb, <www.imdb.com/title/tt0108000/business> and <www.imdb.com/title/tt0112442/business>.
2. IMDb, <www.imdb.com/title/tt0086325/business>.
3. IMDb, <www.imdb.com/title/tt0056875/business>.
4. Pope, "Did Brenda Wed Eric?"
5. Gordon G, "The Star Whose Secret Is Buried in the Sands."
6. Thomas et al., "Names and Faces."
7. "Missile Blows Up in Florida Test," *New York Times*, September 26, 1957.
8. Wikipedia, <en.wikipedia.org/wiki/Cape_Coral,_Florida>.
9. Canby, "Robert Altman's Satire 'Health.'"
10. McGilligan, *Robert Altman*, 474–76.
11. Uricchio, "The Great White Way."
12. IMDb, <www.imdb.com/title/tt0077766/business>.
13. IMDb, <www.imdb.com/title/tt0085750/business>.
14. R. Stanley, *Making Sense of Movies*, 207.

CHAPTER 6. FLORI-DRAMA

1. Méndez, *Cubans in America*, 51.
2. Kaufelt, *Key West Writers and Their Houses*, 77.
3. Ibid., 17; Gee, "Low Keys."
4. Ponti, *Hollywood East*, 40.
5. Welsh, review of *Days of Thunder*, 481–82.
6. London, "Based on a True Story."

CHAPTER 7. FUN IN THE SUN

1. IMDb, <www.imdb.com/title/tt0109040/business>.
2. Miami Dolphins, "Dolphins Name."
3. Pro Football Hall of Fame, "Miami Dolphins."
4. National Football League, "Miami Dolphins History."
5. Bay, "Director's Commentary."
6. Ibid.
7. Ibid.
8. Yancey, "At 50, Venerable Fontainebleau Regaining Its Glitz."
9. Bogdanovich, *Who the Hell's In It*, 148.
10. Ricou Browning, telephone interview, May 13, 2005.
11. Ibid.
12. Ad for *Dr. No*, in Pfeiffer and Worrall, *The Essential Bond*, 21.
13. A. George, *Awaiting Armageddon*, xxiii.
14. Gerstal, "In Defence of Demi."
15. Laytner, "Francis and Me."
16. Francke, "The Crash and Burn Scenario."

CHAPTER 8. FLORIDA AS PARADISE

1. Braden, *The Architecture of Leisure*, 29.
2. Patrick and Morris, *Florida under Five Flags*, 85.
3. Visit Florida, <media.VISITFLORIDA.org/corporate/archives/?1D=55>, February 20, 2003.
4. Doll, *Understanding Elvis*, 99, 103.
5. Doll, *The Films of Elvis Presley*, 60.
6. Floyd, "Closing the (Heterosexual) Frontiers," 99.
7. Irwin, "Fred Neil."
8. Espe, "Paradise Lost."
9. Cheshire, "Victor Nunez: Persistence in Paradise," 18.
10. Kaufman, "Victor's Gold."
11. Doherty, *Teenagers and Teenpics*, 54.
12. Ehrenstein and Reed, *Rock on Film*, 48–50.
13. Ash, "Fort Lauderdale Greets the College Crowd."
14. Wright, "Easter Invasion."

CHAPTER 9. FLORIDA FACADE

1. Rhonda Fleming, e-mail interview, April 12, 2005.
2. Ibid.
3. IMDb, <www.imdb.com/title/tt0301470/business>.
4. Ponti, *Hollywood East*, 84.
5. IMDb, <www.imdb.com/title/tt0098067/business>.
6. Psycho New Jersey, "Florida."

BIBLIOGRAPHY

AAA Florida Tourbook. Heathrow, Fla.: AAA Publishing, 2003.

Acker, Ally. *Reel Women: Pioneers of the Cinema*. New York: Continuum, 1991.

Adamson, Joe. *Groucho, Harpo, Chico, and Sometimes Zeppo: A Celebration of the Marx Brothers and a Satire on the Rest of the World*. New York: Simon and Schuster, 1973.

Allen, Jamie. "Key West: Nothing Dry About This Literary Destination." CNN.com, July 21, 1999. <www.cnn.com/TRAVEL/DESTINATIONS/9907/key.west>.

Allman, T. D. *Miami: City of the Future*. New York: Atlantic Monthly Press, 1987.

Alvarez, Jose, and Leo C. Polopolus. "Florida Sugar Industry." University of Florida, IFAS Extension. Revised June 2002. <edis.ifas.ufl.edu/sc042>.

America's TravelNetwork. "Downtown Panama City History." <www.accessamer.com/Panama_City_Beach/history.html>.

Andrew, Geoff. "Jim Jarmusch Interviewed." *Guardian Unlimited*, November 15, 1999. <film.guardian.co.uk/Guardian_NFT/interview/0%2C4479%2C110607%2C00.html>.

Ansen, David. "Odyssey of Oddballs." *Newsweek*, October 8, 1984, 87.

Armbruster, Ann. *The Life and Times of Miami Beach*. New York: Knopf, 1995.

Armstrong, Richard. "Goodbye to Billy Wilder." *Bright Lights Film Journal*, April 2002. <www.brightlightsfilm.com/36/billywilder.html>.

Arnold, Kathy, and Paul Wade. *National Geographic Traveler: Florida*. Washington, D.C.: National Geographic Society, 1999.

Ash, Clarke. "Fort Lauderdale Greets the College Crowd." *New York Times*, April 10, 1960.

The Astounding B Monster. "After the Fin Man." <www.bmonster.com/profile22.html> (accessed November 27, 2002).

The Astounding B Monster. "Suited for the Role." <www.bmonster.com/horror22.html>.

Authors of Key West Guesthouse. <www.authorskeywest.com/index.htm>.

Bankard, Bob. "The Herschell Gordon Lewis Guide." 2002. <www.phillyburbs.com/hgl>.

Bardèche, Maurice, and Robert Brasillach. *The History of Motion Pictures*. Translated by Iris Barry. New York: Norton, 1938.

Bartow Chamber of Commerce. "Historic Bartow: History and Heritage." <www.bartowchamber.com/heritage.htm>.

Basinger, Jeanine. *The World War II Combat Film*. 1986. Filmography updated by Jeremy Arnold. Middletown, Conn.: Wesleyan University Press, 2003.

Baxter, John. *Woody Allen: A Biography*. New York: Carroll and Graf, 1998.

Bay, Michael. "Director's Commentary." *Bad Boys* DVD, 2000.

Berardinelli, James. "Ace Ventura: Pet Detective." *Reelviews*, 1994. <movie-reviews.colossus.net/movies/a/ace.html>.

Bernhard, Sandra. Interview with David Friedman and Herschell Gordon Lewis. *Reel Wild*. <www.angelfire.com/la/ReelWild/dave.txt>.

Black, Ian. "Desperate Burt Prepares to Revive His Ailing Career." *Advertiser*, March 19, 1987.

The Black Lagoon Website. <www.horrorseek.com/horror/blackylagoon/gillman.html>.

Bogdanovich, Peter. *Who the Devil Made It*. New York: Knopf, 1997.

———. *Who the Hell's In It*. New York: Knopf, 2004.

Bouzereau, Laurent. "The Making of *Cape Fear*." *Cape Fear* (1991) DVD special feature, 2001.

Bowser, Eileen. *The Transformation of Cinema: 1907–1915*. New York: Scribner, 1990.

Bowser, Pearl, Jane Gaines, and Charles Musser, eds. *Oscar Micheaux and His Circle: African-American Filmmaking and Race Cinema of the Silent Era*. Bloomington: Indiana University Press, 2001.

Box Office Mojo. "Brenda Starr." <www.boxofficemojo.com/movies/?id=brendastarr.htm>.

Braden, Susan R. *The Architecture of Leisure: The Florida Resort Hotels of Henry Flagler and Henry Plant*. Gainesville: University Press of Florida, 2002.

Brasell, R. Bruce. "A Seed for Change: The Engenderment of *A Florida Enchantment*." *Cinema Journal* 36, no. 4 (Summer 1997): 3–21.

Breskin, David. *Inner Views: Filmmakers in Conversation*. Boston: Faber and Faber, 1992.

Briant, Don. "Soak Up Ambience of Greek Culture and Learn History of Sponge Diving in Tarpon Springs." *Atlanta Journal-Constitution*, January 25, 2004.

Brode, Douglas. *Woody Allen: His Films and Career*. Secaucus, N.J.: Citadel, 1985.

Brooks, Louise. "The Other Face of W. C. Fields." *Sight and Sound* 40, no. 2 (Spring 1971): 92–96. Reprinted at <www.psykickgirl.com/lulu/wcfields.html>.

Broun, Heywood. "Miami—A Methodist Mining Camp. *Vanity Fair*, February 1936, 13–15.

Brown, Billye Walker, and Walter R. Brown. *Historical Catastrophes: Hurricanes and Tornadoes*. Reading, Mass.: Addison-Wesley, 1972.

Brown, Robert H. "Florida's Lost Tourist Attractions." <www.lostparks.com>.

Buckley, Michael. "John Huston." *Films in Review* 36, no. 4 (April 1985): 210–15.

Buffalo News. "Key Bridge Is Still There." September 4, 1994.

Burleigh, Nina. "Writers' Paradise: 'Papa's Milieu Has Ebbed, Yet Key West Remains an Island of Inspiration." *Chicago Tribune*, November 29, 1988.

Burt Reynolds & Friends Museum. <www.burtreynoldsmuseum.org>.

Canby, Vincent. "Robert Altman's Satire 'Health.'" *New York Times*, April 7, 1982.

Capra, Frank. *The Name Above the Title: An Autobiography*. New York: Macmillan, 1971.

Castle, William. *Step Right Up! I'm Gonna Scare the Pants Off America*. New York: G. P. Putnam's Sons, 1976.

Cerwinske, Laura. *Tropical Deco: The Architecture and Design of Old Miami Beach*. New York: Rizzoli, 1981.

Chamberlain, Ted. "JFK's Island Rescuers Honored at Emotional Reunion." *National Geographic News*, November 20, 2002. <www.news.nationalgeographic.com/news/2002/11/1120_021120_kennedy_pt_109.html>.

Chandler, Raymond. *The Simple Art of Murder*. Boston: Houghton Mifflin, 1950.

Chapman, Ben. "Ben Chapman as Creature from the Black Lagoon." <www.the-reelgill-man.com>.

Cheshire, Godfrey. "Victor Nunez: Persistence in Paradise." *Film Comment* 30, no. 2 (March–April 1994): 10–19.

Chicago Daily Tribune. "She Draws Brenda Starr." March 2, 1941.

Clark, Alexis. "Follow That Dream Parkway." *Gateway to the Gulf*. <iml.jou.ufl.edu/carlson/mmc5015/Homepages/f2000/Clark/page1.htm>.

Cornelison, G. L. "The History of the U.S.S. *Archerfish* (SS/AGSS-311)." <www.ussarcherfish.com/history.htm>.

Coursodon, Jean-Pierre. "Jerry Lewis's Films: No Laughing Matter?" *Film Comment* 11, no. 4 (July–August 1975): 9–15.

Coyote, Peter, official Web site. "Production Notes on *Cross Creek.*" <www.petercoyote. com/creekpn.html>.

Crowther, Bosley. "Collegiate Chase." Review of *Where the Boys Are. New York Times,* January 20, 1961.

———. "Sinatra's 'Tony Rome' Opens." *New York Times,* November 16, 1967.

Culhane, John. *The American Circus: An Illustrated History.* New York: Henry Holt, 1990.

Curtis, James. *W.C. Fields: A Biography.* New York: Alfred Knopf, 2003.

Davis, Ronald L. *Duke: The Life and Image of John Wayne.* Norman: University of Oklahoma Press, 1998.

Death Penalty Information Center. "History of the Death Penalty." <www.deathpenaltyinfo. msu.edu/c/about/history/contents.htm>.

DeMille, Cecil B. *The Autobiography of Cecil B. DeMille.* Edited by Donald Hayne. Englewood Cliffs, N.J.: Prentice-Hall, 1959.

———. "The Greatest Show on Earth." *Circus Magazine and Program,* 81st ed., Ringling Bros. and Barnum & Bailey.

Denby, David. Review of *The Birdcage. New York,* March 11, 1996.

Denton, Clive. "Henry King." In *The Hollywood Professionals,* by Kingsley Canham et al., vol. 2. London: Tantivy, 1974.

Diedrwardo, Judy Alexandra. "Palm Beach Story." <www.worth-avenue.com>.

Doherty, Thomas. *Projections of War: Hollywood, American Culture, and World War II.* New York: Columbia University Press, 1993.

———. *Teenagers and Teenpics: The Juvenilization of American Movies in the 1950s.* Boston: Unwin Hyman, 1988.

Doll, Susan. *The Films of Elvis Presley.* Lincolnwood, Ill.: Publications International, 1991.

———. *Understanding Elvis: Southern Roots vs. Star Image.* New York: Garland, 1998.

Dolphin Research Center. <www.dolphins.org>.

Douglas, Marjory Stoneman. *Florida: The Long Frontier.* New York: Harper and Row, 1967.

Easton, Nina J. "For Hollywood, It's All in the Family." *Los Angeles Times,* July 30, 1989.

Ebert, Roger. Review of *Blood & Wine. Chicago Sun-Times,* February 21, 1997. <rogerebert. suntimes.com>.

———. Review of *Palmetto. Chicago Sun-Times,* February 20, 1998. <rogerebert.suntimes. com>.

———. Review of *Tony Rome. Chicago Sun-Times,* November 22, 1967. <rogerebert.sun times.com>.

Ehrenstein, David, and Bill Reed. *Rock on Film.* New York: Delilah Books, 1982.

Ellis, David. *Rondo Hatton.* <www.rondohatton.com/RONDO.HTML>.

Espe, Troy. "Paradise Lost: Filmmaker Fears Hollywood's Influence on Panhandle." *Panama City (Fla.) News Herald,* August 10, 1997. <www.newsherald.com/LOCAL/FILMB810. HTM>.

Eyewitness Travel Guides. *Florida.* London: DK, 1997.

Eyles, Allen. *The Marx Brothers: Their World of Comedy.* 2nd ed. New York: A.S. Barnes, 1969.

Fentum, Bill. "The Making of Scarface." Brian De Palma Web site. <www.briandepalma. net/scarface/scar2.htm>.

Film Review Annual. "Parenthood." *Film Review Annual 1990,* 971–81. Englewood, N.J.: Jerome S. Ozer, 1990.

Florida Heritage Collection. "Florida, Beauties of the East Coast." State University System (SUS) of Florida, 1892.

Flowers, Charles. "Is Singleton's Movie a Scandal or a Black 'Schindler's List'?" *Seminole Tribune,* March 14, 1997. <www.highbeam.com/doc/1P1:22215514/Is+Singletons+Movie+ A+Scandal+Or+A+Black+%60Schindlers+List%3f.html?refid=SEO>.

Floyd, Kevin. "Closing the (Heterosexual) Frontiers: Midnight Cowboy as National Allegory," *Science and Society* 65, no. 1 (Spring 2001): 99–130.

Flynn, John L. "True Lies: James Cameron's Tribute to the James Bond Films." <www.towson.edu/~flynn/truelies.htm>.

Francke, Lizzie. "The Crash and Burn Scenario." *Guardian*, August 11, 1994.

Franklin, Carl. "Director's Commentary." *Out of Time* DVD, 2003.

Frediani, Michael. "On the Set with Video Assist." *Operating Cameramen*, Fall/Winter 1995–96. <www.soc.org/opcam/07_fw9596/mg07_vidassist.html>.

Fuller, Graham. "Shots in the Dark: Looking Back at 1969, Through the Eyes of a Midnight Cowboy." *Interview* 34, no. 9 (October 2004): 272.

Fury, David H. *Johnny Weissmuller: "Twice the Hero."* Waterville, Maine: Thorndike, 2001.

Gabbard, Alex. *Return to Thunder Road: The Story Behind the Legend*. Lenoir City, Tenn.: Gabbard Publications, 1992.

Garrison, Gordon. "Seeing the Swamp from a Safe Distance." *St. Petersburg Times*, May 4, 1997.

Gauntier, Gene. *Blazing the Trail*. In 4 parts in *Woman's Home Companion*, October 1928–January 1929. Reprinted by Cinema Web at <www.cinemaweb.com/silentfilm/bookshelf/4_blaze1.htm>.

Gee, Jason. "Low Keys." *Guardian Online*, February 24, 2001. <travel.guardian.co.uk/countries/story/0,,442113,00.html>.

George, Alice L. *Awaiting Armageddon: How Americans Faced the Cuban Missile Crisis*. Chapel Hill: University of North Carolina Press, 2003.

George, Paul S. "South Florida: A Brief History." Historical Museum of Southern Florida. <www.historical-museum.org/history/southfla.htm>.

Gerstal, Judy. "In Defence of Demi." *Toronto Star*, August 22, 1997.

Gillespie, Eleanor Ringel. "Director Sayles Keeps His Independent Spirit." *Atlanta Journal-Constitution*, July 14, 2002.

Glassman, Steve, and Maurice J. O'Sullivan, eds. *Crime Fiction and Film in the Sunshine State: Florida Noir*. Bowling Green, Ohio: Popular Press, 1997.

Gleasner, Diana, and Bill Gleasner. *Florida: Off the Beaten Path*. 7th ed. Guilford, Conn.: Globe Pequot, 2003.

Goering, Laurie. "Florida Leads Nation in Wrongful Convictions Among Death Row Inmates." *Chicago Tribune*, February 28, 2000.

Goldstein, Richard. "Gerard Zinser, Last Surviving PT 109 Crewman, Dies at 82." *New York Times*, August 29, 2001.

Gordon G. "The Star Whose Secret Is Buried in the Sands." *Mail on Sunday*, October 6, 1991.

Gorney, Cynthia. "The Price of Illusion: Dar Robinson, His Exploits and His Tragic Death." *Washington Post*, March 19, 1987.

Gregory, Mike. "Gore a Go Go: Herschell Gordon Lewis Speaks." Reel.com. <reel.com/reel.asp?node=features/interviews/lewis>.

Gross, Jane. "An Actor Explores the Fourth Estate." *New York Times*, February 10, 1985.

Guerrero, Ed. Review of *Rosewood*. *Cineaste* 23, no. 1 (Winter 1997): 45.

Guzman, Rafer. "Spring Break: Where the Boys Are Now." *Wall Street Journal*, March 19, 1998.

Gwertzman, Bernard. "U.S. Bids Cuba Take Several Thousand of Its Exiles Back." *New York Times*, May 26, 1983.

Hagan, Pat. "Coral Gables' Historic 'Haunt.'" CruiseMates. <www.cruisemates.com/articles/ports/biltmore.cfm>.

Hamilton, Doug. "True Lies Draws Fire from Muslims Upset Over Its Terrorist Portrayals." *Montreal Gazette*, July 23, 1994.

Hammarstrom, David Lewis. *Behind the Big Top*. South Brunswick, N.J.: A.S. Barnes, 1980.

Hardy, Phil. *The Western*. New York: William Morrow, 1983.

Hart, Martin. The American Widescreen Museum. <www.widescreenmuseum.com>.

Haskew, Michael E. "San Pietro: Capturing the Face of War." *Military History* 17, no. 5 (December 2000), 50–59.

Henry, William A., III. *The Great One: The Life and Legend of Jackie Gleason*. New York: Doubleday, 1992.

Hertzberg, Ludvig, ed. *Jim Jarmusch: Interviews*. Jackson: University Press of Mississippi, 2001.

Higham, Charles. *Cecil B. DeMille*. New York: Scribner, 1973.

Hixson, Richard. Report submitted to the Florida House of Representatives, March 24, 1994.

Hogan, David J. *Dark Romance: Sexuality in the Horror Film*. Jefferson, N.C.: McFarland, 1986.

Holben, Jay. "The Road to Hell: *Jeepers Creepers*." *American Cinematographer* 82, no. 9 (September 2001): 84–92.

Irwin, Colin. "Fred Neil." *Guardian*, July 11, 2001. <www.guardian.co.uk/obituaries/story/0,,519894,00.html>.

James, Henry. *The American Scene*. 1907. Bloomington: Indiana University Press, 1968.

Jones, Maxine. "A Documented History of the Incident which Occurred at Rosewood, Florida, in January 1923." Submitted to the Florida Board of Regents to support the Rosewood victims' claim for damages, December 22, 1993.

Katz, Ephraim. *The Film Encyclopedia*. 4th ed. Revised by Fred Klein and Ronald Dean Nolen. New York: HarperResource, 2001.

Kaufelt, Lynn Mitsuko. *Key West Writers and Their Houses*. Englewood, Fla.: Pineapple Press, 1986.

Kaufman, Anthony. "Production: Victor's Gold; Nunez Wraps Latest Florida-Grown Indie 'Coastlines.'" *indieWIRE*, July 23, 2001. <www.indiewire.com/people/int_Nunez_Victor_010723.html>.

Kempley, Rita. Review of *True Lies*. *Washington Post*, July 15, 1994.

Kendall, Elizabeth. *The Runaway Bride: Hollywood Romantic Comedy of the 1930's*. New York: Knopf, 1990.

Klinkenberg, Jeff. "Cross Creek's Allure May Be Its Downfall." *St. Petersburg Times*, July 9, 1989.

———. "Real Florida: Cross Creek Revival." *St. Petersburg Times*, March 8, 2002.

Knapp, Laurence F., ed. *Brian De Palma: Interviews*. Jackson: University of Mississippi Press, 2003.

Koppes, Clayton R., and Gregory D. Black. *Hollywood Goes to War: How Politics, Profits, and Propaganda Shaped World War II Movies*. New York: Free Press, 1987.

Kronke, David. *Atlanta Journal and Constitution*, 1992.

Lakeland, City of. "Living in the City of Lakeland!" <www.lakelandgov.net/livinghere.html> (accessed April 22, 2004; site discontinued).

Laytner, Ron. "'Francis and Me': Tiffany Bolling, Who Appeared in the 1967 Movie Tony Rome with Frank Sinatra, Tells Ron Laytner About Their Affair and a Love That Has Never Died." *Ottawa Citizen*, January 8, 1998.

Lee, Steve. "The Wilhelm Scream." <http://hollywoodlostandfound.net/wilhelm>.

Levy, Emanuel. *Cinema of Outsiders: The Rise of American Independent Film*. New York: New York University Press, 1999.

Lewis, Jerry. "Dialogue on Film." *American Film* 2, no. 10 (September 1977): 33–48.

Lipper, Hal. "Back to Earth." *St. Petersburg Times*, May 24, 1988.

———. "Cocoon Sequel Won't Be Filmed in St. Petersburg." *St. Petersburg Times*, February 26, 1988.

———. "St. Petersburg Was Never Like This." *St. Petersburg Times*, November 23, 1988.

London, Gabriel. "Based on a True Story: The Making of *Monster*." *Monster* DVD Special Feature, 2004.

Long, Bruce, ed. "Kathlyn Williams." *Taylorology*, no. 48 (December 1996). <www.public. asu.edu/~ialong/Taylor48.txt>.

Longshore, David. *Encyclopedia of Hurricanes, Typhoons, and Cyclones*. New York: Facts on File, 1998.

Louvish, Simon. *Stan and Ollie: The Roots of Comedy; The Double Life of Laurel and Hardy*. New York: St. Martin's Press, 2001.

Maddox, Kaye, and Sandi King. "The Founding of Panama City." In *The History of Bay County Florida*. <www.beaconlearningcenter.com/weblessons/bayhistory/bhis18.htm>.

Maltz, Alan S. *Key West Color*. Key West, Fla.: Light Flight, 1995.

"Marineland of Florida: The Way It Was." <tatooine.fortunecity.com/phlebas/238/>.

Marion County, Florida. <www.usacitiesonline.com/flmarioncounty.htm>.

Martinus, C. "The Creature from the Black Lagoon." <www.umich.edu/~eng1415/intropage/ homepage.html>, under "Gillman."

Maslin, Janet. At the Movies. *New York Times*, February 1, 1985; April 19, 1992.

———. "Helping an Innocent on Death Row." *New York Times*, February 17, 1995.

Maza, Devra. "Preston Sturges: A Screwball Centennial." <wga.org/pr/0898/sturges.html> (accessed July 8, 2005; site discontinued).

McCarthy, Todd. *Howard Hawks: The Grey Fox of Hollywood*. New York: Grove Press, 1997.

McGilligan, Patrick. *Robert Altman: Jumping Off the Cliff*. New York: St. Martin's Press, 1989.

McGinn, Andrew. "The Creature with Two Identities." *Springfield (Ohio) News-Sun*, September 25, 2002.

McLane, Daisann. "Fort Lauderdale for Grown-Ups." *New York Times*, April 9, 2000.

Melbourne, Florida, City of. "About Melbourne, Florida." <www.melbourneflorida.org/info>.

Méndez, Adriana. *Cubans in America*. Minneapolis: Lerner, 1994.

Miami–Dade County. "Vizcaya Museum & Gardens." <www.vizcayamuseum.org>.

Miami Dolphins. "Dolphins Historical Highlights." <www.miamidolphins.com/history/ historicalhighlights/historicalhighlights.asp>.

———. "Dolphins Name." <www.miamidolphins.com/history/dolphinsname/dolphins name.asp>.

Miami Seaquarium. <www.miamiseaquarium.com>.

Miller, Mark. *National Geographic Traveler: Miami & the Keys*. Washington, D.C.: National Geographic Society, 1999.

Miller, Ron. "Woody Allen Makes His TV-Movie Debut with 'Don't Drink the Water' on ABC." Knight Ridder/Tribune News Service, December 9, 1994.

Miller, T. Christian. "The Treasure of Tupelo." *St. Petersburg Times*, June 5, 1997.

The Missing Link. "Midnight Faces." <www.missinglinkclassichorror.co.uk/mar.htm>.

Mix, Olive Stokes. *The Fabulous Tom Mix*. With Eric Heath. Englewood Cliffs, N.J.: Prentice-Hall, 1957. Reprinted at <www.cinemaweb.com/silentfilm/bookshelf/33_mix01. htm> through /33_mix11.htm>.

Monaghan, Kelly. *Orlando's Other Theme Parks: What to Do When You've Done Disney.* 2nd ed. New York: Intrepid Traveler, 1999.

Moore, Deborah Dash. *To the Golden Cities: Pursuing the American Jewish Dream in Miami and L.A.* New York: Free Press, 1994.

Moss, Robert F. "'Blume' and 'Heartbreak Kid'—What Kind of Jews Are They?" *New York Times,* September 9, 1973.

Movie Weekly. "Co-Starring with Death." July 9, 1921. Reprinted in *Taylorology,* no. 48, <www.public.asu.edu/~ialong/Taylor48.txt>.

Moving Picture World. "Lost in the Jungle." October 1911, 109.

MustSeeMiami. "Jackie Gleason Theater of Performing Arts." <www.mustseemiami.com/attractions/jackie-gleason-theater-art.html>.

National Football League. "Miami Dolphins." NFL History Guide. <www.nflhistoryguide.com>.

Navarro, Mireya. "At Home with Carl Hiassen." *New York Times,* July 4, 1996.

Nelson, Richard Alan. *Florida and the American Motion Picture Industry, 1898–1980.* 2 vols. New York: Garland, 1983.

———. *Lights! Camera! Florida! Ninety Years of Moviemaking and Television Production in the Sunshine State.* Tampa: Florida Endowment for the Humanities, 1991.

New York Times. "East Coast Film Taking: Henry King Finishes All Work on His Picture, 'Hell Harbor,' in Florida." December 15, 1929.

———. "Florida Wins Producer." September 22, 1929.

———. "Missile Blows Up in Florida Test." September 26, 1957.

———. "Mr. King's Pirates." October 13, 1929.

———. "That Piratical Film." September 29, 1929.

———. "What the Hurricane Did." October 6, 1929.

Nixon, Rob. "*Smokey and the Bandit.*" Turner Classic Movies. <www.turnerclassicmovies.com>.

Nolan, Robert. "Fort Lauderdale a More Laid Back Spring Break Destination." Knight Ridder/Tribune News Service, April 4, 2004.

Norman, Barry. *The Story of Hollywood.* New York: New American Library, 1987.

Ottawa Citizen. "Raspberry Foundation Tears Strip Off Demi." March 25, 1997.

Parker, Brad, and Victor Salva. "Designing the Creeper." *Jeepers Creepers* DVD special feature, 2001.

Patrick, Rembert W., and Allen Morris. *Florida under Five Flags.* 4th ed. Gainesville: University of Florida Press, 1967.

PCS America. "Welcome to Key West Naval Air Station." <www.pcskeywest.net/dspbasemain.cfm>.

Pearson, Mike. "It's Hard to Forgive True Lie." *Rocky Mountain News,* January 13, 1995.

Pensacola Journal. "Florida-Filmed Movie Premiere Set." March 9, 1962.

Pevere, Geoff. "Scarface was De Palma's Farewell to Coke." *Toronto Star,* April 12, 2003.

Pfeiffer, Lee, and Dave Worrall. *The Essential Bond.* New York: HarperEntertainment, 1998.

Phillips, Craig. *The Captive Sea: Life Behind the Scenes of the Great Modern Oceanariums.* Philadelphia: Chilton, 1964.

Poague, Leland A. *The Cinema of Frank Capra.* South Brunswick, N.J.: A. S. Barnes, 1975.

Ponti, James. *Hollywood East: Florida's Fabulous Flicks.* Orlando: Tribune Publishing, 1992.

Pope, Quentin. "Did Brenda Wed Eric? Yanks Are Anxious to Know." *Chicago Daily Tribune,* December 9, 1942.

Prince, Stephen. *A New Pot of Gold: Hollywood Under the Electronic Rainbow, 1980–1989.* New York: Scribner, 2000.

Pro Football Hall of Fame. "Miami Dolphins." <www.profootballhof.com/history/team.jsp?franchise_id=17>.

Pryor, Thomas M. "Hollywood Review." *New York Times,* July 5, 1953.

Psycho New Jersey. "Florida." <http://psychonj.homestead.com/PAFlorida.html>.

Quin, Eleanor. "*Flipper* on DVD." Turner Classic Movies. <www.turnerclassicmovies.com>.

Rabin, Staton. "Remembering William Powell." *Films in Review* 33, no. 8 (October 1982): 459–63.

Rawlings, Marjorie Kinnan. *Cross Creek.* New York: Scribner, 1942.

———. *Cross Creek Cookery.* New York: Scribner, 1942.

Reisman, Rosemary M. Canfield. "Marjorie Kinnan Rawlings." In *Critical Survey of Long Fiction,* 2nd rev. ed., edited by Frank N. Magill and Carl E. Rollyson, 6:2688–92. Pasadena: Salem Press, 2000.

Reynolds, Burt. *My Life.* New York: Hyperion, 1994.

Riordan, James. *Stone: The Controversies, Excesses, and Exploits of a Radical Filmmaker.* New York: Hyperion, 1995.

Romano, Lois. "'Scarface's Reprieve: Movie Board Reviews Film, Changes X to R." *Washington Post,* November 9, 1983.

Rosenfeld, Jeffrey. *Eye of the Storm: Inside the World's Deadliest Hurricanes, Tornadoes, and Blizzards.* New York: Plenum, 1999.

Ross, Bob. "Nunez Finds That Success Is Sweet." *Tampa Tribune,* July 25, 1997.

Rubin, Steven Jay. *The Complete James Bond Movie Encyclopedia.* Chicago: Contemporary Books, 1990.

Russo, Vito. *The Celluloid Closet.* Rev. ed. New York: Harper and Row, 1987.

Sachs, Lloyd. "New Noir: Auteur Moves Mainstream." *Chicago Sun-Times,* March 1, 1998.

Salva, Victor. "Director's Commentary." *Jeepers Creepers* DVD, 2001.

Sandburg, Carl. "It's the Old Army Game Has Plenty of Background." *Chicago Daily News,* August 2, 1926.

Scheiber, Dave. "PT-109 Bonded Them for Life." *St. Petersburg Times,* May 30, 2000.

Schickel, Richard. *D. W. Griffith: An American Life.* New York: Simon and Schuster, 1984.

Sehlinger, Bob, and Chris Mohney. *Beyond Disney: The Unofficial Guide to Universal, SeaWorld, and the Best of Central Florida.* 3rd ed. New York: John Wiley, 2003.

Selby, Nick, and Corinna Selby. *Lonely Planet: Florida.* 2nd ed. Melbourne, Aus.: Lonely Planet, 2000.

Shales, Tom. "Appreciation: It Was a Wonderful Life." *Washington Post,* September 4, 1991.

Shaw, Arnold. *Sinatra: Twentieth-Century Romantic.* New York: Holt, Rinehart and Winston, 1968.

Shearer, Victoria. *The Insiders' Guide to the Florida Keys and Key West.* Guilford, Conn.: Globe Pequot, 2004.

Sheffield, Skip. "A Spring Break History." Knight Ridder/Tribune News Service, March 24, 1994.

Shepard, Birse. *Lore of the Wreckers.* Boston: Beacon Press, 1961.

Silent Film Society of Chicago. "The Cat and the Canary." Handbill, October 27, 2000.

Singleton, John, et al. "*Rosewood*: Production Notes." <movies.warnerbros.com/rosewood>.

Small, Stacy H. "A Sunshine State Makeover: Fort Lauderdale Sheds Its Spring Break." *National Geographic Traveler,* March 2004, 38ff.

Spehr, Paul C. *The Movies Begin: Making Movies in New Jersey 1887–1920.* Newark, N.J.: Newark Museum, 1977.

Spinrad, Leonard. "Mapping the Growing Wide-Screen 3-D Maze." *New York Times*, April 12, 1953.

Spoto, Donald. *The Kindness of Strangers: The Life of Tennessee Williams*. Boston: Little, Brown, 1985.

St. Andrews, Geoff. "Johnny Weissmuller." <www.geostan.ca/index.html>.

Stanley, John. *The Creature Features Movie Guide*. Rev. ed. New York: Warner Books, 1984.

———. "John Stanley Meets the Composer from the Black Lagoon." *Dark Corridors* 1, no. 8 (2000), at *The Columnists.com*. <www.thecolumnists.com/stanley/stanley35.html>.

Stanley, Robert Henry. *Making Sense of Movies: Filmmaking in the Hollywood Style*. Boston: McGraw-Hill, 2003.

Stevens, Dana. "After the Fall: Trio's *Flops* Launches a Monthlong Celebration of Hollywood's Great Failures." *Slate*, June 4, 2004. <www.slate.com/id/2101789>.

Stone, Jay. "Blue Eyes, Silver Screen." *Ottawa Citizen*, May 16, 1998.

Sturges, Sandy. "Preston Sturges Biography." <www.prestonsturges.com/biography.html>.

Suid, Lawrence H. *Guts & Glory: Great American War Movies*. Reading, Mass.: Addison-Wesley, 1978.

Sullivan, Jim. "Universal Studios Florida Is More Than a Theme Park." *Boston Globe*, June 24, 1990.

Talese, Gay. "Youth Tide Rising on Florida Beach." *New York Times*, March 25, 1962.

Tanner, Louise. Who's in Town. *Films in Review* 41, nos. 6–7, (June–July 1990), 357–58.

Taraborrelli, J. Randy. *Sinatra: Behind the Legend*. Secaucus, N.J.: Birch Lane Press, 1997.

Tare, Peter. "Design and Development of the PTs." <www.petertare.org/ptdesign/pt_design.htm>.

Tatara, Paul. "*Absence of Malice*." Turner Classic Movies. <www.turnerclassicmovies.com>.

Thiltges, Amy. "The Semiotics of Alienation and Emptiness in the Films of Jim Jarmusch." *Organdi Quarterly*, December 2002.

Thomas, Dana, et al. "Names and Faces." *Washington Post*, April 20, 1992.

Thompson, Frank, ed. *Henry King, Director: From Silents to 'Scope*. Based on interviews by David Shepard and Ted Perry. Los Angeles: Directors Guild of America, 1995.

Thompson, Lang. "*They Were Expendable*." Turner Classic Movies. <www.turnerclassicmovies.com>.

Toland, John. "A Profile in Courage, a Background of War." *New York Times*, November 19, 1961.

Travers, Peter. "A Comic Brooke in Distress." *Rolling Stone*, September 19, 1991, 79–81.

Trust for Public Land. "American Beach Preserving Nature, Culture, and History." March 1, 2005. <tpl.org/tier3_cd.cfm?content_item_id=19536&folder_id=250>.

Tunstall, Cynthia, and Jim Tunstall, with Lesley Abravanel. *Florida for Dummies*. 2nd ed. New York: John Wiley, 2003.

TV.com. "*Flipper*." <www.tv.com/flipper/show/324/summary.html>.

Twain, Mark. *The Mysterious Stranger*. New York: Harper, 1916.

Uffelman, Jerry. "USS Queenfish SS393/SSN651." <http://queenfish.org/noframes/index1.html>.

Uricchio, Marylynn. "The Great White Way." *Pittsburgh Post-Gazette*, July 30, 1995.

U.S. Department of the Navy. Naval Historical Center. "Lieutenant John F. Kennedy, USN." <www.history.navy.mil/faqs/faq60-2.htm>.

———. "Report on Loss of *PT-109*." <www.history.navy.mil/faqs/faq60-11.htm>.

———. "USS *Balao* (SS-285, later AGSS-285), 1943–1963." <www.history.navy.mil/photos/sh-usn/usnsh-b/ss285.htm>.

———. "USS *PT-109*, 1942–1943." <www.history.navy.mil/photos/sh-usn/usnsh-p/pt109.htm>.

Van Gelder, Lawrence. "Peter Hyams Awaiting Next Inspiration." *New York Times*, June 27, 1986.

Vesey, Susannah. "Celebrity Buzz." *Atlanta Journal and Constitution*, April 16, 1992.

Villano, David. "Has Knight-Ridder's Flagship Gone Adrift?" *Columbia Journalism Review*, January/February, 1996. <archives.cjr.org/year/96/1/knight_ridder.asp>.

Visit Florida. Media Newsroom. <media.VISITFLORIDA.org>, February 20, 2003.

Wakulla County Tourism Development Council. "Wakulla Springs State Park." <www.wakullacounty.org/wakulla-5.htm>.

Waldman, Carl. *Atlas of the North American Indian*. New York: Facts on File, 1985.

Walker, Gary L. "USS *Balao* SS-285." <www.atule.com/balao_sail.htm>.

Wallis, Hal, and Charles Higham. *Starmaker*. New York: Macmillan, 1980.

Washington Post. "Cocoon: A Good Time." July 16, 1985.

Weber, Bruce. "The Fonda Who Came In from the Cold." *New York Times*, March 22, 1998.

Welsh, James. Review of *Days of Thunder*. *Films in Review* 41, no. 10 (October 1990): 481–82.

Westfall, L. Glenn. "Hell Harbor's 55th Anniversary." *Sunland Tribune*, December 1984.

White, Gayle. "Cypress Gardens: Updated Florida Park Reopens." *Atlanta Journal-Constitution*, December 12, 2004.

Wilkinson, Jerry. "History of Little Munson Island." <www.keyshistory.org/MI-Munson-Island.html>.

Williams, Dakin, and Shepherd Mead. *Tennessee Williams: An Intimate Biography*. New York: Arbor House, 1983.

Williams, Esther. *The Million Dollar Mermaid*. With Digby Diehl. New York: Simon and Schuster, 1999.

Williams, Tennessee. *A Streetcar Named Desire*. New York: New Directions, 1947.

Willis, Donald C. *The Films of Frank Capra*. Metuchen, N.J.: Scarecrow Press, 1974.

Wilson, Robert. "Willeford, A Pro at the Miami Beat." *USA Today*, March 29, 1988.

Windeler, Robert. "Film and TV Empire Is Built on Kingdom of Beasts." *New York Times*, August 2, 1967.

Winn, Marcia. "A Star Reporter Writes About a Starr Reporter." *Chicago Daily Tribune*, January 14, 1945.

Winter, Jack. "How Sweet It Wasn't." *Atlantic Monthly*, June 1995, 68–81.

Wittmer, Paul W. "USS *Balao* (SS-285): Ship's History." Research by Robert Loys Sminkey. <www.subvetpaul.com/USS-Balao-SS-285.htm>.

Wright, C. E. "Easter Invasion." *New York Times*, March 15, 1964.

Yacowar, Maurice. *Tennessee Williams and Film*. New York: Frederick Ungar, 1977.

Yagoda, Ben. "Elmore Leonard's Rogue's Gallery." *New York Times*, December 30, 1984.

Yancey, Kitty Bean. "At 50, Venerable Fontainebleau Regaining Its Glitz." *USA Today*, December 9, 2004.

Yardley, Jonathan. "'Cockfighter': Writer Wins His Spurs." *Washington Post*, December 31, 2004.

Ziggy's Video Realm. "Jaws 3-D." <www.reelcriticism.com/ziggyrealm/reviews/jaws3.html>.

INDEX

Double Deck Turf bar, 155
Douglas, Gordon, 154
Drama, conventions of, 190–92
Dreier, Hans, 71
Drew Field, 326
Drew, Sidney, 11
Dreyfuss, Richard, 260
Driver, Sara, 306
Dumont, Margaret, 256
DuMont network, 335
Duvall, Robert, 211, 212

Eagle Studios, 12–14, 39
Easy to Love, 52–55, 78–79
Ebert, Roger, 83
Ecological issues, as depicted in film, 95–97, 276, 228–31
Eden House, 236
Editing, 174, 183–85, 199, 248–49, 307–8
Edson, Richard, 306
Edwards, Blake, 348
Elbo Room, 316
Elderly, as depicted in film, 191, 196–201
El Mirasol estate, 24–26
Englewood, 96, 106
Ernest Hemingway Home, 284
Estefan, Gloria, 157
Everglades City, 130
Everglades National Park, 43, 50, 78, 111, 276

Fabares, Shelley, 294
Family issues, as depicted in film, 63–64, 68–70, 74–75, 89–90, 124–26, 143–44, 191, 192–96, 201–5, 232–34, 288, 309–11, 350–55, 361
Famous Players–Lasky, 23
Farina, Dennis, 277
Fat and Fickle, 6
Fat Spy, xiii, 161, 172–75, 187–88
FauntLeRoy, Don E., 343
Fell, Norman, 359
Femmes fatales, 82, 84, 92, 115
Field, Sally, 122, 183, 186
Fields, W. C. 23–26
Film noir, conventions of, 81–83, 84, 106–7, 115, 154
Film school generation, 82, 98, 99, 178, 192–93, 296
Fishburne, Laurence, 214

Fisher, Carl, 118, 147
Five Easy Pieces, 192–93
Flagler, Henry, 10–11, 38, 61, 67, 118, 281–82, 285, 286–87
Flagler College, 38
Flagler Dog Track, 158. See also West Flagler Kennel Club
Flagler Museum, 80
Flamingo Hotel, 147
Flash of Green, A, 83, 95–97, 114, 302
Fleming, Rhonda, 332, 333
Flipper (1963), 128–31, 157, 259
Flipper (1996), 130
Flipper (television series), 130, 284–85
Flipper's New Adventure, 130
Florey, Robin, 254
Florida: architecture and 10–11, 38, 67, 119, 120, 126–27, 157, 251–53, 283–84; business and industry of, 2, 10, 47, 72–73, 86, 94, 118, 191–92, 228–31, 276, 288; and ethnic groups (see specific ethnic groups); image of, 10–11, 67–68, 83, 85–87, 95, 98, 101, 106–7, 118–20, 133, 145, 147–48, 200, 204–5, 230–31, 254–56, 264, 269–70, 286–88, 295, 298–99, 300, 305, 308, 313–14; infrastructure of 10, 61, 67, 118, 174–75, 281–82, 286–87; and literature, 83, 98, 141, 206–9, 224, 227, 236, 274; and military, 320–21, 348–49; and natural disasters, 4, 61–62, 79, 281–82, 339; natural history of, 17, 33, 46–47, 97, 104–5, 140, 191, 215–16, 230–31, 320, 329, 331; population of, 83, 118, 119, 175, 195–96, 200, 287–88; and racial issues, 190–91, 220–23, 238; and tourism (see Tourism)
Florida East Coast Railroad, 10, 61, 67, 281–82, 285
Florida Enchantment, 8–11, 38–39
Florida Feud, A; or, Love in the Everglades, 2
Florida land boom, 4, 24, 118, 254–56, 287
Floridian Hotel, 366
Flying Ace, The, 12–14, 39
Follow That Dream, 288–292, 295, 316
Follow That Dream Parkway, 316
Fonda, Peter, 98, 232, 234
Fontainebleau Hotel, 119, 155–56, 240, 250–53, 283–84
Ford, John, 327
Fort Myers, 96, 106

Susan Doll holds a Ph.D. in film studies from Northwestern University and teaches film courses at Oakton Community College in Cook County, Illinois. She has written extensively on film and popular culture for a variety of publications, including the *Encyclopaedia Britannica*, *Literature/Film Quarterly*, and *Magill's Survey of Cinema*. She has also written a book on Marilyn Monroe, *Marilyn: Her Life and Legend*, and several on Elvis Presley, including *The Films of Elvis Presley*, *Elvis: Forever in the Groove*, and *Elvis: American Idol*.

David Morrow is an editor of educational books and general nonfiction, including reference works for the *New York Times*. He has written on film-related topics for the online version of the *Encyclopaedia Britannica* and reviewed popular films for *Insider* magazine. He has also written articles on history, science, and culture for *Cobblestone* educational magazines.